Cases in International Relations

CQ Press, an imprint of SAGE, is the leading publisher of books, periodicals, and electronic products on American government and international affairs. CQ Press consistently ranks among the top commercial publishers in terms of quality, as evidenced by the numerous awards its products have won over the years. CQ Press owes its existence to Nelson Poynter, former publisher of the *St. Petersburg Times,* and his wife Henrietta, with whom he founded Congressional Quarterly in 1945. Poynter established CQ with the mission of promoting democracy through education and in 1975 founded the Modern Media Institute, renamed The Poynter Institute for Media Studies after his death. The Poynter Institute (*www.poynter .org*) is a nonprofit organization dedicated to training journalists and media leaders.

In 2008, CQ Press was acquired by SAGE, a leading international publisher of journals, books, and electronic media for academic, educational, and professional markets. Since 1965, SAGE has helped inform and educate a global community of scholars, practitioners, researchers, and students spanning a wide range of subject areas, including business, humanities, social sciences, and science, technology, and medicine. A privately owned corporation, SAGE has offices in Los Angeles, London, New Delhi, and Singapore, in addition to the Washington DC office of CQ Press.

Cases in International Relations

Pathways to Conflict and Cooperation

Glenn Hastedt
James Madison University

Donna L. Lybecker
Idaho State University

Vaughn P. Shannon
Wright State University

Los Angeles | London | New Delhi
Singapore | Washington DC

Los Angeles | London | New Delhi
Singapore | Washington DC

FOR INFORMATION:

CQ Press

An Imprint of SAGE Publications, Inc.

2455 Teller Road

Thousand Oaks, California 91320

E-mail: order@sagepub.com

SAGE Publications Ltd.

1 Oliver's Yard

55 City Road

London EC1Y 1SP

United Kingdom

SAGE Publications India Pvt. Ltd.

B 1/I 1 Mohan Cooperative Industrial Area

Mathura Road, New Delhi 110 044

India

SAGE Publications Asia-Pacific Pte. Ltd.

3 Church Street

#10-04 Samsung Hub

Singapore 049483

Printed in the United States of America

A catalog record of this book is available from the Library of Congress.

ISBN 978-1-6087-1247-2

This book is printed on acid-free paper.

Acquisitions Editor: Elise Frasier

Development Editor: Nancy Matuszak

Production Editor: Libby Larson

Copy Editor: Shannon Kelly

Typesetter: C&M Digitals (P) Ltd.

Proofreader: Sue Irwin

Indexer: Terri Corry

Cover Designer: Candice Harman

Marketing Manager: Erica DeLuca

Certified Chain of Custody
Promoting Sustainable Forestry
www.sfiprogram.org
SFI-01268

SFI label applies to text stock

14 15 16 17 18 10 9 8 7 6 5 4 3 2 1

To Cathy, Sarah and Guy, and Kelly and Matthew. —Glenn

*To my daughters, Sophia and Catherine Shannon,
whom I hope always will be surrounded by books. —Vaughn*

*To my students, whose creativity
and passion inspire and amaze me. —Donna*

Brief Contents

PART III: HUMAN SECURITY

Detailed Contents

10. Global Monetary Reform after 2008   170

11. Uniting Europe through a Common Currency   191

15. Immigration Tensions over the U.S.-Mexico Border   265

16. Social Responsibility and the BP Oil Spill   287

Preface

Regardless of the name they go by, introductory international politics courses are challenging to teach. Current events outpace the ability of texts to keep up with them, and the course attracts students with a variety of interests. Some are there merely to fulfill a university or departmental graduation requirement. Others have lived abroad or bring with them a curiosity about foreign cultures. Still others have little exposure to international politics but are fascinated with newspaper and media accounts of events overseas.

Adding to this pedagogical challenge is the increasing number of perspectives that exist within the discipline from which to view and evaluate events and the fact that, as the Cold War recedes further and further from view, international politics courses have lost much of their substantive coherence. The high-low politics distinction, as well as that between foreign and domestic policy, no longer serve as effective gatekeepers to what is covered and what is not. Instructors have come to employ a wide range of teaching strategies to address the needs of their varied student audience and accomplish their pedagogical goals. While we can point to a set of best practices to help frame our efforts in the classroom, no single teaching strategy exists today, nor is one likely to emerge.

In *Cases in International Relations: Pathways to Conflict and Cooperation*, we have sought to recognize this complex setting and the diversity of approaches that exist. We believe that our case studies have widespread utility in international politics courses because they provide instructors with assistance in accomplishing what we believe is an underlying goal shared by virtually all: helping students to become critical and independent thinkers who can analyze headlines yet to come.

Consistent with this fundamental objective, our goal is to help students understand that headline events in international politics do not emerge "out of the blue." They have a history and, just as important, they have a future. Our point of departure in organizing our case studies is that conflict and cooperation are not single, stand-alone events, but are part of a stream of activity that creates a pathway from inception to some form of resolution, however temporary, and then continues on to set in motion a new set of foreign policy issues to be addressed.

Case studies are a valuable tool because they permit students to obtain a deeper sense of the dynamics of a problem than is possible in lectures. Through the case studies in this book, students will come to understand that conflict and cooperation are not polar opposites but aspects of foreign policy-making that are universally present. Most importantly, when organized in a consistent fashion, multiple cases studies allow students to discover points of similarity and differences in how conflict and cooperation can evolve and interact. The critical-thinking skills and insights the students develop in doing so can then be applied to helping them understand future problems in world politics.

Organization of Case Studies

The book's first chapter sets the stage for the presentation of the case studies by introducing students to the types of activity that occur. The discussions are not meant to be exhaustive conceptual overviews but are intended to (1) provide students with a firm platform from which to view the unfolding cases and (2) provide instructors with a foundation onto which they can add supplemental conceptual material from lectures or other readings if they so wish. Chapter 1 includes a brief study of U.S. involvement in Vietnam from the end of World War II to the present, which helps students understand how to read the case studies and why they are important. Students also get a sense of the type of critical-thinking questions they will encounter in the case studies that follow.

The case studies are organized under three main parts that address enduring and emerging issues in international politics. Part I: Military Security explores such issues as the long-standing Arab-Israeli conflict and the rapidly developing field of cybersecurity. Part II: Economic Security considers topics such as the creation of a European common currency and the challenges of global hunger. Part III: Human Security examines such issues as immigration on the U.S.-Mexican border, humanitarian relief in Haiti, and the establishment of rules for an Arctic regime. The cases range from the narrowly defined to those of a broader scope. Many were selected for their ability to cross over into the other parts of the book. The South China Sea case study in Part I, for example, contains significant economic elements. Our goal in doing this was to help students see the full complexity of international politics issues and to avoid attaching labels of convenience to problems.

Case study material is structured similarly in every chapter to facilitate the learning process. Each chapter begins with a general discussion that places the case study in a broader context so that students can see its importance to the field of international politics. We then present the case study by breaking down its pathway of conflict and cooperation into three stages: (1) problem setting and origins, (2) problem definition and response, and (3) problem evolution and development.

By first examining problem setting and origins, we recognize three important political realities: foreign policy problems rarely, if ever, come out of nowhere; they are not self-contained challenges existing in isolation from other problems; and the domestic politics of foreign policy problems may differ greatly, even for the same government.

We next explore problem definition and response—how the problem was defined and how the actors involved responded. Individually and collectively, policymakers must determine how critical a situation is. The roles of national and global interests come into play here as policymakers identify how to address a problem, whether to use unilateral or collective action, and when to respond.

The third stage, problem evolution and development, considers the results of the actions taken. Whether disputes are addressed through conflict or cooperation, efforts to deal with them eventually move to some form of resolution, be it a formal or passive settlement.

Presented in this manner, the book's sixteen case studies help stimulate students' thinking about the underlying dynamics of state behavior. They are designed to encourage students to recognize that they are not isolated or stand-alone events that will soon fade from view. The cases are selected with an eye toward their contemporary relevance for world politics and examine the actions of a wide range of actors: powerful states, small states, international organizations, nonprofit organizations, multinational corporations, and individuals.

Features

Our case studies also teach students that understanding the choices made in these pathways requires viewing international politics as more than "connecting the dots." Students need to be able to recognize how global forces and the dynamics of foreign policy-making provide opportunities for, and place constraints on, different lines of conflict and cooperation. Several features in the book help to illustrate these lines, beginning with the Case Summary box that appears at the start of each chapter. This quick overview provides a snapshot of the key issues in play, the global context in which the dispute occurs, key actors and their motives, and relevant key concepts from the study of international politics. A Timeline allows students to note when a case study's key developments occurred.

Recognizing that faculty place various degrees of importance on integrating conceptual material into case studies, a Concept Focus box presents an overview discussion of a relevant key concept or set of concepts that can help students with their analysis. This discussion is kept separate from the case study narrative to allow students to focus on the case and to allow instructors flexibility in the incorporation of theoretical concepts into their course objectives.

A Spotlight box highlights a particular aspect, moment, or event in a dispute's pathway to conflict and cooperation, bringing added depth to the case study. Sometimes the Spotlight focuses on options available or choices made, such as in the selection of a setting in which to discuss monetary reform. In other cases, such as in the study on the creation of the euro, it may highlight the competing views held by key countries. It may examine the development of thinking on a problem, such as Chinese strategy in the South China Sea. This closer look further emphasizes the complexity of the dynamics of state behavior and foreign policy-making.

Finally, each chapter concludes with a series of **Case Analysis** questions that direct students' attention to the factors involved in foreign policy-making and asks them to reflect on the importance of these factors in the case at hand or to apply them to other foreign policy problems. **Suggested Readings** and **Web Resources** point students toward more information they can access on their own about the topic at hand.

For instructors, we have written **Case Notes**, a set of case-specific entries that address why each case was profiled, including a summary and details on the global context, major actors, and themes for class discussion that tie each case to the larger context of international politics. Questions for discussion or assignment are also available, along with recommended videos that highlight aspects of each case. Instructors can access these resources by registering at **http://college.cqpress.com/sites/casesintlrelations-instructor**.

Acknowledgments

The writing of this book was a joint effort, accomplished through many phone calls and e-mails as we determined the best format in which to present the cases. We wish to thank our colleagues Mark McBeth and Erica Allen Wolters, who always took time to help talk through concerns.

This book benefited from an excellent editorial team at CQ Press. Publisher Charisse Kiino, acquisitions editor Elise Frasier, and development editor Nancy Matuszak were full of good suggestions and encouragement. Their expertise and insight were indispensable to moving this project from an idea to a finished product that we believe encourages and facilitates the development of critical-thinking skills. Copy editor Shannon Kelly helped fine-tune the manuscript, and production editor Libby Larson ably managed its final steps on the pathway to publication.

The feedback from our reviewers was very helpful in refining our approach and emphasizing the right angles of the cases. We appreciate the time they took to read our drafts and respond with their insights: Risa Brooks, Marquette University; John W. Dietrich, Bryant University; Michael D. Kanner, University of Colorado, Boulder; Jessica Philipp, University of Phoenix; and Etga Ugur, University of Washington, Tacoma.

About the Authors

Glenn Hastedt holds a Ph.D. in political science from Indiana University. Formerly the chair of the political science department at James Madison University, he is now professor and chair of the justice studies department. He is the author of *American Foreign Policy: Past, Present, Future*, 9th edition (Pearson, 2011) and editor of *American Foreign Policy Annual Edition* (McGraw Hill, 2013). He edited *Controlling Intelligence* (Frank Cass, 1991) and co-edited *Intelligence Analysis and Assessment* (Frank Cass, 1996). Hastedt has also authored articles on intelligence in *Intelligence and National Security, Journal of Intelligence History, Defense Intelligence Journal, and International Journal of Intelligence and Counterintelligence*, as well as chapters in edited volumes on intelligence.

Donna L. Lybecker is an associate professor in the department of political science at Idaho State University, where she specializes in environmental politics and international relations. Her research activities focus on the western United States, the North American borders, and Latin America. Recent publications include articles in *Environmental Politics, International Journal of Sustainable Society and Politics and Policy*.

Vaughn P. Shannon is an associate professor of political science at Wright State University, where he specializes in international security, foreign policy analysis, and Middle East politics. His research has been published in numerous journals, including *International Organization, International Studies Quarterly, European Journal of International Research, Security Studies*, and *Foreign Policy Analysis*. Most recently he is co-editor of *Psychology, Constructivism, and International Relations: An Ideational Alliance* (University of Michigan Press, 2011).

1

Pathways to Conflict and Cooperation

To the casual observer, world politics can seem to be little more than a series of random headlines that appear with little or no warning. Reality is more much complex. Events such as the terrorist attacks on the United States on September 11, 2001; the collapse of the Soviet Union; Western intervention to help remove Muammar Gaddafi from power; and the financial crisis in Greece all have long histories. They will also shape future events in ways that we may not anticipate.

Simply put, problems and opportunities such as these exist in pathways of conflict and cooperation that states travel down during the course of conducting their foreign policies. These pathways are defined by two sets of dynamics. The first has its roots in the structure of world politics. Here, we look to such features as the distribution of economic, political, and military power; the stability of the system; the underlying values of the system; and the presence of nonstate actors. The second set of dynamics has its roots in the way in which foreign policies are made. Key factors here include the world views and personalities of leaders, the structure of the decision-making process, domestic political influences, and bureaucratic competencies.

The pathways of conflict and cooperation created by these two sets of dynamic forces, one rooted in the structure of the international system and the other in foreign policy, do not predetermine the outcome of events. Understanding world politics is not a matter of connecting dots. It is a matter of identifying the key features of the pathways being travelled, assessing the influence of those pathways, and making informed judgments about the direction events might take. Case studies provide an effective way for us to study these features and begin to understand them. By examining the pathways the actors took in a particular event and, with the benefit of hindsight, assessing the influence of their choices, we can come to understand the judgments made at the time that led to the direction taken and begin to apply what we've learned to current events.

Consider the pathway that led the United States into the Vietnam War. During World War II, Vietnamese communist leader Ho Chi Minh was a valuable American ally in the struggle to defeat Japan, and President Franklin Roosevelt was sympathetic to his vision of establishing Vietnam as an independent state after the war and not having it return to the status of a French colony. With the end of the war, however, all of this changed. By 1952 the United States was providing France with $30 million in aid in its efforts to defeat Ho Chi Minh and reestablish colonial control over Indochina. By the end of 1953, that amount had increased to $500 million. This change in outlook and policy came about largely as a result of the structure of world politics, namely the development of Cold War political and military competition between the United States and the Soviet Union. At this time the focal point of this competition was Europe, which had been the central battleground of World War II. The United States needed France to join a European defense system to help contain communist expansion into Western Europe. Southeast Asia had not yet become a Cold War battleground, as the key area of competition there was China, which in the early 1950s was not considered to be a major political or military power. The price France extracted for its support in Europe was American support for its war in Indochina.

Yet American support did not help France hold Vietnam. With its forces surrounded and facing imminent defeat at Dien Bien Phu, France called on the Eisenhower administration to send in troops. Eisenhower refused, in part because of the financial cost of doing so, and France began to withdraw its forces. That exit became official with the signing of the 1954 Geneva Peace Accords, which created a "provisional demarcation line" at the 17th parallel, dividing Vietnam in two parts, and scheduled a 1956 election for the ruler of a single Vietnamese state. Ho Chi Minh's communist forces controlled three-fourths of Vietnam at the time, but they withdrew north of the 17th parallel as agreed. The United States did not sign the agreement but pledged not to use force or the threat of force to disturb it. Yet just six week later, the United States, along with France and Great Britain, created the Southeast Asia Treaty Organization (SEATO) to halt the spread of communism—a goal that affected the status quo in Vietnam. Although Vietnam was not a member of SEATO, a provision of the treaty extended its protection to the "free people under the jurisdiction of Vietnam." With this wording, the United States made the first move to create two Vietnamese states instead of one unified state, as agreed to in the Geneva Accords. It was not long thereafter that the United States supported Ngo Dinh Diem as president of South Vietnam. It also supported Diem's argument that since South Vietnam had not signed the Geneva Accords, it did not have to hold elections in 1956. The temporary truce line was now unilaterally defined as a permanent boundary. Once more, the United States' political and military power, as well as its worldview on the threat of communism, steered the decision-making process behind these actions. By 1960, 1,000 U.S. military advisors were stationed in South Vietnam.

Getting into Vietnam was only one event along the pathway of conflict and cooperation that took the United States through some fifteen years of war until a peace agreement was reached in 1973 and Saigon fell to Hi Chi Minh and his forces in 1975. Along this pathway a series of decisions was made regarding how to define and redefine American interests, what actions to take in order to realize these interests, how to respond to North and South Vietnamese actions, and how to construct an exit strategy from the war. Our first inclination is to think of the Vietnam War entirely in terms of a conflict among countries and ideologies. But what becomes clear when we take a step back and look at it more closely is that the pathway the United States travelled included both episodes of conflict and cooperation. And, as noted above, all along this pathway the structural features of the international system and the nature of foreign policy-making shaped the actions taken. The Vietnam War is not unique is this regard. Very few aspects of foreign policy and international relations consist entirely of conflict or cooperation. In most cases both can be found. We return to the case of Vietnam to examine how U.S. interests were defined, the actions taken to realize those interests, and how the United States chose to respond to the opposition and seek a resolution.

When John Kennedy was elected president in 1960, his primary attention was on Laos, not Vietnam. The Laotian civil war underway was waged between pro-U.S. and pro-Soviet factions, and Kennedy hoped to establish Laos as a neutral country in the Cold War competition between the United States and Soviet Union. This aim redefined U.S. interests in Vietnam from a primary goal of containing the spread of communism to one of establishing a cooperative working relationship with the Soviet Union. From Kennedy's perspective, for this new relationship to succeed, the Soviet Union had to see that there was no real possibility of spreading communism to Southeast Asia. Accordingly, stopping the spread of communism to South Vietnam was not an end goal in Kennedy's foreign policy but a key first step in making Laos neutral and establishing a basis for cooperating with the Soviet Union. Standing in the way of this strategy was the fact that the U.S-supported South Vietnamese government was having difficulty defeating communist guerrilla forces. To address this problem, Kennedy began sending combat troops to South Vietnam.

A U.S.-Soviet neutrality agreement on Laos was signed in 1962, but it soon unraveled and the civil war resumed. U.S. attention focused once again on stopping the spread of communism to South Vietnam. Kennedy's successor, Lyndon Johnson, continued the policy of sending troops and expanded U.S. actions to include the bombing of North Vietnam. The global system in which Johnson made his Vietnam decisions was different from that in which Kennedy had operated. With each passing year, China was considered a more powerful and influential political and military force in Asia. China often disagreed with the Soviet Union and thus had to be viewed as an independent actor, not as one of the Soviet Union's subservient allies.

The key event in this escalation was a disputed attack on U.S. naval vessels in the Gulf of Tonkin. This attack provided the political basis for a U.S. congressional resolution authorizing the use of "all necessary force" to prevent further aggression from North Vietnam. Operation Rolling Thunder, a massive and sustained bombing campaign against North Vietnam, soon followed, along with a substantial increase in the number of U.S. forces in South Vietnam. By 1967 over 485,000 troops were stationed there. The escalation did not produce the desired results. In January 1968 North Vietnam launched the Tet Offensive, a nationwide assault on South Vietnam that succeeded in penetrating Saigon. The attacks did not achieve their objective of defeating U.S. forces, but they succeeded in demonstrating the degree to which U.S. policy had failed and showcasing the dim prospects for U.S. victory. At the same time, a large antiwar protest movement was gaining strength in the United States and deeply dividing the American public.

As more and more U.S. troops were committed to Vietnam and as U.S. casualties grew, a gradual change in U.S. goals also took place. By 1967 a secret Defense Department memo defined U.S. goals as 70 percent avoiding a humiliating defeat, 20 percent keeping South Vietnam from falling to China, and 10 percent to permitting the people of South Vietnam to enjoy a better way of life.

Like Kennedy, Richard Nixon looked at Vietnam in terms of the bigger issue of U.S.-Soviet (and now also Chinese) cooperation. Détente—Nixon's cold war foreign policy strategy of increased cooperation—required reducing the U.S. presence in Vietnam and ending the war. To this end, the Nixon administration adopted a policy of Vietnamization, through which South Vietnam would take on the bulk of the fighting, and entered peace talks in Paris with North Vietnam. The Paris peace talks, which began in 1969, were not the first attempt at cooperation between the two sides. The Johnson administration had begun holding discussions in 1968, and, some two years before, there had been a Polish-Italian peace initiative that received tentative support in the United States and North Korea. Known as Operation Marigold, it collapsed as a result of continued U.S. air strikes against North Vietnam.

Fearing that North Vietnam would take advantage of Vietnamization and try to militarily defeat South Vietnam before its military forces could stand up and fight effectively in the absence of U.S. support, Nixon stepped up U.S. bombing of the North and supported an invasion of Cambodia, which had provided safe passage for North Vietnamese troops and supplies headed to South Vietnam. This escalation failed, and North Vietnamese forces came through the demilitarized zone separating the Vietnams in spring 1972. This action prompted the United States to reengage its fighting forces in Vietnam—a re-Americanization of the war—to avoid South Vietnam falling to the communists.

In early December 1972, the peace talks collapsed in Paris as South Vietnam objected to the terms of an impending agreement. North Vietnam had become increasingly isolated from its Soviet and Chinese allies, who now also valued the prospect of détente with the United States. Nixon, aware of the rift between North Vietnam and its supporters, responded by unleashing a massive bombing of the North to demonstrate U.S. resolve to both sides. Talks resumed as 1972 ended, and a peace treaty was signed on January 23, 1973. Two years later, in March 1975, the North Vietnamese military and South Vietnamese communist forces launched an attack on

South Vietnam. Caught off guard by the offensive, South Vietnamese forces provided little resistance. Saigon quickly fell. Vietnam was now one country, and Saigon was renamed Ho Chi Minh City.

The pathway of conflict and cooperation that the United States and North Vietnam travelled did not end with the peace treaty and the reunification of Vietnam. It has continued, although with a new set of constraints and opportunities. A twenty-two-year period of limited engagement ensued between a reunified Vietnam and the United States. Not until 1995 did the United States, under President Bill Clinton, reestablish diplomatic relations with Vietnam. It would be another two years before a U.S. ambassador was stationed there. Points of conflict far exceeded those of cooperation during this period, even though resolving the issues dividing the two countries required cooperation. For its part, Vietnam sought economic recovery aid it believed was promised to it by Nixon as part of the 1973 peace agreement. It also sought compensation for the damages inflicted on its population by the U.S. military in its bombing campaigns against North Vietnam that used Agent Orange, a chemical warfare agent. The United States demanded an end to Vietnam's 1978 invasion of Cambodia and sought Vietnamese help in locating soldiers identified as prisoners of war/missing in action (POW/MIAs).

By the 1980s the constraints on normalizing U.S.-Vietnamese relations had become less pronounced as Vietnam removed its military forces from Cambodia and adopted a more pragmatic economic position that permitted increased foreign investments and opened Vietnam to foreign trade. These mutually beneficial transactions brought about more frequent and positive interactions between the two countries and helped lay a foundation for greater cooperation between them. Relations improved to the point that President Ronald Reagan sent a special envoy to Hanoi to discuss POW/MIA issues. Today, the United States is Vietnam's largest export market and one of its largest sources of foreign direct investment. Both countries are participating in negotiations to establish a regional free trade system in the Pacific, and both are suspicious of Chinese intentions in the South China Sea. Yet points of conflict between the two remain, including U.S. concerns for human rights in Vietnam and suspicions by conservatives in the Vietnamese Communist Party that U.S. foreign policy's long-term goal is to remove them from power. Current relations between the countries, however, are now more balanced than they were in the mid-twentieth century.

Few could have imagined the way in which this pathway unfolded. In looking back at the events that occurred along the way, from the United States first coming to the aid of France in its bid to retake control over its colonial empire to its opening relations with a united communist Vietnam, we can see how the structure of world politics and the dynamics of foreign policy decision-making influenced policy decisions. As is always the case, the influence of these two forces was not constant over time, with one sometimes being greater than the other, but they were both always present. The United States aided France out of a concern for containing the Soviet

Union's influence in Europe, a decision rooted in the emerging Cold War that dominated the structure of world politics. Later decisions were influenced by a desire to work cooperatively with the Soviet Union within this largely conflictual global structure, first by seeking to create a neutral Laos and later in advancing détente. Today we see the influence of the global system in U.S. and Vietnamese efforts to improve relations, with the common goal of containing the spread of China's rising influence in Asia. At the foreign policy decision-making level, such factors as a concern for the economic cost of the war, rising negative public opinion, and a desire to avoid humiliation all played key roles in U.S. policy toward Vietnam.

Case studies such as this brief one on Vietnam are valuable not only for the information they provide but because they can serve as a starting point for asking critical thinking questions, which are found at the end of each chapter. For example, with regard to U.S. involvement in Vietnam, we might ask which U.S. president faced the most difficult decision regarding Vietnam. There may be no correct answer since the choice made will depend on how you define *difficult*. The response requires you do more than name a president. You need to explain why, and that requires consideration of both the structure of world politics and the role of the foreign policy process in decision making. One possible answer would be that President Eisenhower made the most difficult decision by not sending in U.S. troops, thus allowing France to be defeated and risking that Vietnam would fall to communism; many would argue that the later conflict was his fault.

We might also ask questions about how the U.S. experience in Vietnam helps us to understand similar foreign policy problems. For example, how common is it that the goals of U.S. foreign policy change during a conflict, as was the case after 1967 when involvement in Vietnam deepened? A few moments of reflection on events since Vietnam would reveal that the situation the United States faced is one that has repeatedly confronted countries that militarily intervene into affairs: it is easier to enter into a conflict than it is to exit one, and as the involvement deepens with no end in sight, public demands to exit with honor grow. Both the United States and Soviet Union found it easier to send troops to Afghanistan than to bring them home, and the United States has faced a similar situation in Iraq.

Understanding Conflict and Cooperation

Conflict and cooperation, as our brief overview of the pathway travelled by the United States and Vietnam reveals, are central features of world politics. They are the staple of behind-the-scenes interactions between governments, often conducted in secret out of the public's eye, and they are subject to headlines and lead stories on television and in newspapers and on Web sites. Yet for all the attention they receive, disagreements continue over why conflicts occur and under what conditions cooperation is most likely to be realized.

One reason for this is that conflict and cooperation appear to be simple, straightforward concepts. In popular usage, we translate them into polar opposites. They are taken to mean war and peace. But they are not. Conflict, by definition, does not have to involve violence, and cooperation does not have to mean perfect harmony. *Conflicts* do involve disagreements and disputes. They may reach the level of open hostilities and warfare, or they may not. We not only have conflicts with our enemies but also with our friends and allies. In the latter case, they tend to be resolved in an amicable fashion. *Cooperation* entails working together and coordinating one's actions with that of a group in order to achieve a larger purpose. It does not mean an absence of disagreement about the means and ends. One collaborator may try to impose its views on others, while another may threaten to defect from the group unless its demands are met. Complicating matters further is that states may be heavily engaged in conflict and cooperation with the same country.

A second reason for the continuing clash over how to best understand conflict and cooperation is that each tends to be studied separately. Separate textbook chapters are organized around each, with the causes, dynamics, and outcomes presented in isolation from one another, and different frameworks are used to organize the discussion. Conflict studies typically begin with some notion of a conflict cycle, while cooperation studies move quickly to a discussion of stages and strategies of negotiation. Likewise, the major theoretical perspectives used in studying world politics and international relations take different views of conflict and cooperation, with the result that they often appear to be talking past one another rather than to one another (see Box 1.1).

In *Cases in International Relations: Pathways to Conflict and Cooperation*, we seek to clarify the relationship between conflict and cooperation in world politics by presenting the two concepts in such a way that recognizes their differences without treating them as polar opposites. We also link this discussion to insights from varying theoretical perspectives. Our point of departure is that conflict and cooperation are not single, stand-alone events. Instead, they are part of a stream of activity that creates a pathway from inception to some form of resolution, however temporary, and then continues on to set in motion a new set of opportunities for both.

In the chapters that follow, we present case studies that illustrate both conflict and cooperation. Case studies are a valuable tool for studying pathways to conflict and cooperation because they allow us to zoom in on an event or problem and clearly identify forces that constrain behavior and forces that create opportunities for action. They also allow us to identify and contrast points of conflict and cooperation. More importantly, when organized in a consistent fashion, as in this book, viewing multiple cases studies allows us to discover points of similarity and differences in how conflict and cooperation evolve and interact. The insights we gain can then be applied to helping us understand future problems in world politics.

| **Box 1.1** |

Concept Focus

Theories of International Relations, Conflict, and Cooperation

Commentators on world politics employ different theoretical frameworks for studying world politics. Each framework views conflict and cooperation differently. In this section we review the approaches of realism, neoliberalism, and constructivism, three of the most prominent theoretical perspectives on world politics.

Realists see world politics as an arena dominated by anarchy. They believe that there are no fundamental legal rules that govern state behavior. Rather, world politics is governed by the competitive and judicious acquisition and use of power. States are locked into a contest for survival in which they must rely upon their own power resources. Failing to do so, putting one's security in the hands of allies, international law, international organizations, or public opinion, invites war and defeat. Realists turn to the underlying power structure of the international system for guidance in how to formulate foreign policies that ensure their survival. A bipolar international system (one characterized by the presence of two competing superpowers) dictates a different type of foreign policy than does a unipolar international system (one in which there exists a single dominant power). Enduring cooperation is a rarity because of the need to pursue power, and peace is possible only when all states follow these rules and adopt narrow definitions of the national interest.

Neoliberals tend to agree with realists that world politics is characterized by anarchy, but they reach very different conclusions about what this means and how to craft foreign policies in response to it. Realists are pessimists. They see conflict as an inevitable and permanently defining feature of world politics. Neoliberals reject this position. They argue that states can escape the grasp of competitive power politics by engaging in a series of rule-building efforts at the domestic and international levels. Common to these efforts is the notion that individuals (and hence states) are rational. They have the ability to engage in enlightened cooperative behavior when it can be shown that cooperation is a more effective means of achieving goals than is conflict.

The first key neoliberal rule-building effort is the establishment of democracy because democratic leaders are more accountable to the public than are autocratic rulers and the public will stop them from engaging in unnecessary wars. Second, states must promote international trade because trade binds countries together in a mutually beneficial relationship. Going to war with a trading partner is far more expensive to the economic well-being of a country than is going to war with a country that one does not rely on for markets, raw materials, or workers. Third, international organizations and laws must be created to provide states with a routinized and predictable means of solving problems peacefully. In the absence of these mechanisms, states fall back on international power politics. Neoliberals argue that even superpowers need to establish and respect international rules if they wish to achieve important foreign policy objectives at a reasonable cost.

Constructivists comprise the third theoretical perspective. Where both realism and neoliberalism have long been used to study world politics, constructivism is a rather recent perspective. It takes issue with the notion that, in some manner, the international system dictates what states must do. Constructivists place norms and ideas at the center of their analysis. They assert that "anarchy is what you make of it." There are no permanent underlying rules or forces of world politics. Individuals establish their own identities and interests. States make their own realities. World politics changes as ideas and images of what the world looks like and how to define the national interest change through a process of learning, socialization, and inter- action with other people. For constructivists, not only is conflict not inevitable but there are no permanent rules as to how to promote cooperation.

Each case study in this book will include a Concept Focus box like this. The concepts introduced in this feature are designed to help you gain a better understanding of how the case study material highlights key themes in the study of world politics. For example, the topics in this box—realism, neoliberal- ism, and constructivism—all suggest that the conflict in Vietnam lasted as long as it did for different reasons. Realists would point to the distribution of power in the international system having forced the United States to get involved. Neoliberals would point to the absence of effective international norms and established procedures for cooperation between the United States and the Soviet Union as the cause. Peace is only possible once these norms and proce- dures are in place. Constructivists would point to the way in which Americans and North Vietnamese defined each other as enemies. Cooperation became possible once we changed our views and saw the other as a possible ally.

Stages on the Pathway to Conflict and Cooperation

The case studies in this book address pressing military, economic, and human security issues. In order to better capture the key aspects of these cases, we break our discussion of pathways of conflict and cooperation down into three broad stages: (1) problem setting and origins, (2) problem definition and response, and (3) problem evolution and development. In the remainder of this chapter, we will look at each of these stages in more detail.

Stage 1: Problem Setting and Origins

A starting point for understanding the dynamics of conflict and coop- eration is to recognize three important political realities. To begin, *foreign policy problems rarely, if ever, come out of nowhere.* The impression some may have that one day there is calm and the next day brings Pearl Harbor, the 9/11 terrorist attacks, the fall of the Berlin Wall, or genocide in Africa is not correct. Reality is far more complex. Sometimes the conditions that give rise to such problems are deteriorating in the open for all to see. Other times they are incubating beneath the surface, out of sight, not unlike the constant shifting of the tectonic plates beneath the earth's surface that are the result of rising pressures we only become aware of when the earth vibrates with small tremors or explodes with a the force of a major eruption.

It takes only a moment's reflection to realize that any number of factors can lead to foreign policy problems that bring states into conflict with one another and call for cooperation between them. In order to better focus our attention on the fundamental forces at work here, we group these factors into three categories. First, there are background conditions. These are the underlying conditions on which a problem rests. Second, there are the immediate conditions that caused the problematic situation to intensify and come into the open. Third, there is often a triggering event that catapults a problem into full view.

The second political reality is *foreign policy problems are not self-contained challenges existing in isolation from other problems.* Not only is a foreign policy problem often linked to others on the agenda, it may also be linked to earlier issues, creating an issue spiral in which tensions increase and negative images of the enemy harden as issues accumulate. In these cases, positions are put forward not simply with an eye to resolving the dispute at hand but also to redress past grievances and gain an advantage for dealing with future ones.[1]

Finally, *the domestic politics of foreign policy problems may differ greatly, even for the same government.* The politics of a foreign policy problem inherited from a previous government or administration differ significantly from those of a foreign policy problem of one's own making, if for no other reason than in the latter case it is not as easy to shift blame onto others. The domestic politics of a new or unprecedented foreign policy problem are similarly different from those surrounding the decision-making process of one which has reappeared. In the latter case, any of a number of options have been tried and failed, public opinion may have hardened, and interest groups may have coalesced around competing positions, all of which reduce a government's ability to manage a foreign policy problem.

In this chapter's brief case study on the Vietnam War, we see that U.S. policymakers did not see Vietnam as an isolated foreign policy problem but as part of the larger Cold War struggle with communism. Domestic political considerations were also present, as Eisenhower was concerned with the financial costs of containing communism. The conflict with Vietnam did not come out of the blue. American foreign policy had been dealing with how to respond to Vietnam's desire for independence since World War II. Each case study in the book will examine this first stage of problem setting and origins on the pathway of conflict and cooperation.

Stage 2: Problem Definition and Response

After establishing a problem's origins, the case study will next explore how the problem was defined and how the actors involved responded. Recognition that a problem exists may be slow in coming, and once a foreign policy problem is recognized, it does not automatically lead to conflict or cooperation. Individually and collectively, policymakers must determine how critical the situation is. A commonly used point of reference is the concept of the national interest, but this alone does not tell us whether conflict or cooperation will result, as policymakers routinely invoke "the national interest" in justifying both conflictual and cooperative foreign policies. They present themselves as having little or no choice but to engage in war, put economic sanctions in place, or sign a treaty because "the national interest" demands it.

In its most restrictive sense, the **national interest** refers to the core goals and objectives of a state's foreign policy. Most typically this list is limited to the state's physical survival, the preservation of its form of government, and the fundamental economic well-being of its citizens, but it need not be. Two traditional areas of disagreement involve the relationship of societal interests to the national interest and the relationship between the national and global interest.

An old adage in U.S. foreign policy was that "what was good for General Motors was good for America." On the other hand, many critics of U.S. foreign policy before and during the Cold War argued that U.S. foreign policy toward Latin America often was nothing more than cover for the United Fruit Company to make large profits while sowing the seeds of anti-Americanism that would later haunt the United States. Similarly, we can find many examples of ethnic groups lobbying the U.S. government for policies supporting their ancestral homelands by using the argument that it was vital to U.S. interests to do so.

The disagreement over the relationship between the national and global interest is somewhat different. Whereas the national interest is generally defined in possessive and exclusionary terms, the **global interest** is usually defined as referring to goals that are shared by all states and help structure the general "atmosphere" in which states act.[2] Such policies are often referred to as public goods because no one can possess them to the exclusion of others. A stable global economy, a clean environment, and peace are all examples of international public goods. The central problem created by public goods is the question of who pays. The ever-present temptation is for states to become free riders while others pay for them.

Once they have recognized and defined a problem, policymakers must identify a course of action to address it. Doing so involves making a series of judgments about the nature of the problem and one's relationship with others. The judgments reached go a long way toward determining to what extent the problem can be addressed through conflict, cooperation, or some combination of the two. Three stand out as particularly important. A first judgment is made over how the underlying motives of others are viewed. Are the interests and concerns of others seen as just and legitimate, or are they viewed with suspicion? Or is it feared that the foreign policy problem being contested is a test case of the state's will or a product of domestic forces in the other country that will lead to ever-increasing demands for concessions?

A second judgment is made between unilateral and collective action to address the problem. If the second strategy is chosen, the decision then becomes who to ally with. Does the state act through existing bodies and organizations, seek out the help of specific states or individuals to act as mediators, or create a "coalition of the willing" to tackle the problem? Embedded in this judgment is a sense of the strength of the foundation on which joint action will be carried out. Will it be a matter of strategic necessity ("the enemy of my enemy is my friend"), convenience ("it works for both sides even though they do not share many goals in common"), or a long historical track record of political or ideological cooperation?

A third judgment centers on the timing of the problem. Is the issue being contested at a tipping point, when the actions being contemplated will either prevent the conflict from escalating further and/or create conditions that will lead to a more permanent resolution of the problem? Related to this is the question of whether the domestic politics of key states and conditions in the international system make the issue "ripe" for settlement. If not, it may be judged that little or no serious action should be taken since the prospects for success are slim.

Once they have assessed the situation, policymakers must decide what action to take. In combination with interests and judgments, the key determinant here centers on the amount of power resources at a state's disposal. Two truths must always be kept in mind when making decisions about using power. First, the utility of power is dependent on the context in which it is to be used. In this sense, power is not like money, which is equally usable in any store or for any product. Projecting and using power depend on the nature of the problem, the problem's location, and the identity and interests of those involved.[3] The second truth is that power is not static. A state's power resources will change over time, and the direction of change, when coupled with changes in the power resources of other states, can have profound psychological effects on how policymakers approach a foreign policy problem. Policymakers in a declining state engaged in a foreign policy dispute with a rising state may feel compelled to act quickly and aggressively before the balance of power between the two states moves decidedly against them. Policymakers in a state whose power position is rising may become overconfident. They may overreach or fail to appreciate the position of others when making decisions.

In broad terms these power resources may be divided into hard and soft power.[4] **Hard power** is the ability to compel and impose a position or outcome on another state. **Soft power** is the ability to influence another state so that they make the decision to adopt the desired position or accept the desired outcome on their own. Hard and soft power may be brought to bear on an ally or adversary in varying combinations in both cooperative and conflictual foreign policy undertakings. For example, an adversary in a negotiation may be encouraged to accept terms proposed by the stronger power through the promise of economic aid and may be compelled to do so through the threat of an imminent military action. A military opponent may be compelled to accept defeat as a result of battlefield losses and may be encouraged to do so by offers of amnesty for government officials and soldiers.

It is important to stress that regardless of whether policymakers engage in cooperation or conflict, they are involved in a two-level game. They are not simply interacting with another state, they are also engaged in a domestic political process regarding what positions can and cannot be taken in those international settings. A strategy that requires making concessions to another state can be pursued only if key domestic groups and powerful parts of the government will support those concessions. Similarly, the support of important domestic groups may require that those groups receive a side payment of some type, either in the agreement or elsewhere.

Looking back at our brief Vietnam case study in this chapter, it is clear that U.S. policymakers repeatedly saw stopping North Vietnamese aggression as a high-priority national interest problem. We can also see that domestic politics continued to color American decision making and affect both how the national interest was defined and the ability of the United States to wage war. While on one level U.S. power was far superior to that of North Vietnam, in the end it was not sufficient to effect defeat, and peace talks were necessary.

Stage 3: Problem Evolution and Development

The third stage addressed by each case study considers how the problem at hand evolved and developed. Whether they are addressed through conflict or cooperation, efforts to deal with disputes eventually move to some form of resolution. Reaching this point does not necessarily mark the permanent resolution of an issue. A number of endgames are possible. One outcome is characterized as a **passive settlement**. In this outcome all sides realize that no conclusive agreement can be reached, and the result is that the points of dispute persist and only minimal or largely symbolic efforts are made to break the deadlock on the negotiating table, in economic relations, or on the battlefield to move the issue to a conclusion. In essence, all sides have come to accept the status quo and are willing to live with the situation rather than change it. You will see an example of passive settlement in the Chapter 9 case study on world hunger. In cases like this, the issue may be reactivated as domestic and international politics change or become obsolete and no longer serve as a point of contention.

Even when a **formal settlement** to the issue has been reached, such as in a treaty, there is no guarantee that the problem will not reemerge in the future. There are several reasons for this. One has to do with the process by which the outcome was arrived at, as the manner in which an agreement is reached is often just as important as the content of the agreement. Both conflict and cooperation can end through either mutual agreement or with one side imposing a solution on the other. Rather than solving a problem, the end result may only reenergize the conflict or cause it to resurface in a different form. This is often most noticeably the case with military conflicts such as the efforts to combat terrorism since 9/11, discussed in Chapter 6.

The second possible reason a problem might reemerge involves the content of the agreement. The settlement may be incomplete, leaving out key points of dispute, or it may represent a low-level compromise that all can agree to but which is insufficient to address the problem. At times, formal settlement between Israel and the Palestinians has resulted in this outcome, as you will see in Chapter 4. It is also possible that one or more of the states involved in the dispute may seek an agreement in order to achieve a truce that will allow it to reposition its resources for a new round of negotiations or military action. Additionally, few agreements are self-enforcing. The need often exists for states to take responsibility either directly, through their foreign policies, or indirectly, through the creation of an international organization or commission, to ensure that the agreement's terms are being respected. This need is especially great in situation where "spoilers" arise.[5] Spoilers arise because not everyone involved in the dispute has either literally or emotionally signed on to the agreement. Often these spoilers are pictured as renegade forces or neighboring states that are dissatisfied with a peace agreement. They may also be respected political figures who opposed the agreement, voted against its approval, and vowed to undo the agreement through constitutional means.

The third factor that leads to the reemergence of an issue or its continuation after a formal settlement has been reached lies with the nature of the issue being contested. The temptation is for policymakers and the public to view an issue as having been solved when an agreement is reached or victory is pronounced. Yet many problems in world politics do not lend themselves to being solved. One example of this would be organizing a universally acceptable policy for world trade, discussed in Chapter 8. Problems such as this require constant attention and monitoring so that the situations they grow out of can be managed and the resulting risks and negative consequences held in check.[6]

As we saw in this chapter, the Vietnam War ended with a formal peace agreement, but the agreement did not end the conflict. South Vietnam soon collapsed and Vietnam was reunited under communist rule. U.S.-Vietnam relations continued on an uneven path, with new or related conflicts arising and new efforts at cooperation initiated, to the point where, today, the two countries coexist much in the same manner as do most states.

Conclusion: The Dynamics of State Behavior

Conflict and cooperation are challenging topics to study. While at first glance their central dynamics often are clearly visible, beneath the surface there exists a great diversity of motives, influences, strategies, and possible outcomes. In *Cases in International Relations: Pathways to Conflict and Cooperation*, we have selected fifteen case studies to help highlight this complexity and stimulate thinking about the underlying dynamics of state behavior in these two areas. The cases are selected with an eye toward their contemporary relevance for world politics, and they examine the actions of a wide range of actors: powerful states, small states, international organizations, nonprofit organizations, multinational corporations, and individuals.

Each of the chapters is organized in a similar fashion. They begin by noting the contemporary relevance of the case study topic and then analyze one important feature of its pathway to the present through a framework organized around the three common themes just discussed: (1) problem setting and origins, (2) problem definition and response, and (3) problem evolution and development. A brief Case Summary section outlines the key concepts, actors, and issues in the chapter and prepares you for the pathway of conflict and cooperation you are about to travel down, and a Concept Focus box highlights one theoretical topic or issue central to understanding the pattern of conflict or cooperation being discussed. A Spotlight box takes a closer look at an important aspect of the case study.

The Case Analysis section that appears at the end of each chapter contains questions that encourage you to develop and apply your understanding of conflict and cooperation to the individual case under discussion. These questions get you thinking about the case study and the concepts behind it and give you the opportunity to apply what you've learned from the case to similar problems in the world. As you make your own assessments, you will begin to develop the analytical skills that will allow you to make meaningful comparisons among events, more fully understand future issues in world politics, and gain a better understanding of the pathways open to and taken by countries as they engage in conflict and cooperation.

Suggested Readings

Crocker, Chester, Fen Osler Hampson, and Pamela Aall, eds. *Turbulent Peace: The Challenge of Managing International Conflict.* Washington, DC: United States Institute for Peace, 2001. This is a collection of essays on sources of conflict, strategies for addressing these sources, and the process of peace-building.

Hill, Christopher. *The Changing Politics of Foreign Policy.* New York: Palgrave Macmillan, 2003. Hill surveys the literature on contemporary influences on foreign policy-making.

Fisher, Roger. *International Conflict for Beginners.* New York: Harper, 1969. This is a short, classic overview of the dynamics of international cooperation.

Matthews, Robert, Arthur Rubinoff, and Janice Gross Stein, eds. *International Conflict Management.* Englewood Cliffs, NJ: Prentice Hall, 1984. These essays focus on individual, societal, state, and international system influences on conflict management.

Ramsbotham, Oliver, Tom Woodhouse, and Hugh Miall. *Contemporary Conflict Resolution*, 3rd. ed. Cambridge, UK: Polity, 2011. This work is a survey of key concepts and practices in the field of conflict resolution.

Stein, Arthur. *Why Nations Cooperate.* Ithaca, NY: Cornell University Press, 1990. Stein examines the competing influences of structure and choice in the process of international cooperation.

Web Resources

Institute for the Study of War, www.understandingwar.org. This organization is dedicated to advancing the informed understanding of U.S. military affairs and response to emerging threats.

Institute of Peace and Conflict Studies, www.ipcs.org. The institute is a think tank that conducts independent research and analysis on conventional and unconventional security issues.

International Crisis Group, www.crisisgroup.org. This group is focused on preventing and resolving deadly conflict.

Peace Research Institute-Oslo, www.prio.no. This research institution promotes peace through conflict resolution, dialogue and reconciliation, and policymaking.

Social Science Research Council, www.ssrc.org/programs. The council works with policymakers, social scientists, and practitioners on matters that include conflict and peace-building.

United States Institute of Peace, www.usip.org. Established by Congress in 1984, the institute is focused on the prevention of violence and the mitigation of deadly conflict overseas.

PART I
Military Security

2 Power Management in the South China Sea

For the first two decades of the Cold War, Europe was the center stage of world politics, with the United States and Soviet Union as the lead actors. It was here that these two superpowers learned how to compete safely against the backdrop of the ever-present possibility of a nuclear confrontation. Nothing captured the simultaneous presence of superpower conflict and cooperation in those early efforts at power management more than did a series of crises over Berlin, beginning with the Berlin airlift in 1948 and culminating in the building of the Berlin Wall in 1961. Today we are witnessing what many regard as a new and vital experiment in power management that may take us down a pathway of conflict and cooperation that could play out differently from that in Europe. The key actors now are the United States and China, although a large cast of potentially important and independent-minded supporting actors are also present, just as they were in early post–World War II Europe. The South China Sea now provides the center stage where conflict and cooperation are playing out. And, just as in the case of Europe, the danger of military confrontation cannot be dismissed.

There is one significant way in which the European Cold War confrontations differed from today's South China Sea issue. In Europe, dividing lines were easily established. Everyone knew where the iron curtain was located. The South China Sea lacks any such clear markers of national influence. Instead we find multiple and overlapping claims to lands and the seas surrounding them, and the states making those claims have no intention of dropping them. China's case is particularly interesting in this regard for two reasons. First, China's claim to the South China Sea is long-standing. A dashed line outlining China's claim to the sea was drawn in the 1930s and has appeared on maps since 1947, yet the meaning of this demarcation is unclear. The line has been defined as marking the extent of China's "historical claim" to the South China Sea and its "traditional sea boundary line," but neither the Republic of China (Taiwan) nor the People's Republic of China have officially stated that this dashed line is an international boundary line and, if it is, whether it is a maritime or territorial boundary line.[1] Second, today China is the dominant military and economic power in the region.

This chapter's Concept Focus will examine different means of managing power in the international system. The Spotlight section will examine the evolution of China's strategic thinking as it pertains to the South China Sea and help craft a better understanding of the worldview behind the decisions of the makers of China's foreign policy.

Contestation in the South China Sea

The South China Sea is a contested area. Covering some 648,000 square nautical miles, it is one of the largest semi-enclosed seas in the world. Five countries (six if Taiwan is counted) are located around its rim and claim

---

| **Box 2.1** |

Case Summary

Competing territorial claims to resource-rich islands and reefs in the South China Sea have spurred rising tensions over issues of sovereignty, regional security, and economic interest in a region undergoing major shifts in the distribution of military and economic power.

Global Context

During the Cold War, world politics centered on the global competition and cooperative efforts of the United States and Soviet Union. Today, regional powers and regional interests have assumed greater importance. Nowhere is this more evident than in Asia, where China's influence is on the rise.

Key Actors

- China
- Vietnam
- The Philippines
- United States
- ASEAN (Association of Southeast Asian Nations)

Motives

- Countries laying territorial claims in the South China Sea are motivated by the mineral-rich resources that would benefit their economies and the strategic geographic location that could bolster their security.
- The United States, though officially neutral, is concerned for freedom of navigation in the South China Sea.
- ASEAN has sought to provide a forum for the peaceful settlement of disputes among states with conflicting claims to islands in the South China Sea.

Concepts

- Sovereignty
- Globalization
- National interest
- Power

sovereignty over all or parts of it: China, Vietnam, the Philippines, Brunei, and Malaysia. China is the central player and main protagonist in the unfolding drama of how control over the South China Sea is to be allocated. At issue is not only the control of the sea but control over key islands within it. Three factors make the current situation in the South China Sea today different from in the past. One is the more active interest and presence of the United States in the conflict. Under the Barack Obama administration, the United States announced its intention to "pivot" American foreign policy more intensively on Asia. The second factor is the increased value of the energy resources found in the South China Sea, which make it a valuable prize to possess. For example, in early 2013 Chevron Oil Company and the China National Offshore Oil Corporation announced a production-sharing agreement for two shallow-water exploration blocks in the sea. Third, there is a sense of growing frustration with the failure of efforts to curb China's attempts to expand its control over the South China Sea. Particularly note-worthy here is that in 2013 the Philippines announced it was taking its dispute with China over the Spratly Islands to the United Nations Arbitral Tribunal. China's ambassador to the Philippines responded that Chinese sovereignty over these islands was "indisputable."

Viewed from a geographic perspective, the South China Sea is a marginal sea. It is a partly enclosed body of water that is adjacent to and opens onto an ocean. Approached from a political perspective, the South China Sea is anything but marginal. It may well be the front line of the next major struggle for international military and economic hegemony.[2] China's policy toward the sea is seen by many as a key indicator of the overall direction the nation's foreign policy will take in the coming years. To its defenders, China's South China Sea policy is evidence of its peaceful rise. To its opponents, it is evidence of China's rising aggressiveness. Either through miscalculation or deliberate actions, one possible outcome of rising tensions over the South China Sea is war. Should war occur, it may be very different from past conflicts: it will be principally fought at sea rather than on land.[3] One leading regional diplomat voiced the fear that a different future awaited the South China Sea, claiming it was at risk of becoming "Asia's Palestine."[4]

Problem Setting and Origins: History and Occupation

At the turn of the twenty-first century, some 270 million people lived in coastal areas bordering on the South China Sea. Home to a great diversity of sea life and aquatic vegetation, the sea varies greatly in depth from shallow pools of water to the Manila Trench, which reaches a recorded depth of 5,377 meters. Also found within its boundaries are at least 400 and perhaps as many as 650 rocks, reefs, atolls, and islands, some of which are so small that they are only visible at low tide. Only forty-eight to

---

| Box 2.2 |

Concept Focus

Managing Power in the International System

Managing power has traditionally been seen as the core problem in international politics. It holds this position because the presumed anarchic nature of the international system undermines the effectiveness of any rules or institutions that might control state behavior. Sovereignty places ultimate power with the state. State survival thus requires the acquisition of power and the prudent use of that power. The more powerful the state, the stronger its voice in international policy deliberations and the more foreign policy options open to it. The less powerful the state, the fewer foreign policy options it has and the more vulnerable it is to pressure (power) applied against it by others. As is commonly noted, the strong do what they wish; the weak do what they must.

No single strategy or formula exists for managing power relations. The selection of a strategy depends upon the manner in which power is distributed in the global or regional system and the underlying relationship between states. In the first instance, we routinely characterize international systems as being unipolar, bipolar, or multipolar. Within each of these systems, varying patterns of cooperation and conflict can be found. Most problematic for policymakers is when an international or regional system is in transition and does not fit into one of these categories. Without clear-cut rules for managing power, crises have a much greater potential to escalate into military conflict as incorrect actions are taken and the policies of others are misinterpreted.

During the Cold War the international system was **bipolar**, with the United States and Soviet Union as the two dominant rival powers. While fundamentally in conflict, their relationship also contained elements of cooperation, as evidenced by the series of nuclear bilateral arms control agreements they negotiated. With the end of the Cold War, the international system entered into a period that has generally been characterized as **unipolar,** with the United States as the sole superpower. Unipolar systems tend not to be very stable or long lasting. The dynamics of power acquisition and power use tend to produce challengers to the dominant power and cause it to overreach and see its power diminish compared to other states. The erosion of unipolarity has given rise to speculation over what type of power management system might replace it. Some see a return to bipolarity, while others speculate that there might come into existence a **multipolar** system in which several states are relatively equal in power. States in a multipolar system balance each other by entering into shifting coalitions and alliances depending upon the nature of the problem and the identity of the aggressors.

Unipolarity, bipolarity, and multipolarity are forms of international power management that have been found throughout history. It is also possible to think of future forms of managing power at the international or regional level. One such possibility is a **universal community** in which all states are free to join and participate in equally, regardless of their ideology, level of economic development, or

(Continued)

(Continued)

possession of military power. The United Nations General Assembly is a possible model for such a power management system.

Each of these four different types of power management systems has been identified as a future possibility for the Asia-Pacific. The most logical dominant power in a unipolar system would be China. A *Pax Sinica* ("Chinese peace") based on Chinese economic and military power, as well as its geographic location, would place the United States in the position of lead challenger. A second possibility is a bipolar regional system modeled on the relationship that existed between the United States and Soviet Union in the 1970s. Under it, a superpower condominium would exist. China and the United States would be competitors who viewed the other's motives with suspicion but recognized the need to cooperate to maintain regional stability. The two powers would share responsibility for managing Asia-Pacific relations—perhaps each having its own sphere of influence. As in the Cold War, power management would occur through periodic summit conferences and bilateral agreements.

Developments in Asia-Pacific might, however, produce a demand from other states in the region that they too be given a voice in managing power relations in the region. One strategy for dealing with their concerns would be to create a multipolar system—the so-called Concert of Asia. Indonesia, Japan, and India are the three most frequently mentioned candidates for membership in such a coalition. The idea of the Concert of Asia is modeled on the five-power Concert of Europe that came into prominence following the defeat of Napoleon and that managed affairs in Europe until the outbreak of World War I. Its members were Great Britain, Russia, Austria, Prussia, and post-Napoleonic France. A final option is the creation of a Pacific Community in which—at least in theory—all states in the region could belong but none would dominate. Agreements would be reached through consensus and bargaining. Such a power management system would protect the diversity of interests held by states in Asia-Pacific but would do so at the risk of gridlock and indecision. The most prominent organization that might provide a basis for a Pacific Community is the Association of East Asian States (ASEAN), which was founded in 1967 and has become the organizational spearhead for managing state relations in the region.

---

fifty are occupied. The two largest groupings of land are the Spratly Islands and the Paracel Islands. The Spratly Islands consist of 190 to 230 rocks, atolls, reefs, and islands, of which only seven are greater than 0.1 square kilometers in size. The Paracel Islands are comprised of some thirty islets, sandbanks, and reefs.

The number of occupied features is ambiguous and contested because, as we shall see, the term *occupied* is politically significant for territorial claims made by states bordering on the South China Sea but lacks any agreed-upon definition. Vietnam occupies or has a presence (a step below occupying) on twenty-seven features; China has a presence on seven features; Malaysia has occupied three features and has a presence on two others; the Philippines has a presence on nine features; and Taiwan occupies one island. In several cases, food and water must be brought to the inhabitants of the territory, and in others special hardship pay is given to those residing there.

The physical occupation of pieces of land within the South China Sea is only one basis on which claims to national jurisdiction over those lands and their surrounding maritime areas has been made. History is another. In some cases the claims are deeply rooted in past events and self-image. China's claims go back to the Han Dynasty (206 BC–220 AD), and the South China Sea is often simply referred to as one of the "three seas" or the "near seas" (along with the East China and Yellow Seas). Claims such as Vietnam's are based on the actions of the colonial powers that once ruled those countries. France had claimed jurisdiction over the Spratly Islands in 1929 and formally annexed nine islands in 1933, so South Vietnam claimed to have inherited these territories in 1951. Upon unification after the end of the Vietnam War, North Vietnam reasserted these claims on behalf of a united Vietnam. The Philippines claims sovereignty over one set of islands on the basis of the actions of a Filipino fisherman who claimed them in 1956 and then "transferred" ownership to the Philippines. The islands in question were once ruled by Japan, but it was forced to give them up as part of the peace settlements that ended World War II.

Geography is yet another basis on which maritime area is claimed. Both Malaysia and Brunei claim portions of the South China Sea on the assertion that those portions are extensions of the continental shelf or a straight-line projection of their territory. The scope of the disputes is immense. China, Taiwan, and Vietnam claim all of the South China Sea, while the Philippines, Malaysia, and Brunei claim portions of it.[5] Table 2.1 summarizes the competing claims to the Spratly Islands, which are at the center of the current dispute and are discussed throughout this case study.

Not only is the scope of the competing claims extensive, so is the intensity with which they are held. Three geostrategic factors frame interactions in the South China Sea.[6] The first is the sea's position as a critical point of transit for global commercial shipping and naval operations. Within the South China Sea are three major shipping lanes through which oil and other commodities must pass to move from the Middle East, Latin America, and Africa to China, Japan, and Korea. These lanes are the Strait of Malacca, the Sunda Strait, and the Philippine Sea. The amount of oil passing through the Straight of Malacca is six times larger than that passing through the Suez Canal and seventeen times the amount going through the Panama Canal. All totaled, about 60 percent of the energy supplies of Japan and Taiwan pass through the South China Sea. Two-thirds of South Korea's energy does so as well, as do almost 80 percent of China's crude oil imports. Militarily, the South China Sea is important to the United States as a transit point and operating area for U.S. Navy and Air Force units in Asia, the Persian Gulf, and the Indian Ocean.

The second geostrategic factor is the presence of potentially significant natural energy reserves beneath the sea. The Chinese media have referred

Table 2.1	Competing Claims to the Spratly Islands	
COUNTRY	CLAIM	ISLANDS OCCUPIED
China	Claims the entire area on historical grounds dating back to the Han Dynasty and subsequent use by Chinese fisherman	Seven islands occupied; major military garrison established in 1988
Philippines	Claims the Kalayaan Islands, which the Philippines officially made national territory in 1971	Nine islands occupied; major military garrison established in 1971
Vietnam	Claims the entire area. Argues it took sovereignty when it became independent from France (1954), which claimed administrative control over Vietnam in 1929	Twenty-four islands occupied; major military garrison established in 1974
Malaysia	Claim based on the projection of the continental shelf into a portion of the Spratly Islands	Three islands occupied; major military garrison established in 1983
Taiwan	Claims entire area. Claim is similar to that of China since both China and Taiwan officially assert that they are the true government of China	One island occupied; major military garrison established in 1956
Brunei	Claim based on extension of the continental shelf into Spratly Islands	No islands occupied; no military presence established

Source: Ralph A. Cossa. *Security Implications of Conflict in the South China Sea.* Honolulu: Center for Strategic and International Studies, 1998.

to the South China Sea as the "second Persian Gulf." Estimates as to the amount of oil and natural gas present vary, however. While some Chinese estimates place it at 130 billion barrels, a 1991 study concluded that 10 to 14 billion barrels of oil existed beneath the sea. A 1995 Russian study estimated that 6 billion barrels were present. Large fishing stocks are also present. In 1980 alone, 2.5 million tons of fish were harvested around the Spratly Islands.

The final geostrategic feature is the special place that the South China Sea holds in China's national security thinking. China's position in this regard is often compared to that of the United States and its long-held belief in the strategic importance of the Caribbean Sea. As reflected in the Monroe Doctrine and the Roosevelt Corollary, the U.S. government saw the Caribbean Sea as an area of special influence due to its proximity to the United States. Accordingly, it was viewed as a region in which the United

Timeline
Claims in the South China Sea

1930s	China's claims in the South China Sea first appear on maps.
1950	China establishes a presence in the Paracel Islands.
1951	South Vietnam claims it has inherited the Spratly islands that France annexed in 1933.
1956	The Philippines claims ownership of some territory in the Spratly Islands.
1974	South Vietnam and China engage in a brief naval conflict after which China takes control of the islands South Vietnam had occupied.
1988	China and South Vietnam race to establish a presence on unoccupied islands.
1990	China proposes a joint China-Vietnam development of the Spratly Islands.
1992	The Declaration of the South China Sea is signed at a meeting of ASEAN.
1995	China and the Philippines face off over Mischief Reef.
2002	An ASEAN-China code of conduct for long-term stability in the South China Sea is finalized.
2005	A tripartite agreement between China, Vietnam, and the Philippines allows for a joint venture of their national oil companies to survey territory that includes the Spratly Islands.
2008	China launches independent plans to explore and develop oil deposits in the South China Sea and announces that the Spratly and Paracel Islands have county-level status within one of its provinces.
2010	The United States engages in large-scale military exercises with South Korea; China carries out live ammunition exercises at about the same time.
	Secretary of State Hillary Clinton says the South China Sea is "pivotal to regional stability."
2013	The Philippines takes its dispute with China over the Spratly Islands to the United Nations Arbitral Tribunal

States could freely intervene and which other powers had to be kept out of. So too has China come to see the South China Sea as an area of special political and commercial interest that it must dominate and from which others must be excluded. The analogy is not perfect, however, and herein lies the problem for China. Whereas the United States is the lone major power in the Caribbean Sea, with Great Britain, France, and Spain all an ocean away, China is not the lone major power in the South China Sea. Not only is Japan nearby in the Pacific Ocean but technological challenges have reduced the significance of geographic distance so that the United States is also capable of exerting a very real presence in the region.

Problem Definition and Response: Territorial Ambitions and Chinese Policy

The South China Sea was not an area of major regional tensions in the early years of the Cold War. The center of hostilities lay elsewhere.[7] In the 1950s this was Taiwan, where two major crises broke out. In 1954 the first Taiwan Strait crisis began when China started shelling the island of Quemoy. The United States countered by signing a mutual defense treaty with Taiwan, and the Senate passed the Formosa Resolution, which authorized President Dwight Eisenhower to use force to protect Taiwan's offshore islands. The second Taiwan Straits crisis occurred in 1958 and featured limited military engagements between the two sides. It ended when the United States went unchallenged in escorting a supply ship to Quemoy. In the 1960s the Vietnam War commanded center stage. It was only as the war began to wind down that attention shifted to the South China Sea and, in particular, to the Paracel Islands.

China had begun to establish a presence in the Paracel Islands in 1950 when it occupied Woody Island, the largest island in the chain. Chinese premier Zhou Enlai officially claimed the Paracel Islands and the Spratly Islands for China in 1951 as the Allies were negotiating the final peace agreement with Japan. Zhou reiterated China's claim to the territorial water surrounding the Paracel and Spratly Islands in 1958 during the second Taiwan crisis. One year later, South Vietnam moved to establish its claim to the Paracel Islands by capturing Chinese fisherman who frequently operated in the waters offshore and also by setting up a weather station on one of the islands. China's response was muted. It did not directly challenge South Vietnam's claim to the Paracels, but it built up a naval presence on Woody Island and conducted an average of five naval patrols per year in the region between 1960 and 1973.

The situation changed in January 1974 when South Vietnam intercepted two Chinese fishing boats. A brief naval conflict ensued, with Chinese naval forces, consisting largely of four fast attack craft and two minesweepers, defeating South Vietnamese naval forces essentially made up of three destroyers. After the encounter China took control of the islands that South Vietnam had occupied. Evidence suggests that while China did not begin the conflict by firing the first shot and that it repeatedly warned South Vietnamese forces to end their military operations, China did engineer the crisis and lured South Vietnam into it. Following South Vietnam's defeat, China gave high priority to consolidating its control over the Paracel

---

| **Box 2.3** |

Spotlight

China's Strategic Thinking in the South China Sea

The evolution of China's South China Sea strategy can best be understood by approaching it from two different perspectives. The first places the greatest emphasis on the security objectives to be realized by the strategy. Here we see an evolution from a geocentric strategy that emphasized military defense of China's borders to an economic-centered one that emphasizes protecting and promoting China's economic development. China's anti-encirclement concerns, a product of the Sino-Soviet split, drew the nation's attention to the Paracel Islands. The last stages of the Vietnam War often found the Soviet Union and China at odds with one another. Where the Soviet Union largely supported secret negotiations to bring an end to the war, China took a hard line position and opposed peace talks between the United States and North Vietnam. Differences in domestic politics were also pronounced. China under Mao Zedong's leadership launched the Great Cultural Revolution, which radicalized Chinese society, while under Leonid Brezhnev's leadership the Soviet Union became an increasingly status quo society. These circumstances led China to see the Soviet Union as a potential threat to its security. Key additional elements to this threat were the withdrawal of the United States from South Vietnam and the possibility of an alliance between the Soviet Union and North Vietnam that might lead to the establishment of a Soviet naval base there, something that occurred in 1979. One solution that states commonly employ when faced with national security threats is to strengthen their border areas and push those borders out to provide maximum room for maneuver and protection.

As the Sino-Soviet split moderated in intensity and became less central to China's strategic policy, attention shifted to an economic-centered view of the South China Sea. At the heart of this shift in thinking was China's concern for the economic implications of its rapidly growing population, especially as that growth was linked to heavy land use and poverty. Party leaders, including Deng Xiaoping, chair of the Chinese Communist Party, began to speak of the need to develop untapped resources to further China's modernization. Chinese newspaper articles began to discuss the decline in China's land-based resources, the growing size of the global population, and the important role that technical knowledge would play in exploiting deep-sea resources. A 1988 article stated, "In order to make sure that the descendents of the Chinese nation can survive, develop, prosper and flourish in the world in the future, we should vigorously develop and use the oceans. To protect and defend the rights and interests of the reefs and islands within Chinese waters is a sacred mission."[8]

The second perspective in understanding China's shift in South China Sea strategy places bureaucratic interests at the center of the process. The long-established view was that China was a continental power and that the primary mission of its navy was coastal defense. This policy did not require a large navy, and thus the People's Liberation Army-Navy (PLA-N) remained small. Mao's death and the purge of radicals provided the political opening for the PLA-N to break free from these constraints.

(Continued)

(Continued)

It successfully argued that defending China required a modern, powerful, high seas navy to counteract both the United States' and the Soviet Union's Asian naval forces. The PLA-N's modernization and expansion plans were jeopardized, however, as first U.S.-China relations improved and then Sino-Soviet relations did.

It was at this point that Chinese naval strategists began to push in earnest a strategic mission tied to the growing interest in economic development. They proposed that recovering "lost territories" in the South China Sea and reasserting Chinese sovereignty over the rich maritime resources (most notably fish and oil) surrounding them was a core PLA-N mission. From a strategic point of view, reasserting sovereignty translated into defending these territories from foreign incursions. Significantly, the key islands in this strategic posture were the Spratly Islands. They were sufficiently distant from China to require a long-distance, high seas naval capability. This distance, combined with the necessity to protect the islands from hostile takeovers, led to a need for an air support capability as well as amphibious forces that could go ashore. In brief, the PLA-N needed not only a large, modern navy, it needed to become skilled in joint operations.

Islands. Harbors were dredged, gun emplacements were constructed, and storage units were built.

Now in firm control over the Paracel Islands, China's attention shifted southward to the Spratly Islands.[9] A first encounter was with Vietnam. Even before the Vietnam War formally ended, North Vietnam moved to take control over portions of the Spratlys that South Vietnam claimed as its territory. A map produced by Vietnam shortly after unification showed these islands, along with the Paracels, as being Vietnamese territory. China officially protested this position, and in September 1975 the Chinese Ministry of Foreign Affairs delivered a diplomatic note to North Vietnam stating that its attitude was "unreasonable." Two months later, Vietnam replied that the South China Sea islands were definitely Vietnamese territory but proposed that China and Vietnam set up talks on the matter. China again maintained that Vietnam's position was "unreasonable" and soon thereafter declared that "all the islands belonging to China will definitely return to the embrace of the Motherland."[10] Over the next several years, China took a number of steps to make this claim a reality. Among the most visible were conducting test flights of long-range intercontinental ballistic missiles and military encounters with North Vietnam. In one incident two dozen Vietnamese reconnaissance forces came within 500 meters of an island. They were captured and held for almost a year before being released.

Building on its emerging maritime strategy, Chinese foreign policy fell into a predictable pattern as it became more opportunistic and active in advancing China's influence in the South China Sea. Referred to by some as "creeping aggressiveness," this pattern had two parts. First came a period of limited probes and provocations. This was followed by a period of diplomatic delay. The value of limited probes is that they make a forceful military response difficult because of their restricted scope; the incidents do not seem of sufficient magnitude to warrant a large-scale retaliation. Diplomatic delay allows for a reduction in tensions as talks are held, but the qualifications put on what those talks can accomplish means that the most likely outcome is to legitimize and reaffirm the new status quo—a status quo that favors China. The long-term danger for the region is that, when added together over time, these limited probes and provocations could be seen by other states as being a serious challenge that must be met militarily. The immediate regional danger is that no one knows for sure when this conclusion will be reached.

A second round of disputes over control of the South China Sea took place in 1988. In January a Chinese naval task force arrived at Fiery Cross Reef, thereby establishing a Chinese claim to a portion of the Spratly Islands. This action set off a race between China and Vietnam to establish a presence on other unoccupied areas. The two states also exchanged diplomatic notes declaring the actions of the other as illegal and undertook harassing naval and air military operations. These encounters culminated in a deadly fight in March that left seventy-four Vietnamese dead.[11]

China continued to reject Vietnam's proposals for negotiations over the Paracel and Spratly Islands, asserting that its control was "uncontestable." The actions by both countries that followed served to escalate the conflict. China carried out scientific and geological studies of the Spratly Islands, further reinforced and expanded the military installations on Woody Island, and held military exercises. Vietnam countered by twice sending high-ranking civilian and military government officials to visit the islands it controlled. China labeled these actions as a "flagrant provocation against Chinese territorial sovereignty" and called upon Vietnam to "immediately halt."[12] Vietnam responded to Chinese complaints by sending additional troops to the islands and formally incorporating them into Khanh Hao province. China next condemned Vietnam for its brutal violation of Chinese territory and demanded that it withdraw from all islands, reefs, and shoals. China further raised the stakes for controlling the Spratly Islands by announcing that its studies showed 25 billion cubic meters of natural gas and 105 billion barrels of oil lay on the sea floor, an economic boon that any country with a claim would covet.

Evidence suggests that China considered military action against Vietnam in late 1989, but it was unable to act on its plans due to financial problems and fears of becoming a target of even greater international condemnation following the June 1989 Tiananmen Square reform protests, which were violently put down by the Chinese military. These concerns also are credited with a switch in Chinese tactics designed to lessen the growing regional tension surrounding the Spratly Islands.

In 1990 China proposed talks about the potential for joint Vietnamese-Chinese development of the Spratly Islands. While talks were going on, all claims of sovereignty were to be put on hold and China, Vietnam, and the Philippines would remove their troops from the islands. Pointedly, the Paracel Islands were excluded from this proposal. Indonesia took up the idea and organized a quasi-official academic conference in Bandung, Indonesia, in 1991 to examine ways of peacefully managing maritime disputes in the South China Sea. China sent delegates to the conference but indicated that this did not mean it had altered its position on sovereignty over the Spratly or Paracel Islands, only that it was interested in pursuing a peaceful settlement of the disputes. China also stressed that while it supported looking into various types of measures for pursuing a cooperative solution, it was not supportive of establishing an international organization for resolving territorial disputes or allowing states from outside the region to participate in dispute-settlement procedures. Disputes were to be settled by the states involved.

This cooperative posture did not last long. In January 1992 China sent a high-ranking military and civilian delegation to the Spratly Islands to inspect facilities there and plant "sovereign flags." In February China passed legislation officially claiming sovereignty over the Paracel and Spratly Islands and declared that it had the right to use military force to defend these claims. A few months later, China announced that it had entered an agreement with a U.S.-based oil company to explore for oil in the Spratly Islands near Vietnamese-claimed territory. Chinese officials promised the oil company that it would use military force to protect it if need be.

Rising tensions in the South China Sea that resulted from this deal and China's claims of sovereignty again led China to backtrack and engage in diplomacy. The end result of these diplomatic forays was not to resolve the question of sovereignty over the Spratly Islands but to ratify the status quo, which increasingly favored China. The instrument used for this purpose was the signing of the Declaration on the South China Sea at a meeting of the Association of Southeast Asian Nations (ASEAN) in July 1992. In it, all states pledged to promote greater economic cooperation, resolve all sovereignty and jurisdictional issues peacefully, and promote a spirit of kinship and harmony among their peoples. At that same meeting, the Philippines called for a United Nations conference to resolve conflicting South China Sea claims. China rejected such a move. Instead, the ASEAN Regional Forum was created two years later to serve as a vehicle for dialogue and consultation among ASEAN members, as well as to be a focal point for confidence-building measures and preventive diplomacy initiatives. The forum contains twenty-seven members, including the United States and China.

The regional calm produced by these diplomatic maneuvers did not last long, as in 1995 a third confrontation between China and a South China Sea state erupted. This time the adversary was the Philippines and the subject of dispute was Mischief Reef, a small outcropping of rocks 130 miles off the Philippine coast and well within its 200-mile exclusive economic zone.

In 1995 Filipino fisherman reported that they had been detained by the Chinese navy at Mischief Reef. Upon inspecting their claims, the

Philippines discovered that China had secretly built structures on stilts on the reef in 1994 during the monsoon season, when the Philippine navy was unable to patrol the area. The Philippines protested China's action. China rejected the assertion that this was an attempt to claim sovereignty over the reef, stating it was only an effort to provide shelter for the fisherman. From the Philippine perspective, however, this was the first step in the standard Chinese procedure for establishing control. The Philippines engaged in a token military countermove by reinforcing its military presence on another reef, but it was not in a position to do much more. A key limiting factor was the decision by the United States that the 1951 Mutual Defense Treaty did not apply to the defense of Mischief Reef because the treaty was designed to address situations where a common threat to both countries had arisen.

China's actions on Mischief Reef did not go unchallenged. Thailand, which does not have claims to the South China Sea, held China's actions to be overly aggressive. The Philippines sought to bring the Mischief Reef incident up before the ASEAN Regional Forum but was prevented from doing so by China. The United States issued a statement in May 1995 expressing concern about "a pattern of unilateral actions and reactions in the South China Sea that has increased tensions in the region." It went on to note that, while "maintaining freedom of navigation is a fundamental interest of the United States . . . [it] takes no position on the legal merits of competing claims to sovereignty over the various islands, reefs, atolls, and cays in the South China Sea."[13]

China was once again moved to dampen tensions by entering into diplomatic talks. In 1995 it signed an agreement with the Philippines on a bilateral code of conduct for activity in the South China Sea. The following year, in August 1996, tentative agreement was reached on an ASEAN-China code of conduct that was to "lay the foundation for long-term stability in the South China Sea."[14] Progress in formulating a code of conduct was hindered by disagreement over the potential scope of the agreement. A key issue here was whether or not the code extended to the Paracel Islands, a provision to which China objected. Rough drafts were exchanged in 1999, but it was not until 2002 that a final statement, emphasizing the centrality of consensus in the decision-making process, was reached.

Tensions increased once again at Mischief Reef in January 1996 when Chinese and Philippine warships had a minor encounter.[15] More significant incidents followed in April 1997 when Chinese naval vessels appeared near Mischief Reef and China established additional structures on another reef. For its part, the Philippine navy intercepted two Chinese vessels near other contested islands. The following year photographs surfaced showing China constructing larger structures on Mischief Reef, and the Philippines arrested Chinese fisherman near the reef for illegal fishing. In 1998 the Philippines took steps to strengthen its bargaining position vis-à-vis China by signing a visiting forces agreement with the United States that would allow the United States to station military forces there and train Filipino troops.

Problem Evolution and
Development: Same Strategy, New Players

The twenty-first century opened with new efforts by China to lessen regional tensions and solidify is territorial holdings and position in the South China Sea. Its fundamental approach has remained the same, combining aggressiveness with the appearance of accommodation. What has changed is the addition of new, more powerful countries into the contest for control over the South China Sea. No longer are China's primary opponents countries with limited military and economic resources, such as the Philippines and Vietnam. They have been joined by Japan, South Korea, Australia, and the United States. With the involvement of these countries, the possibility has increased that rising tensions resulting from China's repeated limited acts of aggression may lead to calculated or unintended military responses of a greater magnitude than have occurred in the past.

In 2005 China signed a tripartite agreement with Vietnam and the Philippines, establishing a three-year joint venture between their national oil companies to engage in a seismic survey of over 143,000 square kilometers of the South China Sea, including territory associated with the Spratly Islands. The three oil companies split the costs of the research project equally. No provisions were included in the agreement regarding the exploitation of any resources in the area. In 2006, at the second meeting of the ASEAN-China Joint Working Group on the Declaration on the Conduct of Parties in the South China Sea, a series of cooperative joint scientific projects were set up, including one on maritime rescue and recovery (led by the Philippines), a workshop on oceanographic and climate exchanges (led by Vietnam), a workshop on disaster prevention and reduction (led by China), and a training program on ecosystem monitoring (led by China). The limited availability of funding compromised and postponed the implementation of these projects. ASEAN and China have repeatedly revisited the idea of a declaration of conduct and most recently agreed upon vague guidelines for implementing one.

It was not long before China again switched its strategy from accommodation to assertiveness. Economic considerations centering on the rising cost of oil and the beginning of the global economic crisis appear to have played central roles in this change of strategy.[16] In 2007 China began to pressure a joint venture between BP, ExxonMobil, ConocoPhillips, and an Indian oil firm to end exploratory activities with Vietnam off the Vietnamese coast. Soon thereafter, in late 2008, China's national oil company spearheaded a $29 billion venture to explore and develop oil deposits in the South China Sea. China also announced that the Paracel and Spratly Islands now had county-level city status within Hainan Province. This announcement led to a "spontaneous" demonstration in front of the Chinese embassy in Ho Chi Minh City in December 2007.

The conflict in the South China Sea took a new direction in 2009 when the United States became a more central player both diplomatically and

militarily. That year a series of naval encounters took place between the
U.S. and Chinese navies. In one, two U.S. intelligence-gathering ships, the
Impeccable and the *Victorious*, were harassed by Chinese surface vessels
and aircraft. In the other, a Chinese submarine collided with the USS *John
McCain*. In 2010, on the sixtieth anniversary of the beginning of the Korean
War, the United States sent the USS *George Washington*, a nuclear-powered
supercarrier, and three destroyers to South Korea. They later took part in a
large-scale military exercise involving F-22 fighter-bombers and thousands
of U.S. and South Korean troops. For its part, China's South Sea Fleet carried out a live ammunition exercise and an amphibious landing involving
1,800 marines. While these military moves and countermoves did not bring
the region close to war, they did signal that China's opponents might no
longer be as willing to allow China to further its regional influence at a low
military cost.

In 2010 the dispute between the United States and China also moved to
the diplomatic arena. At the 2010 meeting of the ASEAN Regional Forum,
Secretary of State Hillary Clinton asserted that resolving the territorial
disputes in the South China Sea was a "leading diplomatic priority" and
"pivotal to regional stability." She added that freedom of navigation in the
South China Sea was in the U.S. "national interest." The Chinese army
responded with a statement that China has "indisputable sovereignty" over
the South China Sea. The dispute was further intensified because China had
asked the United States not to bring the matter up at the meeting. In 2011
China reiterated its claim of sovereignty over the Spratly Islands in a verbal
statement made to the Law of the Sea Convention commission that was
reviewing maritime claims, stating that China was "fully entitled" to territorial waters, an exclusive economic zone, and a continental shelf.

The question of control over the South China Sea brought continued controversy in 2012. In July, at the meeting of the ASEAN Regional Forum,
China warned attending countries not to bring up the subject of territorial disputes, saying it was not "an appropriate venue," while Secretary of
State Clinton called for moving ahead with formulating a code of conduct
and voiced the concern that settling issues bilaterally "could be a recipe for
confusion and even confrontation." [17] These contrasting views on control
over the South China Sea followed a decision by China to begin developing
oil and gas reserves in a region in which Vietnam had already awarded a
contract to a multinational oil consortium that included ExxonMobil and
Gazprom, the Russian oil giant. In September tensions rose after Japan purchased three tiny islands from a private Japanese owner.[18] Both China and
Japan claimed sovereignty over them and in 1972 had agreed not to take any
unilateral action to settle the matter. China saw Japan's action as an attempt
to do just this. For its part, Japan argued that China was misinterpreting its
action. The move, Japanese leaders argued, was an attempt to preserve the
status quo by preventing local Japanese governmental officials from acquiring the islets and using them to provoke China. Japan's explanation did
not calm the situation, and some argued that the matter was the "the most

serious for Sino-Japanese relations in the post-war period in terms of the risk of militarized conflict."[19] Tensions rose further as 2013 ended. China announced the creation of a new air defense zone over contested South China Sea waters requiring that foreign aircraft must inform Chinese authorities of any overflights before undertaking them. In protest the United States dispatched military aircraft into the zone without doing so.

Conclusion: Managing China's Power

The South China Sea presents policymakers with a problem that crosses time: How does one manage power in international politics? No one-size-fits-all answer exists; each pathway of conflict and cooperation has its own unique traits as well as points of commonality. Context matters, and our review of efforts to manage power in the South China Sea reveals several important dimensions to the problem as it exists here. First, it is clear that the problem is managing Chinese power. Second, the focal point of that conflict and the countries involved have changed frequently. Third, China's foreign policy of limited probes and delay diplomacy has proved quite effective by making it difficult for other counties to respond effectively. Fourth, diplomacy has succeeded in doing little more than providing a breathing space that has allowed tensions to reduce. It has not laid the foundation for resolving the underlying issue.

What this legacy means to the future is uncertain. Pessimists see it as Asia's Palestine, with an endless continuation of limited probes and provocations followed by failed diplomacy that leaves conditions unchanged and increases the possibilities of violence born of frustration. Stalemate exists with no clearly defined power management system for the South China Sea in place. Optimists see this legacy as being overcome by the imperatives of globalization. China's growing demand for oil, the necessity of open shipping lanes for global commerce, and the damage that would befall Asian and global markets should naval conflict break out in the South China Sea are seen as forcing Asian states to overcome their disagreements. In between are those who see military and national security considerations triumphing over economic ones. They see war of some sort as becoming increasingly likely as dissatisfaction grows and military power increases. Where they are uncertain is over the consequences of such an outcome: Will it confirm China as the dominant power in a unipolar system, will it result in the emergence of a balancing power or coalition of states, will it bring about a system of power sharing, or will it leave the situation worse than before and set the stage for a new round of conflict?

Case Analysis

1. How should the United States respond to the Chinese "Monroe Doctrine" asserting that the South China Sea is similar to the Caribbean Sea and that foreign powers should stay out of it?

2. In looking to the future of the South China Sea, which of the four types of international systems identified in this chapter's Concept Focus box—bipolar, unipolar, multipolar, or universal community—is in the best interests of the United States? Why?

3. What three states outside of the South China Sea region have the most at stake in how power relations there are managed and why?

4. In considering Chinese strategic thinking, which should take precedence: controlling the South China Sea or securing its land borders from an attack by a hostile power? Why?

5. What is the likelihood that China's policy of limited probes and diplomatic delay will continue to succeed in the future? What changes in strategy would you recommend?

6. Was there a point in the pathway of expanding Chinese influence in the South China Sea that other states could have acted to stop it, or was the expansion of Chinese influence inevitable?

7. Does China or the United States have more to lose should a military conflict break out in the South China Sea?

8. Rank in order of most important to least important the various ownership claims countries have made over islands in the South China Sea as presented in this case study. Justify your rankings.

Suggested Readings

Emmers, Ralf. "The Changing Power Distribution in the South China Sea: Implications for Conflict Management and Avoidance." *Political Science* 62, no. 2 (2010): 118–131. This article examines ASEAN's model of conflict management and conflict avoidance.

Fravel, M. Taylor. "China's Strategy in the South China Sea." *Contemporary Southeast Asia* 33, no. 3 (2011): 292–319. Fravel examines the strategy China has used to advance and consolidate its claims in areas of maritime jurisdiction and to deter others from advancing their own claims.

Gallagher, Michael. "China's Illusory Threat to the South China Sea." *International Security* 19, no. 1 (1994): 169–194. Fears of a looming conflict over the Spratly Islands are seen as premature due to domestic and foreign constraints that limit China's military advantages.

Garver, John. "China's Push through the South China Sea: The Interaction of Bureaucratic and National Interests." *China Quarterly* 132 (December 1992): 999–1,028. This article examines the important role that military bureaucratic interests have played in developing China's South China Sea policy.

Kaplan, Robert D. "The Geography of Chinese Power: How Far Can Beijing Reach on Land and at Sea?" *Foreign Affairs* 89 (May–June 2010): 22–41.

Storey, Ian James. "Creeping Assertiveness: China, the Philippines and the South China Sea." *Contemporary Southeast Asia* 21, no. 1 (1999): 95–118. Storey describes how China has advanced its claims using a policy that combines assertiveness and diplomacy.

Thao, Nguyen Hong, and Ramses Amer. "A New Legal Arrangement for the South China Sea?" *Ocean Development and International Law* 40, no. 4 (2009): 333–349. This article examines major efforts toward conflict management in the South China Sea and assesses their progress.

Web Resources

Association of Southeast Asian Nations (ASEAN), www.aseansec.org. The official ASEAN Web site contains information about the organization, its members, and its activities

The Center for a New American Security, www.cnas.org. Explore research and analysis intended for the public and policymakers about U.S. national security and defense policies, including Asia-Pacific security.

Center for U.S.-China Relations (Tsinghua University), www.chinausa .org.cn/en. Access news and reports in English and Chinese from this research institute focused on U.S.-China relations.

Shanghai Institute for International Studies, http://en.siis.org.cn/. This China-based organization focuses on international politics, economy, and security in the nation, as well as in the United States, Russia, Japan, and Europe. Explore information on regional and topical issues.

3 Interstate War with Iraq

T he case study in this chapter explores the 2003 Iraq War, an interstate war. An interstate war is traditionally defined by political scientists as the organized violence by two or more national armed
forces resulting in 1,000 or more battle-related combatant fatalities.[1] The
Iraq War also has been called by some a "war of choice," making it an
excellent case study to explore pathways to conflict. If war is not inevitable,
what pathways make it more or less likely? Our analysis of this case starts
long before Operation Iraqi Freedom, which was launched in March 2003.
This study examines the conflict and cooperation that led up to the war and
discusses how the hostilities came about.

Our focus will be on a particular episode in the build-up to the war: the
search for weapons of mass destruction (WMD) in Iraq. We examine how
WMD arrived on the U.S. and international agenda; how the problem was
defined by American, Iraqi, and United Nations (UN) leadership, and what
positions were taken on the issue by key players of the George W. Bush
administration, Saddam Hussein's Iraq, and relevant members of the UN
Security Council. We assess how the problem was temporarily resolved—
at first through renewed UN inspections—before the point of war was
reached. The nature and implementation of an inspections agreement ultimately failed to convince the United States that Iraq did not possess WMD,
and the failure of that process, which was perhaps inevitable, paved the way
for the U.S. decision to go to war.

Our Concept Focus in this chapter considers the laws of interstate war
that are laid out in the Charter of the United Nations and how those laws
structure world politics when countries go to war. The Spotlight section
takes a closer look at the domestic debate and the U.S. congressional resolution regarding going to war in Iraq.

Understanding the 2003 Iraq War

Understanding the Iraq War is important for many reasons. It is first and
foremost an example of interstate war, an all-too-familiar phenomenon that
has driven much of international relations scholarship over the past century.
However, interstate war has become notably rare in recent years. Some suggest this is a sign of the "obsolescence" of war or the triumph of the "better
angels of our nature."[2] Others suggest that instances of interstate war are

---

| **Box 3.1** |

Case Summary

After twelve years of multilateral cooperation involving UN sanctions, inspections, and diplomacy with regard to Iraq's weapons of mass destruction programs, the United States led several countries into war against Iraq in 2003.

Global Context

In the aftermath of the first U.S. war with Iraq in 1990, Iraqi president Saddam Hussein remained in power. He possessed vast oil resources and was suspected to possess weapons of mass destruction (WMD). After terrorists attacked the United States in 2001, security concerns gained greater global prominence and tolerance shrank for leaders who flouted international law in pursuit of WMD.

Key Actors

- Iraq
- United States
- Saudi Arabia
- United Nations

Motives

- The United States sought regional stability and perceived Iraq as a potential threat to U.S. influence in the Middle East and U.S. access to Persian Gulf oil
- Iraq sought to exert its sovereignty rather than be constrained by rules from the UN, and it wished to increase its power in the region through the use of political, economic, and military might, which potentially included the possession of WMD

Concepts

- Laws of war
- Multilateralism
- National interest
- Power
- Security
- Sovereignty

---

waning due to the dominance of U.S. power, fear of nuclear weapons, or both these reasons. Understanding the causes of war remains vital for scholars, diplomats, and the victims of war.

The causes of interstate war are numerous. Realists suggest that war happens because there is no world authority to stop it—a condition they call anarchy[3]—and that it occurs when those with power have the motive to wage it. Under the current international system, termed *unipolar* by many realists, there is an inequality of power, which invites the lone superpower (the United States) to attack the weak as it likes. Power and anarchy alone, however, do not "cause" war directly. Stephen Van Evera argues that the best explanation for war comes from misperceptions in power.[4] In the instance of this case study, misperception about WMD capability played at least some role in the unfolding of the Iraq War.

Another perspective of war focuses on the rules of war established by international law. Different rules about going to war evolve over time, arguably constraining even powerful states' behavior. In this regard, the Iraq War is a case study in multilateral governance and the rules of war within the UN system. Foreign policy analysis suggests that war is a product of decisions made within political contexts. From this perspective, the Iraq War serves as a case in U.S. foreign policy-making, driven by decision makers within the Bush administration and their different personalities and varying perceptions and concerns about the public and foreign responses to war.

Box 3.2

Concept Focus

The Laws of War in the Charter of the United Nations

War as an institution has rules, and those rules have changed over the course of human history. Since 1945 the preeminent rules for the use of force have been those written into the Charter of the United Nations, to which 193 countries are signatories. The relevant sections of the charter are Article 2.4, Article 51, and Chapter VII. Article 2.4 set the tone for the use of force after the two world wars, stating that "all Members shall refrain in their international relations from the threat or use of force against the territorial integrity or political independence of any state, or in any other manner inconsistent with the Purposes of the United Nations."[5] In essence, states are not supposed to attack other countries, gain land, or change regimes in power. The sovereignty of countries is enshrined in the charter.

But there are exceptions to the banning of force, located in at least two places in the charter. Article 51 states that "nothing in the present Charter shall impair the inherent right of individual or collective self-defence if an armed attack occurs against a Member of the United Nations, until the Security Council has taken measures necessary to maintain international peace and security."[6] So if self-defense is permitted, this raises the issue relevant to our case: the notion of **preemption**. Can a state not strike first to guarantee its survival? What if waiting would court annihilation? Three criteria are commonly cited for preemption to be justified: necessity, immediacy, and proportionality. Is war the only way to resolve the issue? Is the threat immediate, justifying action now? And is the response proportional to the threat?

Analyses of the 2003 Iraq War have concluded that Operation Iraqi Freedom fell short of the criteria of legal preemption (necessity, immediacy, and proportionality) and that it is more appropriately considered a preventive war.[7] A **preventive war** is one that is initiated not because of an immediate threat but because of the

(Continued)

(Continued)

belief that a delay in attacking a possible enemy is a greater risk. The United States could not make the claim it was under immediate threat of attack. The U.S. administration certainly was frustrated by twelve years of cat and mouse with Iraq, but that is different than a "last resort" necessity in which all options are exhausted. Finally, regime change and occupation arguably go beyond proportionality—that is, the required actions to remove a potential immediate threat.

That leaves a second legal avenue for the legitimate use of force: UN Security Council authorization. Under Article 39 of the charter, "The Security Council shall determine the existence of any threat to the peace, breach of the peace, or act of aggression and shall make recommendations, or decide what measures shall be taken . . . to maintain or restore international peace and security."[8] If lesser measures fail, Article 42 states that the Security Council "may take such action by air, sea, or land forces as may be necessary to maintain or restore international peace and security."[9] The debate in 2003 centered on whether the UN authorized force in the case of Iraq. Those saying it did note Iraq's continued lack of cooperation with the Security Council and its material breach of the 1990 resolution that suspended armed force, UN Resolution 687. They also note the "serious consequences" warned in Resolution 1441, passed in 2002, which provided Iraq a final opportunity to comply with disarmament obligations. Those arguing consent was not given note that Resolution 1441 did not give explicit authorization for the use of force and that when the United States tried to obtain such an authorization, it failed to muster Security Council support.

These and other points about the use of force are not entirely clear or settled, but knowing the broad rules of war helps us to understand what motivates countries to act in certain ways and to understand the relative role of power and law in international relations.

Problem Setting and Origins: Perceived Threats and Rivalry

Though the Iraq War is conventionally viewed as part of the so-called U.S. Global War on Terror, the origins of the problems that the United States and Iraq's regional neighbors have had with Iraq date back long before the outlook that arose in the aftermath of the September 11, 2001, attacks. To some degree, the Iraq War that began in 2003 was an extension of the pathway of conflict and cooperation that stemmed from the 1990–1991 Persian Gulf War. That war ended with a resolution that left Saddam Hussein in power but under a set of obligations to open his regime up to UN inspections to verify and dismantle various chemical, biological, and nuclear weapons (WMD). As we shall see, much of the problem definition and response of the 2003 conflict is tied to perceived threats posed by the Iraqi regime on the one hand and Iraq's views of the United States and regional rivals on the other.

To understand the Gulf War and its aftermath, we must situate U.S. policy and strategy in the Persian Gulf region itself. Middle East scholar Shibley Telhami calls the U.S. strategic position "oil denial,"[10] which means the United States seeks to ensure that no other country is able to conquer and dominate the oil-rich Persian Gulf and Caspian Sea basin, within which rests two-thirds of the world's known petroleum reserves.[11] As the petroleum constitutes a strategically vital resource for industrial society and its mechanized armed forces, the United States cannot accept enemies seizing this oil in a way that could deny it to world markets. In short, the United States has sought to ensure the free flow of fair-priced oil from the Persian Gulf. The United States has been a net importer of oil for decades, though the amount it imports has decreased in recent years.

This strategic posture has meant being flexible about local allies and threats. After the British withdrew their colonial presence from the Persian Gulf in the early 1970s, the United States backed Saudi Arabia and the shah of Iran as "twin pillars" against rising Arab nationalism. After the shah's ouster in the Iranian revolution and Iraq's invasion of Iran in 1980, the United States increased its support to Iraq. At the time, the United States was not sure about Saddam Hussein and preferred a return to the prewar status quo of its alliance with Iran, but U.S. distrust of revolutionary Iran in the wake of the hostage crisis of 1979–1981 led the United States to arm and aid Iraq to avoid Iranian dominance in the Persian Gulf.

Not long after the Iran-Iraq War ended in 1988, a new crisis in the Gulf arose. This time Iraq invaded neighboring Kuwait, a fellow Sunni Arab regime and oil-rich state. In line with its policy of oil denial, the United States opposed Iraq and viewed Saddam Hussein as a potential threat to the region's stability and open markets. In response to the Iraqi invasion, the United States mustered 500,000 forces in Saudi Arabia to defend the oil monarchy, which feared Hussein's ambitions of being a unifying Arab nationalist could lead him to push into the rest of the oil-rich Arabian Peninsula. The United States worked together with a large UN coalition to expel Iraq's forces from Kuwait under the authorization of UN Resolution 678, which called for "all necessary means" to restore Kuwait's sovereignty.

The nature of the 1991 Gulf War and its resolution are important to the Iraq War of 2003 because the terms of peace in the former affected the path to conflict in the latter. From the U.S. perspective in 1991, Iraq had become an unpredictable, aggressive threat to Gulf stability. Iraqi biological, chemical, and nuclear weapons programs were confirmed and targeted during combat and became subject to the postwar peace enshrined in UN Resolution 687. Passed on April 3, 1991, the resolution required Iraq to accept, without conditions, the "destruction, removal or rendering harmless, under international supervision," of "all chemical and biological weapons and all stocks of agents and all related . . . facilities," as well as "all ballistic missiles with a range greater than 150 kilometers." Iraq also had to "agree not to acquire or develop nuclear weapons" or weapon-usable materials and declare all such materials and sites related to these programs to the UN for verification and monitoring.[12] Resolution 687 was not a peace treaty per se, but Iraq's acquiescence to it was the condition of suspending allied operations and ending the Gulf War.

The rest of the 1990s involved implementing the resolution. The U.S. administrations of George H. W. Bush and Bill Clinton monitored Iraq through a policy of "dual containment," backing UN Special Commission (UNSCOM) inspections and instituting no-fly zones that, while nominally set up to protect northern Iraqi Kurds and southern Shi'a from Hussein's

Timeline
Conflict Leading to the Iraq War

1979		Saddam Hussein comes to power in Iraq.
1980		Iraq invades Iran, beginning an eight-year war.
1990	August 2	Iraq invades Kuwait.
1991	January	Operation Desert Storm begins under a multilateral, U.S.-led coalition.
	February	The Desert Storm land war begins.
	April	UN Resolution 687 lays out the terms of Iraq's surrender.
1998	December	Operation Desert Fox is launched with the goal of targeting Iraq's weapons capabilities.
2001	September	The first proposals to attack Iraq after 9/11 are made in the U.S. government.
2002	January	President George W. Bush labels Iraq as part of an "axis of evil," claiming it is in possession of WMD and has ties to terrorism.
	October	The U.S. Senate authorizes the president to use any means necessary against Iraq.
	November	UNSC Resolution 1441 demands Iraq either unconditionally comply with new UN inspections or face "serious consequences."
2003	January	Hans Blix's report raises questions about Iraq's weapons capabilities but does not confirm the existence of WMD.
	March	The U.S.-led invasion of Iraq begins.

forces, had the effect of protecting northern and southern Iraqi borders from any potential threats from Hussein as well. There were occasional skirmishes, but containing Iraq and keeping Hussein "in his box" served as sufficient U.S. policy during the Clinton administration. The policy endured even after a violent blip in 1998 when UN inspectors complained about Iraqi intransigence over access to suspected weapons sites. After the inspectors reported that Iraq's stalling tactics prevented them from completing inspections, the United States asked the inspectors to step aside. Accusing Iraq of noncompliance with Resolution 687, in December 1998 the United States and United Kingdom targeted suspected Iraqi weapons sites with missile strikes and aerial assaults in what was called Operation Desert Fox. Hoping to coerce Iraq into cooperation, or, failing that, to degrade Iraqi capabilities, the U.S. "containment plus" approach sought to keep Iraqi forces degraded and unable to threaten the region. Iraq did not comply with UN and U.S. demands and instead kicked out the UN inspectors. From 1998 to 2002, Iraq's regime conducted itself without UN inspections oversight.

Problem Definition and Response: UN Inspections and the U.S. Outlook

The problem for the United States, then, was what to do with an Iraq that had stopped cooperating with the UN before fulfilling its obligations under UN Resolution 687. The Clinton administration had been willing to maintain the status quo of containment, but the incoming administration of George W. Bush contained advisors who proposed regime change. The differences in approach stemmed from the problem being defined differently by American policymakers. Broadly, the Bush administration included realists and hawks (also called neocons or Reaganites). The realists, one of whom was Secretary of State Colin Powell, were conventionally geared toward containment and the status quo and were interested in multilateral coalition-building when considering policy options in the vital Middle East. The hawks, notably represented by Vice President Dick Cheney, Defense Secretary Donald Rumsfeld, and Deputy Secretary of Defense Paul Wolfowitz, were skeptical of those approaches and advocated unilateral and assertive U.S. military options to remake the Middle East to better serve U.S. interests. Cheney and Wolfowitz went on record advocating the use of military might to drive Hussein from power, using as justification Iraq's WMD programs, noncooperation with the UN, and humanitarian record against Kurds and Shiites within Iraq's borders in the 1980s and 1990s. Wolfowitz had previously posed the idea of preemption as a strategic option in the 1992 Defense Planning Guidance document written during the administration of George H. W. Bush. Additionally, during the Clinton administration, an open letter signed by Wolfowitz, Rumsfeld, and others in 1998 advocated military action against Iraq specifically, arguing that containment wasn't working.[13]

As evidenced by these examples, the regime change perspective on Iraq preceded 9/11, although it did not dominate policy prior to the 2001 attacks. The events of September 11, however, soon drove Iraq back into the policy spotlight. A mere four days after 9/11, at a war council meeting at Camp David, Wolfowitz suggested potential ties existed between the attacks and Iraq, and he encouraged the United States to consider Iraq a target.[14] Powell and General Hugh Shelton, the Joint Chiefs of Staff chair, countered that Iraq was not a priority as no compelling evidence tied it to the events of that day.[15] The agreed-upon outcome was to conduct a war in phases, focusing on Afghanistan first since al-Qaeda, the terrorist organization based there, had been identified as the perpetrator of 9/11. Dealing with Iraq would come later.

Given the suspicions about Iraq's nuclear, chemical, and biological weapons programs; its known support for terrorist groups (although not al-Qaeda); and a rash of anthrax attacks in the United States in the fall of 2001 that Wolfowitz wrongly assumed Iraq was complicit in,[16] the Bush administration seemed convinced that Iraq posed a national security threat. Bush's 2002 State of the Union address famously lumped Iraq, Iran, and North Korea into an "axis of evil" that was "arming to threaten the world." Bush claimed Saddam Hussein was working with al-Qaeda, while Cheney insisted that Iraq possessed WMD that it intended to use against the United States and its allies. Invoking the doctrine of preemption, the Bush administration vowed not to wait when "facing clear evidence of peril" for "the final proof, the smoking gun, that could come in the form of a mushroom cloud."[17] To not wait for an attack was to advance the idea of U.S. security through preemption, which was formally indoctrinated as policy in the United States' 2002 National Security Strategy.

The aggressive posture coming out of Washington, based on the notion of preemption and assumptions of Iraq's intents regarding terrorism and WMD, was not shared by many other nations. Allies from the Gulf War, who at the time of that war comprised a coalition lauded for its widespread cooperation, cautioned the United States against aggressive action toward Iraq. The Saudis, a key ally in the first Gulf war, refused to allow U.S. forces to station there in 2003, warning that an invasion would "encourage people to think . . . that what [the United States is] doing is a war of aggression rather than a war for the implementation of the United Nations resolutions."[18] The rest of the Arab world, except for Kuwait, followed suit, with the Arab League issuing an opposition to war and calling on the UN to safeguard Iraqi sovereignty.[19] Turkey, a NATO ally on Iraq's border to the north, refused to allow U.S. troops to operate from Turkish bases and ports.[20] European allies largely saw the issue as a matter of compliance and diplomacy, not an existential threat. France and Germany advocated for time for weapons inspectors to search for banned arms in Iraq.[21] The multitude of disparate positions created conflict that minimized international support in 2003. The shared understanding and aims in 1990–1991 had allowed for a widespread coalition of support to form through which the international community could act. The cooperation in 2003 was much more limited. The United States, however, was not completely without supporters. Britain, Spain, and several Eastern European countries were among those who sided with the United States in what would be called the "coalition of the willing."

Iraq's position was that there were no WMD and that the UNSCOM mission was composed of U.S. spies—the latter of which was confirmed by former weapons inspector Scott Ritter. Indeed, covert operations were directed at Saddam Hussein's regime as early as 1996 when a CIA-sponsored coup plot was foiled.[22] The 1998 Iraq Liberation Act called explicitly for funds and activities directed at regime change, including $100 million aimed at aiding and arming opposition groups in Iraq. As the 2005 Presidential Commission on the Intelligence Capabilities of the United States Regarding Weapons of Mass Destruction reported, the intelligence community was criticized for being "dead wrong" about Iraq's capabilities, and it was suggested the administration's daily briefs were alarmist and one-sided.[23] No arsenal of old weapons or programs for more advanced new weapons were found by the UN inspectors before the war began in 2003, nor were any found by the U.S. Iraq Survey Group that was sent in after the war.[24]

This is not to say that Hussein's government was entirely innocent. Members of the regime confessed to designing illegal missiles and concealing plans and research for the resumption of weapons programs once inspections had ended. Hussein infamously balanced claims of no WMD with veiled threats to the contrary. Acknowledging he had been coy about the state of Iraq's weapons programs, Hussein later told FBI interviewers that openness with UN inspectors would have shown Iran "where to inflict maximum damage in Iraq."[25]

Problem Evolution and Development: The Use of Force

Due to a combination of the U.S. hawks' desire for a clean break in the Middle East, which dated back to the 1990s; lingering issues of WMD; and the new earnestness that came with 9/11, Bush administration officials pushed for regime change in Iraq. Wolfowitz in September 2001 publicly discussed the desire for "ending states" with ties to terrorism. The logic was that the only way to be certain that Iraq had no WMD was to remove the government of Hussein, find the WMD, and put in place a new, friendlier regime that would respect international law.

Others in the administration cautioned against a military operation as they were skeptical of Iraq's supposed tie to 9/11 and concerned about the consequences of going to war without widespread international support. Secretary of State Powell spent much time rebutting the hawks and promoting the policy of containment. In August 2002 Powell pleaded with President Bush to try diplomacy and build a coalition grounded in international law and supported by the UN. Powell got his chance to make the case to the UN in the fall of 2002 when he made a multilateral call for resumed inspections in Iraq.

The attempt to build consensus through the United Nations bore some fruit but also revealed grave differences in the approach to Iraq. The result of Powell's efforts was UN Resolution 1441. Adopted November 8, 2002, the resolution accused Iraq of being in "material breach of its obligations" under Resolution 687 for failure to comply with UN inspectors, and it gave Iraq "a final opportunity to comply with its disarmament obligations" under enhanced inspections.[26] The key phrase tied to the new call for an accurate, "full, and complete declaration of all aspects of its" WMD and ballistic missiles programs was that Iraq would "face serious consequences as a result of its continued violations of its obligations."[27]

Just what "serious consequences" meant varied by country and leader. For the Bush administration hawks, these words implied war and regime change. Iraq agreed to the new resolution's demands, and inspections resumed under the reconstituted UN Monitoring, Verification, and Inspection Commission (UNMOVIC).[28] Lead inspector Hans Blix's January 2003 report to the United Nations was a mixed bag. UNMOVIC found no WMD, but there were discrepancies in the record. What inspectors had previously found did not match what Iraq declared to possess, resulting in several cases where inspectors were unable to verify the whereabouts of weapons material. The report also included a material breach of Resolution 687 in the form of ballistic missiles whose range exceeded 150 kilometers.

The combination of the missiles and the absence of clear proof that there were no WMD led the United States to conclude that Iraq was again noncompliant with UN resolutions. However, countries such as France, Russia, and Germany, when pressed by the United States to authorize force against Iraq, refused. In early March 2003, the United States circulated a draft document to authorize force, but it could not get the nine votes necessary from the UN Security Council. Furthermore, France and Russia threatened to veto any use of force authorization, which rendered the exercise futile. The United States ultimately withdrew the draft resolution and proceeded to act outside of the UN Security Council. The "coalition of the willing," including the United Kingdom, signed on to the U.S. view. When war began, it came after a U.S. ultimatum on March 18, 2003, for Saddam Hussein and his sons to leave Iraq within forty-eight hours.[29] The ultimatum was not accepted and the United States invaded Iraq on March 20.

| Box 3.3 |

Spotlight

Authorization for the Use of Force in Iraq

Much was made during the 2004 U.S. presidential election about the congressional position on the Iraq War. Democratic nominee John Kerry said he had campaigned against the Iraq War. George W. Bush, the incumbent seeking a second term, reminded Kerry that he had voted for congressional authorization of the use of force in Iraq. Could both men be right? And who has the power to declare war in the United States?

The authorization in question was a congressional joint resolution "to authorize the use of United States Armed Forces against Iraq" (H.J. Res. 114), which was passed in October 2002. The resolution states that "the President is authorized to use the Armed Forces of the United States as he determines to be necessary and appropriate in order to (1) defend the national security of the United States against the continuing threat posed by Iraq and (2) enforce all relevant United Nations Security Council resolutions regarding Iraq.[30] The resolution passed, and the Bush administration interpreted it as an authorization to go to war. Critics of the war say the resolution gave the administration authority to go to war under certain circumstances but that those circumstances were not met. They claim, in short, that the resolution was abused by the executive branch.

The more general question related to the authorization of force in Iraq is, do presidents need congressional authorization for war? The Constitution of the United States explicitly gives the power to make war to Congress, but the president has been constitutionally designated as commander in chief. Increasingly since World War II, presidents have put American forces in harm's way by invoking their power as commander in chief, even without congressional approval. Presidents from Harry Truman to Barack Obama have defended the right to deploy military power in the name of national security, be that deployment a police action or just the "use of force." The Vietnam War challenged this swing toward executive authority, however, due to the seeming "blank check" Congress gave Lyndon Johnson to prosecute military activity there as he saw fit. After dramatic escalation and years of war, in 1973 Congress passed the **War Powers Resolution** to clarify expectations for when a president can go to war. It demands presidential consultation with Congress prior to deployment of forces if possible, or within forty-eight hours otherwise. It also requires congressional approval prior to deployment of forces if possible—either through a declaration of war or resolution—or within sixty days of the engagement of U.S. forces into hostilities. After sixty days, or sooner if Congress says so, the lack of congressional approval means the operations must be ceased within another thirty days. The War Powers Resolution is an imperfect document—some critics call it a "parchment barrier" and others call it unconstitutional—but it is the current reigning law on presidential use of force.

What this means for the future use of force remains to be seen. But in the case of the congressional resolution of 2002, the resolution made explicit reference to the War Powers Resolution, claiming that "consistent with section 8(a)(1) of the War Powers Resolution, the Congress declares that this section is intended to constitute specific statutory authorization within the meaning of section 5(b) of the War Powers Resolution."[31] Candidate Kerry may not have agreed with the president's determination that "reliance . . . on further diplomatic or other peaceful means alone either (A) will not adequately protect the national security of the United States against the continuing threat posed by Iraq, or (B) is not likely to lead to enforcement of all relevant United Nations Security Council resolutions regarding Iraq,"[32] but under that language, the Bush administration seemed to meet the requirements for use of force. The 2008 election resulted in the victory of Barack Obama, a candidate who had opposed the war from the beginning, leaving the question of congressional complicity behind for the time being.

Conclusion: The Unpredictability of War

The likelihood of war is influenced by structural conditions (U.S. power in the post–Cold War era), material conditions (oil as a strategic resource), and the flaunting of legal institutional frameworks (the violation of UN resolutions and treaties). But the decision to choose conflict or cooperation is ultimately made by leaders, in this case especially George W. Bush and Saddam Hussein, whose personalities and beliefs perhaps make conflict unavoidable. The pathway toward conflict and away from cooperation was partly set by the leaders themselves. Compromise and respect for institutional constraints were not the hallmarks of either leader: Hussein willfully defied inspections; Bush willfully pushed ahead with war despite the lack of UN authorization. Why Hussein did not accede to the U.S. ultimatum, or to any others, such as the UN's Resolution 678, may speak to his personality or his calculations of risk or bluff.[33] Having survived the Iran-Iraq War of the 1980s and the Gulf War of 1990–1991, perhaps Hussein thought he could ride out this one too, coming across as a hero to the region and appearing strong against neighboring enemy Iran.

On the other side of the coin, why did the United States choose war despite international opposition and questionable legality? Realists are not surprised that a superpower would do as it pleased regardless of international law or opinion, but others suggest that normative behavior is mitigated by leaders' beliefs and decision-making styles. According to one study, unilateral war advocates Bush, Cheney, Wolfowitz, and Rumsfeld were less sensitive to the political and legal context of the issue and had higher levels of distrust than the multilateralist Powell, thus they were more likely to violate international norms if rules and other actors were seen as threatening obstacles.[34]

War, once begun, is famous for its ability to be unpredictable. Despite early conventional victories, the Iraq War soon turned unconventional, and the United States found occupation and insurgency daunting tasks that divided the country and jeopardized the regional stability long sought in U.S. strategy in the Gulf. Ten years after the start of Operation Iraqi Freedom, Iraq is a very different country. It has a new government, constitution, and leadership. It is friends with neighbors that used to be enemies, such as Iran. It is also highly unstable and prone to recurring political violence and terrorism. The war, which estimates say cost between 176,000 to 189,000 lives, including armed forces, insurgents, and foreign civilians, and also resulted in the deaths of 111,000 to 134,000 Iraqi civilians,[35] has become a defining event in twenty-first-century world affairs, U.S. foreign policy, and the Middle East.

As of 2013, fewer than 300 active-duty U.S. troops remained inside Iraq. Most forces were withdrawn at the end of 2011 under the terms of the 2008 Status of Forces Agreement. The minimal presence of U.S. troops has led analyst Fred Kagan to conclude, "We have largely stripped ourselves of any meaningful influence [in Iraq and the region] that we might've had."[36] The pathway of conflict and cooperation that the United States and Iraq have traveled up to this point has been filled with moments of alignment and discord as the countries' interests have merged and parted, and that remains the case today. The United States does not have its once-hoped-for base to station troops in the region, nor did the Iraq War help contribute to greater stability in the Middle East. Iraq, for its part, has had two sets of national elections under the new constitution, but it continues to struggle with sectarian and ethnic violence while it tries to rebuild its national infrastructure, economy, and political and civic life.

Case Analysis

1. Was the invasion of Iraq in 2003 justified? Why or why not?

2. Describe where the United States succeeded with its aims in Iraq and where it fell short.

3. Iraq cooperated with UN inspections numerous times between 1991 and 1998 and between 2002 and 2003. Why did Iraq cooperate then, and why was this not enough for the United States in 2003?

4. Consider this chapter's discussion of preemptive war and the elements needed to justify it: necessity, immediacy, and proportionality. Are there current or past wars that meet these criteria and, if so, how do they do so?

5. Considering the structure of world politics, why would a country be motivated to follow the rules of law laid out in the Charter of the United Nations?

6. Given your understanding of the War Powers Resolution, was the Bush administration justified in the use of force against Iraq in 2003? Explain your reasoning.

7. How would you amend the War Powers Resolution to remove ambiguity and implement clearer standards for the pathway to war?

8. Given past U.S. support for Iraq and Iraq's experiences during and after the 1990–1991 Gulf War, explain what you think may have been Saddam Hussein's perspective when it came to policymaking in response to U.S. demands and UN inspections.

9. Why do you think the U.S. Senate gave the Bush administration the right to resolve the Iraq situation "by any means necessary?"

Suggested Readings

Ajami, Fouad. *The Foreigner's Gift: The Americans, the Arabs, and the Iraqis in Iraq*. New York: Free Press, 2007. This book analyzes how and why Iraqis did not respond well to the U.S. invasion.

Daalder, Ivo, and James Lindsay. *America Unbound: The Bush Revolution in Foreign Policy*. Rev. ed. New York: Wiley, 2005. This book lays out the major foreign policy advisers in the Bush Administration as they built the case for war in Iraq.

Fawn, Rick, and Raymond Hinnebusch. *The Iraq War: Causes and Consequences*. Boulder, CO: Lynne Rienner Publishers, 2006. An edited collection that looks at various reasons for the war and its outcomes.

Harvey, Frank. *Explaining the Iraq War: Counterfactual Theory, Logic and Evidence*. Cambridge: Cambridge University Press, 2012. A scholarly account of the various hypotheses explaining the Iraq War.

Mearsheimer, John, and Stephen Walt. "An Unnecessary War." *Foreign Policy* (January–February 2003): 51–59. An article written by American realist scholars arguing against going to war in Iraq.

Woodward, Bob. *Plan of Attack*. New York: Simon & Schuster, 2004. A journalistic "inside" account of the decision making in the Bush Administration from 9/11 to the start of the Iraq War.

Web Resources

United Nations Special Commission, www.un.org/Depts/unscom. Documents and timeline of events related to the inspection team charged with finding and dismantling Iraqi WMD after the Persian Gulf War.

National Security Strategy 2002, http://georgewbush-whitehouse.archives .gov/nsc/nss/2002/index.html. The George W. Bush administration's 2002 National Security Strategy provided the foundation of the Bush Doctrine and "preemption" against Iraq.

The Security Council, 27 January 2003: An Update on Inspection, www .un.org/Depts/unmovic/Bx27.htm. Hans Blix testified to the United Nations after new inspections were reintroduced into Iraq. It is from this testimony that the United States concluded Iraq to be in "material breach" of previous resolutions.

The Iraq War 10 Years After, The National Security Archive, www.gwu .edu/~nsarchiv/NSAEBB/NSAEBB418. Explore an extensive archive of declassified documents from the U.S. government related to the 2003 Iraq War.

4 The Cyclical Arab-Israeli Conflict

This chapter considers the phenomenon of enduring and cyclical conflict that involves two or more parties engaging in multiple episodes of violence interspersed with repeated periods of rest but never accomplishing a permanent state of reconciliation. Negative peace—the lack of actual war or violence—is temporary if prolonged, but positive peace is absent and elusive. What happens to conflict and cooperation in an enduring rivalry in which states make war, stop fighting but do not make peace, then make war again? When do states decide to end this cycle and why? In this chapter we explore these questions in the context of the Arab-Israeli conflict.

The pathway of conflict and cooperation between Israel and its Arab neighbors began before there was an Israel and after British attempts at promoting cooperation failed during the years of Britain's control of the mandated territory known as Palestine after World War I. With Jewish and Arab nationalists pushing for independence in the same area of Palestine, located between the Mediterranean Sea and the Jordan River, the British attempted to manage aspirations in a manner that also served their own interests in gaining a foothold in the Middle East. When no solution proved acceptable and the costs of occupation became too high, the British withdrew from the region in 1948 and conflict filled the vacuum. The Arab-Israeli conflict has endured in various forms since Israel's founding in 1948 and illuminates the nature of nationalism (loyalty or devotion to a nation) and ethnic discord (conflict between two or more distinct religious, cultural, or linguistic groups). Theories of ancient hatreds driving conflict coexist with political explanations rooted in institutions and decisions of political actors. Whether ethnic conflict is inevitable or a matter of design is important for students to consider. Because this chapter is about cyclical conflict, we employ our framework of the conflict cycle in multiple iterations in two sets of rivalries: Arab-Israeli and Palestinian-Israeli. The first conflict in the cycle was between Zionist forces and both Palestinians and the broader Arab world that was opposed to Israel's founding in 1948. The second set of conflicts we focus on occurred between the new Israel and its Arab neighbors and spanned the period from the Six-Day War of 1967 to the October War of 1973. Issue settlement of these conflicts was facilitated by U.S. shuttle diplomacy, which yielded genuine settlement and reconciliation between Israel and Egypt at Camp David in 1978. The third set of conflicts we investigate involve the Palestinian-Israeli dynamic, from decades of raids and terror attacks abroad by the Palestine Liberation Organization to the uprisings in the occupied territories. Attempts at issue settlement took an historic turn with the 1993 Oslo Accords and their resulting negotiations. Final settlement and reconciliation remain elusive, however, which has led to a second *intifada* and a turn toward unilateral measures to solve the seemingly intractable problems of Israel-Palestine.

The case is also significant for the United States, whose government has long tried to resolve the conflict out of its own interest in regional stability. In the 1970s the United States recognized that solving the Arab-Israeli conflict would benefit its image and its security in the Middle East. Some argue U.S. policy toward the conflict is too pro-Israel and is a major issue fueling anti-American grievances in the Arab and Muslim world.[1] Ending the conflict, then, would have local, regional, and global implications for many.

The Concept Focus in this chapter examines nationalism and ethnic conflict and particularly their roles in cyclical conflicts such as the one considered in this case study. The Spotlight section looks more closely at the Palestinian Authority's pursuit of statehood, which it seeks to achieve not through negotiations with Israel but through recognition at the United Nations.

Box 4.1

Case Summary

Israel was founded in 1948, carved out of Palestine after World War II in order to create a homeland for Jews. This caused conflict with Palestinian Arabs and its Arab, Muslim neighbors, who rejected Israel's existence and protested the resulting disruption of life for Palestinians in the territory now belonging to Israel.

Global Context

In the wake of World War II and the Holocaust in Europe, the Allies engineered a homeland for Jews in their ancestral lands, but in a Middle East still largely in the grip of Western colonial powers, Israel's creation was another example of Western hegemony seen at the expense of local Arab and Palestinian interests and aspirations.

Key Actors

- The Allies—the Western powers victorious in World War II, namely the United Kingdom and the United States
- Israel
- Palestinians
- Arab nations

Motives

- After World War II, the Allies wanted to provide a safe haven for Jews; as Israel's existence became contested, at times violently so, these Western

powers offered their support both to protect the nation—and ally—
they had helped form and also to protect their own interests in the
region
- Israel is dedicated to protecting its sovereignty and right to exist. It seeks possession of Jerusalem and parts of the West Bank for a combination of security, political, and religious reasons
- Palestinians uprooted by Israel's founding or confined to territories Israel now occupies wish to gain their sovereignty with the creation of a separate Palestinian state, preferably with Jerusalem as its capital for political and religious reasons
- Arab nations such as Egypt, Jordan, Lebanon, and Syria objected to Israel's creation; once Palestinians fled the new Israeli lands, the issue also impacted the economies and societies of these other Arab nations, which became strained by an influx of refugees

Concepts

- Conflict cycle
- Ethnic conflict
- Nationalism
- Right of return
- Security

The Arab-Israeli Conflict

The *Arab-Israeli conflict* is a long-standing term for a decades long, occasionally violent rivalry playing out in the Middle East. But the term is misleading in that it is not all Arabs—or only Arabs (Iran is Persian)—that are in conflict with Israel, and the amount of actual violence varies among a handful of Arab actors. While many Arab nations are in an official state of war with Israel, most of the Arab world has arrived at a de facto cold peace with Israel since the 1970s. Only a few Arab actors, including Palestinian Hamas and the Lebanese Shiite group Hezbollah, engage in periodic hostilities with Israeli forces. The "Arab" designation also belies an important subcategory of the conflict we call the Palestinian-Israeli conflict. While Palestinians are Arab, their fight is local and nationalist. Yet the term *Arab-Israeli conflict* came into use due to the lack of peace between Israel and its neighbors since the country's founding in 1948, and it still persists today.

Any single war in the Arab-Israeli conflict can be analyzed for its origins, conduct, and resolution, as has been done numerous times elsewhere. Conflict scholars Greg Cashman and Leonard Robinson, for example, articulate multiple "long-term" root causes of the Six-Day War—including religion, ethnonationalism, territory disputes, and the presence of regional arms races and enduring rivalries—and proximate causes of domestic and regional politics, as well as examine psychological factors at play.[2] Moving beyond a single case, we can track changes in these multiple factors with changes in the nature of the cyclical conflict.

It is interesting to note changes in conflict cycles. In 1978 Egypt made peace with Israel, yet as of 2013, Syria still has not. The 1990s brought a good deal of optimism about the Palestinian-Israeli conflict coming to a realistic close. Middle East scholar Avraham Sela hailed and analyzed the "decline of the Arab-Israeli conflict."[3] Political scientists Hemda Ben-Yehuda and Schmuel Sandler suggested that the Arab-Israeli conflict had been "transformed" in the 1990s, noting Israel's peace with Jordan compared to the enduring rivalries between Israel and neighboring Syria and the Palestinians.[4] Yet despite this optimism, each participant in the conflict maintains positions on issues from which it will not compromise, talks continue, and the conflict endures.

Problem Setting and Origins: Competing Land Claims, 1948

The root sources of the Arab-Israeli conflict are numerous and complex. The conflict, contrary to common misconception, is not ancient, though some of its roots are grounded in claims to land dating back a few thousand years. There is a base level at which the conflict is about territory: Who rules in the land between the Mediterranean Sea and the Jordan River? Those who think that space should include only a sovereign Jewish state are at odds with others who think it should include only sovereign Arab land. In this first conflict cycle, the end was the establishment of a sovereign Jewish state known as Israel in 1948. Arab attempts to undo this action resulted in a war that ended in armistice in 1949.

The Zionist viewpoint built on the writings of Theodor Herzl, whose 1896 *Der Judenstaat* spoke of the "futility of combating anti-Semitism." Herzl witnessed the Russian pogroms against Jews and the Dreyfus affair that saw a Jewish man scandalously convicted of treason in France and claimed they were part of a history of relentless persecution across time and space. *Zionism* is the term defining the movement for Jewish people to return to their historic homeland in Israel. The World Zionist Organization and Jewish National Fund were founded to turn Herzl's vision of a Jewish state into a reality, and they debated where and how to realize a Jewish state and raised funds to buy land and help Jews immigrate to the eventual homeland. Arab nationalism also has roots in the latter nineteenth century. References to "Palestine" date back to the sixteenth and seventeenth centuries, and the editorial line in the Palestinian newspaper *Filastin* in 1913 advocated for Palestinian nationalism and voiced alarm over encroaching Zionist land purchases and immigration.[5]

Add to these brewing nationalist movements the important matter of shifting geopolitical tides. The 500-year-old Ottoman Empire was in its twilight as these movements began to rally for independence within its confines. Siding with the Central Powers of Germany, Italy, and Japan in World War I sealed the empire's fate: battling with the British and French opened the door for European designs to pick apart the empire when it suffered defeat in 1918. It also spurred the British to undermine the Ottomans from within by courting the empire's Arab constituents. Notable for our study are two promises that involved Palestine: the McMahon-Hussein correspondence and the Balfour Declaration. In the former, Sharif Hussein bin Ali of Mecca was convinced to stage an Arab revolt within Ottoman borders; in exchange for victory, the British promised Arab rule over ambiguously defined parts of Arab Ottoman territory. And in 1917 British foreign secretary Arthur Balfour, in an attempt to court Jewish and Zionist sympathy and force of arms against the Ottomans, declared that his government would "view with favor the establishment in Palestine of a national home for the Jewish people, and will use [our] best endeavors to facilitate the achievement of this object."[6] Importantly, the declaration added that "nothing shall be done which may prejudice the civil and religious rights of existing non-Jewish communities in Palestine," suggesting that the status of Arabs there was a matter of consideration.

The British made a third agreement regarding Palestine with their French allies. The Sykes-Picot Agreement (1916) divided Arab lands into French and British spheres of control or influence, with the area of Palestine designated an international zone. By the time the postwar peace was formalized and endorsed by the League of Nations, the British had obtained the mandate of Palestine and were facing at least two nationalist movements seeking the same piece of land: Zionist and Palestinian. To this add the broader Arab aspirations for independence in the land of Palestine, such as those expressed by the General Syrian Congress, which in 1919 rejected the "pretensions of the Zionists" and asked that "there be no separation of the southern part of Syria, known as Palestine"[7] The result was a recipe for conflict over the fate of the land.

Problem Definition and Response: A Two-State Proposal

To the Zionists, the problem was the need for a Jewish homeland. The Jewish Agency set up an office in Palestine to work with the British and help facilitate land sales and immigration for Jews to Palestine. The League of Nations mandate that granted the British authority over the mandate of Palestine also designated the Jewish Agency "a public body for the purpose of advising . . . the Administration of Palestine."

To Palestinians, the problem was the desire for Palestinian independence and resistance to both British rule and the Zionist project. There were authorized Palestinian authorities, such as the Arab Higher Committee and the grand mufti of Jerusalem, Hajj Amin al-Husayni, but these British-favored bodies and individuals did not represent the popular aspects of Palestinian society and were not given the same status and privileges as the Jewish

---

| **Box 4.2** |

Concept Focus

Nationalism, Ethnic Conflict, Cyclical Conflict

Much conflict in the world has had to do with the search for self-determination by groups seeking an independent state. Nationalism can be defined as "devotion to one's nation or a policy of national independence," with a nation being a community of persons "closely associated with each other by common descent, language or history," forming a sense of distinctiveness.[8] Different scholars emphasize the importance of religion, blood ties, and more constructed notions of psychological bonds in nationalism, but key is the sense of community and the quest for self-rule. Zionism was the pursuit of a Jewish state in Palestine, and Palestinian nationalism was at the heart of the Palestinian-Israeli conundrum.

While ethnicity is one basis for nationalism, other nationalist movements rally around religious identities or are driven by a common ideology. Also, ethnic nationalism does not necessarily mean ethnic conflict. While the Arab-Israeli conflict appears to be ethnic, pitting Arab against Jew, it is more appropriate to see it as a nationalist political conflict in which the lines of conflict are ethnonationalist in nature. The difference is important in that political conflicts over territory are more likely to be resolved than an "ancient hatreds" view of fundamental sectarian or ethnic animosity.

This chapter considers the phenomenon of cyclical conflict, when a cycle repeats itself again and again. The literature on conflict discusses several concepts for such dynamics, chief among them the notion of enduring rivalries, or ERs. More than half of interstate wars in the nineteenth and twentieth centuries were between enduring rivals, such as India and Pakistan, and disputes between enduring rivals are almost twice as likely to end in war as those between other pairs of states.[9] A related concept is that of intractable conflict, defined as having "persisted over time and refused to yield to efforts—through either direct negotiations by the parties or mediation with third-party assistance—to arrive at a political settlement."[10] This is a matter of degree and does not mean the conflict is impossible to resolve, only that there are psychological obstacles or incompatible interests that make resolution particularly difficult. An example of this is the decades-long conflict over Kashmir among India, Pakistan, and Kashmiri insurgents.

With such conflicts, opportunities for cooperation can seem slim or impossible. Third-party mediators become important to provide political cover for talks and for providing incentives to make peace (see the Camp David Accords discussed in this chapter). But outside powers can't want peace more than the conflict parties themselves. Often warring parties come to the table only in a "hurting stalemate" in which both are tired and no victory seems plausible to either side.[11] There are certain ripe moments, such as in 1978 and 1993, which we will examine, where these conditions make peace possible.

Agency. Anti-British forces such as Sheikh Izz al-Din al-Qassam fueled uprisings against the British. In 1920 and 1921, violent protests by Arabs in Jerusalem and Jaffa signaled that the mandate was not a welcome change.

To the British, the problem was defined in terms of stability and the desire for a foothold in the Levant. In the 1921 Cairo Conference, it was decided that this territory would be split, with Sharif Hussein bin Ali's son Abdullah leading the new state of Transjordan. The Churchill White Paper of 1922 questioned the British position laid out in the Balfour Declaration in the face of Arab opposition and British desires to retain a foothold in the area. In 1929 violence broke out as Arabs protested the World Zionist Organization calling at its annual meeting for settlement in Palestine "by the great colonizing masses" of the Jewish people. In 1936 the death of al-Qassam and others led to protests and strikes that put more pressure on the British and spiraled into the Great Revolt of 1936–1939. In response, the Peel Commission, a British royal commission of inquiry that concluded in 1937, offered a two-state proposal that included a continued British presence. A follow-up proposal by the Woodhead Commission, another British investigative commission, reduced the size of a proposed Jewish state in a two-state solution, but this still did not satisfy the Arab and Palestinian position. A sea change in British policy came with the White Paper of 1939, which formally rescinded the Balfour Declaration and the partition proposals, limited Jewish land sales and immigration, offered more jobs to Palestinian Arabs in the British mandatory government, and called for Palestinian independence in ten years.

1939 brought the beginning of World War II, so the British role in Palestine was further strained. The weight of the Holocaust led the Zionist movement to redouble its efforts to assure a Jewish state in Palestine. The 1942 Biltmore Declaration vowed its creation and, as the conference that produced the declaration took place in the United States, signaled the intent of the Zionists to lobby the Americans for support for their cause. Added to this was the rise of violent Jewish nationalist groups such as the Irgun and the Stern Gang, who viewed the White Paper as a betrayal of the Zionist cause. The British were now under double the pressure from Arab and Jewish quarters, and in 1946 the British headquarters in the King David Hotel became the target of an Irgun bombing.

Problem Evolution and Development: Partition

Whether the British seriously wanted to leave Palestine in 1948 is debatable, but leave they did after a few postwar efforts to come up with solutions. In 1947 the British turned over the matter to the new United Nations (UN). The solution offered by the international body was a partition plan that was adopted in UN Resolution 181 on November 29, 1947. The Zionist government was not pleased with the size of the state proposed for the Jews but ultimately decided to accept the plan as better than nothing. Skeptical that it would be implemented, the Zionists further reasoned that in the ensuing conflict more land could be acquired. For their part, the various Palestinian constituencies had agreed to boycott the UN commission that interviewed parties in preparation for making its recommendations.[12] After Resolution 181 was approved by the UN, the Arab parties rejected the idea of a Jewish state in the UN solution.

Confrontation came in two phases. Almost immediately after the vote on Resolution 181, violence in Palestine flared up. On January 20, 1948, Britain announced it was ending all security responsibilities in the mandate and urged "both sides to take measures to defend their respective communities," fueling a security void that spurred an escalation in violence.[13] On May 14, 1948, when Britain formally ended its mandatory control, the State of Israel was declared and phase two of the war began. The first full-blown war between Israel and the Arabs broke out, dubbed by Israel as the War of Independence. Contrary to standard accounts that suggest multiple Arab armies invaded Israel to destroy it, only Syria and Egypt crossed the borders of the new Israeli state, while Jordan, Iraq, and Lebanon limited themselves to engagements in what the UN demarcated as Arab territories.[14] Rather than a concerted plot to destroy Israel, Benny Morris characterizes the "first Arab-Israeli war" as a "general land grab," with everyone—Israel, Transjordan, Egypt, and Syria—"bent on preventing the birth of a Palestinian state" and "carving out chunks for themselves."[15] In fact, a "Zionist-Hashemite non-aggression pact" was sanctioned by the British, in essence keeping Israel and Jordan from coming to blows.[16]

A cease-fire was brokered in June–July 1948, but it did not hold. UN envoy Count Folke Bernadotte in September 1948 proposed new schemes to redistribute the land of Palestine, but he was assassinated and his plans died with him.[17] The UN called for a cease-fire in late November 1948, and Israel and Jordan agreed to one shortly after in December. By early 1949 armistice was in place throughout the land between the Jordan River and the Mediterranean Sea. There was a Jewish state of Israel, but not a state of Palestine. The West Bank was in Jordan's control; the Gaza Strip was held by Egypt.

The refugee plight of Palestinian Arabs remained a vital question that recurred in future cycles of conflict. An estimated 600,000 to 760,000 Palestinians fled their homes and lands between the end of 1947 and early 1949.[18] UN Resolution 194 addressed, among other things, the status of Palestinian refugees, suggesting that "refugees wishing to return to their homes and live at peace with their neighbors should be permitted to do so at the earliest practicable date" and noting that compensation would be paid to those choosing not to return.[19] This became the basis for Palestinian claims of the "right of return" (discussed below). While there was settlement of the issue after 1948 in the form of armistice, there was no reconciliation. Instead, a second conflict cycle began where this one ended—in the uneasy state of armistice between Israel and the neighborhood of Arab states that did not recognize its right to exist.

Timeline

The Arab-Israeli Conflict

1516		Ottoman rule over Palestine begins.
1880s		The first modern wave of Jewish immigration to Ottoman Palestine takes place.
1896		Theodor Herzl publishes his influential *Der Judenstaat*, calling for the establishment of a Jewish state.
1897		The first Zionist congress meets and establishes the World Zionist Organization, which begins to promote Zionist settlement in Palestine.
1915		McMahon-Hussein correspondence promises British support for Arab self-determination in exchange for an Arab revolt within the Ottoman Empire.
1917	November	The Balfour Declaration provides British support for the establishment of a Jewish national home in Palestine.
	December	The British capture Jerusalem and Ottoman Palestine.
1920		The San Remo Conference grants Palestine to Britain, a move later enshrined in a 1922 League of Nations mandate.
1921		The British separate Palestine from Transjordan.
1936–1939		Arab revolt in Palestine
1937		The Peel Commission recommends the partitioning of Palestine into Arab and Jewish states.
1939		The British White Paper limits Jewish immigration and land sales, disavows the Balfour Declaration, and rescinds plans for partition.
1942		The Biltmore Declaration of the World Zionist Organization calls for a Jewish state in all of mandated Palestine.
1947	May	The UN General Assembly Special Committee on Palestine (UNSCOP) is formed to investigate a solution to the Palestine problem.

(Continued)

(Continued)

	November	UN General Assembly Resolution 181 endorses UNSCOP's plan for partition.
1948	May 14	Israel declares its statehood and the United States recognizes it; Arab armies attack the next day.
	December	UN Resolution 194 creates the Conciliation Commission for Palestine and calls for Palestinian refugees' right of return.
1949		Armistices are signed with Egypt (February), Transjordan (March), and Syria (July).
1956		Egypt nationalizes the Suez Canal; Israel invades the Sinai before the United States compels it to leave.
1964		The Palestine Liberation Organization (PLO) is established.
1967	June	The Six-Day War takes place.
1973	October	The Yom Kippur War begins; Egypt and Syria attack Israeli forces in Sinai and the Golan Heights.
1978		The Camp David Accords bring peace between Egypt and Israel.
1982		Israel invades Lebanon.
1987		The *intifada* begins.
1993		The Oslo Accords are signed.
2000		Camp David II talks fail; the second *intifada* begins.
2002		The Arab Peace Initiative is publicized. A "Road Map for Peace" is offered by the United States, UN, European Union, and Russia.
2005		Israel withdraws from Gaza.
2006		Hamas wins Palestinian legislative elections.
		Israel wars with Hezbollah in Lebanon.
2008-2009		Israel wars with Hamas in Gaza.
2012		Palestine wins observer state status in the UN General Assembly.

Arab-Israeli Cycles after the 1948 Armistice

Conflict in the area did not end in 1948, the dynamic just changed from nationalist groups protesting to wars between states—namely Israel and its Arab neighbors. There have been several Arab-Israeli conflicts since 1948, including two major ones in 1967 and 1973. We focus below on the lead-up to these two wars as two cycles and show how the issue evolved and was (partly) resolved after the second war.

Problem Definition and Response: Unsettled Issues, 1967

The years between 1949 and 1967 represented a rather placid period of time involving no real war between Israel and its Arab neighbors, but also no peace. Cashman and Robinson note the Arab perspective that "armistices agreements dealt purely with military matters," and thus "the final status of political issues . . . were still unresolved." By contrast, Israeli leaders considered the armistice a de facto agreement of the "final borders of the states in the region," with Israel free to "carry out any activities [it] deemed necessary" therein.[20] This difference in perspective provided the foundation for the conflicts that followed.

The issue was managed through various low-level militarized disputes spurred by rising Arab nationalism under Egypt's Gamal Abdel Nasser, as well as the Palestinian issue, which Arab governments used to harass the "Zionist entity." In response to cross-border raids by Palestinian *fida'iyyun* (self-sacrificers), Israeli decision makers created rules governing the use of force in the conflict with their Arab neighbors.[21] In 1953 Israeli forces launched reprisal raids in the West Bank town of Qibla, and in a 1955 raid of Gaza attacked Egyptian forces in an effort to halt the raids and quell Egypt's permissive attitude towards them. Instead, historian Michael Oren says the raid "inaugurated the countdown to war."[22] In 1956 a staged war occurred that pitted Israel, Britain, and France against Egypt over Nasser's nationalization of the Suez.

After a full decade of peace from 1957 to 1967 (a notable reminder that the rivalry, however bitter, is not a perpetual conflict), war came again to the area as a case of what Cashman and Robinson call a "multilateral security dilemma."[23] Each side feared the buildup of the other's military. To resolve the 1956 crisis, Israel had needed assurances that the United States was obliged to give, such as freedom of navigation in the Strait of Tiran. Additionally, the United Nations Emergency Force (UNEF) was created to monitor and keep the peace on the Sinai to assure Israel that Egypt would not attack.

Problem Evolution and Development: Escalating Attacks[24]

Beginning in late 1966, Palestinian raids from Syria combined with occasional Syrian incursions into Israeli airspace, which provoked Israeli retaliation. This dynamic escalated through early 1967, and Syria called upon Egypt to honor its stated obligation to come to Syria's defense. Egyptian president Nasser obliged, if somewhat reluctantly. Once committed, Egypt took steps to assure its reputation and the situation escalated. Egypt blockaded Israel's access in and out of the Gulf of Aqaba, which Israel called an act of war. Nasser asked for UNEF troops to move from part of the Sinai and, when the UN responded that either they all stayed or they all went, Egypt chose the latter. Tensions and rhetoric increased, and the Arab governments and Israel mobilized troops for potential war.

On May 30, 1967, Nasser publicly vowed that

> the armies of Egypt, Jordan, Syria and Lebanon are poised on the borders of Israel . . . to face the challenge, while standing behind us are the armies of Iraq, Algeria, Kuwait, Sudan and the whole Arab nation. This act will astound the world. Today . . . the Arabs are arranged for battle, the critical hour has arrived. We have reached the stage of serious action and not of more declarations.[25]

Scholars dispute the seriousness of the Arab desire for war, as well as the opportunism on the Israeli side to use the crisis to strike first and obtain desired lands from Arab hands. But with the failure of diplomacy and the intensity of the situation, a restless Israel decided to strike first on June 5, 1967. Due to quick, early Israeli victories on the battlefield, by June 7 Jordan accepted a cease-fire. Egypt and Syria were not so eager to acquiesce, however. On June 9 the Israeli invasion of Syria began, despite U.S. calls for peace. At this point the Soviets threatened to stop Israel with military action, but before the superpowers could consider their next moves, on June 10 Syria signed a truce and the fighting subsided by the next day.

The United States worked with the Soviets to secure a lasting cease-fire. After months of negotiations and diplomacy, on November 22, 1967, UN Resolution 242 passed unanimously in the Security Council. The resolution called for the following:

1. Withdrawal of Israeli forces from territories occupied in the recent conflict

2. Termination of all claims of belligerency and respect for and acknowledgement of the sovereignty, territorial integrity, and political independence of every state in the area and their right to live in peace within secure and recognized boundaries free from threats or acts of force[26]

This framework, which has been referred to as "land for peace," importantly did not clarify whether Israel should withdraw from *all* or *some* of the territories it occupied during the Six-Day War. It also did not stipulate whether the mutual recognition of every state's right to exist should come *before* or *after* Israel's withdrawal from the occupied territories.

Israel expected recognition prior to withdrawal, whereas Arab states often expected the withdrawal first as a condition.[27] So, although UN Resolution 242 offered issue settlement in theory, peace did not come yet in practice.

While the war was over almost as quickly as it had begun, the consequences were monumental and formed the basis for all subsequent references to the Arab-Israeli conflict into the twenty-first century. Israel now possessed what many refer to as the occupied territories: the Golan Heights (from Syria), the Sinai Peninsula (from Egypt), and the Gaza Strip, East Jerusalem, and the West Bank. These latter three territories had been controlled by Egypt and Jordan since 1949, and their populations were heavily Palestinian nationalist. Israel's occupation of these territories has played a central role in subsequent cycles of the conflict, affecting both the peacemaking with Arab neighbor states (land for peace) and the plight and militancy of Palestinians under Israeli military occupation.

Problem Definition and Response: Enduring Disputes, 1973

Unresolved issues from the Six-Day War spilled over into the October War of 1973. The Israelis were ecstatic over their win in 1967. The victory was decisive and the territorial gains substantial and, to some, religiously invaluable. Jerusalem, the holiest city of Judaism, was now entirely within Israeli control. On the other hand, 1967 was humiliating to the Arab world. Arab leaders sought the return of their territories as well as of some pride to redress the balance. New fighting arose intermittently through 1968–1970 in what has been called the War of Attrition.[28]

The Arab-Israeli conflict was not just a regional problem. As Arab nationalism swept the region in the 1950s and 1960s, the Soviet Union sponsored Egypt's and Syria's efforts to break from traditional Western influence in the Middle East. The United States found itself backing the shah of Iran and regimes such as Saudi Arabia as a counterweight to these revolutionary trends. It also began funneling arms and aid to Israel in the 1960s, seeing Israel as a useful ally in a strategic region where the Cold War was being played out. The consequence was that any Arab-Israeli conflict, such as the Six-Day War, could conceivably become a superpower conflict.

The fighting continued after 1967, and the prospects of superpower confrontation brought new urgency to U.S. policy. The result was a United States renewed in its quest for peace and balance in the Arab-Israeli calculus. Throughout the 1970s, the shuttle diplomacy of U.S. secretary of state Henry Kissinger and others famously tried to end the wars and promote peace, culminating with the Camp David Accords between Egypt and Israel in 1978 in which the two sides officially declared peace with one another.

In a first run at a peace plan, the Richard Nixon administration produced the Rogers Plan in 1969. It proposed an Israeli withdrawal from occupied territories in exchange for an Arab contractual arrangement for permanent peace, a plan that Secretary of State William Rogers called "balanced" between the Arabs and Israelis. Balanced or not, it was a State Department-inspired plan that was at odds with the U.S. view after the Six-Day War, as it called for withdrawal without a prior, explicit formal treaty of peace. It also questioned the refugee situation, which had been made worse under the 1967 war, and suggested that Jerusalem's "civic, economic and religious life" be jointly managed by Israel and Jordan—both points said to have alarmed Israel.[29] It also raised eyebrows in the White House. President Nixon sent private assurances to Israeli prime minister Golda Meir that "we [will] not press our proposal" and assured a meeting of Jewish leaders in Washington that "an agreement can be achieved only through negotiations."[30]

Alienated in the Arab world, the United States sought to prop up and strengthen the few friendly regimes in the area, notably Iran and Israel.[31] By 1972 Nixon had increased aid to Israel to $500 million, partly in fear of "Soviet-inspired" Syrian and Egyptian governments.[32] This new relationship with the United States afforded Israel new status and new aid that tilted policy in its favor for years to come.[33] Yet the United States' increased links to Israel also increased the difficulties associated with such a relationship. The relationship did not improve the U.S. image in the broader Arab and Muslim world, particularly when the Arabs and Israelis came to blows in 1973.

Problem Evolution and Development: Geopolitical Strategy

Egypt's successor to Gamal Abdel Nasser, Anwar Sadat, sought to restore Egyptian pride and force compromises from the Jewish state and the international community. On October 6, 1973, Egypt and Syria attacked Israeli positions in the Golan Heights and the Suez. Within a few days, the Nixon administration was forced to consider the possibility of Israel's defeat. The loss of Israel would be a blow to U.S. domestic and strategic interests; Israel was a reliable, strong, anticommunist ally in a vital region and, additionally, was adored by a powerful constituency in the U.S. political landscape. As evidence surfaced of a Soviet airlift of arms to the Arabs, the United States commenced its own flow of direct arms aid to Israel.

Nixon viewed the situation geostrategically for an opportunity to resolve outstanding issues once and for all—facilitated in his mind by a "battlefield stalemate" that would "make it easier to reach an enforceable settlement."[34] Thus, the United States withheld from a full-scale commitment so that the Israeli government would acquiesce to a cease-fire, which it did on October 12. Sadat, however, rejected any cease-fire. Nixon then ordered a full-scale airlift of military equipment to Israel. The Soviets threatened a unilateral intervention, sparking a U.S. response that included a conventional and nuclear force alert and the warning that unilateral action by Moscow would be "of the gravest concern, involving incalculable consequences."[35] At the same time, the United States threatened to cut off aid to Israel for its intransigence. On October 22, 1973, UN Resolution 338 called for a cease-fire, the implementation of UN Resolution 242, and negotiations for establishing "a just and durable peace in the Middle East."[36] Hostilities ended October 27th.

The combination of the real threat to Israel, the superpower flare-up and escalation, and an oil embargo placed against the United States by Arab members of the Organization of Petroleum Exporting Countries (OPEC) led the U.S. government to rethink its role in the Arab-Israeli conflict. While the United States had long been seen as biased toward Israel, there was now a real, tangible price being paid with regard to U.S. economic health. Coupled with continued instability in the region and the perpetual threat of losing regional states to the Soviet bloc, there was new urgency to settle the thorny problem and save American face in the process.

The first step in the new climate of Middle East politics was to disengage the forces that had been locked over the Suez since the cease-fire at the end of October 1973. Henry Kissinger began his famous shuttle diplomacy in negotiating with all parties to avoid new hostilities and to bring resolution to the immediate battlefield land-grab problems. The fruits of this round of talks came in January 1974 with the Sinai I agreement, whereby Israel retained control of the Mitla and Gidi Passes while Egypt was allowed to maintain substantial forces east of the Suez. In exchange, the United States vowed to support UN 242 and also forgave Israel $1 billion in debts. By March 1974 the oil embargo was lifted, in part because of U.S. gestures but also due to the strain the embargo put on the exporting countries dependent on U.S. petrodollars.[37] The next step was to disengage Israeli and Syrian forces, which occurred in May 1974.

With forces now disengaged, the process began to make peace among the enemies. Kissinger's shuttle diplomacy yielded a deal in September 1975 whereby Egypt committed to a peaceful resolution with Israel, Israel committed to a pullout of Sinai passes, and the United States pledged to increase aid to both Israel and Egypt and promised not to recognize or negotiate with the Palestine Liberation Organization (PLO), a nationalist group led by Yasser Arafat and violently opposed to Israel, until it recognized Israel and UN resolutions 242 and 338.[38] This secret deal was leaked and was never pursued to its conclusion. Nonetheless, Kissinger had laid the groundwork for a workable peace.

Jimmy Carter assumed the U.S. presidency in 1977 and broke with Kissinger's step-by-step diplomacy, instead opting for a comprehensive approach involving high-level meetings between Anwar Sadat and new Israeli prime minister Menachem Begin. In September 1978 Carter, Sadat, and Begin isolated themselves at the presidential retreat known as Camp David and produced two accords, one on Israeli-Egyptian relations and the other on the matter of the West Bank and Gaza. The Framework for the Conclusion of a Peace Treaty between Egypt and Israel extended Egyptian diplomatic recognition to Israel in exchange for the return of the Sinai to Egypt's possession. It also called for Israeli settlements in the Sinai to be dismantled, economic relations to be established, and for all future problems to be resolved peacefully. This framework, under the spirit of UN Resolution 242, was declared the basis of subsequent negotiations for a formal treaty within three months of signing.

A second document, the Framework of Peace in the Middle East, called for the autonomy of peoples in the West Bank and Gaza through the elected, self-governing Palestinian Authority (PA), which was to replace the Israeli military governance there. While this pushed the Palestinian question forward symbolically, no action was taken by Israelis, Arabs, or the United States to make a Palestinian homeland a reality anytime soon. The issue of the political fate of the Palestinians had been a sticking point that almost derailed the talks, and, ultimately, the issue was tabled and separated from the bilateral talks with Egypt related to Sinai, which was a higher priority for Sadat.[39]

The Camp David Accords and the peace between Egypt and Israel have represented an enduring testament to the possibility of ending conflict cycles. After wars in 1948, 1956, 1967, and 1973, Egypt and Israel got off the merry-go-round and forged a lasting peace that persists to this day.

However, just as wars don't last forever, neither is peace guaranteed to last. The so-called Arab Spring that shook Egypt and the Middle East in 2011 threw Egyptian president Hosni Mubarak from power, ushering in popular government in an Egypt whose populace still views Israel with hostility and resentment. The regime that emerged, first in transition (the Transitional Council) and later through elections, was headed by Mohammed Morsi of the Muslim Brotherhood. Although Morsi agreed to abide by all existing international agreements, including the treaty with Israel, he also allowed Iranian warships to pass through the Suez Canal and seemed unable to contain new violence against Israel from the Egyptian border. After a military ouster of Morsi in the summer of 2013, the situation became uncertain. Even if peace endures in this dyad of Egypt and Israel, the broader Arab-Israeli conflict remains. Unresolved at Camp David were outstanding issues related to Syria and the Golan Heights, and the particularly thorny issue of the fate of the Palestinians. Until these issues are resolved, the larger conflict will endure.

Palestinian-Israeli Cycles of Uprising: *Intifada*

The Palestinian conflict, as mentioned earlier, predates Israel and shares the same roots as the Israeli conflict with the broader Arab world. We consider two cycles of conflict between Israel and the Palestinians. The first involves the PLO, introduced above. The PLO took up the cause of war for the "liberation" of Palestine in the 1960s, which fused with the *intifada* of the 1980s until peace was made in the Oslo process of the 1990s. The term *intifada* describes the uprising of Palestinians in the West Bank and Gaza against Israel. The second cycle of violence stemmed from the failure of the Oslo process and involved the second al-Aqsa *intifada*, which spiraled into great violence, numerous international plans, and hardened, unilateral postures from the Palestinian and Israeli camps.

Problem Definition and Response: The Palestinian Question

While Arab-Israeli peace was breaking new ground at the interstate level with the forging of the Camp David Accords, the lingering issue of the Palestinian question remained. In this phase of the conflict, Palestinian politics and dispute returned to the foreground, and aspects of this included the establishment of the PLO in 1964 and demands for the realization of Palestinian nationalist aspirations. Unresolved from the 1948–1949 period of conflict was the status and fate of Palestinian Arabs from the mandate area, including the 750,000 refugees settled in Gaza, the West Bank, and adjacent Arab countries Egypt, Jordan, Syria, and Lebanon. The 1967 war only added to the Palestinian crisis, generating hundreds of thousands more refugees and placing Palestinian Arab territories (Gaza, the West Bank, and East Jerusalem) under Israeli occupation.

The problem from the Palestinian vantage point was the continued dispossession of the Palestinian Arabs and the unresolved issue of the allocation of territories from mandatory Palestine. For Israel, the problem remained how to win secure, legitimate peace in the Arab world, plus the additional 1967 issue of what to do with newly acquired lands teeming with Arab populations hostile to Israeli presence. The Israeli occupation of various territories since the Six-Day War opened a new chapter in the Arab-Israeli conflict with regard to the plight of the Palestinians. The status of refugees had been a recurring theme since 1948, but now that Israel had a physical military presence over the lives of Palestinian Arabs, the flames of Palestinian nationalism kindled anew. New militant groups emerged, including the Popular Front for the Liberation of Palestine (PFLP) and the Popular Democratic Front for the Liberation of Palestine. The PLO, created by the Arab League in 1964 to deal with Palestinian issues, was brought under the leadership of Fatah leader Yasser Arafat in 1969. Fatah, the Movement for the National Liberation of Palestine, was founded in the late 1950s with the goal of pursuing Palestinians' freedom from Israeli occupation through low-intensity warfare. Agitating for Palestinian sovereignty, the PLO engaged in various political and paramilitary activities, including terrorism and raids on Israel and its military, the Israeli Defense Force (IDF), in the West Bank.

Israeli settlement policies, which aimed to claim the lands Israel occupied by populating them with Israeli settlers, and Israel's extended military occupation of Gaza and the West Bank stoked the fledgling Palestinian nationalism. Despite UN resolutions calling for the contrary, Israel embarked on an open-ended annexation of occupied conquered lands and settled civilians in those lands. Defense Minister Moshe Dayan ordered the creation of settlements in order to avert future ideas of partition in the area between the Jordan River and the Mediterranean Sea.[40] By 1977, 500,000 Israeli Jews had settled in the territories, and by 1981 Israel had declared East Jerusalem and the Golan Heights to be annexed territories of the state.[41]

The PLO's 1973–1974 debate over Palestinian participation in the Geneva Peace Conference demonstrates how both peacemaking and peacebreaking can be the product of competition within the same non-state group. During this era, the question of who spoke for the Palestinians remained unsettled. Fatah warmed to joining the peace process, at least in part to ensure the political survival of the PLO under its leadership. At the same time, opposition factions rejected the peace process, at least in part to ensure their own political survival within the PLO. Negotiating for peace and spoiling those negotiations, therefore, were part of a common dynamic by Palestinian groups motivated not only by their goals of statehood but also by their desire to remain politically relevant in the Arab-Palestinian arena.[42]

The U.S. administration of President Ronald Reagan sought to carry the momentum of the Camp David Accords into new areas of the Arab-Israeli conflict, namely Lebanon and the Palestinian question. A new focus on the fate of the Palestinians was central to an early peace proposal dubbed the Reagan Plan that rejected both an independent Palestinian state and the notion of Israeli sovereignty over the West Bank and Gaza, choosing instead "self-government by the Palestinians of the West Bank and Gaza in association with Jordan."[43] Israelis and Palestinians disagreed with the plan, the latter because existing settlements in the occupied territories were not to be touched, in addition to the independence issue. Defense Minister Ariel Sharon considered the proposal a threat to Israel's existence, and Foreign Minister Yitzhak Shamir accused the United States of "showing maximum consideration for the Arabs" and abandoning Israel in the process.[44] In the effort to demonstrate a more balanced approach, the United States ended up pleasing neither side and the plan failed.

At the same time, a more pressing issue came to occupy the minds of all participants. Israel invaded Lebanon in 1982 in what was called Operation Peace for Galilee, officially to create a buffer zone between Israel and the PLO. The PLO had used southern Lebanon for operations since it was expelled by Jordan in 1970, and Israel had raided the region in 1978 to push the PLO north of the Litani River. In 1982 Israel invaded again to finish off the PLO. A U.S.-brokered cease-fire guaranteed the peaceful withdrawal of the PLO out of Lebanon. The PLO found itself exiled to Tunis, far from the Palestinian front lines. Israeli occupation of southern Lebanon continued, and with it came a new actor in the maze of conflict: Hezbollah, a Lebanese Shiite militia born out of the Israeli invasion and occupation. Hezbollah received support from Syria and Iran and grew in stature as a resistance movement and political force in Lebanese politics.

Palestinians operating in the occupied territories conducted activities against Israeli occupation forces or helped foster pro-PLO sympathies. In 1985 Israel carried its search for PLO operatives into the occupied territories with new resolve. With the so-called iron fist policy, Defense Minister

Yitzhak Rabin implemented measures to increase detention and expulsion of activists and suspects linked to PLO sympathies in an effort to quash pro-PLO activity. This was at a time when Israeli settlements were proliferating in the occupied territories, provoking further Palestinian resentment and conflict. By 1987, 175,000 Israelis were estimated to be living in 130 West Bank settlements, and 2,500 lived in nineteen Gaza settlements.[45]

Despite Israel's aggressive actions against the PLO and continued pursuit of settlements, the United States pushed forward with the Schultz Initiative, which called for (1) an international conference in spring 1988 to get the ball rolling on discussions of the issue of the Palestinians and broader final peace among the regional powers and (2) negotiations between Israel and a Jordanian-Palestinian delegation to discuss a three-year interim arrangement for the West Bank and Gaza. These negotiations were to be followed by direct negotiations beginning in December 1998 to reach a permanent final settlement on the status of the territories.[46] Israeli prime minister Yitzhak Shamir vehemently opposed the proposal, and the initiative ultimately stalled on the Israeli front so long as the conservative, hard-line Likud Party was in charge.

At the same time, everyday Palestinians were going on twenty years of military occupation, which culminated in an explosion of strikes, protests, and violence known as the uprising, or *intifada*.[47] The trigger event occurred when an Israeli tank transporter collided with Palestinian vehicles lined up at a military checkpoint, killing four and injuring seven others. Protests led to confrontation with Israeli forces in which a Gazan was shot, fueling violence that spread and spiraled. IDF forces met protests and rock-throwing with live ammunition, and in the first two weeks of confrontation, two dozen civilian Palestinians were killed. Water, phone service, and electricity to refugee camps were cut off in a form of collective punishment that further stoked civilian Palestinians' rage and resentment. Some 8,500 were detained, and after thirty months the dead included forty-five Israeli soldiers and civilians and some 837 Palestinians.[48]

The *intifada* spawned several different responses. Part of the Palestinian frustration was not just with Israeli military occupation but also with perceived ineffectual leadership in the West, the Arab states, and the PLO. Yasser Arafat sought to rally his PLO leadership around this frustration in a forged alliance with other Palestinian groups under the banner of the Unified National Leadership. This emboldened Palestinian leadership took up the banner of resistance and asserted its cause internationally and locally. The 1988 meeting of the Palestinian National Congress included a declaration of the state of Palestine, a move that was recognized by several states in the region and international community, though not by the United States, whose veto kept Palestine from winning a seat in the United Nations. A related effect was the militarization of Hamas, an Islamist organization that called for resistance against Israel and challenged the PLO as a major force in Palestinian politics. This motivated Arafat to seek international avenues to legitimacy on behalf of the Palestinian people.

From Israel's perspective, the *intifada* revealed the burden of occupation and the moral hazard of fighting young boys wielding stones. The costs of administrating the territories now were bundled with the costs of pacifying a disgruntled population and the renewed international criticism for Israel's perpetual military rule and the blood it was shedding. The more right-wing, nationalist Likud Party offered no fundamentally new plan for solving the conflict, but the more leftist (and more willing to compromise) Labor Party floated the idea of negotiating for the eventual Palestinian autonomy of the occupied Gaza and the West Bank, either through Jordan or a Palestinian delegation that did not include PLO members (still deemed terrorists and enemies of the state). For its part, Israel debated the status of the territories and the future and character of Israeli demography versus geography. Those who wanted to annex the occupied territories risked absorbing millions of Arabs into the "Jewish State," but leaving the territories to potentially hostile Arabs jeopardized Israeli settlements and the strategic depth afforded by the extra territory between potential enemies and vital Israeli population centers.

For the United States, the new violence of the *intifada* and Israel's predicament posed a potential opportunity to foster a new round of negotiations. The idea broached in the early Reagan years of initiating contact with the PLO, rejected at the time, gained new momentum amidst the uprising. The United States demanded that the PLO accept the tenets of UN Resolution 242 and renounce terror before establishing a dialogue. Arafat, who did not start the *intifada* and who sought to reassert PLO relevance in the occupied territories, became interested in shoring up the PLO's legitimacy as the voice of the Palestinians. In November 1988 the Palestinian National Council declared a Palestinian state and also recognized Israel.[49] Arafat stated explicitly that the PLO accepted UN resolution 242 and fully renounced terrorism. Hours after the press conference, U.S. secretary of state George P. Schultz announced that the United States would open a dialogue with the PLO.

The 1989 Baker Plan was the George H. W. Bush administration's first stab at the Arab-Israeli dilemma. The proposal called for Israel to set aside its vision of keeping all of the occupied territories, demanded that the PLO formalize the end to calls for Israel's destruction, and created a list for Israel of Palestinians that could serve as representatives for negotiations on a final peace.[50] The PLO rejected the plan because it did not permit the PLO to represent the Palestinians. To place pressure on the Israeli decision-making process, Secretary of State James Baker announced that loan guarantees would be conditioned on the cessation of Israeli settlement activities, which the Bush administration had begun to conclude were illegal as well as a hindrance to the peace process.[51] This was a sign that the new administration felt free from domestic and traditional Cold War constraints to play hardball with Israel if so needed.

Meanwhile, the United States had carried on back-channel talks with Israeli Labor Party representatives, notably Defense Minister Rabin, but the Israeli settlements issue stalled any progress. Secretary Baker testified to Congress that a $400 million loan guarantee request should be approved for Soviet Jewish immigrants,[52] provided that Israel halt construction of new settlements in the territories. But in 1990 Israel's National Unity government fell and was replaced by an ultranationalist coalition under hard-liner Yitzhak Shamir that virtually guaranteed no real progress in the diplomacy of the peace process.[53]

At the same time, Israel was under increasing pressure from the international community about its tactics against the *intifada*. The United States had been willing to repeatedly shield Israel from UN Security Council condemnations, but this did not mean the United States was happy about Israel's behavior; the pressure was such that the United States sought finally to apply some pressure on Israel to change the situation for the benefit of all.

Problem Evolution and Development: Oslo and Wye River Accords

It was not American diplomacy that turned the tide, however, but secret bilateral talks between out-of-power Labor Party Israelis and PLO emissaries in Oslo, Norway. Secret understandings were reached so that, when Labor came to power, a new negotiating process could be implemented. This was to happen by mid-1993. The so-called Oslo Accords promised much, though in reality delivered very little that was tangible. On the one hand, the PLO recognized Israel and its right to exist. Unlike the Camp David Accords, this was not land for peace. Israel did not give the Palestinians statehood or the occupied territories but only the promise to negotiate with the PLO about all outstanding issues with a goal of final settlement by the end of 1999.

Palestinian critics found the Oslo Accords a bad deal for Palestinians. Many Israelis also felt the deal was bad because it involved talking to Arafat and the PLO (deemed terrorists by many) and held out the potential of withdrawal from parts of Gaza and the West Bank. Rabin paid for Oslo with his life at the hands of an Israeli assassin in 1995, but on the White House lawn in the fall of 1993, the handshake of Rabin and Arafat over the accords signified the possibility of resolution. The agreement helped pave the way for Jordan to make peace with Israel in 1994, thus showing Israelis the benefits of progress on the Palestinian issue. Negotiations continued over the next few years, and interim agreements parceled out portions of the West Bank and Gaza for Palestinian administration. The Palestinian Authority was created to govern parts of Palestinian territories in the West Bank and Gaza, and it had local administrative authority. It held elections for president and featured a Palestinian Legislative Council. Arafat presided over this fledgling government as its first president, and in 1998 the Palestinian Authority was given observer status in the UN, which came with the right to debate and co-sponsor resolutions in the UN General Assembly.[54]

What did not come from the Oslo process was final settlement, however. Hard-liners opposed to compromised peace painted the negotiators as traitors or appeasers to the enemy. In Israel hard-liners won the 1996 elections and the talks slowed to a crawl under Likud's Benjamin Netanyahu (prime minister again at the time of this writing). The U.S. administration of Bill Clinton pressed for negotiations, and the 1998 Wye River Accords transferred more territory to Palestinian rule, though sovereign statehood remained elusive at the end of 1999. Eager to finalize a deal, Clinton brought Arafat and the newly elected Labor government's leader, Ehud Barak, to Camp David in the summer of 2000. Despite claims that Israel made ambitious offers of a two-state solution, nothing was agreed to on paper. Arafat has been famously attributed with single-handedly dooming the peace process from that 2000 meeting through the last-gasp offers of the Clinton administration in January 2001.[55] What kept Arafat from taking the offer and making a Palestinian state a reality? The offer—generous from the Israeli view—included 96 percent of the West Bank, but this was still perceived as unjust from the Palestinian vantage. The Palestinians felt they had already lost 78 percent of Palestine to Israel, and now they were being asked to forfeit 4 percent more of the West Bank for Israeli settlements that most of the world declared were illegal and unjust. The status of East Jerusalem, which contained the Al-Aqsa Mosque and a sizeable Arab population, was not offered as a sovereign part of a Palestinian state. Despite whether Arafat should have taken the deal(s) offered in 2000–2001, he did not, and then new events overcame the negotiation process. A second *intifada* helped to usher in a hard-line Israeli government that declared in 2001 that the Oslo process was dead.

Box 4.3

Spotlight

Recognition at the United Nations

Our focus in this chapter has been the manner in which Arabs, including Palestinians, have pursued conflict and cooperation with Israelis and Zionists in the pursuit of their goals of self-determination. After the failure of the Oslo Accords to produce results, Israelis and Palestinians pursued unilateral agendas, with each side thinking there was no partner in peace to deal with. Israel's policy after Oslo was to disengage—disengage from talks, disengage from occupation of Gaza, and disengage from the Palestinian West Bank by erecting a security barrier meant to keep terrorism out and settlements inside Israeli control.

For its part, the Palestinian Authority pursued various measures of nonviolent resistance to reframe the moral high ground after the second *intifada*. Its major initiative at this time was an attempt to achieve statehood through the United Nations, circumventing the need to negotiate and compromise with the hard-line Likud government that seemed opposed to statehood and that continued to expand Israeli settlements in the occupied territories despite international protest. In 2011 Palestinian Authority president Mahmoud Abbas launched a campaign for statehood in the UN, but the Security Council tabled the subject and deferred action. Only the United Nations Educational, Scientific, and Cultural Organization (UNESCO) acted, voting 107–14 (with fifty-two abstentions) to admit Palestine into the organization.

Falling short of his goal and frustrated by U.S. opposition in the Security Council, Abbas tried again in 2012, this time bypassing the Security Council and lobbying for a General Assembly vote on statehood. A/Res/67/19 was approved, according Palestine "non-member observer status in the UN." The vote, 138–9 (with forty-one abstentions) elevated the status and legitimacy of Palestine but fell short of total sovereign statehood, which required Security Council approval. The United States vowed to oppose any such bid, saying the only road to statehood had to be through negotiations with Israel. Why the United States continues to insist on the negotiated route is a matter of debate, with many pointing to the "Israel Lobby"—a domestic set of interests that puts pressure on Congress and presidents alike to ensure Israeli interests in U.S. policy.[56] Regardless, the U.S. veto effectively blocks Palestinian statehood in the UN.

While the UN route seemed to be a dead end, and perhaps even self-defeating since it led to Israeli and U.S. aid cuts to the Palestinian Authority, it did bring the issue of Palestinian statehood to the foreground and put the United States and Israel on the defensive in the court of world opinion. It affords the entity of "Palestine" legitimacy in the world's eyes on a par with that of the Vatican and even gives Palestinians the ability to pursue claims in the International Criminal Court, should there be cause in its conflict with Israel. Given the legally contested nature of Israeli settlements and occasional Israeli military actions, the possibility of new pressure on Israel from international institutions is very real. All of this may spark renewed interest in bilateral negotiations, which were set to begin at the time of this writing.

Conclusion: Long Push for Peace

With the failure of the Oslo process and renewed violent confrontation in the second *intifada* from 2000 onward, the Arab-Israeli conflict has entered into another cycle. During the escalating violence in 2001–2002, Israel reoccupied West Bank territories under the Palestinian Authority's control. For some time, Israel's view was that it had no partner in peace, and it acted unilaterally through a policy called disengagement. This involved a withdrawal from the Gaza Strip in 2005 and the erection of a security barrier between Israel and Gaza, as well as a security "fence" around areas of the West Bank. Some of the walled area appeared to annex parts of the territory taken in the 1967 Six-Day War, which only exacerbated the tensions with Palestinians.

Palestinian responses varied by actor. Arafat has been famously described as either unwilling or unable to stop the violence perpetrated by the likes of

Hamas and Fatah's own al-Aqsa Martyrs Brigade. Such groups resorted to violent unilateralism in response to Israeli actions, which in turn clearly fed into Israel's reluctance to trust and deal with the Palestinians.

The outside world has renewed calls for peace over the years. In 2002 the Saudis offered up a deal that became known as the Arab Peace Initiative. Endorsed by the Arab League in 2007, it essentially called for peace with Israel in exchange for Israeli withdrawal to the so-called Green Line of pre–Six-Day War borders and recognition of a Palestinian state in Gaza and the West Bank, with East Jerusalem as its capital. Regarding refugees, the plan called for either the right of return or just compensation, in line with UN Resolution 194. In addition, the 2002 "Road Map to Peace" was offered up by the United States, UN, European Union, and Russia. This road map was incremental and required an end to violence and settlements before moving on to a tentative Palestinian state. Arafat died in 2004 and Mahmoud Abbas succeeded him as president of the Palestinian Authority. Abbas defended the Palestinian people's right to "express their rejection of the occupation through popular and social means" but declared that "using weapons is harmful and has got to stop."[57]

The Palestinian situation has been complicated by 2006 legislative elections that swept Hamas into power. With a PLO president in the West Bank and Hamas, which continues to deny Israel's right to exist, claiming authority in the Palestinian Legislative Council, gridlock resulted. The Israelis and Americans cut off aid to Hamas, calling it a "terrorist group," and backed Abbas and the PLO as the moderate alternative. This led to a violent rift between the PLO and Hamas in 2007. Attempts at unity between the factions have been unsuccessful. Negotiating without unity may lead to an unenforceable deal; negotiating with unity may require the United States or Israel to change their views on Hamas or for Hamas to change its views on violence and the right of Israel to exist.

The Israeli position of unilateralism since the second *intifada* is held under the belief that Israel has no reliable, unified partner in peace. Embracing the demography versus geography conundrum, Likud's Ariel Sharon formed a new party, Kadima, that advocated a withdrawal from Gaza and the construction of the wall separating Israel and its settlements from the rest of the West Bank. Israel has waged skirmish-level wars against Hezbollah (2006) and Hamas (2008–2009, among others). Sharon's successor, Ehud Olmert, pursued potential peace proposals under the urging of the United States, but his term was cut short by corruption charges that led to his resignation.[58] Subsequent Israeli governments have been run by coalitions led by the more hard-line Likud Party, and peace prospects have been dim ever since.

The Arab League endorsed a U.S. proposal for indirect Palestinian-Israeli talks through U.S. mediator George Mitchell in 2010. Direct negotiations were still anathema to the Arab position, in large part due to Israel's continued building of settlements in West Bank territories, including the government-authorized construction of 600 new homes in East Jerusalem. The Arab League met in July to assess this new attempt at discussions. In September 2010 Israel's ten-month moratorium on new settlement construction in the

West Bank came to an end, and with it any chance of talks died also.

In spring 2013 the U.S. administration of Barack Obama seemed intent on renewing an active role in negotiations and showed possible signs of being open to unity between the PLO and Hamas.[59] In June 2013 Secretary of State John Kerry made his fifth visit to the region to push for peace, warning that "if we do not succeed now . . . we may not get another chance."[60]

As for Arab-Israeli peace, the Arab Peace Initiative offered a route to normalization should Palestinian peace be reached. Syria still has outstanding issues with Israel related to the Golan Heights. Given Syrian president Bashar al-Assad's domestic crisis—a popular uprising stemming from the Arab Spring—it is unlikely to be resolved soon. But the common threat of Iran to Israel and the broader Sunni Arab world may help facilitate normalization, with U.S. assistance. Jordan and Egypt have ended the cycles of conflict with Israel. If and when others will do the same remains to be seen.

The pathway to cooperation between Israel and Palestinians, as well as Israel and its Arab neighbors, is long, winding, and complicated, illustrating the nonlinear and path-dependent nature of our pathways of conflict and cooperation. Each instance of conflict can inhibit future cooperation by fostering a sense of pessimism, anger, and injustice. But conflict also breeds fatigue and weariness, as we saw after the 1973 war and the *intifada*. With outside assistance, as was provided by the United States in those cases, peace talks can become a reality and peace becomes a possibility. If the parties are ready again, and the United States and others assist and aid the process, this conflict may indeed someday no longer be intractable, cyclical, or enduring.

Case Analysis

1. What are the most significant causes of the Arab-Israeli conflict—religious, ethnic, and political—and why? How do the answers to this question frame your understanding of the prospects for ending the conflict?

2. How does each cycle in the Arab-Israeli conflict affect the next, and what does this mean for the prospect of ending the conflict? How has each cycle in the conflict been similar, and how have they differed?

3. How did nationalism and ethnic conflict fuel the impetus for Israel's founding, and how do they inform the policies of the Israeli government in response to hostility from its Arab neighbors?

4. Compare how Israel achieved recognized independence with the Palestinians' failure to do so. Is there a way to achieve independence for Palestine without negotiations with Israel?

5. What factors have hurt the Palestinians' pursuit of sovereignty in the eyes of the international community? Consider the refugee status of many Palestinians, the geographic and political divisions of the West Bank and Gaza, and the oftentimes violent methods of resistance used against Israel.

6. Why do you think Egypt made peace with Israel? Could the same process work with Syria? Why or why not?

7. What role has the United States previously played in the Arab-Israeli conflict? Can it be an "honest broker" in negotiations? How can it help promote the pathway to cooperation?

8. Explain why you think the Arab-Israeli conflict can or cannot be resolved.

9. Identify and describe one or two other conflicts in world affairs—past or present—that can be described as cyclical or enduring.

Suggested Readings

Bickerton, Ian, and Carla Klausner. *A History of the Arab-Israeli Conflict.* 6th ed. (Upper Saddle River, NJ: Pearson, 2009. A solid history of the conflict, including primary documents.

Dowty, Alan. *Israel/Palestine.* Cambridge, UK: Polity Press, 2008. An excellent, balanced account of the politics of the Israeli-Palestinian conflict, from the perspective of both sides.

Khalidi, Rashid. *The Iron Cage: The Story of the Palestinian Struggle for Statehood.* Boston: Beacon Press, 2007. A critical account of how the Palestinians have been let down by the British, Zionists, and Palestinian leaders themselves.

Quandt, William. *Peace Process: American Diplomacy and the Arab-Israeli Conflict since 1967.* 3rd ed. Washington DC/Berkeley and Los Angeles: Brookings Institution Press/University of California Press, 2005. Authoritative account of U.S. diplomacy in the Arab-Israeli conflict.

Ross, Dennis. *The Missing Peace: The Inside Story of the Fight for Middle East Peace.* New York: Farrar, Straus and Giroux, 2004. Clinton Administration insider account of U.S. diplomacy between Israel and Palestinians, especially during the Oslo era.

Said, Edward. *The End of the Peace Process: Oslo and After.* New York: Vintage Books, 2000. Critical account of the Oslo era from a Palestinian viewpoint.

Web Resources

Arab-Israeli Conflict, Primary Source Documents, www.historyteacher.net/ Arab-Israeli_Conflict.htm#Docs. An overview and repository of links to key documents of the Arab-Israeli conflict throughout history.

Bitterlemons International, www.bitterlemons.net/. An online, self-described "Middle East Roundtable," this site offers content from prominent Israeli and Palestinian authors who present multiple perspectives on numerous past and present issues of the Arab-Israeli conflict.

Is Peace Possible?, www.ispeacepossible.com. This interactive Web site informs viewers of the concerns of both sides of the Israel-Palestine conflict and lets viewers try to create a workable map to solve the conflict.

The "Question of Palestine," United Nations, www.un.org/Depts/dpa/ qpal. A repository of documents and maps from the United Nations compiled since the 1948 War of Israeli Independence.

Iran's Nuclear Ambitions

I ran has been embroiled in complex diplomatic and economic entanglements for the better part of the last decade, chiefly because of its nuclear program. Highlighting the complex weave between conflict and cooperation, the past decade has included occasional agreements, proposed solutions, and threats and incidences of cyberwarfare and assassination. One example of this is the Stuxnet computer worm (discussed in Chapter 7) that famously disrupted Iran's centrifuge activity, which was revealed to be an Israeli-American joint effort to thwart Iran's nuclear program.[1] What has led to this cycle of diplomacy, sanctions, and threats of war? What are the prospects for cooperation in resolving issues that matter not only to the United States and Israel but to Iran, the Arab states, and the rest of the world? This case study investigates previous attempts at resolving the conflict of a nuclear-capable Iran, the difficulties stemming from different definitions of the problem, and the prospects for peace in the future. We examine the issue of nuclear proliferation through the various international mechanisms associated with the Non-Proliferation Treaty (NPT). Through the case of Iran, we explore the application of the NPT and the disagreements that exist about the rights and obligations of states abiding by the treaty.

Iran's nuclear actions are viewed here in the broader context of the Middle East regional balance of power. An American audience may look at the crisis in terms of Iran and the United States, but it is also an issue of regional security that involves conflict and cooperation in a neighborhood of states. This case also considers the challenge that Iran presents to regional security in the Middle East and how this situation evolved, focusing on U.S., United Nations (UN), and regional efforts to deter Iran militarily, diplomatically, and economically. The chapter's Concept Focus explores nuclear nonproliferation, and the Spotlight section examines Iranian supreme leader Ali Khamenei's 2003 fatwa that allegedly bans nuclear weapons in Iran.

Iran and the World Today

In August 2013 a man was arrested at New York City's John F. Kennedy airport with uranium lining the inside soles of his shoes. He was charged by the U.S. government with attempting to broker a sale of yellowcake to

┌──── **Box 5.1** ──┐

Case Summary

Iran seeks to enrich uranium for its nuclear program. Many in the international community maintain Iran should not possess uranium for fear of it developing nuclear weapons and threatening regional, if not global, security.

Global Context

With its primary regional competitor Iraq destabilized in the wake of the 2003 Iraq War, Iran may become an influential leader in the Middle East. However, the United States and others with interests in the region prefer a steadier, friendly ally to dominate, and Iran's history with the West has meant they are often in opposition.

Key Actors

- Iran
- Israel
- Saudi Arabia

- United States
- United Nations

Motives

- Iran is compelled by domestic and regional concerns to enrich uranium for energy production (and possibly weapons production), a right it says it has been unjustly denied by the UN Security Council.
- The international community, including the United States, wants assurance that Iran will not use enriched uranium to build a nuclear bomb.
- Israel, Saudi Arabia, and the United States aim to control Iran's ambition to become a regional power.

Concepts

- Balance of power
- Diplomacy
- Nationalism

- Nonproliferation
- Sovereignty

└───┘

Iran. Yellowcake is a concentrated uranium powder that is the first step in the process of enriching uranium for nuclear-capable weaponry. The arrest, which was the result of an undercover U.S. Department of Homeland Security operation and did not involve any actual Iranian agents, was a recent example in an ongoing conflict between the United States, Iran, and the international community. Although the Iranian government has repeatedly announced that it intends to use uranium for civilian energy purposes only, the United States and many others in the international community continue to suspect Iran has a military, weaponized aim.

International law has laid the groundwork when it comes to the possession of nuclear weapons, and the results are enshrined in the Nuclear Non-Proliferation Treaty of 1968. This international agreement has been signed by nearly all of the world's nations—including Iran—and lays out clear conditions for the transferring or receiving of weapons, weapons-grade materials, and weapons technologies between nuclear and non-nuclear states. The United States asserts that Iran is not adhering to these conditions. For its part, Iran disagrees that it even has weapons aims. However, Iran lacks the trust of the international community, including that of many of its Persian Gulf neighbors. Who has the most power and influence in the Middle East is important not only to the nations in the region but to countries such as the United States who rely on a steady flow of oil to keep their economies moving.

The United States and Iran were allies in the mid-twentieth century, but the pathway of conflict and cooperation that they have traveled since—spurred by new leadership and new motivations, as well as by changes in the structure of world politics with the end of the Cold War—has led to what for now appears an intractable situation with potentially very high stakes. The current conflict is only part of a longer rivalry that has its roots in the mid-twentieth century.

Problem Setting and Origins: Long-Running Rivalry

Sandwiched between Iraq and Afghanistan, Iran is a majority Persian nation in a region dominated by Arabs, and its residents are overwhelmingly Shi'a Muslim in a region dominated by Sunni Muslims. Over the centuries Iran has been buffeted between outside powers and politics, including British and Soviet occupation during World War II and a CIA-influenced coup in 1953, which fueled anti-Americanism that came to the fore in the 1979 Iranian revolution. Since World War II, the traditional Middle East regional system has been dominated by competition among Iran and multiple Arab powers for regional primacy through shifting balances and alliances. These regional rivals have been backed by military assistance and political support from extra-regional patrons (such as the United States and Soviet Union during the Cold War) to ensure that no one regional power or ideological bloc could dominate the region and, most critically, its oil supplies. In what author Malcolm Kerr dubbed the "Arab Cold War," Arab nationalist political forces, led by Gamal Abdel Nasser's Egypt and backed by Soviet military aid, were pitted against the traditional Persian Gulf monarchies, backed by the United States, who feared losing power and stability in a wave of pan-Arab revolution.[2]

In the 1970s Iran became another pillar in the U.S. strategy to preserve the status quo in the Persian Gulf. Iran's unchallenged leader since the 1950s, Shah Mohammad Reza Pahlavi, was a strong Western ally whose oppressive tactics at home garnered increased opposition. U.S. meddling in Iranian politics and support for the often ruthless shah generated the distrust and hatred of many Iranians. The shah departed Iran amidst revolution in 1978–1979, and U.S. president Jimmy Carter announced diplomatic relations with the successors to the shah's regime, led by former exile Ayatollah Rouhollah Khomenei. As Khomenei's Revolutionary Council consolidated power under the new Islamic Republic of Iran, however, mutual distrust and hostility between the new republic and the United States mounted.

Khomenei's new government executed hundreds from the previous regime, which generated protests from the United States. But it was the U.S. decision to admit the sick and exiled Pahlavi of Iran for medical treatment in the United States that incited the Iranian regime and public. On November 4, 1979, the American embassy in Tehran was overrun and hostages taken, prompting President Carter to cease oil imports from Iran, freeze Iranian assets, and issue threats of military action should the hostages be put on trial in Iran. The United States broke off relations with the new Islamic regime in 1980 after a failed hostage rescue mission that likely contributed significantly to Carter's loss in the next U.S. presidential election. (The hostages would not be released until after President Ronald Reagan's inauguration in 1981.) The tense relationship between the two countries has continued until today, with little to thaw the mutual chill.

U.S. fears of anti-American fundamentalist revolution elsewhere in the Middle East led the Reagan administration to back Saddam Hussein's war against Iran in the 1980s. Officially, the United States remained neutral, calling for a cease-fire between Iran and Iraq as the status quo, but unofficially it worked to block arms sales to Iran, provided battlefield intelligence to Iraq, and engaged in low-level battles with the Iranian navy in an attempt to protect oil shipments in the Gulf from Iranian attacks.[3]

Iran's ties to Hezbollah, a Lebanon-based Shi'a terrorist group, have created tensions between Iran and Saudi Arabia. After Hezbollah's 1983 bombing of the U.S. Marine barracks in Lebanon, the U.S. State Department labeled Iran a state sponsor of terrorism, which by law banned direct U.S. financial assistance and arms sales. Under President Bill Clinton, the United States moved to further isolate Iran as part of a strategy of dual containment aimed at both Iran and Iraq. In 1995 and 1996, the Clinton administration and Congress levied sanctions on Iran in response to growing concerns about Iran's weapons of mass destruction, its support for terrorist groups, and its efforts to subvert the Arab-Israeli peace process. The Republican-controlled Congress in 1995 allocated appropriations to fund CIA covert action to overthrow the Iranian regime, prompting the Iranian Majlis, or legislature, to fund covert operations against the United States.[4] Two bombings of U.S. military complexes in Saudi Arabia in 1995 and 1996 raised U.S. suspicion of Iran's role and led to discussions about a military response, but, as hard evidence was lacking, action was deferred.[5]

For all their disagreements and increasingly confrontational interactions, there were measures of cooperation between Iran and the United States between the 1980s and 1990s. The 1981 Algiers Accords officially ended the Iran hostage crisis and called for noninterference in each country's internal affairs. By the end of the Iran-Iraq War and after the death of Ayatollah Khomenei in 1989, Iran sought a measure of normalization with the United States. After reformist Mohammad Khatami won Iran's 1997 presidential elections, he called for a "dialogue among civilizations."[6] Secretary of State Madeline Albright subsequently acknowledged past U.S. interference in Iran and announced some minor concessions in the U.S. trade ban with Iran.

From a wider perspective, with the Islamic revolution in 1979, Iran's position in the regional equation shifted dramatically. Iran went from a modernizing U.S. ally to an anti-American Islamic republic and began quickly to promote "exporting revolution" abroad, including to Iraq and its neighbors in the Gulf. What the Iranian revolution meant for the region, however, depends on which country you ask. While much of the Arab world was startled by this change of events, some countries expressed more alarm than others. Especially concerned were those in the Persian (or Arabian) Gulf or those with significant Shi'a populations that could be swayed by Iran's call to arms. While most Sunni nations in the Middle East have kept their distance from Iran, Syria today remains an exception, having forged a relationship with Tehran partly because of Syria's historic rivalry with Arab neighbor Iraq and partly because Syria's ruling elite are themselves not Sunni but largely the religious minority of Alawite, a Shi'a offshoot. In John Limbert's words, Iranians "enjoy correct if not warm relations with their Qatari and Omani neighbors," relations with Saudi Arabia and Bahrain are "icy," and relations with the United Arab Emirates and Kuwait fall "somewhere in the middle."[7]

Beyond the Arab world, Israel has had an odd, occasional alliance with Iran, the result of shared suspicions of their Arab neighbors, which has led to intermittent cooperation despite the rhetoric of hostility from Tehran about the "Zionist entity."[8] Israel and Iran's mutual concerns with Arab powers and ambitions led to their cooperation in targeting Saddam Hussein's illicit nuclear weapons program at Osirak in 1981, which Israel bombed, and mutual support for Kurdish opposition in Iraq in the 1960s and 1970s.

In sum, there is a history of and context for regional rivalries and distrust preceding the advent of the "nuclear crisis" highlighted in this case, and that context has influenced how Iran's neighbors in the Middle East perceive its actions, how they respond to those actions, and how the role of the United States is received. In terms of when the current crisis over nuclear nonproliferation arose, however, the case of suspicious Iranian nuclear activity flared in 2001, and the urgency about Iran's future picked up pace after the fall of Saddam Hussein in 2003.

| Box 5.2 |

Concept Focus

Nuclear Nonproliferation

Proliferation, in the context of arms, refers to the spread of weapons from one entity to another. Nonproliferation is the idea of preventing the spread of weapons. **Nuclear nonproliferation** thus refers to the attempts to stop the spread of nuclear weapons and weapons-grade materials. By the 1960s five nuclear powers had emerged, and predictions were made by the likes of President John F. Kennedy that fifteen to twenty-five countries could obtain nuclear weapons capabilities by the 1970s.[9] The centerpiece of international efforts at nuclear nonproliferation is the Nuclear Non-Proliferation Treaty (NPT). Founded in 1968 and signed by all the countries of the world except Israel, India, Pakistan, and—since 2003—North Korea, the NPT lays out conditions for nuclear "have" states and "have-not" states to forego transferring or receiving weapons or weapons-grade materials and technologies.

Pertinent to the case of Iran, Article 4.2 of the NPT calls on the "have" countries to "facilitate . . . exchange of equipment, materials & scientific & technological information for the peaceful uses of nuclear energy. Parties . . . shall co-operate in contributing . . . to the further development of the applications of nuclear energy for peaceful purposes . . . in the territories of non-nuclear-weapon States Party to the Treaty." And Article 4.1 states that "nothing . . . shall . . . affect the inalienable right of all the Parties . . . to develop research, production & use of nuclear energy for peaceful purposes without discrimination and in conformity with Articles I and II of this Treaty."[10] From Iran's position, Article 4.1 permits enrichment and Security Council resolutions demanding it stop are unfair given its NPT rights. The UN reply notes that this right exists "in conformity with Articles I and II" that pertain to the transparent nonpursuit of weapons programs. If the International Atomic Energy Agency (IAEA) suggests Iran is violating these articles, the right to enrich uranium no longer is sacrosanct.

Optimists hail the NPT for limiting the number of weaponized states from the dire predictions of the 1960s, creating legal norms and inspections mechanisms (through the IAEA), and for providing the basis for enforcement against violations. Pessimists note that those states that have not signed the NPT have developed nuclear weapons outside the framework without punishment and that some countries, such as Iraq, Syria, and Libya, have covertly attempted nuclear programs despite being party to the NPT. The concern over Iran is whether it is doing the same.

Problem Definition and Response:
The Purpose of Iran's Nuclear Program

The nuclear aspect of the conflict became a defining feature by the late twentieth and early twenty-first centuries.[11] Although the Western-friendly shah of Iran built nuclear reactors in the mid-1970s, Iran suspended its nuclear programs after the revolution. During the Iran-Iraq War, Iraq used chemical weapons against Iran and was revealed to have a secret nuclear weapons program, which Iran helped Israel destroy at Osirak in 1981.[12] A few years later, Iraq struck Iranian facilities and partially completed reactors in raids from 1984 to 1988.[13] Iran's nuclear energy program resumed in 1992 when Russia was contracted to build a nuclear reactor at Bushehr and lease fuel for its operation.[14]

The issue of whether Iran's nuclear program is merely civilian has been a major concern for several parties, such as the United States, Israel, and the Sunni Arab Gulf states who fear radicalized Shi'a revolution from Iran. Pakistan's leading nuclear scientist, Abdul Qadeer (A. Q.) Khan, has said his network of scientists supplied Iran with key components to make specialized centrifuges for enriching uranium. Pakistan also gave Iran bomb-related drawings, parts for centrifuges to purify uranium, and a secret worldwide list of suppliers.[15] Well before 9/11, some analysts speculated that Iranian civilian nuclear energy programs merely "serve as the foundation for a nuclear weapons program."[16] U.S. and Israeli analyses from 1992 to 1993 estimated that Iran could potentially develop nuclear weapons within eight to ten years, a number revised in 1995 to an estimated seven to fifteen years "at its present pace."[17]

Though covert, unauthorized nuclear activity in the Islamic Republic can be traced back to the mid-1980s, it wasn't until 2001 that Iran was accused of running illicit programs. Unconfirmed allegations from anti-regime sources, combined with CIA estimates, convinced the U.S. administration of George W. Bush to add Iran to the "axis of evil" that Bush identified in his 2002 State of the Union address. Iran, Iraq, and North Korea were, in essence, lumped together as countries combining support for terrorism with pursuit of WMD. This significantly impacted the conflict with Iran by emphasizing nuclear weapons as a driving issue. The politics of the 2002 U.S. speech notwithstanding, the International Atomic Energy Agency (IAEA) verified at least some of the allegations. In 2003 the IAEA uncovered a pilot centrifuge plant at Natanz, Iran, and a heavy water reactor fuel plant in Arak, neither of which Iran had disclosed to the agency as required under the NPT.[18] In addition, weapons-grade traces of highly enriched uranium (HEU) discovered in Iranian plants were traced to Pakistani parts and centrifuge technology. All of these unreported activities violated the NPT. Iran's defense minister admitted to the centrifuges and clandestine program but claimed they were for civilian use.[19]

After the Iraq War in 2003, the United States perceived that, with Iraq no longer an obstacle to Iranian ambitions, Iran's influence in the region could more easily spread. Some experts, however, question the notion that Iraq ever served as a serious bulwark to Iran, but "the psychological effect [in Washington and the Sunni Arab capitals of the Gulf] of the demise of a stable Iraqi state and the rise of a Shi'a-dominated government with long-standing ties to Iran is significant."[20] The Iraq War and the resulting significant American military presence in the region have also turned the United States into a de facto regional power.[21]

From Iran's position, the conflict remained one of a Shi'a Persian republic existing in a region dominated by Sunni Arab states; the global unipolar power, the United States; and the United States' regional ally, the nuclear state of Israel. Iran's definition of the situation was one of new opportunities and new threats. On the one hand, with Hussein gone, a nemesis neighbor became a Shiite-led potential ally within Iran's Shi'a orbit of influence. On the other hand, U.S. forces were now poised on either side of Iran's borders in Afghanistan and Iraq. Some neoconservatives in the United States dreamed of using U.S. bases in the region as a staging ground for toppling other enemies, including Tehran, either by direct force or covert agitation and encouraged revolution. Middle East scholar Fouad Ajami notes Iran's predictable concerns with the U.S. invasion and occupation of Iraq, suggesting that "what America had brought along, loaded up with the military gear, was a threat that the clerical revolution that had triumphed in Iran a quarter-century earlier could be undone."[22]

Iran considers nuclear energy and production to be an NPT right—one threatened by the United States and Israel. The Iranians claim not to want nuclear weapons. The supreme leader himself allegedly said in a religious ruling, or fatwa, that nuclear weapons are un-Islamic (see Box 5.3). Iran's position on nuclear energy rights, negotiations, and foreign policy comes from a combination of pride and a siege mentality exacerbated by regional Arab, Israeli, and U.S. hostility.[23] According to a Gallup poll taken December–January 2012–2013, 63 percent of Iranians think their government should continue to develop nuclear capabilities, and 47 percent of the poll's respondents primarily blame the United States for the sanctions Iran faces, compared to one in ten that blame their own government.[24] Yet Iran's neighbors, including Israel, are uncomfortable with the possibility of a nuclear-capable Iran.

The differing views of Iran's intentions play into different threat perceptions of Iran. Concerns about a nuclear-weaponized Iran range from the strategic—tilting the regional balance of power toward the Persian state at the expense of the Arab world—to existential fears by some Israelis that Iran wishes Israel to be "wiped off the map" (though this oft-cited quote by Iranian president Mahmoud Ahmadinejad is commonly seen as a misinterpretation of Iranian policy to confront Zionist ideology rather than to literally destroy the state of Israel).[25]

Of course, Israel and the United States maintain nuclear and conventional capabilities in the region. Israel is a nuclear-armed state that lives in a condition of deliberate "nuclear opacity," neither confirming nor denying its weapons program.[26] There have, however, been leaks, disclosures, and declassifications confirming the Israeli program. The CIA concluded in 1974 that Israel had become a nuclear state,[27] but the origins of the program date to the 1960s. In 1969 Israeli prime minister Golda Meir told U.S. president Richard Nixon that Israel had developed nuclear weapons, and the U.S. administration agreed to "look the other way" if Israel would "neither test nor declare its nuclear weapons."[28] Pakistani scientist A. Q. Khan said of his support for an Iranian bomb program, "Iran's nuclear capability will

Timeline
Iran's Nuclear Program

1953		Iran's democratically elected prime minister, Mohammad Mosaddegh, is ousted in a CIA-led coup. The pro-American shah of Iran assumes control of the country.
1950s		Eisenhower's Atoms for Peace program uses U.S. technology to assist countries and leaders with civilian nuclear energy, including the shah of Iran.
1979		The Iranian revolution takes place; Ayatollah Khomenei suspends nuclear programs begun by the shah. Iranian revolutionaries attack the U.S. embassy in Tehran and take hostages.
1980		Saddam Hussein's Iraq attacks Iran, beginning the Iran-Iraq War.
1981		The U.S. and Iran sign the Algiers Accords. Iran releases the American hostages and the U.S. pledges nonintervention in Iranian affairs.
1983		Chemical weapons are first used by Iraq against Iran.
1984		By some accounts, Iran begins a covert nuclear weapons program, acquiring covert nuclear equipment from Pakistani supplier A. Q. Khan in 1987.
2002		U.S. president George W. Bush places Iran in an "axis of evil" of state sponsors of terrorism.
2003		IAEA reports "credible information" indicating that Iran has carried out activities "relevant to the development of a nuclear device."
2006		UN Resolution 1696 becomes the basis for a series of UN sanctions; the UN demands Iran cease uranium enrichment or face compliance measures
2007		A U.S. National Intelligence Estimate leak suggests Iran ceased a nuclear weapons program in 2003.
2009	June	Iranian presidential elections are disputed, leading to unrest in Iran.
	October	Geneva talks between Iran and the P5+1 lead to a deal for Iran to send enriched uranium to Russia and France in exchange for fuel; the deal is scuttled by Iranian domestic politics.
2010		Turkey and Brazil offer Iran a deal to ship uranium to Turkey; the West rejects the deal.
2012		
2013		Two rounds of talks occur in Almaty, Kazakhstan.
	June	Iranian presidential elections bring to power moderate Hassan Rohani.
	October	A new round of talks begins between Iran and the P5+1 in Geneva.

neutralise Israel's power."[29] This was not merely a reference to a general regional balance of power but also to the worst-kept secret in the region—Israel's long-standing possession of nuclear weapons.

As has been noted, it is not only the United States and Israel that fear Iranian power and intentions. Many of the Sunni Arab states in the Middle East are anxious as well. As a regional issue, the 2003 Iraq War was a pivotal part of what has been called by different authors "the Shi'a Revival" and the "Eclipse of the Sunni."[30] The Persian Gulf regional subsystem shifted from a balance of power between Iraq and Iran to one of Iranian regional preeminence in relative power with the decimation of Iraqi forces in the Iraq War.

Iran's power in the region is not attractive to its neighbors. Indeed, WikiLeaks published cables that revealed hostility and distrust toward Iran by high-ranking Arab officials from around the region. In an April 17, 2008, meeting with U.S. diplomats, the Saudi ambassador to the United States reportedly recalled "the King's frequent exhortations to the U.S. to attack Iran and so put an end to its nuclear weapons program."[31] In 2009 Mohammed bin Zayed Al Nahyan, a crown prince of the United Arab Emirates' Abu Dhabi, likened Iranian president Mahmoud Ahmadinejad to Hitler, and the UAE foreign minister is described as viewing Iran "as a huge problem that goes far beyond nuclear capabilities."[32]

For its part, Iran has tried to ingratiate itself to the Arab world while putting Arab rival governments on the defensive by being a vocal proponent of the Palestinian cause and of independence from U.S. influence. A Zogby Research Services survey shows that Arab support for Iran declined from 2006 to 2011, with a majority of those polled in twenty Arab states possessing a negative view of the country. These detractors cite Iran's support for Syria during Syria's crackdown on Arab Spring proponents, which began in 2011 and still continues.[33]

In spring 2003 Iran offered the United States a "grand bargain" that the Bush administration rebuffed. Iran sought an end to hostile U.S. behavior and sanctions imposed by the United States after the hostage crisis, as well as recognition of Iran's "legitimate security interests" and rights to peaceful nuclear technology. In exchange, Iran would offer "full transparency" and "full cooperation" with IAEA concerns, take "decisive action against any terrorists on Iranian territory," support political stabilization in Iraq, and pressure "Palestinian opposition groups to stop violent actions against civilians" in Israel.[34] This sort of approach tied the nuclear question to a larger regional context that the United States did not want and did not trust.

With its rejection of this bargain, the United States seemed to shift toward a hard-line confrontation with Iran. The EU3 of France, Germany, and the United Kingdom led the way in negotiating with Iran after U.S. president George W. Bush refused direct talks. Iran agreed to a cessation of enrichment activities in 2003, and in 2004 the EU3 worked out a deal with Iran to discuss "a range of nuclear, security, and economic issues as long as Tehran suspended work on its uranium enrichment program and cooperated fully with an investigation by the International Atomic Energy Agency."[35] That agreement was scuttled in 2005, however, after the election of Mahmoud Ahmadinejad. Under Ahmadinejad's leadership, the Iranian position took a nationalist turn whereby the right to enrich uranium was upheld as a proud statement of Iranian policy.

Box 5.3

Spotlight

The Supreme Leader's Nuclear Fatwa

In October 2003 Iran's supreme leader, Ayatollah Khomenei, issued a fatwa that declared the possession of nuclear weapons a sin, leading many observers to say it effectively banned nuclear weapons and other weapons of mass destruction in Iran. A fatwa is an edict or ruling provided by a religious authority. With Khomenei's nuclear fatwa, Iranian foreign minister Ali Akbar Salehi announced that Iran was ready to "translate the fatwa into a secular, binding document" and "to transform it into a legally binding, official document at the U.N."[36]

Iran's neighbors and the international community received the fatwa with various degrees of skepticism. One debate is over the seriousness of the decree; another is over what it truly says. As for what it exactly says, some say it is clear and obvious. According to one text, the exact words of the statement are as follows:

> The Iranian nation has never pursued and will never pursue nuclear weapons. . . . There is no doubt that the decision makers in the countries opposing us know well that Iran is not after nuclear weapons because the Islamic Republic, logically, religiously and theoretically, considers the possession of nuclear weapons a grave sin and believes the proliferation of such weapons is senseless, destructive and dangerous.[37]

As for its validity, one argument is that because of the

> strong bond between religion and politics in Iran, the supreme leader's religious fatwas carry both legislative and religious importance. According to the Iranian constitution, the supreme leader has the ultimate authority over all three branches of government. As such, the fatwa has the status of law and cannot be subject to review of any kind.[38]

Others note that the statement was oral, not written, and that translations leave the wording open to interpretation. One study also points to fatwas being "altered in response to changing conditions" and notes that subsequent statements "have been ambiguous with regard to the development and stockpiling of nuclear weapons."[39] Whatever the merits of the fatwa, it is unlikely that it will assure those who are already suspicious of Iranian intentions.

Problem Evolution and Development: UN Sanctions

With enrichment resumed and the first attempts at a solution resulting in no progress, the Iranian nuclear issue became more confrontational in the world arena after 2005. After alternating between promises to freeze enrichment plans and asserting a sovereign right to enrichment, Iran broke the UN seals on its nuclear facilities and resumed uranium conversion in Isfahan in August 2005.[40] Iran announced in April 2006 that it had successfully enriched uranium for the first time but that it had no intention of developing nuclear weapons.

By 2006 the Bush administration backed down from a policy of no direct talks and made overtures to Iran, but only with the precondition of the Iranian regime completely and verifiably suspending its enrichment and reprocessing of uranium. Iranian nuclear negotiator Ali Larijani said in response, "If they want to put this prerequisite, why are we negotiating at all?"[41] Despite the awkward start, the United States, China, and Russia joined the three EU3 countries in June 2006 for what became the United States' first direct talks with Iran since the revolution. The talks became known as the EU3+3 or, alternately, the P5+1 (referring to the same countries: five permanent members of the UN Security Council plus Germany). By this time the IAEA could not conclude that Iran's nuclear program was "exclusively for peaceful purposes,"[42] and the UN Security Council responded with the adoption of six resolutions over the next two years. With the adoption of Resolution 1696 in July 2006, the council first demanded that Iran suspend its uranium enrichment-related and reprocessing activities. The following three resolutions, 1737 adopted in December 2006, 1747 adopted in March 2007, and 1803 adopted in March 2008, imposed incremental sanctions on Iranian persons and entities believed to have been involved in Iran's nuclear and missile programs. Resolution 1835, adopted in September 2008, reiterated the demands made in resolution 1696 without imposing additional sanctions.

When Barack Obama took control of the White House after the elections in 2008, the shift in U.S. leadership offered a chance for change in the Iranian dynamic toward a pathway of greater cooperation. Obama, who had sent a letter to Iranian supreme leader Ayatollah Khomenei before assuming the presidency, hoped to signal a willingness to engage in negotiations and resolve outstanding issues.[43] Letters to and from Obama and Ahmadinejad furthered the sense of possibility, and each side prepared for the first substantive direct talks since the Iranian revolution. Ahead of the formal talks in Geneva, Switzerland, set for October 2009, proposals and confidence-building measures were suggested back and forth. The warming in relations, however, was hindered especially by the Iranian presidential elections in June 2009, in which Ahmadinejad was declared the winner in a highly suspicious election. Iranians protesting the vote count were met with violent resistance in the streets, images of which made their way to YouTube and the wider world media. The Obama administration walked a line between criticizing antidemocratic and oppressive measures in Iran while still preserving the opening for progress in nuclear talks.

Nonetheless, talks took place that fall in Geneva that yielded the first concrete proposal between the United States and Iran. Specifically, Iran would export 1,200 kilograms of low-enriched uranium (LEU) to Russia and France, who would enrich it to 20 percent for fuel rods that would be delivered back to Iran.[44] Iran agreed in principle to this deal, creating hope of an end to the cycle of confrontation. But it did not happen. Iran delayed giving the IAEA and the P5+1 a definitive response to the proposal, and prominent Iranian politicians publicly opposed the deal. Iranian officials called for different fuel swap proposals, such as staggering the export of Iran's LEU over the course of a year.[45]

After the failure of the Geneva talks, cooperation became politically difficult for the Obama administration, as it had appeared to reach out a hand to Iran only to be rebuffed for its efforts. In 2010 an innovative new proposal emerged among Iran, Brazil, and Turkey. The May 17 "Tehran Declaration" affirmed "the right of all State Parties, including the Islamic Republic of Iran, to develop research, production and use of nuclear energy," including enrichment, and gave Iran the option to transfer LEU to Turkey to be held in escrow. In exchange, the P5+1 countries would transfer the equivalent amount of uranium enriched to 20 percent within a year. If such a transfer did not take place, Turkey would give the LEU back to Iran for its own use. Uninvolved in the talks and feeling rebuffed, France, Russia, and the United States did not accept the declaration.

In discussing diplomacy employed in the Iranian nuclear situation, we should not forget about **coercive diplomacy**. Defined as the use of threats to influence another country into changing policy, coercive diplomacy suggests a variety of mechanisms for punishing a country's behavior. The threat and use of sanctions is one avenue of coercive diplomacy, as is the threat and (perhaps escalating) use of force. By defining red lines and not ruling out the use of force, the United States employed coercive diplomacy in attempts to compel Iran to adopt desired policies for fear of the economic and military consequences that could follow if it did not.[46] Yet for all that the United States has threatened force and Iran's neighbors have indicated they would support such efforts, no one has been willing to rush to overt action.

As negotiations, coercive diplomacy, and covert action have failed to successfully resolve the crisis, rhetoric about the use of force has escalated. U.S. vice president Joseph Biden went on record in 2009 saying the United States would not stand in the way of Israeli action against Iran.[47] In response, leading Iranian Majlis speaker Ali Larijani replied, "We will consider the Americans responsible in any adventure launched by the Zionist entity."[48] Yet despite such rhetoric, signs point to the United States restraining Israel, not encouraging it. Reports note "a series of sharp, behind-the-scenes exchanges between the Israelis and top American intelligence and military officials," dating back to 2007 and spiking for a time in 2012, indicating that Israeli officials privately believe "the Obama administration is deluding itself in thinking that diplomacy will persuade Iran to give up its nuclear program."[49]

Iran also has made clear its potential to make mayhem. Iranian-provided assets and weapons in Iraq and Afghanistan could, and occasionally did, make U.S. operations there more difficult. Hamas, Hezbollah, and Syria are potential allies that could be activated in a regional war. Iran has at times threatened to close the Strait of Hormuz, a vital and narrow passageway from the Persian Gulf out to the world's seas through which flows over a third of global oil exports. In 2008 five Iranian Revolutionary Guard patrol boats harassed a three-ship U.S. Navy convoy in the strait, coming within 200 yards of a U.S. ship and demonstrating how surprise and swarming could catch U.S. power off guard.[50] Iran also continues to rely on strong rhetoric, indicating just how little progress has been made in resolving the conflict over Iranian nuclear capabilities despite all of the coordinated diplomatic efforts and covert actions. In reply to Israeli threats of military action, Ayatollah Khomenei vowed in 2013 that "the Islamic Republic will raze Tel Aviv and Haifa to the ground."[51]

Conclusion: Status Quo

On April 2012, the P5+1 and Iran began another series of talks in which negotiators proposed individual steps of progress that would be reciprocated with steps by the other side and culminate in a long-term solution. Yet with U.S. presidential elections in 2012, the chance for a breakthrough seemed slim. The initial hope was that the reelected Obama, free from the political concerns about having to run again, would be willing to take a more realistic approach to resolving the conflict. The two sides, however, remained far apart, and the violent fighting between Arab-backed rebels and the Iranian-supported regime in Syria increased regional tensions and diplomatic intractability. After Obama's reelection, prospects for a renewed path of cooperation were heightened with talks in Almaty, Kazakhstan, in spring 2013. While no new deal was made, the positions of each side were clarified. Iran sought an end to sanctions and the recognition of the right to enrich. But Iran itself was in the midst of a presidential election season, and most assumed no new talks would be fruitful until the Ahmadinejad era came to a close.

What will come from future talks remains to be seen. The June 2013 election of a new, moderate Iranian president, Hassan Rohani, may provide an opportunity to change the dialogue on this conflict. Rohani, who took office in August 2013, rejected caving in to sanctions but declared a pathway to cooperation through "a dialogue on an equal footing, confidence-building which should be mutual, and mutual respect as well as reducing antagonism and aggressiveness."[52] In October Iran met with the P5+1, including the United States, in the first of many rounds of anticipated talks. But even if Rohani is serious about substantive talks, Ayatollah Khomenei remains the supreme authority in Iran and it is not yet clear that the supreme leader's position on the issue has changed. Whether the United States or Israel trust Iran is yet to be determined, but talks are surely forthcoming. The urgency of the situation depends on beliefs about Iranian intentions and the broader issues of the region.

With pessimists warning of a pending point of no return in the Iranian uranium enrichment cycle, the pressure to act will surely persist, and the outcome—either new cooperation or continuing conflict—is far from assured. Fear of a Middle East arms race should Iran go nuclear drives concerns beyond the Arab Gulf.[53] Some experts suggest an arms race is less likely than the need of other Middle Eastern countries to harness nuclear energy to support the needs of their citizens. Egypt, for instance, plans to build four nuclear power plants by 2025 to provide more energy to support its growing populace and infrastructure.[54] Whether talks with Iran can be resolved on narrow issues of enrichment and sanctions or must approach a grand bargain of regional and outstanding issues, forces that fear the bomb will continue to push for conflict, while forces that fear regional war will push for cooperation.

Case Analysis

1. What motivates the common regional views of Iran's nuclear program and what to do about it? What about these views are different and what conclusions can you draw about the motivations of the countries holding these views?

2. Does the fact that states such as Pakistan and India are signatories to the Nuclear Non-Proliferation Treaty and yet have obtained nuclear weapons negate the effectiveness of the agreement? Explain your reasoning.

3. What is Iran's position on its nuclear program? What are the sources of this position, and do you think it will change? Why or why not?

4. Explain which you think is the greater impetus for conflict: the possession of nuclear weapons or the desire to attain them.

5. Describe what actions Iran has taken since the 2003 nuclear fatwa issued by its supreme leader that would justify the international community's skepticism of Iran's stated intentions.

6. A major aspect of the 2008 U.S. presidential campaign with regard to foreign policy was how to approach the Iranian nuclear question. Compare and contrast the Bush and Obama approaches to Iran. Has either proven to be better or worse, and why?

7. On the pathway of conflict and cooperation traveled by the United States and Iran with regard to nuclear weapons, identify missed opportunities for cooperation that may have occurred in 2003, 2006, and/or 2009.

Considering the structure of world politics and the dynamics that play into the way foreign policies are made, what do you think accounts for these missed opportunities?

8. Given Iran's history and the nature of its relationship with the United States and United Nations, should there be reason for optimism with a newly elected president in Iran in 2013? Why or why not?

Suggested Readings

Jervis, Robert. "Getting to Yes with Iran: The Challenges of Coercive Diplomacy." *Foreign Affairs* (January–February 2013). Analysis of the use of threats and promises to achieve successful diplomatic results with Iran.

Kaussler, Bernd. *Iran's Nuclear Diplomacy: Power Politics and Conflict Resolution*. New York: Routledge, 2014. Up-to-date analysis of the politics and power dynamics underlying Iran's nuclear program.

Nasr, Vali. *The Shia Revival: How Conflicts within Islam Will Shape the Future*. New York: W.W. Norton & Company, 2007. Insightful regional perspective of changing power dynamics after the Iraq War, with Iran and the Shi'a perceived as a threat to Sunni, Arab areas.

Palmer, Michael. *Guardians of the Gulf: A History of America's Expanding Role in the Persian Gulf, 1833–1992*. New York: Free Press, 1992. Overview of the rise of U.S. interests and responsibilities in Persian Gulf security.

Parsi, Trita. *Treacherous Alliance: The Secret Dealings of Israel, Iran and the U.S.* Cambridge: Yale University Press, 2007. Analysis of the power balance between Israel and Iran that defines the rhetoric and politics of nuclear diplomacy.

Rubin, Barry. *Paved with Good Intentions*. New York: Penguin Books, 1980. Classic analysis of the U.S. role in Iran before and after the revolution.

Web Resources

International Atomic Energy Agency, www.iaea.org/NewsCenter/Focus/IaeaIran/index.shtml. Track the ongoing status of Iran's nuclear program through this Web site maintained by the IAEA.

Non-Proliferation Treaty, United Nations, www.un.org/disarmament/WMD/Nuclear/pdf/NPTEnglish_Text.pdf. The text of the Nuclear Non-Proliferation Treaty is available from the United Nations.

2010 Nuclear Force Posture Review, www.defense.gov/npr/docs/2010%20nuclear%20posture%20review%20report.pdf. This document presents President Obama's roadmap for reducing nuclear risks to the United States and the international community and specifically addresses U.S. nonproliferation aims.

"Iran: Nuclear Intentions and Capabilities," U.S. National Intelligence Estimate, November 2007, www.dni.gov/files/documents/Newsroom/Reports%20and%20Pubs/20071203_release.pdf. Examine the U.S. Office of the Director of National Intelligence's estimate on Iran's nuclear capabilities and interpretation of its intentions.

6 Responding to Terrorism after 9/11

I n previous chapters we have dealt with interstate war and recurring wars between states, both of which involved the policies of sovereign governments toward other sovereign governments. In this chapter we look at a different dynamic—states pitted against transnational nonstate actors. Specifically, we examine how the United States has responded to the militant Islamist group al-Qaeda, especially after the attacks of September 11, 2001. Those attacks changed the nature of the way the United States has responded to threats from al-Qaeda and terrorist groups generally. Under the leadership of George W. Bush, the United States launched a so-called Global War on Terror (GWOT) aimed at attacking al-Qaeda and affili- ated individuals and organizations around the world. Under the Barack Obama administration, the GWOT label has been dropped, but the United States remains engaged in pursuit of al-Qaeda and its allies in Afghanistan, Pakistan, Yemen, and Somalia, among other places.

Has the American way of countering terrorism since 9/11 been effec- tive? The pathway of conflict and cooperation between the United States and al-Qaeda is not new and began with the two parties collaborating against the Soviet presence in Afghanistan in the 1980s. It has since grown increasingly oppositional, with the goals of each in direct opposition to the other. This chapter traces how al-Qaeda evolved, examines the group's agenda, and discusses how al-Qaeda's interests and ideas have grown to increasingly clash with those of the West. We then turn to the attacks of 9/11 and the U.S.-led response. Although violence had occurred prior to 9/11, the events of that day, in which al-Qaeda members hijacked four passenger jets and killed nearly 3,000 people by crashing the jets into the World Trade Center in New York City, the Pentagon near Washington, D.C., and a field in Pennsylvania, signaled a new level of action for al-Qaeda. Likewise, 9/11 prompted a new response framework for the United States, and policymakers shifted from viewing terrorism as a legal issue and form of criminal activity to viewing it as a form of warfare. We conclude the case study with an examination of the efforts to end the con- flicts that have sprouted from waging war on terror and the prospects for reconciliation.

While the conflict after 9/11 seems to defy analysis under our frame-work involving cooperation or negotiation—after all, governments claim not to negotiate with terrorists and al-Qaeda seems uninterested in compromise and political haggling—we can explore how the framing of the war against al-Qaeda led to a wider war that eventually also involved the Taliban of Afghanistan. We also examine the use and effect of counterterrorism tactics against al-Qaeda, including the targeting of al-Qaeda leader Osama bin Laden in 2011. We also explore the attempt to negotiate and find a political solution amidst a long-standing, grinding war between North Atlantic Treaty Organization (NATO) forces and Taliban insurgents from Afghanistan to Pakistan. Why the various sides decided to attempt talks with the Taliban, and why these efforts failed, is an aspect of our case study.

How to fight, whether to fight, and who to fight remain key questions when confronting nonstate actors using terrorist tactics. Even the idea of fighting only al-Qaeda becomes complicated by the proliferation of its various associated organizations: al-Qaeda of the Arabian Peninsula (AQAP) is thriving in Yemen, and al-Qaeda of the Islamic Maghreb (AQIM) stepped up attacks and kidnappings from Mali to Algeria in 2013. Our Concept Focus in this chapter considers asymmetric conflict and counterterrorism. The Spotlight section examines the spread of al-Qaeda, including how the organization has adopted and supported likeminded groups around the Islamic world.[1]

| Box 6.1 |

Case Summary

After the radical group al-Qaeda executed the largest attack in history on U.S. soil on September 11, 2001, the United States launched a massive counterterrorism offensive against the rise of militant groups that use terrorist tactics to achieve their goals.

Global Context

Once supported and used by the United States and its allies during the Cold War to wage a proxy fight against the Soviet Union in Afghanistan, al-Qaeda shifted its focus in the 1990s to opposing corrupt Islamic regimes and foreign presence in the Islamic world.

Key Actors

- United States
- Al-Qaeda
- Taliban

- Afghanistan
- Pakistan

Motives

- Al-Qaeda is driven by militant, religious ideology as it seeks to eliminate foreign, particularly U.S., influence and power in the Middle East.
- The United States is motivated by the desire to protect its national security and, more broadly, to have influence and stability in the oil-rich Persian Gulf area of the Middle East.
- Afghanistan under Hamid Karzai seeks stability and aid and to ward off threats from the Taliban and al-Qaeda.

Concepts

- Counterterrorism
- National security
- Terrorism
- Unconventional warfare

Terrorism and Unconventional Warfare Today

The United States has long dealt with the problem of terrorism, be it domestic, international, nationalist, ideological, or religious. Terrorism, in the form of bombings, shootings, and hijackings, among other means, was more frequent in the United States in the 1970s than at any time since, but fatalities were low compared to the events of September 11, 2001.

Terrorism, traditionally defined as the use of violence to achieve political aims, is a tactic of unconventional warfare. The goal of **unconventional warfare** is to coerce, disrupt, or overthrow a government or occupying power through methods that do not rely on traditional military weaponry but employ other means, including, in the case of al-Qaeda and 9/11, the use of commercial aircraft as a weapon. Prior to the rise of al-Qaeda, terrorism was employed by resistance movements in Northern Ireland, Chechnya, Peru, and Sri Lanka, to name a few. Such movements and their use of unconventional warfare to achieve a political purpose still exist today. Al-Qaeda, however, marks a dominant shift from a political aim to one that is more ideologically based.

Al-Qaeda's founder, Osama bin Laden, had wider goals beyond the removal of a regime. His vision was more ideological—to battle corrupt Muslim regimes and the intrusion of foreign presence anywhere in the Muslim world. As the sole remaining superpower, with a vested interest in the Middle East and its rich oil resources, the United States became al-Qaeda's main target. The first documented al-Qaeda strike against the United States occurred in 1992 with the bombing of a hotel in Aden, Yemen, where U.S. troops were staying. This was followed a year later by the first attack against the World Trade Center, for which the Kuwaiti-born Ramzi Yousef was arrested and convicted. From 1992 to 2000, the United States continued to treat terrorism as a criminal act and responded to al-Qaeda's attacks through its law enforcement and judicial systems. After the attacks of 9/11, the approach took a military shift as the administration of George W. Bush went to war against the perpetrators—al-Qaeda—and against terrorism itself.

The problem of al-Qaeda is part of the rise of conservative, militant Islam as a political force. There are two broad schools of theory about the causes of militant Islamist terrorism aimed at the United States. One is the "their fault" school, which focuses on the ideological extremism of the groups and their antipathy toward the West based on value differences. The second is the "our fault" school, which focuses on U.S. and Western policies as the source for antipathy toward the West in general and the United States in particular.[2] The "our fault" school emphasizes the role of the United States and Western powers' militarism, colonialism, and support for Israel over the Palestinians, all of which have drawn the ire of many in the Muslim Middle East.[3] The "their fault" outlook emphasizes the extreme ideology of the Islamic revivalist movement, which is driven by moral conservatism and seeks to implement Islamic values in all spheres of life—by radical means if necessary.[4]

Of course, the answer may not rest with one camp or the other; both external intervention and internal radical ideology may be necessary components of militant Islam. Taqi al-Din ibn Taymiyya (1263–1328), called by some the spiritual father of revolutionary Islam, announced a religious fatwa after the thirteenth-century Mongol conquest of the Islamic world, declaring the Mongols subject to rightful jihad, or struggle against nonbelievers.[5] Twentieth-century variants of Taymiyya's thinking have emerged in response to Western imperialism or to secularized regimes serving Western interests. In an illustration of this division within the Middle East, Egypt's King Farouk, installed by the British in 1936, faced the opposition of the Muslim Brotherhood (MB) and its founder Hassan al-Banna, who proposed an Islamic system for Egypt under the MB banner. According to al-Banna, "God is our objective, the Quran is our constitution; the Prophet is our leader; struggle is our way; and death for the sake of God is the highest of our aspirations."[6] The MB's Sayyid Qutb became a disillusioned critic of later Egyptian nationalist president Gamal Abdul Nasser, setting the stage for conflict between Islamists and secular military forces that continues to this day and can be seen most recently in Egypt's summer clashes of 2013. It is in this context of political Islam and Western influence in the Muslim world that al-Qaeda's precursor emerged.

Problem Setting and Origins: The Rise of Al-Qaeda

The Soviet invasion of Afghanistan at the end of 1979 became a magnet for Muslim forces in the region in need of a common cause. The "Arab Afghanis" came from all corners of the Middle East to focus energy on ejecting the Soviet superpower from Muslim land. The Afghan Services Bureau, which operated out of neighboring Pakistan, was created to help train fighters and channel funds, arms, and resources to the battle.[7] The United States, keen to wage a proxy war against its rival superpower, provided support to the group through Central Intelligence Agency operations. Pakistan's Inter-Services Intelligence (ISI) was responsible for distribution of the U.S. funds and favored radical groups over the more moderate ones in existence in the 1980s.[8] The Muslim Brotherhood also reportedly funneled funds to Afghanistan's fundamentalist resistance parties. These trends helped to ensure a Soviet defeat but also allowed for the entrenchment of more fundamentalist and radical Muslim elements in an otherwise moderate Afghan population.[9] General Hameed Gul of the Pakistani ISI referred to the soldiers fighting the Soviets in Afghanistan as "the first Islamic international brigade in the modern era."[10]

By 1989 the Soviet Union withdrew from Afghanistan, and the country spiraled into civil war between liberal, moderate, and conservative forces. With the Soviet withdrawal and the end of the Cold War in the early 1990s, U.S. support dried up, and the remnants of the Afghan Services Bureau needed a new cause. Osama bin Laden, a Saudi who had fought against the Soviets in Afghanistan, presented the militants with a new, wider cause when he founded al-Qaeda, which is Arabic for "the base." The group's purpose went beyond ejecting an occupying force from one country and instead focused on a far-reaching scope of corrupt Muslim regimes and all foreign presence in the Muslim world. Al-Qaeda began training militants for various battles against infidels and apostates (nonbelievers) from Chechnya to Bosnia—anywhere Muslims were seen to be oppressed by outside, non-Muslim, or nonpious rulers.

At the same time, U.S. attention turned away from Afghanistan to other post–Cold War concerns. Yet Islamic extremist groups that had once received indirect support from the United States found a new cause in targeting the sole remaining superpower. To justify designating the United States as al-Qaeda's main enemy, bin Laden pointed to U.S. dominance of the Middle East as demonstrated through the 1991 Gulf War, the establishment of U.S. forces and bases in Saudi Arabia and much of the Persian Gulf, and U.S. support for the Saudi regime and monarchs of the Gulf, which bin Laden found offensive. From the perspective of bin Laden and his supporters, the stationing of U.S. forces in Saudi Arabia represented an infidel occupation of the holy lands of Islam. In addition, bin Laden believed that U.S. support for regimes in Egypt and Israel confirmed that Muslims were denied independence and spiritual purity because of U.S. support and presence in the region.

Thus motivated, al-Qaeda and other militant Islamists increasingly used unconventional methods to target the United States. They did so largely through bombings of U.S. financial interests, as in the 1993 bombing of the World Trade Center, and U.S. military forces, such as the 1996 attack on a housing unit in Saudi Arabia. While responsibility for the latter attack could not be definitely proved, the 1993 World Trade Center attack was ultimately traced to an Egyptian cleric (called "the Blind Sheikh") and his associates, who condemned U.S. ties to Israel and the perceived oppressive regime in Egypt.

In 1998 al-Qaeda made a religiously based appeal when it announced a public call to arms:

> The ruling to kill the Americans and their allies—civilians and military—is an individual duty for every Muslim who can do it in any country in which it is possible to do it, in order to liberate the al-Aqsa Mosque and the holy mosque [Mecca] from their grip, and in order for their armies to move out of all the lands of Islam, defeated and unable to threaten any Muslim.[11]

From this declaration came a sense of motive and mission, as it emphasized al-Qaeda's goal of forcing the United States to leave the Middle East. This launched a new campaign against U.S. targets, realized in August 1998 with the bombings of U.S. embassies in Kenya and Tanzania, which killed 200 and injured thousands of local residents, and the October 2000 suicide bombing of the USS *Cole* docked in Yemen, which killed seventeen U.S. sailors and injuring thirty-nine.

As al-Qaeda stepped up its attacks, the United States began to covertly search for bin Laden and to respond more militarily to the terrorist threat. In response to the embassy bombings, President Bill Clinton ordered strikes against al-Qaeda camps in Afghanistan and a pharmaceutical plant in Sudan that the United States believed was tied to the organization.[12] (The latter claim turned out to be unfounded.) In some cases the United States prosecuted those found responsible for attacks, convicting Wadih el-Hage, a U.S. citizen, of facilitating the embassy bombings.[13] The Clinton administration also placed sanctions on the extreme fundamentalist Taliban regime that had taken over Afghanistan in 1996 and had given safe haven to al-Qaeda that year. Military actions against those responsible for the bombings have continued, and in October 2013 the United States conducted a daring operation in Libya to capture another senior al-Qaeda member, Nazih Abdul-Hamed al-Ruqai, who was alleged to be tied to the bombings.[14]

Yet despite its more active military response, prior to 9/11 the United States had not fundamentally reordered its foreign policy orientation and continued to handle al-Qaeda's attacks as an issue of law, not war.[15] From the U.S. perspective, the big threat from the Cold War had been vanquished and there was nothing of similar scale on the horizon; al-Qaeda was a growing problem but could be dealt with in the traditional way. The United States continued to focus on homeland defense, foiling a planned millennial attack for New Year's Eve 2000, though it was unable to stop the attack on the USS *Cole* later that year. Upon succeeding Clinton to the presidency, George W. Bush followed the status quo in the early months of 2001, but that would change on September 11, 2001.

Box 6.2

Concept Focus

Counterterrorism

The war that George W. Bush declared in 2001 against al-Qaeda and related militant Islamist groups is a different kind of war from those fought by the United States in the past. Compared to interstate war, where conventional armies compete for victory, here we have a type of **asymmetric conflict** (fighting between parties whose military power, strategy, and/or tactics differ significantly) and unconventional warfare involving irregular forces (nonstandard military) on at least one side. Unconventional warfare is carried out over the long term through military and/or paramilitary operations by forces organized, trained, equipped, and supported or directed by an external source. According to the U.S. Department of Defense, it "includes, but is not limited to, guerrilla warfare, subversion, sabotage, intelligence activities, and unconventional assisted recovery."[16] This definition can include terrorism.

Terrorism, as a potential tool within a broader unconventional campaign, is a type of politically motivated violence that is conceptually distinguished by a relatively small number of nonstate actors who engage in violence against government, civilians, or property to achieve their aims.[17] **Counterterrorism**, then, is the strategy of disrupting a group and its operations to minimize the chance of it carrying out attacks.[18]

Counterterrorism has always been a multifaceted program that ranges from homeland defense to intelligence gathering to the struggle to address the root causes of terror.[19] The British used military and intelligence efforts to combat the Irish Republican Army (IRA) in Northern Ireland in the mid- to late twentieth century. The IRA sought to free Northern Ireland from British rule and used bombings, shootings, and riots to try to bring about this end. For its part, the United Kingdom was determined to protect its interests and its territory and employed strong measures using British military and intelligence forces and local law enforcement. Israel has done similarly in response to what it perceives as terrorist actions from Palestinians in the West Bank and Gaza and from groups within the region that support the Palestinians. Both are motivated by the need to defend the homeland and their citizens from violent aggression. Yet both faced (and in the case of Israel, continues to face) the challenge of combating an enemy with no distinct geographic borders, no formal armies, and no central banks. Financing, weapons, and other support flow to terrorist groups from sources around the world, requiring nations engaged in counterterrorism to consider all facets of such groups' operations in their attempts to prevent future attacks.

As this case study discusses, U.S. counterterrorism efforts have moved from the legal approach that dominated the period prior to 9/11 to a more militarized effort. Before 9/11 attacks on American soil incurred far fewer deaths and were usually treated as crimes against persons or property to be handled by the Federal Bureau of Investigation and/or the local police. An exception is the 1986 U.S. response to the bombing of a German disco that killed American servicemen. The attack was tied to the Libyan government, and U.S. president Ronald

(Continued)

(Continued)

Reagan responded with an airstrike against Libya. It was more than ten years later when the United States again responded militarily to a terrorist attack with the cruise missile strikes against targets in the Sudan and Afghanistan after the 1998 embassy bombings. The perception of terrorism as a tactic to be handled through law enforcement and the courts was a long-standing one, and it took a drastic change in terrorist tactics to effect a similar change in counterterrorism perspective.

The attacks of September 11, 2001, effected that change. Prior to 9/11, terrorists had only ever used airplanes to hijack them, hold passengers for ransom or, as occurred over Lockerbie, Scotland, in 1988 with Pan Am Flight 103, simply blow them up. On September 11 al-Qaeda members hijacked four jetliners with the intent to crash them into notable U.S. landmarks such as the World Trade Center and Pentagon and cause a significantly higher death toll than that of most terrorist attacks. Indeed, nearly 3,000 people were killed at the World Trade Center alone, making 9/11 the largest attack on U.S. soil in the nation's history. The government—and its people—felt vulnerable and afraid, which was exactly the response terrorism is intended to achieve.

It was this singular event that altered the U.S. perspective, redefining an act of terrorism as an act of war and prompting a military response against a nonstate entity such as al-Qaeda. The Bush administration knew that al-Qaeda received safe haven from Afghanistan's extremely conservative Taliban government and demanded that it give up al-Qaeda. When the Taliban refused, Bush declared that state sponsors of terrorism were just as responsible for the damage done by terrorists as the terrorists themselves, and the United States prepared to go to war against Afghanistan to get at al-Qaeda. The Taliban fell quickly, though its forces marshaled in Afghanistan's remote and rocky terrain. However, al-Qaeda continued to carry out attacks in pursuit of its goal. U.S. counterterrorism's new military response has included Special Forces missions, airstrikes, large ground operations, and, more recently, controversial targeted drone strikes. The goal of a drone strike is to stealthily eliminate a target and, in theory, minimize civilian casualties, but the accuracy of such an attack is questionable and has raised the question of at what cost terrorists are pursued. How should ethical considerations constrain the ways in which legitimate adversaries are pursued? And how might the United States be harmed—or harm itself— by not giving due consideration to these ethics? The drone-targeted killing of American Anwar al-Awlaki raised the issue of due process for Americans,[20] and in spring 2013 hearings were conducted about the secretive nature of procedures behind the use of drones.[21]

War and peace scholar Richard Betts warns of responding to terrorism in ways that play into the "strategic judo" of turning one's strength against oneself and compromising one's own purpose.[22] Combating extremism is said to be a collective effort of international society, led by the world power, the United States,[23] so much attention is now focused on U.S. efforts, U.S. allies, and other actors engaged in addressing the globalizing nature of al-Qaeda and its offshoots.

Problem Definition and Response: 9/11 and a Global Offensive

The conflict that emerged slowly in the 1990s exploded into full bloom on September 11, 2001. The events of that day altered U.S. thinking on terrorism in particular and global strategy more generally. Members of al-Qaeda forcibly gained control of four U.S. passenger jets, piloting two of them into New York City's World Trade Center and one into the Pentagon near Washington, D.C. The fourth plane crashed in rural Pennsylvania after the hijackers struggled with passengers; its destination was unknown but it was suspected to be heading to Washington, D.C., towards targets such as the White House or U.S. Capitol. The attacks killed nearly 3,000 people.

President George W. Bush assembled a war cabinet on the evening of 9/11 and made his first public statement, noting that the United States was at war. Identifying who the United States was at war with was a crucial step. Early signs indicated al-Qaeda, and it was quickly decided that it would be a target of military action. But al-Qaeda was not itself a country. It made its center of operations in the country of Afghanistan, then run by the Taliban, a conservative Islamist group supported by neighboring Pakistan and rooted in local politics of the ethnic Pashtuns of both Pakistan and Afghanistan. The fates of the Taliban and al-Qaeda were tied through a relationship formed from 1996 to 2001, when Osama bin Laden found refuge for his organization in Afghanistan after it was forced out of Sudan and his home country of Saudi Arabia. The Taliban offered bin Laden protection to train the "second generation of Arab Afghans" preparing to wage jihad against infidel and apostate alike in the Middle East and beyond.[24]

After 9/11 Bush demanded that the Taliban hand over bin Laden and his lieutenants or share in their fate. The Taliban's ambassador to Pakistan refused and demanded evidence of al Qaeda's culpability, contradicting an earlier statement by Afghanistan's Muslim clerics that bin Laden could perhaps be persuaded to leave the country. On October 7, 2001, the United States and its allies initiated Operation Enduring Freedom to oust the Taliban and destroy al-Qaeda bases, camps, and operations in Afghanistan. Members of the Taliban were treated as enemies alongside al-Qaeda, and President Bush rejected an October 14 offer by the Taliban to discuss turning over bin Laden in exchange for a U.S. cessation of hostilities.[25] The Afghan capital of Kabul fell to allied hands by November 13, and the chase headed south toward Kandahar and east toward the mountainous borders of Pakistan. As U.S. forces and the Northern Alliance, long-time opponents of the Taliban, swept through the rest of the country, a final stand ensued at Tora Bora on the Pakistani border, but both bin Laden and Taliban chief Mullah Omar escaped. Nonetheless, by December 17, 2001, Afghanistan was entirely in allied hands, and by year's end a UN-sponsored meeting of Afghan leaders selected Hamid Karzai to head a new transitional regime.

Bush's controversial declaration of a war on terror was a marked departure from the United States' traditional approach to dealing with acts of terrorism, made even more significant when Bush noted the war would not be limited to only al-Qaeda but also to potentially numerous other organizations and state governments that supported terrorism. Military action against the perpetrators—al-Qaeda—was expected by the international community and received widespread support. But Bush went beyond the old rules of counterterrorism in announcing a global war, and international reaction to that remained ambivalent. The emphasis of the war, as articulated in the 2002 National Security Strategy of the United States, was on using military power in various locations and in various degrees. The United States would act preemptively if necessary to confront terrorist groups and their state sponsors ahead of any potential future attack. The 2003 National Strategy for Combating Terrorism declared the U.S. goal of using legal, diplomatic, economic, and military assets to go on the offensive against terrorist groups of global reach in the hopes of reducing the scope and capability of such groups to the point that they were no longer a threat to the United States.

The primary U.S. focus in this war remained on al-Qaeda. The same 2001 UN-sponsored meeting that selected Karzai to head Afghanistan's transitional regime also introduced the next, multilateral phase of Afghanistan operations. A NATO force, the International Security Assistance Force (ISAF), was created to provide security around the capital and help the new Afghan government establish control over Kabul. This mission was later expanded to broader areas of Afghanistan in 2005 to assert control over rural provinces.[26] U.S. operations in Afghanistan did not end with the ousting of the Taliban and routing of al-Qaeda but continued both in Afghanistan and in neighboring Pakistan with the aim of countering and foiling future al-Qaeda plots and operations. One of the main goals of U.S. counterterrorism efforts at this time was to capture or kill bin Laden and his right-hand man, Ayman al-Zawahiri. The CIA missed a chance to nab al-Zawahri in 2003, and he subsequently survived a bombing by Pakistani military planes one year later. A well-publicized U.S. missile strike aimed at him in 2006 also failed because he did not turn up at the attack site.

U.S. counterterrorism efforts were not solely concentrated on al-Qaeda and Afghanistan. In 2003 the United States launched a war against Iraqi leader Saddam Hussein, who the United States feared was harboring weapons of mass destruction (WMD) as well as offering support to al-Qaeda or its offshoots. This arm of U.S. counterterrorism strategy received markedly less support from the international community, which remained skeptical of U.S. claims of Iraqi WMD. The coalition that supported the U.S. endeavor in Iraq was much smaller than the 1991 coalition in the Gulf War, and while the United States toppled the Hussein regime relatively quickly, it failed to win the people. This effort at regime-building had a rocky and unpredictable result. While Iraq successfully elected a new leader, U.S. forces battled Iraqi resisters before finally pulling out in 2011 to questionable success.

With the United States increasingly drawn into a widening conflict in Iraq, al-Qaeda and its erstwhile hosts the Taliban had a chance to regroup and challenge the new Afghan regime and its protectors, the United States and NATO. Within a few years, al-Qaeda, the Taliban, and local Afghan warlords and allies joined forces to carry out terrorist attacks not just in Afghanistan but also in Pakistan, which was now seen to be aiding the United States. The Pakistani army launched a massive crackdown against them in the north-western areas and other parts of the country, which dragged Pakistan into its own spiral of violence and put it at odds with the United States over the direction of the war.[27] By 2009 a resurgent Taliban had NATO, Pakistan, and Afghanistan against the ropes and searching for a new approach.

Timeline
The Rise of Al-Qaeda

1979		The Soviet Union invades Afghanistan, sparking a local resistance led in part by the Afghan Services Bureau; the United States funnels aid to the rebels.
1989		The Soviet Union leaves Afghanistan. This year is the approximate date during which Osama bin Laden founds al-Qaeda.
1991		The United States leads a multinational coalition in war against Iraq.
1993		The World Trade Center is bombed; Ramzi Yousef is later convicted of the crime.
1996		The bombing of Khobar Towers in Dharhan, Saudi Arabia, targets U.S. troops stationed in the country.
1998	February 23	Osama bin Laden issues a fatwa declaring holy war against the West and Israel.
	August 7	U.S. embassies in Kenya and Tanzania are bombed.
2000		A suicide bomber attacks the USS *Cole* in Aden, Yemen.
2001	September 11	Al-Qaeda members fly passenger jets into the World Trade Center, the Pentagon, and a field in Pennsylvania.
	September 20	President George W. Bush declares the Global War on Terror.

(Continued)

(Continued)

	October 7	The Bush administration launches Operation Enduring Freedom against al-Qaeda and the Taliban in Afghanistan.
2003		The United States widens its War on Terror with an invasion of Iraq.
2009		U.S. President Barack Obama orders an increase in U.S. forces in Afghanistan.
	July 2	A U.S. offensive in Afghanistan's Helmand Province tries to root out Taliban forces and the poppy fields they control for opium revenue.
2011	May	A Secret U.S. raid on a bin Laden compound in Abbottabad, Pakistan, kills the al-Qaeda leader and others.
2013		
	July	The United States pledges to withdraw troops from Afghanistan by the end of 2014.

Problem Evolution and Development: The Obama Surge

The incoming administration of Barack Obama attempted a new approach to dealing with terrorism in 2005: a surge in U.S. and NATO forces, combined with the rise of drone warfare to target al-Qaeda leaders and operatives. In February 2009 Obama authorized 17,000 additional troops to Afghanistan, boosting the U.S. total to 55,000. With this surge came a new strategy to address some of the root causes of terrorism by bringing a degree of stability in the country. Success was to be defined as the ability "to disrupt, dismantle, and defeat Al-Qaeda in Pakistan and Afghanistan and to prevent their return to either country in the future."[28] In February 2010 American and Afghan troops began large-scale combat operations against resurgent Taliban positions in southern Afghanistan, including an effort to bring the heavily infiltrated south under coalition control. Along with the military buildup came a similar effort to increase the presence of U.S. State Department employees and aid contractors paid by the United States, who would serve as stabilization teams.[29] Afghan and NATO forces staged a new push, called Operation Dragon Strike, to drive Taliban militants out of their stronghold around the southern city of Kandahar. This was part of the air-and-ground phase of an anti-Taliban offensive that involved weeks of fighting.[30]

At the same time, neighboring Pakistan grappled with its own troubles from al-Qaeda and the Taliban. Under pressure from a Pakistani offensive begun in May 2009, Taliban elements in that country threatened to move into Afghanistan and launch a war against Pakistan from there. In 2009 a truce was offered that permitted autonomy for the Taliban in the northwest of Pakistan, but they broke the cease-fire and waged an offensive that pushed within miles of Islamabad.[31]

Frustrated by Pakistan's uneven response to al-Qaeda and the Taliban— at times assisting the United States and at times seemingly abetting its enemies—the United States increased the use of unmanned, armed drone strikes in Pakistan, to varying effect. U.S. military helicopters also launched attacks into Pakistani territory against those associated with the anti-American insurgency in Afghanistan. U.S. military commanders also pondered ground raids into Pakistan, which the Pakistani government opposed.[32] By some Pakistani Taliban accounts, the twin pressures of U.S. drone attacks and the Pakistani offensive forced the group underground and created fractures in the group over how to proceed. At the same time, such sources threatened to continue strikes "if the drone attacks are not stopped."[33] Pakistan's Taliban threatened to launch attacks in the United States and Europe, and the United States added Tehrik-e-Taliban Pakistan (TTP), or the Taliban Movement of Pakistan, to its list of foreign terrorist organizations.[34] The Obama administration blamed the TTP for an attempted car bombing in New York's Times Square in 2010, and the bomber, naturalized U.S. citizen Faisal Shahzad, admitted he was trained in militant tactics while in Pakistan.

The biggest victory for the Obama administration came not from the stalemate surge or the increased use of drones but from the targeted special operations against al-Qaeda and Taliban elites. After 9/11 the CIA pursued leads about bin Laden's whereabouts, eventually tracing a courier to a compound in Abbottabad, Pakistan, in August 2010. Built five years prior, the compound's walls, security, and inhabitants raised suspicion about its occupants. The courier and his brother had no known source of income, yet lived in a secretive and enormous structure with another family, the composition of which by one account matched bin Laden's. By February 2011 the CIA assessed that it had determined bin Laden's location, and on April 29, 2011, President Obama ordered an operation involving four U.S. military helicopters carrying elite troops from Navy SEAL Team Six, a top counterterrorism unit. Bin Laden, the al-Qaeda courier, the courier's brother, and one of bin Laden's sons were killed in the assault.[35] The ten-year manhunt for the figurehead behind the 9/11 attacks was over.

Whether leadership decapitation was a game changer or not for the Global War on Terror begun under George W. Bush in 2001, it was the best news the United States had received in an otherwise continuing stalemate with the Taliban. For years the United States had struggled with a lack of progress in countering the Taliban's resurgence in Afghanistan and in rooting out al-Qaeda in the region, all while al-Qaeda's influence spread to other countries. This frustration, combined with the unpopularity of escalating war in the public opinion of Americans and the Middle East, led U.S. officials to begin thinking about negotiations. Lt. Col. Brett Jenkinson suggested that "we are not going to kill our way out of this war,"[36] and General David Petraus reiterated the need for political reconciliation in September 2010.[37]

In 2008 reports arose of Saudi-mediated talks between the Afghan Taliban and the Afghan government, including suggestions that the Taliban was "severing their ties with al-Qaeda."[38] President Karzai established a peace council to foster negotiations between his government and the insurgents. Some dismissed the high-level talks as propaganda, suggesting the stringent list of U.S. conditions (renounce violence, cut ties with al-Qaeda, respect the Afghan constitution) precluded any prospect for evenhanded talks.[39] The talks, facilitated by NATO forces between Afghan officials and the man thought to be representing the Taliban, led to an embarrassing situation when the man turned out to be an impostor. President Karzai denied meeting with him, and a U.S. official suggested that the United States never trusted the impostor or had faith that he could deliver anything to the talks.[40]

Karzai included eventual talks with the Taliban as part of a wider reconciliation plan to bring peace to Afghanistan, but Afghan and U.S. officials have played down confused and unconfirmed reports about talks with high-level insurgents. Karzai's peace plan included the goal of Afghan forces taking over complete security responsibility of the country by 2014 and for U.S. and NATO withdrawal.[41] Despite these efforts at diplomacy, there is little hope of reconciliation with al-Qaeda as a whole. In August 2013 Karzai met with the Pakistani president to stress the need for joint cooperation to facilitate peace talks with the Taliban and to put aside bitter accusations and rivalry amidst the prospect of a U.S. withdrawal from the region in 2014.[42]

| Box 6.3 |

Spotlight

The Spread of Al-Qaeda

One of the problems of a war on terror is choosing whom to target. Al-Qaeda may have begun as a limited-reach organization, but it is no longer merely Osama bin Laden's group in Afghanistan and Pakistan. Al-Qaeda today is a decentralized network of autonomous and inspired organizations in locations ranging from the Maghreb to Somalia to Yemen. The United States disclosed in 2008 that since 2004 U.S. Special Forces have carried out "nearly a dozen previously undisclosed attacks against al-Qaeda and other militants in Syria, Pakistan,"[43] Somalia, Yemen, and elsewhere. This followed a classified order from Secretary of Defense Donald Rumsfeld, approved by President Bush, giving the U.S. military authority to attack the al-Qaeda network in countries not at war with the United States.[44]

A prime example of this authorization in action was directed at al-Qaeda of the Arabian Peninsula (AQAP), which is based in Yemen. AQAP's original leader, Abu Ali al-Harithi, was killed in a 2002 strike by an unmanned CIA drone in Yemen. His replacement, Muhammad Hamdi al-Ahdal, was tracked down and surrendered to Yemeni authorities, which seemingly ending the group's influence in Yemen by 2003. But in February 2006, twenty-three al-Qaeda suspects tunneled out of a maximum-security prison there, two of whom reinvented the branch of AQAP in Yemen.[45]

Yemen has become a central front for U.S. counterterrorism efforts against al-Qaeda and its affiliates. AQAP attacked the U.S. embassy in the capital city of Sana'a in 2008 and plotted to blow up a plane in the United States on Christmas 2009. An American-born cleric in Yemen, Anwar al-Awlaki, served as an English-speaking conduit and helped to recruit and spin al-Qaeda's message in the Western world.[46] To help combat AQAP's growing influence in Yemen, the Obama administration provided support to the regime of Ali Abdullah Saleh (and its successor after the Arab Spring).[47] The United States also authorized Yemen to engage in operations to kill or capture Anwar al-Awlaki, but it was ultimately a U.S. drone strike that killed him in September 2011.[48] After dozens of attacks on security forces in 2013 alone, the Yemeni government is now stepping up its effort to confront this insurgency with U.S. help.[49]

Another example of al-Qaeda's spread can be found in Somalia with the group al-Shabaab. Ethiopia's U.S.-supported 2006 invasion of Somalia, intended to remove Islamists from power there, led to an offshoot organization—al-Shabaab—that became more radical and more powerful. Al-Shabaab controls most of central and western Somalia and claimed responsibility for the attacks in Uganda's capital on July 11, 2013, that killed seventy-six people gathered to watch the World Cup final.[50] Angry at U.S. involvement in the invasion and the targeting of al-Qaeda-linked individuals in Somalia, the group is anti-American and has become involved in operations on U.S. soil. In August 2010 fourteen people in the United States were indicted on charges of aiding al-Shabaab, some of whom were believed to be in Somalia fighting for the group.[51]

On the Mediterranean coast of Africa, yet another group, al-Qaeda of the Islamic Maghreb (AQIM), originated in the 1990s as an offshoot of the Armed Islamic Group (GIA) "as an armed Islamist resistance movement to the secular Algerian government."[52] It called itself the Salafist Group for Preaching and Combat (GSPC) until Sept. 11, 2006, when Ayman al-Zawahiri, al-Qaeda's second in command, officially endorsed it in a video message, making it part of Osama bin Laden's global jihad.[53] AQIM has conducted suicide attacks on Algeria's government and security establishment and has resorted to kidnapping European hostages in the promotion of its cause.[54]

As these examples attest, Osama bin Laden's vision to combat corrupt Muslim regimes and oust foreign presence from the Muslim world has spread beyond al-Qaeda and now provides motivation to extremists on several continents. As the United States continues to pursue counterterrorism efforts against al-Qaeda, its battle will increasingly widen as the ideas that inspire the group's members spread to others.

Conclusion: Combating Extremism

The long path of conflict and cooperation traveled by the United States and al-Qaeda has no easy resolution. The United States, as well as other Western and, indeed, world governments, are faced with a multipronged transnational blend of global and local militant Islam. Al-Qaeda's franchising of terrorism offers new challenges and threats that make conflict resolution and reconciliation all the more difficult.[55] Ideological aims such as al-Qaeda's to remove foreign presence from the Muslim world cannot realistically be attained, nor can such beliefs be easily tamped out. So where does victory lie? While in the past states handily suppressed insurgencies, studies find that they have been increasingly less likely to do so as a result of the mechanized state militaries' force structures, which inhibit information collection among local populations and selectively apply rewards and punishment among citizens.[56] In other words, the ways in which militaries operate may engender more enmity among the populations they seek to win over.

Extremist groups such as al-Qaeda do not give way easily to compromise. Their ideological purpose provides them with strong motivation, and their goals may be so stark, inflexible, or beyond rational expectation that compromise or rational dialogue is impossible. The best some hope for is to peel off moderates from extremist organizations through dialogue, diplomacy, and concessions, leaving a weaker, though still radical, fringe behind to contain and pursue. Here we consider efforts at issue settlement in the various venues discussed above. In Somalia a Sufi Muslim group joined Somalia's government to tackle the al-Qaeda-inspired al-Shabaab insurgents who control large parts of the country. The Yemeni government launched a media campaign aimed at countering al-Qaeda's message and has recruited popular televangelist Amr Khaled to help dissuade Yemenis from joining the cause.[57] Fusing military operations with campaigns for "hearts and minds," and balancing U.S. and local power in the cause, is the core of the dilemma of current counterterrorism efforts.

The drive pushing al-Qaeda and the Taliban in Afghanistan and Pakistan may be lessened in short order as the United States has pledged a 2014 withdrawal from Afghanistan. NATO's planned withdrawal of combat troops could reduce violence by removing Western targets or it could lead to a Taliban takeover of the shaky Karzai regime and result in civil war. Some say U.S. counterterrorism efforts there were a failure because U.S. actions alienated the people and the (democratically elected) government without achieving battlefield victory.[58]

In terms of negotiations with the enemy, it may be useful to sort through the parties in various conceptual ways. First, the distinction between al-Qaeda and the Taliban must be kept clear. Lumping the latter in with the former created a much more complicated and unpopular war for the United States than if it had remained attentive only to al-Qaeda and counterterrorism operations. Second, the Taliban has Afghan and Pakistani variants, which complicates the nature of cooperation with governments in both countries. Knowing who you can talk to, and in what situation, may determine the difference between success and failure in negotiations. In this case, the failure of force *and* talks—or, rather, of conflict and cooperation—has left the United States quietly preparing an exit and hoping to avoid a return to power of the very forces that brought it there in the first place. Time will tell if this limited goal will be achieved.

Case Analysis

1. How are nonstate threats such as terrorism similar to and different from conventional threats of war and violence as they are depicted in other chapters in this book?

2. In the pathway of conflict and cooperation concerning the United States and al-Qaeda, how important is international cooperation to the U.S. Global War on Terror? Consider the case of Afghanistan and Pakistan, and even Iraq, to illustrate your answer.

3. Should the United States fight the Taliban or negotiate with it to instead focus more narrowly on counterterrorism against al-Qaeda? Explain your reasoning.

4. How does an ideological goal differ from a political one, and how are they similar?

5. Given the uncertainty over Afghanistan's future after 2014, did the troop surge under the Obama administration help the war effort or not?

6. Should the U.S. withdraw in 2014 or not, given the state of affairs in Afghanistan?

7. Identify two modern conflicts in which unconventional warfare is used and describe how this is done.

8. Describe what you think is the best way to combat terrorism: through legal means, as the United States did prior to 9/11, or through military means?

Suggested Readings

Benjamin, Daniel, and Steven Simon. *The Age of Sacred Terror*. New York: Random House, 2002. Comprehensive overview of America's pre-9/11 struggle with Islamist terrorism.

Bergen, Peter. *Holy War, Inc.: Inside the Secret World of Osama bin Laden*. New York: The Free Press, 2001. Overview of the original al-Qaeda and its founder, Osama bin Laden.

Caldwell, Dan. *Vortex of Conflict: U.S. Policy toward Afghanistan, Pakistan, and Iraq*. Stanford: Stanford University Press, 2011. Comparison of American military actions after 9/11.

Chandrasekaran, Rajiv. *Little America: The War within the War for Afghanistan*. New York: Random House, 2012. Investigates the American domestic and bureaucratic politics behind the war in Afghanistan.

Merari, Ariel. "Terrorism as a Strategy of Insurgency." *Terrorism and Political Violence 5*, no.4 (1993): 213–251. General overview of concepts of terrorism and insurgency.

Pillar, Paul. *Terrorism and U.S. Foreign Policy*. Washington, DC: Brookings Institute, 2001. Pre-9/11 analysis of how the U.S. conducted counter-terrorism.

Rashid, Ahmed. *Taliban: Militant Islam, Oil, and Fundamentalism in Central Asia*. New Haven: Yale University Press, 2001. Overview of the origins of the Taliban.

Web Resources

Al-Qa'ida (the Base), FAS Intelligence Resource Program, www.fas.org/irp/world/para/ladin.htm. The Federation of American Scientists provides science-based solutions to threats to national and international security. Access an extensive compilation of information on al-Qaeda, its history, and its operations.

National Commission on Terrorist Attacks upon the United States, http://govinfo.library.unt.edu/911/report/index.htm. Formal, detailed report on the September 11 attacks as issued by the independent, bipartisan commission created to investigate them.

North Atlantic Treaty Organization, www.nato.int/cps/en/natolive/topics_8189.htm. Explore NATO's role in Afghanistan under the International Security Assistance Force, including its mission, its troop force, and the transition to Afghan security leadership.

"A New Strategy for Afghanistan and Pakistan," The White House, www.whitehouse.gov/blog/09/03/27/a-new-strategy-for-afghanistan-and-pakistan. Official White House blog report and video on Obama's new strategy for Afghanistan, unveiled March 2009.

Council on Foreign Relations, www.cfr.org/publication/9126. This site provides background information from the Council on Foreign Relations on al-Qaeda and its origins, operations, leaders, and future prospects.

7 Cybersecurity's Uncertain Battleground

Michael Hayden, former head of the Central Intelligence Agency (CIA), once remarked about cybersecurity that "rarely has something been so important and so talked about with less clarity and less understanding."[1] In large part this is because neither those who have carried out a cyberattack nor the attack's victims are anxious to reveal many details. Attackers do not wish to publicly admit responsibility and become the target for reprisals or have their capabilities known. Victims fear that in providing details of a successful attack they will reveal what information has been compromised or alert others to weaknesses in their systems, thereby inviting further attacks. For example, the March–April 2010 cyberattack on computers used by Iran to produce nuclear power, about which we will have much more to say later, was only uncovered in June 2010. The United States and Israel are generally considered to have perpetrated the attack, but neither has officially assumed responsibility and Iran has not confirmed the extent of the damage done.

Cyberthreats—dangers to the security of a country's electronic and computer-related activities that result in the unwanted manipulation of data or compromise operating systems—used to be the stuff of science fiction novels or the imagination. And in many regards they still are. One forecaster of world politics recently presented a detailed account of a twenty-first-century world war started by Japan that began with a cyberattack in outer space against the United States.[2] Japan lost. But today cyberthreats are also very real.

On June 8, 2013, U.S. president Barack Obama and Chinese president Xi Jinping met in California for a get-to-know-you retreat that was part of an overall effort by the two governments to define their relationship with one another in an era in which Chinese economic and military power is on the rise and the United States is facing increasing domestic and global limitations on its exercise of power. While the meeting was described as cordial and productive, with each side promising to work with the other to solve common problems, the talks contained a dark underside. President Obama voiced concerns over industrial espionage and cases of computer hacking linked to China. He pointedly observed that this continued cyberactivity could become "a very difficult problem" and an "inhibitor" to the development of good relations.[3]

Obama's warning was not entirely unexpected. In the months preceding the meeting, complaints about Chinese cyberattacks on the United States had become more direct and vehement, with an editorial by *The New York Times* asserting that "both nations need to take steps to avoid an all-out cyberwar."[4] In early April, without directly mentioning China, the Pentagon announced that it would increase spending for cyberoperations from $3.9 billion to $4.7 billion in the 2014 defense budget, with the majority of that increase going toward developing greater offensive capabilities. Later that month U.S. and Chinese military leaders held their highest-level talks in nearly two years, and a senior Chinese general observed that the consequences of a major cyberattack "may be as serious as a nuclear bomb."[5] Then, in early May, the Obama administration publicly charged China's military with mounting attacks on U.S. government and private sector computer systems in an effort to obtain "military capabilities that could be exploited during a crisis."[6] Chinese officials denied involvement in any attacks directed at the United States and countered that "China has repeatedly said that we resolutely oppose all forms of hacker attacks."[7]

Growing evidence pointed to the conclusion that U.S. concern about Chinese cyberattacks was well founded.[8] Ten major American energy firms had been the target of cyberattacks that provided China with valuable information about oil production technologies and potentially saved it years of research. Pentagon officials have asserted that over the past six years, "Chinese computer spies raided the data banks of almost every major U.S. defense contractor."[9] Among the weapons systems now believed to have been compromised in some way due to cyberattacks were the Patriot missile system, the Black Hawk helicopter, and the F-35 Joint Strike Fighter.[10] Other U.S. computer systems that have been compromised include that of the National Aeronautics and Space Agency (NASA); State Department computer networks, especially those at the Bureau of East Asian and Pacific Affairs; U.S. Naval War College computers, possibly those involved with running war games; the e-mail system of the Office of the Secretary of Defense; and computers at the Oak Ridge National Lab, which is run by the Department of Energy.

The U.S. government is not the only target of Chinese cyberattacks. The private sector has been hit hard as well. Chinese hacking is estimated to cost the American economy more than $300 billion per year. Coca-Cola fell victim after it failed to acquire a Chinese juice company. Google has been the target of several attacks, presumably because dissident political groups in China have used it as a method of communication. *The New York Times* came under attack probably for its reporting on political events in China. Cyberattacks have the potential to build on one another. When the computers at the security services firm RSA were compromised, the Chinese hackers also gained access to Lockheed Martin, a major defense subcontractor.

| Box 7.1 |

Case Summary

Cyberthreats have emerged as the newest security problem facing states, and great uncertainty exists over how to both define and respond to them. The most significant issues surround cyberwarfare. Unilateral, regional, and global responses to cyberthreats are being explored.

Global Context

Debates over how to respond to cyberthreats and promote cybersecurity are taking place in an international system undergoing rapid change as a result of globalization. State monopolies on key power resources and the importance of state boundaries are disappearing as globalization has created an international system in which cyberspace has become a new and uncharted arena for conflict and competition.

Key actors

- United States
- China
- Russia
- Iran
- Israel

Motives

- Russia has used cyberpower as part of its military and political strategy to secure its borders as well as for economic and domestic political reasons.
- China is a major source of cyber-related espionage and cybercrime; many of its cyberattacks are conducted to add to its military power, speed the growth of its economy, and control political dissidents.
- The United States, Israel, and Iran have all been linked to stand-alone cyberattacks that reflect their national and regional security interests; for the United States and Israel, that includes preventing Iran from acquiring an operational nuclear capability.
- All states are concerned with the lack of international norms and rules governing the use of cyberpower and have begun to explore national and international strategies for dealing with cyberthreats.

Concepts

- Information and international relations
- Military strategy
- Nature of war
- Technology and international relations

Were the story to stop here, the United States would appear to be the victim seeking justice, and to some extent this is true. The emerging cybersecurity case study, however, also contains evidence of the United States as an aggressor. Along with Israel, the United States has been linked to the Stuxnet virus that attacked Iran's computer system. The Obama administration also considered but ultimately rejected using cyberattack capabilities in helping to remove Muammar Gaddafi from power during Libya's uprising during the Arab Spring. Russia and Iran have also been linked to cyberattacks, as have scores of criminals and hacktivists (political and social groups) located around the world. By one estimate, over thirty countries have created cyberunits within their militaries.

In this chapter we will travel down a pathway of conflict and cooperation that is far less well defined than those we encounter in other case studies. As a result, when it comes to cybersecurity, policymakers, analysts, and the public at large find themselves trying to understand both the problems they face and the direction the path they are travelling is taking them. The resulting uncertainty of how to proceed greatly expands the room for disagreement over what is feasible and what is desirable when formulating cybersecurity policy.

We will begin moving down the pathway of cybersecurity conflict and cooperation by first outlining the dimensions of the problem and defining key terms. We then examine in more detail key cyberattacks that have brought us to this point in time. We next consider how the United States and others are thinking about cybersecurity and conclude by speculating what directions the cybersecurity pathway may take in the future. Our Concept Focus looks at a current method used by strategists to characterize different levels of cyberattacks. The Spotlight section examines Russia and China as rising cyber superpowers.

The Nature of the Cybersecurity Problem

Policymakers often look to what has worked in the past for guidance in solving new policy problems. In the case of cybersecurity threats, this has led to warnings of cyber-Pearl Harbors and cyber-9/11s. In developing cybersecurity strategies, the historical analogy most frequently relied upon is the development and use of nuclear weapons. The nuclear era ushered in a new age of military strategy and redefined power relations among states. The cyberpower era is expected to do the same.

Tempting as historical analogies might be, however, they are also potentially dangerous because the pathways of present and future conflict and cooperation are not likely to duplicate any single road already travelled. For instance, nuclear weapons are immensely destructive in their own right, but cyberweapons are not. They cannot destroy buildings or kill large numbers of people in an instant. They do their damage by crippling computers, blocking communications, and manipulating information.

Despite these differences, there are similarities between nuclear technology and cybertechnology.[11] Most important is the fact that nuclear technology changed and developed over time and nuclear offensive and defensive strategies changed with it. As with nuclear arms control efforts, we may see periods in which most states agree on the nature of the problem of cyberthreats and the consequences of inaction but lack the cooperation to prevent unwanted futures from occurring.

Another approach to understanding cybersecurity is to break it down into four component parts: cyberspace, cyberpower, cyberthreats, and cyberstrategy. Cyberspace, along with air, sea, land, and space, is now accepted by strategic planners as one of five geographical domains for war and peace. Although it was created by the Pentagon to provide a secure means of communication for the military, early civilian advocates believed that the Internet would be a force for cooperation and mutual benefit.[12] Unlike the other four domains, cyberspace is a human creation. Land, sea, space, and air would still exist without human activity, but cyberspace came into existence as a result of manmade technological innovations. It is the physical infrastructure of networked computers, cellular technologies, fiber optic cables, and space-based communications that link people together. Because of its manmade nature, the boundaries and properties of cyberspace as a domain of policymaking are capable of undergoing far greater and more rapid changes in character than are land, sea, air, and space domains, thus complicating the development and execution of cybersecurity policies. As one commentator has noted, "Nothing is final in cyberspace." [13]

| Box 7.2 |

Concept Focus

Cyberthreat Conflict Ladder

A common method employed by strategists and military observers to assess the range of threats and security challenges facing a country is to create a threat contingency ladder with the most threatening scenarios at the top and the least threatening at the bottom. The idea of a conflict ladder is not meant to suggest that conflicts move up or down one rung at a time. It is designed to help organize thinking and prioritize problems. As we have noted, concepts such as cyberwarfare, cyberthreats and cybersecurity are far from precise and lend themselves to multiple interpretations. Below is one possible way to think about the range of cybersecurity challenges and threats that a country could face.

Types of Cybersecurity Threats	
THREAT	DESCRIPTION

15. Full-Range First-Strike Cyberattack
  a. stand-alone attack
  b. as part of coordinated military attack
	A widespread, offensive attack carried out against military, economic, and societal targets
	
	Damage: temporary, although if accompanied by military attacks, it could be extensive

(Continued)

(Continued)

THREAT	DESCRIPTION
14. Selective First-Strike Cyberattack	An offensive attack carried out against a limited set of societal targets
a. stand-alone attack b. as part of coordinated military attack	Damage: temporary and not extensive unless accompanied by military attacks

13. Full-Range Preemptive Cyberattack
    a. stand-alone attack
    b. as part of coordinated military attack
	A widespread, offensive strike in self-defense against military, economic, and societal targets; carried out in anticipation of imminent war
	
	Damage: temporary, but could be extensive if accompanied by military attacks

12. Selective Preemptive Cyberattack	An offensive, self-defense strike with a limited target set
a. stand-alone attack b. as part of coordinated military attack	Damage: temporary and not extensive, although more significant damage would occur if accompanied by military attacks

11. Full-Range Retaliatory Cyberattack
    a. stand-alone attack
    b. as part of coordinated military attack
	A widespread strike against military, economic, and societal targets carried out in response to an adversary's attack
	
	Damage: temporary, but could be extensive if accompanied by military attacks

10. Selective Retaliatory Cyberattack	A strike against a limited set of targets carried out after an adversary has attacked
a. stand-alone attack b. as part of coordinated military attack	Damage: temporary and not extensive unless accompanied by military attacks
9. Full-Range International Terrorist Cyberattack	An offensive strike delivered by a centrally organized terrorist group(s) Damage: extensive but temporary; no military component
8. Selective International Terrorist Cyberattack	An offensive strike, most likely delivered by a single terrorist cell or loose alliance of cells Damage: limited but temporary; no military component
7. Symbolic Cyberattack	A statement attack intended as a warning to an adversary of further action—cyber and military—should tensions continue or undesirable policies not change

THREAT	DESCRIPTION
6. Crisis Management Cyberattack	An attack by states outside of a conflict for the purpose of stabilizing a crisis situation and allowing for the restoration of civil order and regional security
5. Sabotage Cyberattack	Carried out either as stand-alone activities designed to weaken an enemy or an attack in conjunction with a planned military maneuver designed to defeat the enemy
4. Espionage Cyberattack	An attack aimed at obtaining otherwise secret national security information from an adversary that is carried out by government and military agencies or civilians working in alliance with state officials
3. Criminal Cyberattack	An attack aimed at gaining information that will lead to a financial profit
2. Hacktivist Cyberattack	An attack initiated by political and social groups as part of a global campaign to advance their cause
1. Mischief Cyberattack	A recreational and isolated cyberattack carried out by individuals with no political or financial motive

Source: Compiled by the author.

Cyberpower, at its most elementary level, is information used in order to inflict harm, persuade, or more generally gain an advantage. Unlike traditional military technologies that achieve their objectives through the physical destruction of a target, information power achieves its objectives by temporarily capturing its target and providing it with misleading or false information that reduces its effectiveness. Cyberattacks gain entry into networks by exploiting previously unknown computer vulnerabilities known as zero days. Typically, these zero days are identified by individuals who, in return for their silence, sell their discovery. Software firms seeking to protect their products by fixing the vulnerability before it became known were once the primary purchasers of this information. Today, governments play a major role as they seek to protect their military systems from attack and create an inventory of vulnerabilities that can be used against adversaries on short notice. For example, the Stuxnet virus that attacked Iran's nuclear processing system made use of four or five zero days to gain entry into the system.

Cyberweapons are attractive instruments of influence because in their most generic form they can literally be purchased off the shelf at affordable prices and delivered via messages to personal computers or through portable thumb drives.[14] The cyberweapons employed against Iran's nuclear capability in March or April 2010 were virtually identical to those employed by cybercriminals seeking to ferret out secret information from companies or government offices. For example, in 2011, as a result of Operation Ghost Glick, the FBI arrested six Estonians and charged them with running an Internet fraud scheme that operated in over 100 countries and infected more than 4 million computers. By infecting the computers with a virus, the hackers were able to manipulate Internet advertising and steal $14 million in illegitimate fees.[15]

Cyberthreats and risks, from a national security policy perspective, come in two forms. The first are risks and threats to the infrastructure of cyberspace. Virtually all individuals, corporations, and governments face these risks and threats and are concerned about protecting computers and other information-processing systems from being covertly captured, disrupted, disabled, or deceived. The second set of risks and threats involve the information that flows through cyberspace, which is perceived and evaluated to different degrees. For authoritarian political systems, the information in cyberspace may be a potentially serious threat to their ability to rule. It may also seriously harm a country's economy through its ability to influence investment, savings, and purchasing decisions. Finally, information in cyberspace may be seen as threatening fundamental societal values, as is often perceived to be the case with child pornography.

The fourth and final dimension to cybersecurity is cyberstrategy. Strategy is the lynchpin that unites policy goals with tactics. Tactics without strategy means winning the war and losing the peace. Wars are fought for political purposes that go beyond simply defeating the enemy. Failing that, wars, even if they are won on the battlefield, can be lost. Pearl Harbor was a tremendous military success for Japan, but it did not prevent that country from losing World War II. One of the major critiques of cyberstrategic thinking is that it is overly concerned with tactics and not strategy. Too much emphasis is given to what cyberpower can and might do, without adequate attention paid to whether or not its use will make a country more secure or whether its side effects might create even greater security threats in the future.

Military strategists have no agreed-upon answers regarding the strategic effectiveness of cyberpower. Three major areas of disagreement exist, and the chosen conclusions will help determine the nature of the cybersecurity pathway that countries travel in the coming decades. The first area of dispute is over whether or not cyberweapons can be used defensively. For some, given the speed and stealth of cyberpower, there is no effective defense against it. Cyberweapons are by their very nature first-strike weapons. Advocates of defense argue that while offense has the advantage now, this may not be the case in the long run since cybertechnology is in its infancy and will mature, change, and stabilize over time.

The second debate is over whether cyberweapons can be used alone—that is, can a war in which only cyberweapons are used be fought and won? The low cost, relative ease of use, and covert nature of cyberattacks make them attractive weapons of choice that are sought by military establishments around the world. At the same time, critics ask what country is likely to surrender or abandon its position simply as a result of a cyberattack. From this perspective, cyberweapons are valuable only when used in conjunction with other weapons systems.

The third and most finely tuned debate is over the possibility of cyberdeterrence, a concept that gained great prominence with the advent of nuclear weapons. Deterrence seeks to prevent a country from taking unwanted actions by threatening an immediate and unacceptable level of retaliation. Threatening like retaliation for a cyberattack has become a standard part of the language of cyberstrategy. Yet problems exist in carrying out this

Timeline
Cybersecurity Attacks

1998	U.S. Defense Department computers are penetrated by hackers.
1999	Hackers target NATO computers in response to the NATO bombing of Kosovo.
2001	Russian hackers penetrate U.S. Defense Department computers.
2007	Estonia suffers a cyberattack linked to Russia.
2008	Georgia suffers a cyberattack as part of military conflict with Russia.
2009	A cyberattack linked to China attacks computers used by supporters of the Dalai Lama.
2010	The United States and Israel are linked to the Stuxnet virus that attacks Iranian computers used in its nuclear weapons program.
2011	The Obama administration releases its International Strategy for Cybersecurity. The London Conference on Cyberspace is held.
2012	Iran undergoes a second cyberattack linked to Israel. Saudi Aramco oil company suffers a cyberattack linked to Iran. The Pentagon announces Plan X, designed to give the United States the ability to launch retaliatory or preemptive cyberattacks
2013	President Obama and Chinese leader Xi Jinping meet and discuss cybersecurity issues.

strategy, the most profound of which is the difficulty of detecting who was behind an attack. Simply because the attack came from country X does not mean the government of country X was responsible for it. Without firm proof, a retaliatory action can turn into an offensive act of war.

Problem Setting and Origins: The Beginning of Cyberwarfare

The exact date at which cyberconflict became an important aspect of world politics is subject to debate. Numerous starting dates exist to choose from. In 1998 computers believed to be in the United Arab Emirates succeeded in penetrating the Defense Department's security system (later it was discovered the computers were in fact controlled by teenagers in Israel and California). In 1999 NATO's computer system was overwhelmed by hackers protesting the NATO bombing in Kosovo. In 2001 Russian hackers penetrated Defense Department computers in what are referred to as the Moonlight Maze attacks. Some treat the 2007 cyberattacks on Estonia as the beginning of a new era in warfare, while others say the notable date is for yet a different attack or has in fact not yet even occurred. In this section we examine these and other examples of cyberconflict that mark the pathway of conflict and cooperation policymakers find themselves on today. They are significant as much for the questions they raised as for what actually happened.

The cyberattacks on Estonia began on April 27, 2007, and continued into mid-May. The spark that ignited these attacks was the decision to relocate a bronze statue of a Russian soldier from the center of Tallinn, Estonia's capital, to a war cemetery. Russians saw the statue as commemorating the sacrifices made in fighting Nazi Germany during World War II, but Estonians considered it to be a symbol of Soviet-enforced communist rule. Rioting by ethnic Russians living in Estonia and by Nashi, the government-sponsored youth group in Russia, broke out over the statue's relocation. The Russian government protested the action and then put in place a series of limited economic reprisals such as cutting railroad service between the two countries.

At the same time, a flood of junk e-mail was sent to parliamentary Web sites in Estonia as well as those of the president and prime minister. In the following weeks, newspaper and broadcasting Web sites crashed, online access to Estonia's largest bank was blocked, telephone exchanges were attacked, and Web sites were defaced with cybergraffiti and Russian propaganda. On May 5 Estonia announced the attacks had originated in Russia, which denied responsibility. However, it is generally held that the attacks could not have been carried out without the approval and support of the Russian government. Among those known to have participated in the attacks were individuals affiliated with Nashi and "script kiddies," individuals located around the world who followed Russian-language chat rooms, which provided information on how to attack Estonian Web sites.

The key question raised by the cyberattacks on Estonia was how the event should be classified. The question is significant because how it is defined legitimizes some responses and places others off limits. Initial accounts referred to it as a cyber-riot. Estonians officials took a more somber view, arguing that these cyberattacks were no different from a physical attack on their country.

The following year cyberattacks surfaced as part of a traditional military operation. On August 8, 2008, Russian troops invaded Georgia, an independent country on its borders that had been part of the Soviet Union. The invasion was the culmination of growing tensions between Georgia and Russia over South Ossetia, a breakaway province of Georgia containing large numbers of ethnic Russians. On August 7 Georgia sent troops into South Ossetia in an effort to reestablish control over it. Russia retaliated by invading Georgia and quickly overran the country.

In carrying out its military operation, Russia also engaged in a two-phase cyberoffensive, the goal of which was to isolate and silence Georgia.[16] In the first phase, Russian hackers unleashed a brute force denial-of-service attack. Unlike a semantic attack, which targets specific software systems, a brute attack seeks to overwhelm the target by increasing Internet traffic to the target to a point where its system fails. Groups of computers known as botnets that have had their command and control systems infected are taken over and used for this purpose. In the Georgian brute force attack, the botnets used were linked to Russian criminal organizations. In the second phase of the cyberoffensive, Russia concentrated its efforts on a more specific set of Web sites used by businesses, financial firms, Western media outlets, and educational institutions. CNN, for example, was hit with over 300,000 e-mails from individuals supporting the Russian invasion. The primary sources of cyberactivity in this phase were Russian "patriotic hackers," many of whom were members of Nashi and other youth movements. As with the Estonia cyberattack, they received guidance and instruction from Web sites such as StopGeorgia on how to launch denial-of-service attacks to the point where a user-friendly button (FLOOD) was made available to them. Evidence suggests that these sites were overseen by professionals who sought to counter Georgia's efforts to repair the damage done or to block the attack. A key question the Georgian attacks raised was the definition of neutrality in a cyberconflict. How were other states supposed to respond, especially since Russia denied responsibility for the cyberattacks? Moreover, was there any form of global responsibility to aid the victims of a cyberattack?

Another milestone in cyberwarfare occurred in 2010 with Operation Olympic Games.[17] Beginning in 2007, during George W. Bush's administration, the United States and Israel began working together with the goal of finding a means of crippling Iran's efforts to obtain nuclear capability. A secondary goal for the United States was to convince Israel that war with Iran would not be necessary to achieve this, thus averting the possibility of a widening and escalating conflict in the Middle East. The tool used to achieve this objective became known as Stuxnet. Five different organizations in Iran were identified for attack, with the Natanz uranium enrichment facility being the primary one. After the Stuxnet attacks, Iran confirmed that about 30,000 IP addresses had been infected. Evidence points to a reduction in the number of operational enrichment centrifuges in Iran from some 4,700 to 3,900 and a reduction in operational capacity at Nantz of 30 percent.

Stuxnet's objective was to penetrate and attack Iran's nuclear industrial control systems through a multistep process. First, it exploited several previously unknown vulnerabilities (referred to as zero-day exploits) in the Windows operating system. It then used stolen digital certificates to target specific industrial codes made by Siemens. By capturing the Siemens industrial codes, Stuxnet was able to issue instructions to computers controlling the uranium enrichment centrifuges to change the speed of the centrifuges and break them. The virus is initially attached to a host via a USB drive or other removable device. Once present, it self-replicates, infecting other local networks of computers that might not be connected to the Internet and sending information back to its operators.

Stuxnet's significance to the future of cyberconflict is found in several different issues surrounding its use. First, it was a preventive attack. There was no significant rise in tensions and war was not imminent. According to conventional international laws of war, a preemptive attack, striking first in self-defense when war is about to happen, is justified. A preventive attack is not. Second, it produced directed and limited damage. Stuxnet did not silence Iran nor cripple its entire cyberspace as the attacks on Estonia and Georgia sought to accomplish. Third, the damage done was repairable and more limited than early public accounts suggested, leading to questions about the wisdom of the attacks.

In May 2012 a second U.S.-Israeli cyberattack on Iran occurred. It also was developed as part of Olympic Games. Known as Flame, its primary purpose was intelligence gathering. Masquerading as a Windows updating program, Flame can activate computer microphones and cameras, take screenshots, log keyboard strokes, get location data, and send and receive commands, making it a valuable tool for constructing future attacks. It is estimated that 1,000 computers in Iran were infected. Other infected targets were found in Syria, Sudan, and the West Bank. Flame was discovered after Iran was hit with a series of cyberattacks on its oil fields. These attacks were apparently organized and carried out by Israel without U.S. knowledge.

Suspicion focused on Iran itself as the source of a cyberattack uncovered in 2012. The target was Saudi Aramco, Saudi Arabia's national oil and gas company.[18] The virus, referred to as Shamoon, did not cause any physical damage to Saudi Arabia's oil production facilities and has been described as relatively amateurish, but it did affect Saudi Aramco's business operations by randomly destroying drilling and oil production data. It took the company two weeks to fix the problem. Iran officially denied any involvement in the Shamoon attacks. Unlike the earlier attacks surveyed in this case study, this attack had the potential for disrupting the global economy if Saudi Aramco's oil production had been severely damaged. The question raised then became whether the potential scope of the consequences of the cyberattack changed the manner in which other states could and should respond to it.

To date, no significant act of cyberwarfare can be included in this over-view of cyber-related events, although fears of cyberterrorism occupy a prominent place in both public and governmental rhetoric on cyberse-curity.[19] Instead, the most common form of cyberwarfare by al-Qaeda, Hamas, and other extremist groups has been the release of videos calling for an electronic jihad.

Problem Definition and Response: Coordinating and Structuring a Strategy

The United States undertook several initiatives in 2011 to address the problems of cybersecurity.[20] In May the Obama administration released its International Strategy for Cyberspace. Its conceptual starting point is that cyberspace is a global commons that cannot become the possession of any one country or set of countries. The United States' ultimate objective is defined as an open and secure information and communications infrastruc-ture that supports international trade, strengthens international security, and fosters the free flow of ideas. According to this strategy document, the United States believes that these goals can be achieved through the applica-tion of long-standing international norms of peaceful behavior and behavior that is permitted during conflict. The United States does not see cyberspace as requiring the creation of new norms or as having made existing norms obsolete. The strategy reaffirms that "when warranted the United States will respond to hostile acts in cyberspace as we would to any other threat to our country. . . . We reserve the right to use all necessary means . . . as appro-priate and consistent with applicable international law in order to defend our Nation, our allies, our partners, and our interests."

Two months later, the Government Accountability Office (GAO) released its study on the Defense Department's efforts to bolster U.S. cyberdefenses. The GAO acknowledged the immense scope of this challenge, noting that the Pentagon possessed over 7 million computer devices, linking together more than 10,000 networks. The primary finding of the GAO's report was that the Defense Department lacked both a coherent command structure to coordinate its cybersecurity efforts or a coherent strategic doctrine to guide planning and assess the resources needed to succeed in cyberdefense.

Two concrete steps have been taken to address these concerns. The first was the creation of the U.S. Cyber Command in 2010. It is charged with the direction of Defense Department information networks for conducting a full spectrum of cyberspace activities in all domains, thereby ensuring the United States and its allies freedom of action in cyberspace and denying such use to U.S. adversaries. Responsibility for federal civilian information networks rests with the Department of Homeland Security. Second, in October 2012 the Pentagon announced the start up of Plan X by the Pentagon's Department's Defense Advanced Research Projects Agency (DARPA), an organization established in 1958 in order to ensure that the United States would have a technological edge over any adversary and to prevent a surprise technological attack.[21] The conventional strategy for protecting information networks is to build firewalls around them to thwart any attack. Plan X is a five-year, $100 million research program designed to create a global map of cyberspace that will provide military commanders with the ability to identify and track threats continuously and allow them to retaliate or preemptively attack cybertargets instantly using preplanned scenarios.

The Defense Department issued a report to Congress in November 2012 detailing its cyberstrategy policy. The report noted that a cyberattack had to be of "significant" scale in order to justify a retaliatory strike, but it did not present specifics on at what point an attack moved from being an annoyance or limited engagement to qualifying as an action meriting a response. It was also silent on when that response should entail the use of military force and, should that be the case, at what point the provisions of the War Powers Resolution requiring that the president obtain the consent of Congress became relevant.[22]

Efforts to address cybersecurity issues have also taken place at the international level.[23] In 2010 the United Nations Group of Governmental Experts, in this case diplomats and military officers from cyberstates, issued a report titled "Developments in the Field of Information and Telecommunications in the Context of International Security," which called upon states to undertake confidence-building and risk-reduction measures in order to protect critical national and international information infrastructures. This group has continued to meet on ways to improve cybersecurity.

The following year Russia and China jointly introduced a proposal to the United Nations General Assembly calling for a code of conduct among cyberstates. The objective was to keep cyberspace from becoming a battleground, prevent a cyber arms race, and promote dialogue as a means of settling cyber-related disputes. A key aspect of this proposed code was the right of states to protect their information space from attacks and sabotage. Later in the same UN meeting, Russia introduced the separate Convention on International Information Security. The wording and spirit of the codes raised concern by observers that what one country defined as cyberspace sabotage might strike another as a legitimate exercise of free speech.

These concerns were very much in evidence at the 2011 London Conference on Cyberspace, which was attended by government officials from sixty countries, including Russia and China, and representatives from the private sector. Although the conference officially focused on cyberattacks and cybercrime, the discussion quickly turned to questions of free speech, with one participant asserting that the threat to the Internet was not cybercriminals but misguided or overreaching government policy. U.S.

and British officials urged that governments not use cybersecurity as an excuse for censorship and warned against the dangers of a "repressive global code."[24]

Whereas Russia and China have sought the establishment of global codes of conduct, the United States and many of its allies have looked to regional organizations as the most appropriate site for developing such standards of behavior.[25] Primary attention has focused on the Organization for Security and Cooperation in Europe (OSCE). Now with almost sixty members, the OSCE was established during the Cold War as an organization dedicated to conflict reduction and risk management. Cybersecurity issues are seen as a logical next step for this organization due to its long experience in dealing with Cold War conventional and military security issues. ASEAN (the Association of Southeast Asian Nations) is viewed as the logical partner organization for addressing cybersecurity concerns among Asian states. Other regional and international organizations have also directed their attention to cybersecurity issues. Three of the most prominent are the Group of 8 (G8), the European Union, and NATO.

| Box 7.3 |

Spotlight

Russia and China: Cyber Superpowers

China's approach to cybersecurity encompasses a full range of activity.[26] The first major Chinese statement regarding the military uses of cyberpower came in 1998 with the publication of *Unlimited Warfare*, which argued that U.S. military dependence on information and communication technology was a weakness that China could exploit. Today, Chinese military thinking integrates electronic warfare and cyberwarfare into the concept of information confrontation, and there are special units within the People's Liberation Army dedicated to carrying out hacking operations. Political dissidents are a prime target of Chinese cyber-related espionage operations. While many blogs are tolerated by the Chinese government, especially those on foreign affairs that are highly nationalist in tone, blogs on democracy, religion, and Tibet tend to be taken down. Ghost Net, discovered in 2009, was a cybersystem suspected of being linked to the Chinese government that targeted the computer systems used by supporters of the Dalai Lama. It infected 1,200 computers in 103 countries.

The popular perception is that Chinese hacking is highly sophisticated, but in fact much of it is considered to be rather sloppy and easily detected. Cyberattacks from China tend to occur only from 9:00 a.m. to 5 p.m., Beijing time; hackers do not hide their activity very well; and many attacks are noisy because they are carried out by multiple hackers in search of the same information. This stands in contrast to Russia, where hacking occurs 24/7 and is harder to identify as a result of carefully scripted targeting of sites.

(Continued)

(Continued)

Finally, China also engages in cyber-related sabotage. "Patriot hackers" (private citizens who are believed to act with the encouragement of the government) have attacked en masse the Web sites of organizations such as CNN for its reporting on riots in Tibet in 2008. Additionally, the Chinese government has blocked Internet access in parts of China by establishing firewalls and gateway controls that prevent IP addresses from getting through.

Russian thinking on the military uses of cyberpower has several dimensions. As evidenced by its operation against Georgia, the Russian military embraces an offensive strategy that emphasizes informational warfare to achieve political objectives, but it is also developing plans for regional cyberdefense systems. It is a major source of cyber-related espionage, with motivation being an important distinguishing feature separating the Russian and Chinese efforts.[27] In China the profit motive is very much present but exists alongside an organized effort by the Chinese government to obtain secret information from foreign businesses in order to strengthen China's world military and economic standing. In Russia the profit motive is far more pronounced. A recent example was uncovered in 2013 when four Russians and one Ukrainian were charged with stealing 160 million credit card numbers between 2005 and 2008. One of the leading Russian crime organizations is the Russian Business Network (RBN), which is said to be responsible for about 40 percent of all global cybercrime committed in 2007. The net worth of its efforts that year was put at over $100 billion. RBN is also the reported to be the world's largest spammer, accounting for 20 percent of all spam in 2008. It was also involved in Russia's cyberattack on Georgia in 2008.

Russian authorities have employed many of the same techniques used on Georgia and Estonia against their domestic opponents. Some of the prominent voices that have been subject to cyber-related sabotage are involved with Russia's anticorruption movement, such as Alexei Navalny's blog site; the People's Freedom Party, which was set to post an anti-Putin report on LiveJournal; and opposition leaders' Web sites that were hit on the eve of the 2012 Duma elections.

Countries are considered to be military superpowers because of the range of weapons they possess and their ability to inflict harm. So it is with cyber superpowers. Russia and China, along with the United States, have a far more extensive range of cyberweapons at their disposal than do most countries. As the China and Russia cases illustrate, one important difference between conventional military superpowers and cyber superpowers is that cyber superpowers need not rely on the military to exercise their influence. They can work through patriot hackers, criminals, and private citizens, making it very difficult to assign responsibility for their actions and thus clouding retaliatory efforts as well as arms control undertakings.

Problem Evolution and Development: A Pathway under Construction

Unlike many other case studies in this book, our overview of the cybersecurity pathway of conflict and cooperation being travelled has brought us to the present. We have not seen the next wave of conflicts that will allow us to judge whether cyberdefenses or deterrence work or whether certain forms of cyberweapons will be used more often than others. Much more than those studied in our other cases, the cybersecurity pathway is under construction. In this it very much resembles the period right after World War II when strategists began to struggle with understanding the power and limits of nuclear weapons as an instrument of foreign policy. Those debates lasted into the 1960s before a consensus on nuclear strategy was developed. Rather than speculate on the direction that the cybersecurity pathway will take, we will identify four of the leading possibilities under discussion.

The two end points of the debate are that (1) cyberwar has fundamentally changed the nature of war and (2) while it is a new tactic, at the strategic level nothing has changed. The possibility that cyberwar will usher in a new era of warfare was put forward a decade before the attacks on Estonia, Georgia, and Iran.[28] This position argues that managing, obtaining, and denying information is a potentially transformative strategic asset whose full realization will require reorganizing military structures from ones based on hierarchy to ones organized around networks. Cyberwar is also seen as requiring a change in military doctrine so that political and psychological factors are fully integrated with the military aspects of war. The definition of the boundaries of a battlefield, what constitutes an attack, and how to define victory and defeat are three elements of military doctrine which will need to be reconsidered.

At the opposite end of the spectrum is the view that cyberwar is business as usual.[29] Proponents of this belief argue that cyberweapons, while swift and covert, are not deadly. Scenarios built around catastrophic damage done by the stand-alone use of cyberweapons are not found to be persuasive. Instead of being rooted in transformative information power, cyberpower is here treated as just information. Military strategy is unchanged by cyberpower and the fascination with new technologies should not obscure that. Cyberpower is just another weapon.

In between these two positions can be found two others of note. In one perspective cyberwar is seen as an extension of the Cold War, and thus the debate over the extent to which cyberpower has altered the nature of warfare is off target. Just as in the Cold War, we are not likely to see major confrontations between opposing global powers. Instead, we will see indirect conflicts, local wars, and wars fought by proxies.[30] These wars may become commonplace and will include cyberpower, but it will be used in a limited and constrained fashion so as not to provoke the anger of the global powers. Cyber-related subversion and espionage will flourish and cyberstates will routinely deny their involvement in these disputes.

The final alternative future sees cyberpower as being transformative in its impact on military strategy, but not in the way in which the first perspective we introduced in this section views it. Here cyberwar is transformative not because of the damage it can do, which is seen as temporary in nature, but by the uncertainty it creates in other states.[31] Accordingly, the target of a cyberattack is not the adversary's information systems but the adversary's confidence in the ability of its information systems to engage in successful offensive or defensive action. Without such confidence, there is no reason to go forward with developing a cyberwar capability. The development of such an offensive capability by the United States would not dissuade Russia or China from moving forward to develop cyberpower capabilities, nor would it eliminate the problems of cybercrime and cyberhacking, but it would serve as an effective deterrent to the majority of the world's countries from obtaining a cyber-related military capability.

Conclusion: An Evolving Cyberthreat

The cybersecurity pathway we have explored began with an overview discussion of the different component parts of cybersecurity and moved to an examination of key cyberwar incidents that elevated cybersecurity from an abstract problem to a concrete national security issue. We then looked at efforts by countries and international organizations to create cybersecurity strategies and place limits on cyberconflicts. As we noted in our look into future developments, although much has transpired, cybersecurity is still in its formative period and uncertainty exists over the future direction it may take.

Regardless of which direction the cybersecurity pathway takes, elements of conflict and cooperation will be present. Particularly challenging for countries as they continue on this journey will likely be the higher-than-usual degree of suspicion and uncertainty that will surround their interactions (both peaceful and conflictual ones). Suspicion grows out of the stealth nature of cyberattacks and the difficulty of assigning responsibility for them: Who really is an ally and who is an enemy? Uncertainty grows out of the newness of cyberattacks. Will cyber arms control really work? How much damage will a cyberattack produce and how quickly will the enemy recover from it?

Case Analysis

1. In our discussion, we noted that the cybersecurity pathway was under construction. Rank in order of likelihood and desirability the four possible directions the cybersecurity pathway might develop. Justify and compare your rankings.

2. Does China, Russia, or the United States represent the greatest cyberthreat to global security? Why?

3. What would you include in a code of conduct for cyberspace? What would you want excluded?

4. Are separate national, regional, or global efforts the best way to go in making cyberspace secure?

5. Should different rules govern cyberspace as it exists in the global commons and within national state boundaries?

6. At what point in the cyberthreat conflict ladder do we cross over to cyberwar?

7. In looking at the cybersecurity pathway, which cyberattack is most relevant for thinking about the future: Estonia, Georgia, or Iran? Why?

8. Assume that you are the national security advisor and have been asked to develop a cyberstrategy for the United States. What are the key issues that must be addressed in this document? What is your position on them?

Suggested Readings

Arquilla, John, and David Ronfeldt. "Cyberwar Is Coming." *Comparative Strategy* 12, no. 2 (1993): 141–165. This is an early classic statement of the conflict-transforming potential of cyberpower.

Deibert, Ronald, and Rafal Rohozinski. "Risking Security: Policies and Paradoxes of Cyberspace Security. *International Political Sociology* 4, no. 1 (2010), 15–32. This article provides a conceptual overview of the concept of cybersecurity and the debates over its meaning and implications.

Gray, Colin. *Making Strategic Sense of Cyber Power: Why the Sky Is Not Falling*. Carlisle Barracks, PA: U.S. Army War College Press, 2013. This work argues that concerns with the uniqueness and destructive potential of cyberpower are overstated.

Klimburg, Alexander. "Mobilising Cyber Power." *Survival* 53, no. 1 (2011): 41–60. Klimburg presents an overview of the concept of cyberpower and discusses Russian, Chinese, and U.S. cyberpower resources and polices.

Nye, Joseph S., Jr. "Nuclear Lessons for Cyber Security?" *Strategic Studies Quarterly* 5, no. 4 (2011): 18–38. Nye presents a balanced account of the parallels and dissimilarities between strategic thinking for nuclear weapons and cyberweapons

Rudner, Martin. "Cyber-Threats to Critical National Infrastructure: An Intelligence Challenge." *International Journal of Intelligence and CounterIntelligence* 26, no. 3 (2013): 453–481. This article presents an overview of threats from international terrorism, state-sponsored terrorism, malevolent hacking, and insider threats.

Web Resources

Center for Strategic and International Studies, http://csis.org/category/top ics/technology/cybersecurity. This bipartisan nonprofit organization presents an overview on policy, research, and news coverage on cybersecurity.

CyberDomain Security and Operations, U.S. Department of Defense, www
.defense.gov/home/features/2013/0713_cyberdomain. Access articles,
speeches, news, and more from this DOD site, including links to U.S.
Cyber Command.

Royal United Services Institute, www.rusi.org. Explore research, analysis,
and publications from this independent think tank based in the UK.

Strategic Studies Institute, U.S. Army War College, www.strategicstud
iesinstitute.army.mil/. Access research, analysis, and other publications
on a range of security topics, including cybersecurity.

U.S. Department of Homeland Security, www.dhs.gov/topic/cyber
security. The DHS provides an overview on cybersecurity, U.S. policy,
privacy, and more.

Comprehensive National Cybersecurity Initiative, the White House, www
.whitehouse.gov/cyber security/comprehensive-national-cyber security-
initiative. Read the Comprehensive Cybersecurity Initiative presented by
the White House and explore related White House blog posts.

PART II
Economic Security

8 Organizing World Trade

Widespread agreement exists that free trade is the best way to organize international trade. This consensus reflects both contemporary and historical conditions. Free trade is central to the operation of today's globalized economy, which requires the unrestricted movement of people, goods, services, money, and ideas across national borders. The absence of free trade and the popularity of state-controlled trade policies are also seen as having contributed to the Great Depression of the 1930s, which produced widespread poverty and suffering among people around the world, and to the rise of fascism. Often overlooked, however, are two important points about free trade. First, free trade is not the only option open to policymakers in constructing their international economic policies. A variety of policy alternatives exist, and which one is selected will be influenced by both domestic and international factors, many of which will not be economic in nature. Second, free trade strategies may be applied in a variety of settings.

Since the end of World War II, policymakers have travelled down a long pathway of conflict and cooperation as they seek to put a global free trade system in place. The primary method in use to bring about such a system is a series of international trade negotiations. The most recent of these negotiations is known as the Doha Round. Begun in November 2001, the Doha Development Agenda talks adjourned in July 2008 without an agreement. The deadlock in Doha is important for understanding the future direction of international politics for at least two reasons. First, since the Doha Round has yet to produce a new agreement, this leads some to question the value of international conferences to manage global issues. Others remain convinced of the value of large international conferences and attribute the failures of the Doha Round to specific decisions and negotiating strategies adopted by countries. Second, disagreement exists over the consequences of a failure to reach a new trade agreement. Opinions here range—some are indifferent because they see free trade as firmly established as the basis for international trade, some fear a global retreat to protectionist and antidemocratic national policies, and some see the Doha Round as irrelevant because free trade has been undermined by a new generation of state-controlled trade policies. The result of these varying outlooks has been to produce doubt over the pathway that international trade negotiations may travel in the future.

In this case study, our Concept Focus will consider different trade strategies that a country may adopt. The Spotlight section will examine in greater depth the controversies surrounding the Doha Round of negotiations on agriculture policy that took place in Cancun in 2008.

| Box 8.1 |

Case Summary

The Doha Round of trade talks has stalled over agenda disagreements between advanced economic countries and less developed countries on a wide variety of issues ranging from trade in agriculture to trade in services and investments. Many of these issues have also created divisions within these two groups. Neither has been willing to compromise much, thus blocking further reforms in international trading policies and leaving many in doubt as to the value of global international trade negotiations.

Global Context

Disagreement between countries and from antiglobalization demonstrators led to the collapse of the Seattle Millennium WTO trade talks in 2000, but one year later, after the September 11, 2001, terrorist attacks, global trade talks were energized by a renewed sense of unity. The original issues of contention from 2000, however, have remained.

Key Actors

- Advanced economies, including the United States
- Developing nations

Motives

- The United States views the Doha talks as part of a global strategy to defeat terrorism as it believes that promoting global economic growth would reduce the appeal of terrorist rhetoric in less developed countries.
- Less developed countries want to redress the imbalance of GATT trade negotiations that systematically favored the trade concerns of advanced economies.

Concepts

- International political economy
- Trade strategies (protectionism versus free trade)
- Globalization

Trade and Power: National Interests Affect the Doha Round

Viewed from a global perspective, it is tempting to see trade policy as being about allocating scarce resources and creating wealth. Viewed from the perspective of states, a different and competing picture emerges. Trade policy is also about power and national interests. The link between trade, state power, and national interests is long established. Christopher Columbus had the support of the Spanish monarchy in his effort to find a faster trade route to Asia. In 1600 Queen Elizabeth I gave Britain's East India Company a charter granting it a monopoly on all trade with countries east of the Cape of Good Hope and west of the Strait of Magellan. In time the company would come to have its own army and be the de facto ruler over large parts of India. During the Cold War, the United States sought to deny the Soviet Union access to critical military and commercial goods by passing the Trading with the Enemy Act. It also gave favorable trade terms to key countries to prevent them from entering into the Soviet sphere of influence.

Neither the end of the Cold War nor the advent of globalization changed this. Consider two recent examples. In 2005 the Chinese National Offshore Oil Corporation, the third-largest oil company in China, presented Unocal (Union Oil Company of California) with an unsolicited $18.5 million dollar cash offer to purchase it, topping an offer on the table from Chevron Texaco. Members of Congress quickly organized in opposition to the proposed purchase, arguing that China had questionable motives in making the purchase since Unocal possesses sensitive deep-sea exploration technology that could have military uses and that U.S. firms could not make a similar purchase in China. In 2013, as the United States and Europe were exploring the possibility of establishing a regional free trade system linking them together, France raised objections to allowing U.S. firms to have unrestricted access to its market on the grounds of needing to protect "cultural diversity."

As these examples attest, although today countries often attempt to coordinate their economic and trade policies, conflicts continue to exist. National interests, such as the desire to protect a domestic market from outside influences, are often at play. Countries who find themselves with similar domestic interests may band together to present a more powerful front as they advocate for their position, as is the case with the Doha Round, in which less developed countries (LDCs) have combined forces to push for a change in trade policies. On their own, their policy goals may have been easily overlooked by more economically advanced countries in Europe, the Americas, and elsewhere, but because the LDCs have coordinated their voices and their efforts, they have succeeded in getting their concerns on the radar of the Doha Round. Advanced economies, however, continue to wield more economic might, and the agenda of the talks has lingered in stalemate for years. The issue of opposing agendas has come to a head during the Doha Round, but the dynamics in play are not new. They have built up over time, changing as events have influenced them and as interests and priorities have changed.

| **Box 8.2** |

Concept Focus

Trade Strategies

Countries have a variety of choices in constructing their international trade policy. Today, **free trade** is the most prevalent strategy. It is a strategic outlook that emphasizes allowing the international marketplace and the forces of supply and demand to set the price for any and all goods and services being traded. Government involvement in setting prices, aiding firms, or determining what is to be produced within a country's national borders is to be avoided. The role of government is to create an open and level economic playing field in which national and foreign firms are treated alike and can fairly compete with one another.

In the post–World War II era, global free trade strategies were the preferred orientation to world trade and domestic economic growth. They tended to be built around three core principles. The first was nondiscrimination. Government rules and regulations should make no distinction between domestic products and imported products; a car was a car regardless of where it was made. The second was reciprocity. Governments should respond in kind when a trading partner reduced tariffs or other trade restrictions on its products. The third core principle was most-favored-nation (MFN) status, now referred to in the United States as permanent normal trade relations. This designation was designed to speed up the process of creating a global free trade system. When a country received MFN status, it did not have to engage in trade negotiations to receive improved trade terms. It automatically received the best trade terms given.

Free trade can also be practiced at a regional level, where it takes place within a closed grouping of states that are able to create a barrier to trade around them. A regional free trade agreement is a form of preferential trade agreement (PTA) and can also be bilateral in form. Uncertainty exists over the future of PTAs. From a global perspective, PTAs are seen by many as a decidedly second-best solution to the dangers of protectionism (discussed below) and have significant drawbacks when compared to global free trade, perhaps the greatest of which is the need to define the "nationality" of a product in order for it to qualify under the rules of the bilateral or regional trade agreement. The dispute resolution system presents an additional problem. Since, typically, bilateral and regional agreements link weak economies to strong ones either directly or through a hub-and-spoke system, it is difficult for weaker states to effectively challenge the actions of the stronger ones.

The concept of **strategic trade** considers trade to be something more than economics; it sees it as a key ingredient in domestic political stability and national security. Where advocates of free trade stress its ability to efficiently allocate resources and its potential for creating positive and peaceful relationships between countries, supporters of strategic trade policies emphasize the existence of competition among countries and the insecurity that this creates. They advocate using government power through such measures as tax breaks, tariffs, and subsidies

(Continued)

(Continued)

to promote and protect key economic sectors from foreign competition and give domestic firms an advantage in competing for foreign markets. Typically this is done to protect old and decaying industrial sectors that have lost much of their competitive advantage (steel, autos, textiles) or to help new industries (computers, electronics) survive foreign competition in their early years of existence. It can also take the form of targeting certain foreign markets for "capture" to prevent firms in competing countries from gaining a foothold there or dominating that market.

A third trade strategy option open to countries is **protectionism**. Free trade and strategic trade are outward-looking trade strategies. They differ over the terms by which the competition for markets should take place. Protectionism is at heart antitrade. It seeks to cut off foreign competition by protecting the home market for national firms. At the same time it shows little interest in expanding into foreign markets or extending the global reach of its economy. For this reason it is often described as antiglobalist. During the period between world wars, the United States and many other countries adopted protectionist policies in an attempt to protect their economies from the devastating social and economic effects of the Great Depression. In essence, they sought to "export" these problems to other countries. Quotas (numerical limits) and high tariffs (taxes) on foreign goods caused American consumers to buy American-made goods, thus keeping Americans employed and increasing unemployment in other countries.

Problem Setting and Origin: The Long Road to Doha

The Doha Round is the first round of trade negotiations to be carried out under the mandate of the World Trade Organization (WTO), but it is not an isolated or unique event in the history of post–World War II international trade politics.[1] Seven previous negotiating rounds were carried out under the sponsorship of the General Agreement on Tariffs and Trade (GATT). GATT was created to temporarily organize international trade until the International Trade Organization (ITO) came into existence. Along with the World Bank and the International Monetary Fund (IMF), the ITO was to be part of the Bretton Woods system that the United States helped create after World War II to ensure that the global economy would not slip back into protectionism. Each organization had a special role in the Bretton Woods system: the IMF provided financial stability; the World Bank provided economic recovery and development funds; and the ITO was to promote free trade while also permitting states to take protective measures with the permission of other states.[2]

The ITO never came into existence. It ran into opposition in the Senate from a coalition of protectionist forces that feared that by joining the ITO the United States would be forced to adopt trade policies that would hurt U.S. firms and free traders who felt that the ITO did not eliminate enough restrictions on free trade. With the ITO sidetracked because of U.S. opposition, GATT became the primary vehicle for organizing a global free trade system.

In order to accomplish its mission of promoting global free trade, GATT organized a series of international conferences commonly referred to as negotiating rounds. This label was applied to them because the conferences were made up of a series of meetings spanning several years. With the passage of time, these negotiating rounds took longer and longer to produce an agreement. The first GATT round, the Geneva Round (1947), was completed in less than one year; the Kennedy Round (1964), which had sixty-two members, took thirty-seven months to complete; and the eighth and final GATT round, the Uruguay Round (1986), which had 123 members, required seven years to produce an agreement. This agreement included a call for establishing a new international organization, the World Trade Organization (WTO), to manage international trade relations.

The GATT negotiating rounds created a mixed legacy for the Doha Round. On the positive side, they produced an impressive reduction in the size of tariffs (taxes) on manufactured goods. On the negative side, they were less successful in reducing nontariff barriers to trade such as red tape, licensing requirements, health and safety standards, requirements that goods enter a country on ships registered in that country, and government procurement policies. Perhaps most significantly in the eyes of developing economies, GATT came to be seen as a "rich man's club."[3] Less developed countries were excluded from the decision-making process, and their interests were largely ignored. Final draft agreements were presented as a take-it-or-leave-it package, with many delegations not getting a copy of the agreement until after it was officially announced. LDCs found it necessary to turn to the United Nations (UN) for development help. Under its auspices the first Development Decade was announced in 1961, and in 1964 it established the United Nations Conference on Trade and Development (UNCTAD).

By the end of the Uruguay Round in 1994, the negatives of GATT were far more politically significant than were its earlier positive achievements. This was clear for all to see in the first meeting of the WTO in Singapore in 1996, where developed and developing countries clashed over the agenda for a new round of international trade talks to be held in Seattle and labeled the Millennium Round. The LDCs wanted to address GATT's unfinished trade agenda: agriculture and services (banking, investment, insurance). These were issues they felt developed countries benefitted from at their expense. Advanced economies countered by advancing a new set of trade issues for international negotiation that would provide them with greater access to developing country markets. These issues included transparency in government procurement, trade facilitation (customs issues), investment, and competition, and, collectively, they came to be known as the Singapore issues.

The less developed countries opposed adding these issues to the agenda of the next round of international trade talks, but the advanced economies remained adamant that the Singapore issues would have to be included on the agenda of the upcoming Seattle WTO talks.

The WTO Seattle conference began on November 30, 1999, and adjourned in failure on December 3. It is best remembered for the large-scale antiglobalization demonstrations that surrounded virtually every aspect of the meeting.[4] Demonstrators blocked the opening meeting, impeded the ability of delegates to attend meetings, and protested in the streets.

Among the many reasons for the failure of the Seattle talks were the conflicting positions held by key countries. The deep divisions between advanced economies and less developed countries that had surfaced in Singapore continued in Seattle. Neither Europe nor Japan was interested in seeing major modifications made to open up free trade in agriculture, as sought by the LDCs. Farmers are a potent voting bloc in many European states, and their support rests heavily on the continuation of price supports and export subsidies. Citing the need for self-sufficiency, Japan has a long history of protectionist policies that prevent rice from entering its market. Many developing countries found that the costs of opening up their markets to foreign goods as required by the Uruguay Round agreements were greater than they anticipated. They also felt that many advanced economies were slow to fully implement provisions that offered LDCs the most benefits.

Hope for progress on an international trade agreement in Seattle was further undermined by the ambivalent position adopted by the United States.[5] On the one hand, the United States was a strong advocate of expanding the scope of free trade. On the other hand, a series of domestic constraints caused the United States to adopt a cautious approach. President Bill Clinton lacked fast-track authority (FTA), which would have required that Congress vote only yes or no on trade treaties put before it. Congress could not propose amendments or otherwise insert modifying language into trade agreements while FTA was in effect. The 2000 presidential election presented an additional complication. American foreign policy tends to come to a halt in the run-up period to elections. Candidates seek votes by promising a strong defense and a strong economy. Agreements that might be accused of weakening the United States or "costing too much" are avoided.

The negotiating roadblocks to a new international trade agreement encountered at the failed Seattle WTO conference were overcome by the events of September 11, 2001. The terrorist attacks on the World Trade Center and the Pentagon altered American perceptions of the world. The limited security challenges of the post–Cold War era had overnight been replaced by a "war on terrorism." A new international trade conference came to be seen as a means for promoting global cohesion and jump-starting a global economy shaken badly by the terrorist attacks; 2001 showed the lowest growth in global output in more than two decades.

Timeline
GATT and WTO Trade Meetings

1947	The General Agreement on Tarrifs and Trade (GATT) is founded in Geneva.
1948	Congress rejects the International Trade Organization (ITO).
1949	Second-round GATT talks occur in Annecy, France.
1950	Third-round GATT talks occur in Torquay, England.
1956	Fourth-round GATT talks occur in Geneva, Switzerland.
1960–1962	Fifth, Dillon Round GATT talks
1964–1969	Sixth, Kennedy Round GATT talks
1973–1979	Seventh-round GATT talks occur in Tokyo, Japan.
1986–1994	Eighth, Uruguay Round GATT talks
1995	The World Trade Organization (WTO) is founded.
1996	The first WTO meeting is held in Singapore.
1998	The second WTO meeting is held in Geneva, Switzerland.
1999	Third, Millennium Round WTO meeting in Seattle, Washington
2001	The fourth round of WTO trade talks kick off in Doha, Qatar.
2003	The WTO meets in Cancun as part of the Doha Round.
2004	WTO Doha Round meeting in Geneva
2006	Hong Kong hosts a WTO meeting of the Doha Round.
2007	Doha talks continue in Potsdam, Germany.
2008	Geneva hosts another meeting of the Doha Round.
2013	The WTO Doha Round meets in Bali, Indonesia.

Problem Definition and Response: The Changing Balance of Power

The new round of trade talks began on November 9, 2001, in Doha, Qatar, far removed from the potentially disruptive effects of antiglobalism protestors.[6] The decision to go forward with a new round of multilateral trade talks left unanswered the question of its agenda. The issues that divided advanced economies and less developed countries in the lead-up to the ill-fated Seattle meeting persisted. In the end the Doha meeting produced a twenty-one-point agenda that provided something for everyone but also required concessions from all. The LDCs agreed to place foreign investment, competition, and environmental issues on the agenda. The European Union (EU) agreed, in principle, to discuss phasing out farm subsidies, and the United States agreed to a nonbinding declaration that intellectual property rules could not be used to stop LDCs from obtaining low-cost medicines to treat AIDS and other diseases.

This compromise agenda formed the basis for the Cancun ministerial conference that took place in September 2003.[7] The Cancun meetings brought into full focus the extent to which the underlying dynamics of the politics and economics of international trade had undergone fundamental changes since the beginning of the GATT system. Then, the trade concerns of the advanced economies had dominated the meetings through a variety of informal mechanisms, including the so-called green room discussions. Attendance at these pre-negotiation sessions was at the invitation of GATT's director general and generally excluded advanced economies. Decision making at the negotiating sessions was led by the Quad (the United States, Great Britain, Japan, and Canada). Decisions were approved by the full membership by consensus rather than voting with silence being interpreted as agreement.

The LDCs eventually countered this arrangement by creating their own informal negotiating coalitions to oppose the agenda of advanced economies.[8] Initially, the Quad was able to blunt LDCs' influence through a policy of divide and conquer. For example, in the deliberations to set up the Uruguay Round, many LDCs joined together in a coalition known as the Informal Group of Developing Countries. Two of its goals were to get trade in agriculture and textiles included on the agenda and to keep trade in services and intellectual property rights off the agenda. The group split when some LDCs (who, together with the advanced economies, came to be known as the Café au Lait coalition) broke away from this position and agreed to enter into discussions on an agreement in services while others (known as the Group of 10, or G10) continued to take a hard-line stance that excluded trade in services from the agenda.

As the Cancun meetings approached, advanced and developing countries came to view one another with distrust and hostility. Advanced economies saw LDCs as engaging in grandstand diplomacy and confrontational tactics designed to influence their home populations rather than negotiating in a spirit of solving global trade problems. For their part, LDCs accused advanced economies of not negotiating in good faith and seeking to obtain one-sided concessions from LDCs.

An important hardening of positions in the trade negotiations occurred in August, just one month before the Cancun talks began. A joint U.S.-EU declaration of August 13 on agriculture was viewed as entirely unsatisfactory by the LDCs. India and Brazil, soon to be joined by China, took the lead in drafting a developing states rebuttal. Signed on September 2, this document signaled the founding of the G20.[9] At the top of the G20's agenda was a call for significant cuts in U.S. and EU agricultural subsidies, special treatment for LDCs, and greater market access for nonagricultural exports from LDCs.

The formation of the G20 was significant because it injected a strong North-South dimension (developed and developing nations) into the GATT talks. Unlike the Café au Lait group, the G20 was a coalition of LDCs, not a mixed grouping of states. And, unlike previous coalitions of LDCs that showed limited interest in coordinating their policy proposals with other developing states (such as the G10), the G20 engaged in a policy of active consultation that created a broad alliance of LDCs. A consequence of this outreach was the formation of two broader groupings of developing countries, the G90, which linked together many of the regional groupings of developing states, and the G33, made up of poor states that were particularly worried about the impact cuts in tariffs would have on their agricultural sectors.

Whatever chance of success may have existed was further lessened by the manner in which an agreement was to be reached at Cancun. It was to be a single undertaking, meaning that all agreements were to be contained in a single package. The benefit of this approach was that it permitted and even encouraged trade-offs among different categories so that losses in one could be offset by gains in another. The difficulty was that, with over 140 countries participating in negotiations over such a wide range of contentious topics, not only was it hard to keep track of who was winning and who was losing but lack of progress in any one area could short circuit and undermine negotiating process in other areas. A further problem was that the success of a single undertaking negotiating strategy presumed crosscutting coalitions. When groups are aligned in bipolar fashion, as they increasingly were at Cancun (rich versus poor), few side deals are likely to be made.

The Cancun Ministerial talks adjourned in July 2008 without any agreement. Many attributed this failure to a lack of political will on the part of key participants in both advanced and developing economies. At the outset of the Doha Round, the United States had a far-reaching trade agenda that included increased market access for nonagricultural goods in LDCs and furthering trade in services. As the talks progressed, however, the United States adopted a narrower position brought on by the twin political realities that President George W. Bush's fast-track authority would in all likelihood expire before the talks ended and that any agreement would have to include U.S. concessions to reduce agricultural subsidies. Such a reduction was certain to be politically expensive given the opposition of U.S. farmers, who had just secured passage of the 2002 U.S. Farm Bill that promised to increase agricultural support to American farmers. In addition, the EU's agricultural export support policies placed it at odds with both the United States and LDCs. Internal decision-making procedures in the EU limited its ability to offer concessions to LDCs that went beyond those already in place. Japan was also a defensive-minded participant in the Doha Round

---
| **Box 8.3** |

Spotlight

Trade Issues at Cancun

The difficulty in making strategy linkages can be seen in a short overview of four of the main items on the agenda at Cancun. Perhaps no issue was more central to the Cancun Ministerial conference than trade in agriculture. The Doha Declaration identified three pillars of agriculture policy where reforms were necessary: (1) improved market access, (2) reducing and phasing out market subsidies, and (3) reducing trade-distorting domestic support for agriculture, better known as subsidies. A variety of antagonistic positions characterized negotiations on these issues. The most significant ones were U.S. and EU opposition to cutting out domestic support systems that were demanded by LDCs and U.S. and developing state support for cutting out export subsidies for agricultural products, which was opposed by the European Union. Disagreements also existed over the extent to which LDCs needed to open up their markets. The United States pushed for substantial cuts in LDC tariffs, with those in Brazil and India being singled out as particularly in need of lowering.

A second and related point of disagreement over agriculture involved cotton. An agreement on cotton trade was not in the Doha Declaration but was added to the agenda just before Cancun. A coalition of Central and Western African states had singled out the United States, EU, and China for having subsidy policies that drove down the world price of cotton. The sectoral initiative put forward at Cancun called for immediately eliminating cotton subsidies and setting up a mechanism to compensate cotton farmers in LDCs for their losses. No resolution of the problem was reached at Cancun, and the failure to do so was of great symbolic importance to many developing states who saw this issue as a key test of the willingness of advanced economies to address agriculture issues more generally.

The Singapore issues (investment, competition/antitrust policy, transparency in government procurement policies, and trade facilitation) were a third area of controversy. Here, three groups were unable to reconcile their positions. One group, led by the EU, Japan, and South Korea, wanted all four of the above issues negotiated at Cancun. A second group composed of LDCs opposed any discussion of the Singapore issues. India was a leading advocate of this position. A third group of states, to which the United States and some developing nations belonged, wished to divide the Singapore issues. The United States was particularly interested in starting negotiations over transparency in government procurement and trade facilitation.

A fourth area of controversy concerned making special treatment for many LDCs a high priority. A significant narrowing of points of disagreement was reached in this area, but this was not enough to produce an agreement. The Doha Declaration recognized the right of LDCs to receive special and differential treatments in making the concessions demanded by WTO agreements. What was lacking was what this meant in concrete terms. Advanced economies tended to favor a needs-based approach in which special provisions would be tailored to the economic needs of specific countries. Many advanced economies advocated the adoption of more broadly stated and universally applied exceptions. Eighty-eight different proposals were presented at Cancun, with twenty-four special and differential proposals being forwarded to the next scheduled ministerial meeting in Geneva in 2004.

talks, interested primarily in protecting its domestic rice market and other politically sensitive agricultural areas from foreign competition.

China and India, two of the countries that organized the G20 (China having just joined the WTO at the Doha meeting), took leading roles in negotiating the position of LDCs, but each had little at stake in terms of making the negotiations a success. The result was that, while along with Brazil they were willing to aggressively advance the interests of LDCs to cement their place as leaders in trade negotiations, they adopted a generally defensive position on key issues involving questions affecting their economies. One estimate calculated that a Doha agreement would only add the equivalent of three days of growth to the Chinese economy and twenty-one days of growth to the Indian economy.

Problem Evolution and Development: The Stalemate Continues

The Doha Round did not officially end in Cancun. In the months that followed, a new Group of 5 (G5) formed to try and save the Doha Round. It was made up of the United States, EU, Brazil, India, and Australia. The United States facilitated movement toward a new set of talks in Geneva by proposing that market access and the elimination of agricultural subsidies be the primary focus of these talks. Further progress was made when the EU agreed to end agricultural subsidies "at some date" and the Singapore issues were removed from the Doha agenda. These negotiations led in July 2004 to a four-page framework agreement that set out guidelines for constructing the final Doha Round agreement. The new deadline for reaching this agreement was set for December 2005 in Hong Kong.[10] This date was crucial because President George W. Bush's fast-track authority was set to expire in June 2007, and December 2005 was the last date by which Bush could inform Congress that an agreement requiring its approval under fast-track procedures had been signed.

Negotiations resumed in Hong Kong as scheduled but with diminished hopes of reaching an agreement. The month before it had been announced that a comprehensive package agreement was unlikely and that delegates would concentrate on reaching agreements where consensus existed. Hong Kong set December 2006 as the new deadline for a Doha Round agreement. This date came and went with no results. Negotiating sessions in Potsdam (2007) and Geneva (2008) were deadlocked over agricultural trade issues, the foremost of which centered on the establishment of special safeguard provisions to protect poor farmers in developing countries.

The Hong Kong talks also set 2013 as a deadline for eliminating subsidies on agricultural exports, as LDCs desired. In the lead-up to the December 2013 Bali meeting, WTO secretary-general Pascal Lamy urged countries to manage their expectations and keep their ambitions in check. He also put forward a set of guidelines the simplicity of which indicates the great distance that remains to be traveled after over a decade of talks. Most important, Lamy called for a policy of "no surprises.[11] In the end, a minimalist agreement was reached at Bali to promote trade by reducing customs regulations. Still, the agreement was reached only after overcoming threats to block it by India among others. It sought to protect domestic industries from increased foreign competition. Prior to implementation the agreement would have to be approved by WTO members.

Conclusion: Distribution of Economic Power

The perceived need for a new round of global trade talks was a product of both long-term forces and short-term shocks to the international system. Free trade is a core ingredient of a globalized world economy. Free trade is also about power and influence. It is not simply about prosperity. For those who seek to avoid repeating the past, free trade is necessary to ensure the existence of democratic and prosperous countries.

There are many reasons for the inability of the Doha Round to produce a meaningful agreement. They include the changing distribution of economic power in world politics, the uneven benefits that countries have experienced as a result of previous agreements, and the expansion of the negotiating agenda to include trade issues not tackled in previous rounds. The problem remains how to bring free trade about and ensure its effectiveness. Global conferences carried out over several years in different locations and attended by representatives from some 150 states that produce agreements that then must be ratified by home governments are seen as ill-suited for the task of managing a global economy in an era in which problems appear with suddenness and great impact.

As they look to the future and try to determine the pathway that global free trade talks may take, supporters of the Doha Round put the best face possible on the inability to reach a new trade agreement.[12] They argue that even a limited or partial agreement would be critical to solidifying the gains in free trade and would reaffirm the legitimacy of the WTO process. One of the recommendations supporters put forward is to split the negotiating agenda into smaller pieces. Rather than have one all-encompassing agreement, states would pick and chose which agreements they would sign. A second recommendation is to limit the number of states participating in the negotiations. One suggestion calls for creating "critical mass" negotiations so that those states with the most at stake are present and negotiate an agreement that other states will have to accept out of necessity. Another suggestion to limit size calls for "coalitions of the willing" negotiations, whereby only those states interested in the outcome will negotiate the issue.

Critics openly raised the possibility that Doha's failure signaled the end of global free trade.[13] The major challenger to a global free trade system is one organized around preferential trade agreements (PTAs) such as the North American Free Trade Agreement (NAFTA) or Mercosur, a regional free trade area established between Argentina, Brazil, Uruguay, and Paraguay. More such agreements are on the horizon. The United States is involved in discussions with Asian states about creating the Asia-Pacific Free Trade Agreement, and with the European Union on creating the Transatlantic Free Trade Agreement. In principle, preferential trade agreements retain a strong commitment to free trade principles. Membership, however, is limited, thus creating the potential for competition and conflict among trade areas. This potential is reinforced by the fact that the establishment of a preferential trade agreement is often driven by political and security concerns as much as by economic ones. Together, these factors have led to disagreement over how valuable they are from an economic perspective and the extent to which they are compatible with global free trade.

A second challenger to the future of free trade agreements is the growth of state capitalism, which is an international trading system in which states dominate markets for political gain. The primary tools of state capitalism today are state-owned corporations; privately-owned "national champions," companies that receive favorable treatment by governments as they pursue overseas investments; and sovereign wealth funds that invest in foreign countries. In the view of those who view the development of state capitalism with alarm, the end result is an unequal competition between free market companies and state-supported or state-dominated firms.[14]

Case Analysis

1. Must Doha succeed? Why or why not? Do advanced economies or developing economies have the most to lose if Doha fails?

2. Which is the greatest danger to globalization: regional free trade agreements or the growth of state capitalism? Why?

3. Are advanced economies or developing economies most responsible for the problems encountered in reaching an agreement in the Doha talks?

4. Rank in order three factors that led to the success of the early GATT talks that are absent in today's trade discussions. Explain why you chose these factors.

5. What might a compromise Doha trade agreement look like? What countries will have to give up the most in order for it to be accepted?

6. What issues should be on the negotiating agenda for the next round of international trade talks after the Doha Round?

7. Select a current trade issue that divides countries. What are the positions taken by those involved? What is the potential for agreement over what should be done? What do you think should be done to end the dispute?

8. If a "coalition of the willing" was called together to construct an international trade policy agreement, what group of twelve countries would
   you invite? Why?

Suggested Readings

Andersson, Erik. "Who Needs Effective Doha Negotiations and Why."
    International Negotiation 17, no. 1 (2012): 189–209. Andersson argues
    that the interests of most states are fulfilled by stalling at the Doha talks
    because the goals of GATT have been largely fulfilled.
Baldwin, David. *Economic Statecraft*. Princeton, NJ: Princeton University
    Press, 1985. Baldwin's book is a classic account of the intersection of
    economics and politics in the conduct of foreign policy.
Capling, Ann, and Richard Higgott. "Introduction: The Future of the
    Multilateral Trade System." *Global Governance* 15, no. 3 (2009):
    313–325. This is an overview essay for a special issue that examines
    the problem of governing the global economy, with special attention
    given to the role of the World Trade Organization.
"Empty Promises, What Happened to 'Development' in the WTO's Doha
    Round?" Axfam Briefing Paper. July 16, 2009. Available online at
    www.oxfam.org/sites/www.oxfam.org/files/bp131-empty-promises
    .pdf. This paper argues that while Doha was intended to rebalance
    decades of unfair international trade policies, the negotiations have
    betrayed this promise.
Low, Patrick. "Potential Future Functions of the World Trade Organization."
    Global Governance 15, no. 3 (2008): 327–334. Low examines six key
    issues in thinking about the WTO's role in the future governance of a
    global trading system.
Mead, Walter. "America's Sticky Power." *Foreign Policy* 141 (March
    2004): 46–53. Mead offers a contemporary discussion of how trade
    serves as a source of power in world politics.
Nenci, Silvia. "The Rise of Southern Economies: Implications for the WTO-
    Multilateral Trading System." UNU-Wider Research Paper 2008/10.
    February 2008. Available online at www.wider.unu.edu/publications/
    working-papers/research-papers/2008/en_GB/rp2008-10/. Nenci reviews
    the participation of developing states in multilateral trading systems and
    examines the impact of the BRICS on the world economy.

Web Resources

Apostrophe

CATO Institute, www.cato.org. This public policy research organization
    site contains research and analysis on issues related to development,
    finance, monetary policy, foreign policy, and more.
Council on Foreign Relations, www.cfr.org. This think tank and publisher
    provides articles and reports in areas of development, economics, gov-
    ernance, and security.

Organisation for Economic Co-operation and Development, www .oecd.org. Access databases and reports on everything from agriculture and industry to development and economics in order to compare country performances.

United States Trade Representative, www.ustr.gov. Explore U.S. trade policies and agreements with other countries and access recent speeches and reports on various trade topics.

World Trade Organization, www.wto.org. Learn more about the WTO and its policies and actions and access data on international trade, tariffs, and more.

9

Food Aid as a Solution to World Hunger

World hunger is a persistent problem that defies simple definition or one-size-fits-all solutions. In some cases hunger is due to the absence of sufficient food supplies. Other times it is due to a lack of money. Sometimes both of these factors are at play. It can also be the result of natural or man-made disasters, or military conflict.[1] In the eyes of some, world hunger is looked at strictly in terms of the onset of a famine, a slowly developing disaster of mass starvation.[2] Even this broad definition leads to disagreements over whether famine in Indonesia is the same as famine in Africa. For others, world hunger includes periodic events such as famine but is not limited to them. World hunger as seen from this perspective is about ongoing problems such as malnutrition that reflect a long-lasting lack of access to food. Progress has been made in addressing world hunger defined as malnutrition, but problems remain. For example, the proportion of children under the age of five who suffer from malnutrition fell from 45 percent in the 1960s to 31 percent in the late 1990s, yet because of population growth the number of malnourished children has only fallen from 187 million to 167 million.[3]

Given both the repeated occurrences of famine and continued problems of malnutrition, it strikes many as surprising that relatively little progress has been made in setting up a system of global governance to more effectively manage world food supplies and establish safety nets for those in need.[4] It is not for lack of effort. Over 140 international conferences have been called to address problems related to global hunger. They have often been marked by the existence of wide disparities in power among those who attend, with those countries receiving food aid having little say, and by ideological positions that range from the endorsing of free markets to the embracing of a rights-oriented approach that stresses access to food as a fundamental right. As a result, what we find is the focus of this case study—a fragmented global governance system that attempts to deal with the problem of global hunger.

Our focus in this chapter is on the pathway of conflict and cooperation that states are travelling in their search for agreement over how to define the problem of world hunger and devise a global management system of rules, regulations, and organizations to put a solution into place.

We will take a somewhat different approach in examining this pathway then we have in other chapters. While we will continue to examine events as instances of conflict and cooperation, our primary focus in this chapter is on charting the evolution of ideas that have been put forward as the basis for cooperative global action to bring an end to hunger. At the center of our discussion is the movement leading up to the 1974 World Food Conference and developments on the pathway that followed the conference. Called in the aftermath of rapidly rising global food prices, the World Food Conference stands as a crossroads in the pathway that countries have travelled in addressing global hunger. It signaled a change in thinking about this problem. No longer would the needs of food donors be the conceptual centerpiece; from this point forward, the central focus would be on the needs of the hungry.

Our Concept Focus examines international institutions as instruments of global governance, as in this case study international institutions are the primary means by which the issue of global hunger is addressed. The chapter's Spotlight section takes a closer look at how a food crisis develops.

Defining Global Hunger: A Moving Target

Ideas matter. In the short run, they help frame policy options and aid policymakers coping with the inherent uncertainty involved in selecting among competing options when the outcome is unknown. In the long run, ideas become institutionalized in organizational rules and laws. They become part of the overall structural context in which policymaking takes place. Since organizational behavior and laws are slow to change, ideas continue to influence policy long after they are first introduced into the policymaking process. The result can be thought of as a layering of ideas that can pull policy in multiple directions and dilute the innovativeness of any single new idea later introduced. The influence of ideas is widespread and crosses policy areas. We continue to talk about trade policies in terms of protectionism and free trade even though it is increasingly difficult to determine what it means to be an American firm in an age of globalization. We also see the long-lasting influence of ideas today in efforts to understand cyberwarfare in which early Cold War concepts of deterrence, containment, and first strike are used to discuss cyberthreats.

In one sense, the pathway of ideas to addressing the problem of world hunger can be said to have begun with British cleric and scholar Thomas Robert Malthus. He argued in a 1798 essay that the human population was growing at a rate greater than the ability of the earth's resources to provide food to support it. The inevitable results were that population growth

---

| **Box 9.1** |

Case Summary

Global hunger is a problem that has defied solution despite the numerous international conferences that have addressed the issue. These meetings face a major challenge in defining the problem of global hunger, and ideas about how to fight hunger have changed over time, moving from a focus on the concerns of food aid donors to the needs of those receiving the aid.

Global Context

Global efforts to end hunger through food aid are made up of several different elements: the response to some sort of international food crisis, the donor's use of food aid to influence politics and affairs to its advantage, and the domestic needs of aid recipients.

Key Actors

- World Food Conference
- World Food Council
- World Food Summit
- United States

Motives

- The United States wanted to organize global food aid in such a way that it maximized U.S. control over the global supply and price of grain.
- The goal of United Nations (UN) officials and of countries receiving food aid was to shift the focus of global food aid away from the needs of donors to the needs of the poor, as well as to maximize the power of international organizations.
- Over time, advocates of increased food aid sought to broaden the context within which food aid was given to include issues of poverty and income rather than just the supply of food.

Concepts

- Food security
- Human security
- International regimes
- International organizations
- National interest
- Role of ideas in world politics

---

would sooner or later be stopped by famine and disease and that poverty would be a constant feature of society as people struggled to obtain food. While not unchallenged, the logic of Malthus's position made famines and food shortages appear as normal occurrences.

The poverty and hunger that engulfed much of Europe after World War I changed this passive acceptance of widespread hunger and unleashed three competing sets of ideas on how to respond to it. One set of ideas built on the arguments made by Malthus. This perspective argued for pursuing nationalist and protectionist trade policies that would isolate a country from world markets. Self-sufficiency in food became the goal, and where self-sufficiency could not be achieved, a country's foreign policy should try to obtain control over the needed foreign resources. The extreme statement of this logic is found in the ideas of *lebensraum* ("living room") that were advanced by Adolph Hitler as a rationale for Nazi Germany's expansion. One of the objectives of setting up the post–World War II free trade system (discussed in Chapter 8) was to ensure that such protectionist and nationalist thinking did not reappear.

Whereas the Malthusian outlook on world hunger is extremely pessimistic and all but denies the possibility of perfecting human society, a second perspective that emerged after World War I took an optimistic utopian outlook, one that was fully confident that the problem of hunger could be solved. The solution was said to lay with advances in scientific and technological research that promised to increase agriculture production to levels needed to support the world's growing population. For example, with the support of the Rockefeller Foundation, agriculture projects were begun in China and plant genetics studies designed to produce high-yield grains were undertaken in Mexico. Additionally, medical research on malaria and yellow fever were carried out in Africa. Efforts to overcome global hunger through scientific discoveries and technological breakthroughs continue today and are evident in efforts to develop genetically modified crops.

The third set of ideas was concerned with the need for food aid. What sets the idea of food aid apart from the Malthusian fatalistic notion of the certainty of future famines and the optimism of scientific solutions overcoming hunger is that food aid is an apolitical problem. There is nothing inevitable about providing food aid to those who need it. Doing so requires that states overcome the conflicts of values and interests that separate them and learn to cooperate. For those who saw food aid as the need to act, the course was clear. As one official asserted at a meeting of the League of Nations in 1921, "Argentina is burning its grain surplus; America is letting is corn rot in its silos; Canada has more than two billion tons of leftover grain—yet, in Russia, millions are dying of hunger."[5]

The Great Depression of the 1930s and then World War II brought a temporary halt to debates over how to deal with the problem of global hunger. The Great Depression turned policymakers' attention inward to addressing the needs of their own people and away from global nutritional concerns. World War II placed national security considerations above all others. As happened after World War I, however, the societal destruction that was left in the war's wake reenergized thinking about the problem of global hunger, the scope of which was immense. The United States sent 6.23 million tons of food to Europe from 1919 to 1926 in an attempt to feed Europe and stabilize European societies.

It is the pathway that the idea of food aid as a leading element in the fight to end global hunger has followed since the end of World War II that we will be concerned with for the remainder of this case study. As we will see, while the idea of food aid has advanced, its meaning has changed several times as it has moved down the pathway of international collaboration.[6] At least three major shifts have taken place in the postwar period. Initial post–World War II thought on food aid first viewed the issue from the perspective of food donors, and their primary concerns were about protecting their farmers and stabilizing the global food market so that prices remained firm.

This outlook changed with the World Food Conference, where primary attention shifted from donors to the recipients of food. The problem of global hunger began to be increasingly defined in terms of the needs of people rather than the needs of countries and the stability of global markets. The impetus behind this change in thinking was a sharp rise in world food prices, which produced fears that the world food system was failing and going out of control.

The third shift in thinking took place in the mid-1980s with a movement away from focusing almost exclusively on food as a solution to global hunger to an emphasis on the broader problem of livelihoods. The driving force behind this change in perspective was the famine that gripped Africa in 1984–1985. Supporters of this position noted that people in Darfur, Sudan, were willing to go hungry in order to keep animals alive and have seed to plant future crops, meaning they would risk starvation to ensure their future livelihoods.

Problem Setting and Origins: Vanishing Abundance

World War II was still being fought when the need for food aid for victims of the war was recognized by both governments and citizens. In 1942 the United States and Great Britain formed the Combined Food Board to supervise the distribution of food to Europe, and Oxfam (the Oxford Committee for Famine Relief) was established to provide food for Greece, which had suffered badly under German occupation. Attention also started to be directed to the broader issue of fighting hunger. The Atlantic Charter, a 1941 statement of war goals issued by U.S. president Franklin D. Roosevelt and British prime minister Winston Churchill, identified freedom from want as a universal human right.

The first major international step in making this goal a reality came in 1943 when delegates from forty-four countries met in Hot Springs, Virginia, to create the Food and Agriculture Organization (FAO) of the United Nations. One of the FAO's guiding principles was the belief that "freedom from want means a secure, an adequate, and a suitable supply of food for every man." In making this declaration, the delegates observed that "there has never been enough food for the health of all people." Accordingly, it was agreed that the starting point for food aid was the expansion of food production and the development of adequate food reserves.[9]

| **Box 9.2** |

Concept Focus

International Organizations as Instruments of Global Governance

International organizations (IOs) are central to many of today's efforts to establish systems of global governance.[7] This has not always been the case. By the end of 1865 there were only five IOs. On the eve of World War I, only twenty-nine existed. But in 2010 the *Yearbook of International Organizations* counted more than 5,000 active IOs. As the number of IOs has risen, so too has their role and influence in global governance.

The first major effort at institution-building for purposes of global governance took the form of multilateral, high-level political conferences known as the Concert of Europe. Composed of the "Great Powers" of the nineteenth century (Great Britain, France, Prussia, Austria-Hungary, and Russia), the concert's leaders came together periodically on matters of common interest and benefit. Most pointedly, they were interested in preserving the post-Napoleonic, politically conservative status quo in Europe. A second significant effort at building international institutions was the Hague Conferences of 1899 and 1907, in which large and small European and non-European states met to address the problem of war, promote the peaceful settlement of disputes, and place restrictions on military weapons inventories. A third and very different effort at international institution-building was the creation of public international unions that sought to bring order to policy areas that were demanding international cooperation to guarantee their smooth operation. Early examples include the International Telegraphic Union (1865) and the Universal Postal Union (1874). Technical expertise rather than political power or ideology was central to their successful operation.

The best-known international organizations for the purposes of global governance were created in the twentieth century: the League of Nations and the United Nations. The League of Nations was created in 1919 by the victors of World War I. Intended to legitimize the postwar distribution of power in the international system and prevent the kind of system-wide breakdown that took place in 1914 and led to war, the League of Nation's effectiveness was severely undermined by the "empty chair problem": the United States did not join the organization, the Soviet Union only joined in 1934 and was expelled in 1939, Germany's membership was limited to 1926–1933, and founding member Japan withdrew in 1933.

Twenty-seven years after its founding, the League of Nations ended. Its successor, the United Nations (UN), came into existence in 1945 and has evolved over time into an organization that in many respects is quite different from that envisioned by its founders. The UN was intended to be an instrument for keeping together the World War II alliance that defeated Germany and Japan, but the onset of the Cold War changed that. At various points in time, the UN has instead served as an instrument of U.S. foreign policy, a force for containing and preventing conflicts that threaten international peace, a platform for developing countries to advance demands for changing the structure of the international economic system, and a voice for human rights.

(Continued)

(Continued)

Two broad strategies exist for studying the role that international institutions play in global governance. The first starts from an instrumentalist perspective. From this viewpoint IOs are created by countries to serve and advance their national interests. As such, IOs prosper in terms of the support they receive from governments to the extent that they continue to serve these interests. When they fail to do so, they become marginalized and replaced as instruments of state foreign policy by other international organizations.

The second perspective for studying international organizations argues that IOs do more than serve state interests. They also exert an independent influence on state conduct. They are able to do so for reasons found inside of them and in the international system. Looking inward, IOs are not "empty shells" but develop value systems, cultures, and outlooks on global problems that influence the positions they take. Looking outward, the complexity of the international system, cross pressures from states on how to act, and information problems often present IOs with a high degree of latitude in terms of how to respond to a problem. As a result, IOs become independent sources of expertise on issues such as development and health. The language they use helps define problems and solutions, such as designating who is a refugee, and their approval lends legitimacy to state action, such as when economic sanctions and interventions are said to fall under the heading of "the responsibility to protect."[8]

Finally, it should be noted that while many see IOs as part of the solution to global governance, others see them as part of the problem. Their concern is what is known as the democracy deficit. This refers to situations in which important state decisions are made in settings that are, for all practical purposes, beyond the reach of citizens in those states. When a democratically elected government makes a decision to impose sanctions or bail out a debtor state, its policymakers can be held accountable for these actions through elections, but when such actions are made in an international organization, no such direct line of control exists. As globalization becomes more prevalent and the demand for coordinated international action more urgent, citizens find more and more important decisions made in political arenas in which they are spectators rather than the ultimate judge of the appropriateness of actions being taken.

Beyond this fundamental point, significant disagreement existed at the Hot Springs meeting on a number of issues that would later reappear on the pathway to fighting global hunger. The most significant disagreement was over the powers to be given to the FAO. The United States, supported by Great Britain, wanted the FAO to be limited in power to collecting data and serving as a consultative body. Many Latin American and non-European states, led by Argentina, favored creating a more powerful organization, one that would do more than redistribute food from producers to hungry consumers. They wanted the FAO to also restructure the international food system to encourage food production by additional countries such as them. No agreement was reached on this point as the meeting ended.

Large-scale global food shortages in the immediate post–World War II period drove home the need for immediate action. An FAO study concluded that a difference of 8 to 10 million tons existed between the amount of bread grain available for import to needy countries and the amount needed. Consequently, on its own initiative in May 1946, the FAO organized a meeting attended by twenty-one countries that created the short-term International Emergency Food Council to purchase food on the international market and distribute it to relief organizations for their use. The meeting also called for greater attention to be given by the international community to long-term food issues. This call led to plans put forth in 1946 for a world food board that would stabilize prices for agricultural goods on the international market and set up emergency stockpiles.

The World Food Bank soon fell victim to divisions based on competing national interests reminiscent of those that had surfaced in the creation of the FAO a few years earlier. Large grain-producing countries such as the United States favored giving aid directly to recipients rather than working through international organizations. Not only did these states fear the price impact of such global distribution agreements but they also wished to more tightly control who received food aid. Typically, conditions, or "strings," were attached to foreign aid. As a U.S. Department of Agriculture official observed at the time, "Governments are not likely to place the large funds needed for financing such a plan in the hands of an international agency over whose operations and price policy they have little or no control."[10] In the case of food aid, this meant that in the 1960s and 1970s significant amounts of food aid went to key allied states such as Israel, South Vietnam, Egypt, South Korea, and India.

Another complicating factor was early signs that the World War II unity of effort was beginning to fray and be replaced by Cold War competition. While the Soviet Union had participated in early FAO talks, evidence was now pointing to its refusal to participate in any global food aid plan. The Soviet Union was a major grain producer, and without its participation in aid plans, those plans were unlikely to succeed.

Both of these concerns contributed to the creation of the Marshall Plan, a foreign aid plan in which the U.S. sent $13.5 billion in foreign aid to Europe from 1948 to 1953.[11] Almost 25 percent of this aid was dedicated to providing food, feed, and fertilizer. In return, aid recipients had to propose and agree upon economic development plans. At first it appeared that the Soviet Union and its allies would participate in the plan, but this ultimately was not the case. The result was a hardening of the growing iron curtain divide of Europe into East (Soviet allies) and West (U.S. allies).

By 1950 the global hunger problem was taking on a different nature. Attention was increasingly directed at problems resulting from the growing surplus of food stocks produced by the leading agricultural exporting states. For example, wheat stocks in the United States, Argentina, Canada, and Australia stood at over 34 million tons in 1955. In 1961 they reached over 58 million tons. In Canada and the United States, coarse grains such as barley, oats, and rye stood at 32 million tons in 1955 and reached almost 82 million tons in 1961. One major concern was that these foods be dispensed in a way that did not create sudden swings in the international prices of food. A surge in demand could lead to increased food production in exporting countries that was not really needed, leading to further over-production. Rapidly declining food prices reduced the ability of developing economies relying on food exports for hard currency to buy other products on the world market needed for development. A second concern expressed by many was that food reserves be used for purposes other than profit or advancing national security goals. Speaking to this point in 1963, President John Kennedy stated that "we have the capacity to eliminate hunger form the face of the earth in our lifetime. We need only the will." [12]

Concern for market stabilization and the United States' own national interest was evident in the creation of the Food for Peace Program, also known as Public Law 480 (P.L. 480), by the Eisenhower administration in 1954. [13] It permitted the United States to sell food to countries in local currency and on concessionary below-market terms. In return, the receiving country could use their scarce hard currency reserves for other purposes, including developing new markets for U.S. agricultural goods, purchasing U.S. military equipment, or purchasing goods from other countries with U.S. permission. Reasonable steps were to be taken to ensure that agricul-tural prices would not be unduly disrupted.

This unilateral U.S. initiative was joined by an international undertak-ing with the 1967 establishment of the Food Aid Convention, which came into existence as part of the Kenney Round GATT (General Agreement on Tariffs and Trade) negotiations that were tasked with the goal of expand-ing global free trade opportunities and policies. By joining the Food Aid Convention, countries agreed to provide a minimum of 4.5 million tons of grain to developing countries, thereby ensuring a steady flow of grain and price stability in the marketplace due to the predictability of grain ship-ments. The governing body was made up entirely of donor countries, with receiving countries only attending occasionally and then only as observers. The operating rules of the Food Aid Convention and the food aid commit-ments of the members were revised and renewed periodically until 1999 when the decision was made to terminate the organization and replace it with the new Food Assistance Convention.

Concern over using food aid for other than national security purposes led to the creation of the World Food Program. [14] Established in 1963 as a three-year experiment, it was made a permanent organization in 1965. The idea for the World Food Program came for a proposal made in 1960 by George McGovern, who was the director of the U.S. Food for Peace Program. He called for establishing a multilateral emergency food aid pro-gram within the UN system that would respond to food emergencies due to famine and natural disasters, improve the nutrition and quality of life of the world's poor, and build self-reliance on the part of aid recipients. McGovern's proposal called for few additional resources to be devoted to the project. Its limited vision ran into opposition at the UN from those favoring a more extensive global commitment. U.S. opposition to these more ambitious efforts saw to their defeat.

The early optimism of the 1950s and 1960s over the scale of food production and the accompanying conviction that the food problem was one of excess production faded in the late 1960s.[15] Signs of trouble began to appear in 1968 when the U.S. corn crop began to shrink as a result of corn blight, a fungus that attacked hybrid corn. In 1972 Illinois, which in 1971 had produced one-fifth of the U.S. corn crop, reported that 25 percent of its corn had been destroyed. By then corn blight had spread to Canada, Japan, the Philippines, Africa, and Latin America. The global impact of this disease on corn supplies was still limited, however, due to large reserves of corn held by the United States.

New problems affecting food production occurred in 1972 when poor weather conditions led to sharply reduced crops in the Soviet Union, Asia, and Africa.[16] Where food supplies had increased by an average of 28 million tons per year for over a decade and had shown a sharp increase of 85 million tons in 1971, world cereal production in wheat, grains, and rice fell by 33 million tons. The Soviet Union responded by engaging in a massive campaign that resulted in the purchase of 28 million tons of grain. It was able to purchase this grain at low prices because it successfully hid the extent of its harvest shortfall and producers continued to assume that overproduction was the problem and were anxious to sell.

When the extent of the shortfall and the Soviet purchase became known, the result was a global buying frenzy that was contained only by dipping

Timeline
Efforts to Control Global Hunger

1941		Atlantic Charter signed
1942		Combined Food board formed
1943		UN Food and Agriculture Organization (FAO) established
1946		World Food Board founded
1947		Marshall Plan begins
1954		Food for Peace Program established
1963		World Food Program founded
1967		Food Aid Convention signed
1974	November	World Food Conference held
	December	World Food Council established
1996		World Food Summit meets
2002		Follow-up meeting (WFS+5) to the World Food Summit

further into global reserves. Yet even after releasing these food reserves, global food prices rose. The situation worsened in 1973 when the Organization of Petroleum Exporting Countries (OPEC) decided to raise oil prices (and thus transportation costs). This sent the price of food even higher. In 1971 the export price of wheat was $42 per ton; in December 1972 it was $104 per ton; in December 1973 it was $199 per ton; and it peaked at $220 per ton in February 1974. The price of rice showed a similar pattern. In 1971 it was $129 per ton; in December 1972 it was $186 per ton; by December 1983 it was $521 per ton; and it peaked at $630 per ton in April 1974.

Problem Definition and Response: A Divided United States

The first alarm bells warning of an impending world food crisis were sounded in February 1973 by the director general of the FAO. That warning was echoed at the meeting of the countries of the Non-Aligned Movement in September, which called for a special emergency joint conference of the FAO and the UN Conference on Trade and Development (UNCTAD) to address the problem of global food shortages and price instability. U.S. secretary of state Henry Kissinger gave added impetus to such a meeting when, in addressing the UN General Assembly that same month, he called for a world food conference that would "discuss ways to maintain adequate food supplies and to harness the efforts of all nations to meet the hunger and malnutrition resulting from natural disasters."[17]

Kissinger's motives for advancing the cause of global food diplomacy were many. First, while his career is most closely identified with Cold War foreign policy issues such as Vietnam, arms control, and covert action, Kissinger was no stranger to food as an international policy area and had used it as an instrument for pursuing his broader Cold War security goals. Second, domestic political considerations appear to have contributed to Kissinger's placing of the United States at the forefront of efforts to deal with the growing food crisis. Senator Hubert Humphrey reportedly dropped his opposition to President Richard Nixon's controversial nomination of Kissinger to secretary of state on the condition that Kissinger would support the concept of a world food conference. Additionally, Kissinger's initiative was designed to keep control of the food issue in the hands of the State Department and away from the Department of Agriculture, as Secretary of Agriculture Earl Butz opposed any expansion of food aid as a threat to food trade.

Spurred on by these calls for action, both the United States and international organizations took action, with the United States calling for the food crisis to be placed on the agenda of the UN General Assembly and the UN Economic and Social Council (ECOSOC) calling for the UN to convene an international meeting. The FAO also supported the concept of a UN conference and urged that the problem of food be discussed within the context of the economic development problems being experienced by many poor states.

The General Assembly agreed, and a resolution setting November 1974 as the date and Rome as the location of the meeting passed in December 1973.

As a prelude to the World Food Conference, the Preparatory Committee, which was open to all interested governments and recognized observers to UN meetings, began the work of forging an agreement on the issues that would come before the conference. It produced a two-part plan of action. The first part focused on food problems growing out of threats of famine, natural disasters, and other unexpected food production problems. The second part addressed the problem of persistent hunger among the world's poor. Here the Preparatory Committee called for a world food production policy and a world food security policy. Specific actions called for included giving the highest priority to increasing food production in developing countries, assuring adequate food availability, stabilizing and expanding world food markets, and creating a world food authority to oversee and coordinate the implementation of policies adopted under these headings.[18]

Such preparatory committee meetings are standard practice for large international gatherings, with the delegates to these meetings coming together largely to ratify the agreements produced in them or to modify the language in some minor way. In a break with the norm, the World Food Conference was also preceded by a meeting of independent experts from fifteen countries, known as the Rome Forum, that met in early November 1974 to examine the Preparatory Committee's proposals and make action recommendations to the upcoming conference. The forum concluded that solving the world food crisis was a question of political will and that the crisis was "more serious than any that has been faced since the end of World War II."[19] It called for immediate action to guarantee access to basic food, fertilizer, and petroleum supplies and long-term action to restore global grain supplies, create a stable pricing system for trade in food supplies, and set up a global grain reserve to deal with food crises. In the final analysis, the forum stated that the chief hope for bringing into existence a stable and reliable food system for the hungry in the developing world was maximizing the developing world's own food production capabilities.

The World Food Conference ran from November 5–16, 1974. Representatives from 131 countries, twenty-six UN organizations, and twenty-five intergovernmental organizations were in attendance. A parallel unofficial conference was attended by 161 nongovernmental organizations. Henry Kissinger gave the keynote address at the conference, asserting that "all governments should accept the removal of the scourge of hunger and malnutrition . . . as the objective of the international community . . . and should accept the goal that within a decade no child will go to bed hungry."[20]

While Kissinger's presence at the conference and his bold words addressing the meeting raised expectations about the United States' willingness to undertake energetic food aid initiative, Kissinger's words did not translate into action. The United States was divided on how to proceed. Opposition to Kissinger's position came both from Secretary of Agriculture Butz, who opposed any form of international control over U.S. food stockpiles and defined the problem of world hunger in terms of increased agricultural productivity, and Secretary of the Treasury George Shultz, who raised financial concerns about a vastly increased global foreign aid effort. Compounding matters further was that President Nixon had been forced to resign from office due to the Watergate scandal only months before, leaving the United States with a new president with a potentially new perspective. In the end, President Gerald Ford supported the position taken by Butz and Shultz that increased food aid would only lead to increases in grain prices, a reduction in the amount of grain available for other programs, and a strain on the U.S. budget.

Indications that Kissinger's call for bold action lacked support in the Ford administration were readily visible. After his speech Kissinger left for the Middle East to continue to seek a peace agreement to the Arab-Israeli conflict. Butz soon left the conference to fly to Egypt and Syria to help arrange grain sales to these countries. Democratic senators attending the conference as observers in the U.S. delegation, led by George McGovern and Hubert Humphrey, protested the lack of commitment to food aid in a cable to Washington, but U.S. policy did not change. The United States did not announce any increase in its food aid program, stating only that it was prepared to increase its level of food production while calling on OPEC countries to increase their funding of global food aid.

The United States was not alone in its unwillingness to commit to a concrete course of action that would realize the objectives set out by the Preparatory Committee. The Soviet Union stated that it was already providing technical assistance and called for domestic economic and social reform as the path most likely to result in increased food supplies. China called upon

---

| Box 9.3 |

Spotlight

Anatomy of a Global Food Crisis

The typical "anatomy" of a global food crisis contains three sets of factors.[21] The first set affects supply. Weather and climate conditions are key contributors to the onset of a food crisis. Floods, hurricanes, and drought are common short-term catalysts to food crisis, yet all can be linked to long-term problems. Extensive deforestation in Haiti, for example, has made that country much more vulnerable to the effects of floods and hurricanes. Soil erosion costs Haiti between 10,000 to 15,000 hectares of fertile land each year. Water scarcity can also dramatically cut agricultural production. Half a billion people live in water-stressed or water-scarce countries. It is estimated that by 2025 this number will increase to 3 billion.

The second set of factors in a global food crisis affects demand. Foremost here is the prevalence of poverty. A 2008 World Bank report estimated that 100 million more people exist below the poverty line due to rising food prices. For those people living at the bottom of the economic pyramid, an estimated 70 percent of their household expenditures are devoted to purchasing food.

Government policies also affect the supply of food available. The problem in developing countries is often the lack of adequate investment in agriculture. In advanced economies, the problem tends to be one of overproduction, in large part due to government policies that directly or indirectly subsidize production by providing for the purchase of agricultural products at guaranteed prices and limiting food imports from developing countries. Total domestic support for agriculture in the United States from 1995 to 2005, for example, was $16.5 million, and in the European Union it was $70 million. Large agricultural surpluses in advanced economies have led to these countries to export foodstuffs or send food abroad as foreign aid. The net result has been to suppress domestic food prices in the importing countries, which reduces the incomes of local farmers, making it difficult for them to escape poverty.

Changing patterns of food consumption also affect demand for food. Here also we can identify two different dimensions to the problem. The first is an intensification of demand for an existing food product due to such factors as increased population growth and wealth. China, for instance, had an annual rice consumption of about 50 million metric tons in the 1960s. By 2001 this had risen to some 137 million metric tons. A second dimension involves the demand for new types of food. Especially important here is the growing global demand for meat and dairy products. It is estimated that more than 75 percent of the increased demand for cereal and meat will come from developing countries. Because grain is a central product for raising meat, poultry and pork growth creates additional demand for grain.

A variation of this cascading effect of demand for grain due to changing consumption patterns is the growing interest in biofuels. From 2004 to 2007, 50 million tons of maize in the United States were harvested for biofuel production. Only 33 billion tons were harvested for food and feeding livestock. By 2020 the world price for maize for food consumption is expected to rise 26 percent as a result of increased investment in biofuels. If aggressive biofuel policies are adopted, some suggest a price hike of 72 percent could occur.

The third set of factors acts as transmission belts linking domestic and international markets. One of these is government hording of food stocks. Rice provides a particularly compelling example since it is described by many as a "political" crop due to the ability of sudden and sharp price hikes in rice to lead to regime-threatening political unrest in many Asian states. In the most recent food crisis, India and Vietnam, which together produce almost 30 percent of the world's rice supply, placed stringent export conditions on rice as the crisis grew. The Philippines, which imports about 6 percent of the world's rice, followed the opposite strategy by aggressively buying up rice on the international market to increase its national stockpile.

Financial speculation acts as a second transmission belt. As stock market prices fell and the housing market crashed, investors around the world increasingly turned to commodity futures as an area of investment. Historically, those engaged in buying commodity futures were direct users of these commodities, seeking to reduce their risk to production shortfalls. Now pension funds, hedge funds, and institutional investors began purchasing commodities futures in large quantities, speculating that prices would rise and produce profits for them from reselling the commodities. From 2005 through March 2008, the value of commodity futures contracts doubled to $400 billion.

developing countries to form a united front against capitalism and for them to become more self-sufficient in food as a step toward true independence. The European Economic Community called for buyers and sellers to enter into negotiations on establishing a global grain reserve but declined to talk about proposals for stabilizing grain prices. The Group of 77 (G77), composed of developing countries, proposed a series of changes in the structure of the international food trading system that it claimed would result in food at reasonable prices on the world market, reduced food consumption in rich countries, preference for developing country exports, the postponement of debt repayments, and an end to restrictive trade practices in developed states.

The World Food Conference passed twenty-one resolutions on topics ranging from fertilizers to reducing military expenditures so that food production might be increased to creating a global information and early warning system on food and agriculture. It was unable to reach an agreement on creating a powerful world food authority, however. The FAO was able to block this threat to its bureaucratic turf by building on general opposition to creating yet another international body within the UN system. At the same time, the FAO was defeated in its attempt to be designated as having primary responsibility for follow-up activities to the World Food Conference meeting, in large measure because its staff and recommendations were seen by many less developed countries as being overly influenced by the views of the developed world.

In place of a world food authority, the World Food Conference recommended creating the less-powerful World Food Council as a way of signaling a political commitment to the food problem.[22] It was to have two subcommittees, one for food aid and the other for food security, and be responsible politically to the UN General Assembly. The United States supported the creation of the World Food Council with the caveat that the council would have not have the ability to force actions upon governments or other UN organizations; its only power was to be moral persuasion. The next month, in December 1974, the General Assembly voted to establish the World Food Council. Its mission was defined as essentially one of political oversight and serving as a global conscience on food security issues. Three main tasks were identified:

- to periodically review major problems and policy issues affecting the world food situation,

- to make recommendations for remedial action, and

- to monitor and coordinate the activities of UN agencies and bodies dealing with food production, nutrition, food security, and food aid policies, with special attention given to the situation of the world's poorest countries.

Notwithstanding the lack of concrete accomplishments in moving the global food aid effort forward and the fact that serious divisions in how countries viewed the matter surfaced, early evaluations of the World Food Conference tended to be quite positive. Supporters noted that the conference had succeeded in emphasizing the importance of the human factor in food aid. No longer would these discussions be defined solely in terms of the needs of donors. The idea of food aid had been successfully publicized and re-invigorated.[23]

Problem Evolution and Development: Rise and Fall of the World Food Council

The World Food Council operated for some twenty years, during which time it held annual meetings. It was terminated in 1993. In its last report in 1992, the council observed that advances had been made in the developing world to reduce the number of malnourished and hungry but that the conditions in sub-Saharan Africa remained a major concern.[24] Additionally, the council urged that international efforts to provide needed food supplies to the breakaway states emerging out of the fall of the Soviet Union and to the formerly communist states of Eastern Europe should not come at the expense of food aid to the developing world but should be new food aid.

World Food Council reports consistently stressed two priorities for food aid: (1) providing help for low-income, food-deficit countries and (2) dealing with emergencies and supporting food production, nutrition enhancement, and food production programs. Its reports also stressed the importance of food trade and took advanced economies to task for policies that placed restrictions on agricultural imports from developing countries and provided export subsidies and price supports to domestic producers. Several of the World Food Council's recommends for remedial action led to institutional and policy innovations.

One recommendation was the identification of food-priority countries. These countries were defined as being at the core of the food problem and were singled out for special attention by international agencies, regional banks, and advanced economies. Forty-three countries were identified as meeting the criteria of a food-priority country, with eight classified as extremely severe cases. Combined, these forty-three countries held more than half the population of the developing world and over half its projected food deficit in the coming decade.

A second major initiative was the formulation of country-specific national food strategies. As the 1970s ended, many less developed countries continued to face a combination of inadequate domestic food production totals and high food import costs. What was needed, according to the World Food Council, was a long-term strategy in which national food policies were developed within the framework of a coordinated international support policy that was targeted on country-specific obstacles to increasing food production and reducing malnutrition. The concept of national food strategies received the endorsement of the UN General Assembly, and by 1982 about fifty developing countries were carrying out food strategy reviews. Thirty-two were doing so with the assistance of the World Food Council.

In spite of these and other accomplishments, the operation of the World Food Council was beset by a number of problems that ultimately led to its termination. Among them was the failure of many countries to send high-level ministerial representatives to the meetings and the tendency for presentations at plenary sessions to do little more that extol a country's accomplishments. At its 1992 meeting, members acknowledged that the World Food Council had not succeeded in realizing the political leadership and coordination role expected at the time of its creation. In the debate that followed, future UN secretary-general Boutros Boutros-Ghali called for the council's termination, asserting that while the council had not met its original and ambitious mandate, the UN system as a whole had succeeded in bringing global attention to food security problems. The United States, Canada, Japan, and Denmark also spoke out for ending the council's existence. This position held and the World Food Council came to an end.

With the termination of the World Food Council, the international community once again turned to periodic international gatherings to try and forge a consensus on food security issues. The inaugural post–World Food Council meeting took place in 1996 with the calling of the World Food Summit.[25] Unlike in 1974, no global food crisis served as a catalyst for this meeting. The FAO had judged the world food situation to have deteriorated only slightly in 1993–1994 from the previous year.

Instead, the principal force behind the conference was the ending of the Cold War, which unleashed a flood of UN-sponsored conferences dealing with a wide range of social, economic, cultural, and humanitarian issues. The World Food Summit was one of these. Other such conferences included the World Summit for Children (1990), the International Conference on Nutrition (1992), and the World Conference on Overcoming Global Hunger (1993). Whatever the merits and successes of these individual conferences, by 1996 they had cumulatively produced a sense of conference fatigue and given rise to a sense that the UN system had become overgrown with institutions that lacked distinct mandates or areas of responsibility. The World Food Summit was no exception to this sense of malaise.

A preparatory meeting for the World Food Summit was held in Rome in November 1996. It produced two documents that were adopted unanimously by the 190 countries in attendance. One of these, the "Rome Declaration on World Food Security," stated that everyone had the right to "access to safe and nutritious food, consistent with the right to adequate food and the fundamental right of everyone to be free from hunger."[26] This document identified poverty as the primary cause of world food insecurity and cited conflict, terrorism, environmental degradation, and corruption as contributing factors. The other document, the "World Food Summit Plan for Action," set 2015 as the target year for cutting in half the number of undernourished people.

In spite of the unanimous support given to the World Food Summit's declarations, the conference itself showed a distinct lack of unity. The United States asserted that the conference was not about generating new resources or institutions, or reopening existing agreements. From the U.S. perspective, the food security problem in the 1990s was large but geographically focused and not global in scope, as had been the case in the early 1970s. Most significantly, the United States stated that in participating in the conference it did not recognize any change in international law regarding the "right to food." It regarded the right to food as an aspirational goal that did not affect the existing responsibilities of countries or people.

Cuba's Fidel Castro spoke to the conference and roundly criticized it for failing to address the true causes of world hunger, which he identified as being rooted in capitalism, neoliberalism, external debt, underdevelopment, and conditions of inequality. He singled out the U.S. economic blockade of Cuba as violating human rights and contributing to hunger and misery in Cuba. Pope John Paul II cited spending on weapons, global indebtedness, trade embargoes, development policies that forced people to become refugees and leave their farms, and policies that stabilized or reduced the global population as among the fundamental causes of global hunger. The Vatican's position paper concluded that food was a universal human right.

The goal to cut in half the number of undernourished people in the world by 2015 was picked up by the Millennium Summit that coincided with the start of the UN's September 2000 meeting. Called for by Secretary-General Kofi Annan, the Millennium Summit was widely seen as the capstone conference that brought together the spirit and agenda of change that had emerged from the series of conferences held in the 1990s. Annan identified four major priority areas that demanded action if the UN was going to apply its founding principles to the twenty-first century: (1) freeing people from poverty, (2) freeing people from the scourge of war, (3) freeing people from the dangers posed by environmental destruction and resource scarcity, and (4) reforming the UN system to make it more effective in meeting these goals. The conference concluded with the passage of the Millennium Development Goals, which set a concrete agenda for global action.

A follow-up summit meeting to the World Food Summit (WFS+5) was held in Rome from June 10–13, 2002, to assess the progress made on achieving the goals laid out at the 1996 World Food Summit, including the goal of hunger reduction. One hundred and seventy-nine countries sent delegates to this conference, which was also attended by representatives from the European Community. Documenting progress was difficult. Instead of reducing the number of undernourished by 22 million a year, only 6 million per year had been helped. At this rate it was estimated that it would take forty-five years to achieve the 50 percent reduction in the number of undernourished that had been called for by 2015. More promising was the finding that since the World Food Summit, 150 countries had begun work on national food security strategies. Additionally, fifty-three countries and the European Community signed the International Treaty on Plant Genetic Resources for Food and Agriculture during the meeting.

The United States participated in the WFS+5 meeting and, though pledging to take action to meet the conferences objectives, it repeated its 1996 concerns regarding the perception that new rights and responsibilities relating to food were being created. The United States announced that it interpreted the "right to access to food" as meaning an "opportunity" and not a "guaranteed entitlement." Furthermore, it voiced the concern that the conference was entering into a sterile debate over the question of voluntary guidelines at the expense of addressing the problem of reducing poverty and hunger.

A parallel conference called by nongovernmental organizations (NGOs) took place alongside the WFS+5 meeting. This group rejected the WFS+5's declaration as disappointing and concluded that little progress had been made over the past five years. For progress to be made, existing liberal trade policies and the international organizations built around them, such as the International Monetary Fund, the World Trade Organizations, and regional trading blocs, had to be abandoned. In their place needed to be a focus on the food needs of people and communities. The NGO conference called for a new convention on food sovereignty that would become part of international law.

Taken as a group, these post–World Food Conference meetings show a slow and hesitant movement away from the idea of solving the hunger problem simply by providing more food to the needy. Instead, thought was modified toward defining the problem of hunger in a broader set of issues, ones we identified earlier as being livelihood issues. It was recognized that a "trickle-down" approach was called for, through which national development would lead to self-sufficiency and food for the poor. What were needed were programs to generate employment and incomes for the poor. A key element of the World Food Council's national food strategy was the notion that success in eliminating hunger required reforming social and economic policies that affected an individual's income and access to food. None of this alleviated the need to focus on creating and maintaining an emergency stock of food or increasing food production, but it did represent a change in the context within which these solutions were pursued.

Conclusion: Continuing Crisis

In summarizing the pathway of efforts to end global hunger, one leading authority on the subject referred to it as "a story of good intentions."[27] The pathway has not ended in abysmal failure. It has not, however, succeeded in putting an end to the problem of global hunger. This became painfully clear in 2007–2008. In the one-year period from March 2007 to March 2008, the world experienced what *The Washington Post* characterized as the greatest food crisis in a generation.[28] During this time the price of meat increased 10 percent, dairy products by 48 percent, rice by 74 percent, soy by 87 percent, and wheat by 130 percent. Prolonged drought in Australia, along with poor harvests in the United States and Europe, were cited as major underlying contributing factors. Countries adopted a variety of responses. Japan, the Philippines, South Korea, and Taiwan placed large orders on international commodity markets. This, in turn, led others to do the same in order not to be left without wheat or other commodities. India banned the export of basmati rice. China announced to its worried public that it had a large rice reserve but fears were not easily calmed. In southern China there were reports of food hoarding, and panic buying of rice occurred in Hong Kong. In many countries people had no choice but to buy lesser quality food supplies or go without. Others took to the streets. Some 20,000 factory workers participated in protests against raising food prices in Bangladesh, and at least fifty people were injured. In all, fifteen countries experienced some form of food violence. In Haiti rioting forced the prime minister to resign. But others profited. Food was "the new gold." So intense was the trading on commodity markets that "some traders were walking off the floor for weeks at a time, unable to handle the stress."[29]

What steps should be taken next? One option that has already drawn much support is to untie food aid.[30] That is, rather than use one's surplus food stocks as food aid, such as the United States does via P.L. 480, donor countries should buy food from national and regional sources. It is argued that this would increase the incentives for local farmers to produce food and get food aid to where it is needed more quickly. Others call for establishing a global food aid compact.[31] This compact would be all inclusive, with both donors and recipients being able to join. Strong monitoring and enforcement mechanisms would be put into place, and, most importantly, binding codes of conduct would be set for all signatories.

From the perspective we have taken in this chapter, the most significant next steps may be found in further development of the ideas about the meaning of hunger that guide action on this pathway. One notable development already occurring is viewing the problem of global hunger in subjective terms: What matters is not whether an individual is hungry in terms of some formal measure of nutrition or food intake. What matters is the individual's subjective perception of the situation.[32]

Case Analysis

1. Is hunger primarily the responsibility of national governments or the broader international community acting through international organizations?

2. If you were asked to measure the amount of hunger in the world, what five indicators would you select? How would they be weighted?

3. Is it better for a country to rely on imported supplies or emphasize self-sufficiency? Why?

4. Should the World Food Council have been terminated? Why or why not? What might have been done to prevent its termination?

5. Should food aid be an instrument of foreign policy used to advance a country's own national interest? Can food aid ever be politically neutral?

6. If you were drafting a global food aid compact, what obligations and responsibilities would you assign to donor countries, international organizations, private nonprofit aid groups, and recipient countries?

7. In looking at the pathway of conflict and cooperation for fighting global hunger, how would you rate the relative importance of ideas versus national interest or power in the search for a policy?

8. Considering the ideas that shaped policymaking on the pathway we outlined in this case study, are there any ideas missing that should have been considered?

Suggested Readings

Clapp, Jennifer. *Hunger in the Balance: The New Politics of International Food Aid*. Ithaca, NY: Cornell University Press, 2012. Clapp examines the history of food aid efforts and prospects for the future. Special attention is given to debates in the United States and questions surrounding genetically modified crops.

Hanjra, Munir, and M. Ejaz Qureshi. "Global Water Crisis and Future Food Security in an Era of Climate Change." *Food Policy* 35, no. 5 (2010): 365–377. This article takes a forward-looking perspective on the problem of food security and calls for added investment in food security.

Kneteman, Christie. "Tied Food Aid: Export Subsidy in the Guise of Charity." *Third World Quarterly* 36, no. 6 (2009): 1,215–1,225. Kneteman examines the issue of tied food aid in the context of World Trade Organization negotiations. The United States is described as the largest donor of food aid and the most consistent user of tied aid policies.

Pinstrup-Andersen, Per, and Anna Herforth. "Food Security: Achieving the Potential." *Environment* 50 (September 2008): 48–60. This article reviews the past, present, and future of food security and presents a framework linking food availability, food security, and nutrition.

Shapouri, Shahla, and Stacey Rosen. *Food Security: Why Countries Are at Risk*. Washington, DC: Economic Research Service, Department of Agriculture, 1999. This is a study of sixty-six countries in terms of food availability and food distribution. The report anticipated an intensification of food insecurity in many countries.

Shaw, D. John. *World Food Security: A History since 1945*. New York: Palgrave Macmillan, 2007. Shaw presents a comprehensive review of efforts to create international bodies to improve world food security.

Web Resources

Center for Global Prosperity, Hudson Institute, http://gpr.hudson.org. The center generates awareness with the public and government leaders about the role of the private sector in the creation of economic growth; the site includes a policy center on global food issues that contains commentary and information.

Economic Research Service, U.S. Department of Agriculture, www.ers .usda.gov. Explore fact sheets, reports, and maps about U.S. agriculture and food production and access information on U.S. food security and other topics.

Focus on the Global South, www.focusweb.org. The site for this organization focused on the developing world and an alternative to globalization offers commentary and information on issues such as climate, land, and trade.

Heritage Foundation, www.heritage.org. This U.S. think tank promoting conservative public policies offers reports, analysis, and videos on issues including agriculture, energy, and the environment.

Institute for Policy Studies, www.ips-dc.org. This U.S.-based progressive think tank links issues of peace, justice, and the environment in the United States and globally and offers reports and commentary on topics ranging from the global economy to foreign policy.

United States Agency for International Development, www.usaid.gov. Access information on U.S. aid efforts in areas including agriculture and food security, as well as data and reports on U.S. aid.

10 Global Monetary Reform after 2008

T he pathway of conflict and cooperation in managing the global monetary system has been a long one that has featured many policy initiatives, and it is one that remains in transition following the 2008 global financial crisis.[1] We have passed through a period in which currencies were identified, defined, and, most importantly, had their values determined largely by the policies of national governments. We thought of currencies as operating within national boundaries. Going abroad meant exchanging one's currency for that of the country you were entering. This imagery, while true for most currencies, was not true for all. A select few, such as the U.S. dollar, held a privileged position and could be used internationally with great ease. It was considered to be "good as gold."

This is no longer the case for even the most highly desired international currencies. What we have seen as a by-product of globalization is increased competition among currencies in cross-border financial and trade transactions. The U.S. dollar is still highly sought after, but users of money now have a choice. They can turn to the euro, the Chinese yuan, or artificial currencies to finance their investments, conduct trade transactions, or calculate their profits. Even more important is the reality that national governments have lost their ability to unilaterally manage the value of their currencies. Increasingly, practical control over the value of currencies has shifted to market forces. Benjamin Cohen has gone so far as to assert that national governments are now "hostage" to abrupt shifts in market sentiment.[2] He goes on to note that market forces are not elected by the public nor are they created equal; there is no market equivalent of equal voting rights. Moreover, markets are not accountable to politicians or the public. They are also subject to abrupt changes in direction often with little warning or apparent logic. Money may flow in one day only to flow out the next, greatly complicating the efforts of national governments to engage in policymaking designed to strengthen their domestic economies. Because of this some now refer to international trade and financial transactions as "casino capitalism."[3]

What is needed for state officials to regain control over international monetary policy is the creation of some form of effective international monetary governance. This need not take the form of a world government or a global organization, but it does require a global consensus on rights, responsibilities, and values. It also requires that the governance system created be seen as legitimate by all countries, both weak and strong, as well as by businesses, investment firms, and banks.[4] These are the types of problems and issues that countries faced in formulating a response to the 2008 financial crisis, which produced a global market collapse on the scale of the Great Depression of the 1930s. By mid-2008 shares of commercial banks listed in Standard & Poor's 500 index had lost about one-third of their value. As we shall see shortly, what began as a crisis for the U.S. financial system went global and forced states to act together, overcoming their differences and cooperating to reach an agreement, if the global economy was to be put back on solid footing.

Our Concept Focus in this chapter explores globalization and examines the perspectives of both supporters and critics. The Spotlight section takes a closer look at the forum chosen for international monetary negotiations and considers options such as the International Monetary Fund, G8, and G20.

The G20 Response to the 2008 Financial Crisis

The 2008 financial crisis did not come as a total surprise as the international monetary system has been shaken by a series of financial crises over the past several decades. For a number of reasons, however, monetary crises do not lend themselves to easy solutions. First, the international economic system is an arena of competition in which individuals, groups, firms, and governments vie for profits, jobs, prestige, and wealth. This competition creates winners and losers. Even if everyone gains, some will gain more than others. Too much competition can be dangerous and can create conditions under which the entire structure of the international economic system collapses, turning everyone into losers. This happened in the 1930s when countries tried to protect their domestic economies through the adoption of protectionist policies as the world slid into a depression. Instead of isolating themselves from global economic conditions, protectionism only made their domestic economic problems worse by inviting retaliation from other countries. Protectionism cut off competition from foreign goods, thereby saving jobs, but it also led to other countries closing off their markets, which resulted in lost jobs.

Second, monetary policy cannot be isolated from a country's broader foreign and domestic policy agendas. One set of foreign policy issues affected by the onset of a financial crisis may be grouped under the heading of "rules of the game." For example, prior to 2008 global economic relations were carried out according to what many called the Washington Consensus. Its central elements included fiscal discipline on the part of governments that minimized global indebtedness, free trade and investment policies, privatization and deregulation of businesses, and flexible

---

Box 10.1

Case Summary

The economic problems experienced in the United States in 2008 spread through the rest of the international system as panicked investors pulled out of other financial markets, setting off a global monetary crisis that required coordinating a response to minimize losses.

Global Context

After the end of the Bretton Woods system in 1970, the international monetary system lacked a strong centralized management system run by states. Instead, the value of currencies fluctuated on the basis of supply and demand. The free market currency exchange structure of the system remained intact, however, despite periodic monetary crises. By 2007–2008 globalization's effects were so widespread that the overall boundaries of the system could not contain the new crisis, forcing states to come together and repair it.

Key Actors

- United States
- European Union
- G20

Motives

- Domestic interests prompted some governments to pour money into their economies to stimulate them and avoid a long-term economic depression and its related costs, such as unemployment and loss of productivity.
- Other nations, also protective of their domestic interests, responded to economic concerns by cutting spending and reducing programs.

Concepts

- Globalization
- Interdependence
- International organizations
- Nationalism
- Protectionism

---

exchange rates. The financial crisis discredited many of these ideas. In the realm of domestic politics, international financial policies may lead to growing poverty and citizen discontent due to the loss of export opportunities, decreased foreign investment, and the institution of austerity measures. Often the result is antigovernment protests that threaten government stability, such as in Argentina in 2000, when an estimated 80,000 protestors took to the streets.

Policymakers were concerned with monetary crises and their consequences when they outlined the post–World War II international economic order that came to be known as the Bretton Woods system. One of the system's key components was the International Monetary Fund (IMF), which was designed to stabilize the international monetary system by linking currencies to gold and setting limits on how much countries could unilaterally change the value of their currency relative to gold.[5] Officially, international transactions in the Bretton Woods system were based on the gold value of currencies, and in theory currencies could be exchanged for their value in gold. But as global trade grew, it became clear that the supply of gold could not match the value of the currencies being exchanged. Instead, the U.S. dollar became the top international currency.

This status proved to be a mixed blessing. On the one hand, it provided the United States with benefits denied to other states. As French president Charles DeGaulle noted, it allowed the United States to run large budget deficits without fear of having the value of its currency collapse because everyone wanted dollars.[6] With the Lyndon B. Johnson administration's decision in the late 1960s to fund both the Vietnam War and the War on Poverty, this became the case. Whereas another country would have been forced to choose between spending money on "guns" or "butter" because of the large debt it would accumulate, the United States was able to do both because of the global demand for dollars. On the other hand, the top currency status of the dollar also created a very real problem for the United States. So many dollars were held outside the United States that it became virtually impossible for the country to correct the large trade imbalance it was running. Whereas another country might adjust downward the value of its currency to make exports cheaper and imports more expensive, the United States could not.

The Bretton Woods system ended abruptly with President Richard Nixon's August 1971 decision to suspend the convertibility of dollars into gold. With the end of Bretton Woods, international monetary relations came

Timeline
International Financial Crises and Response

1929–1939	The Great Depression
1948	The Bretton Woods system is implemented, setting the international monetary system on the gold standard and creating the International Monetary Fund.

(Continued)

(Continued)

1970s		Mortgages begin to be bundled together into investment pools that are bought and sold on the stock market.
1971		The Bretton Woods system ends; the U.S. dollar "floats," its value set by the market.
1974		Oil prices drastically increase under an OPEC embargo; Western nations respond by cutting interest rates, which leads to global stagflation.
1982		A rise in interest rates on loans to developing economies in Latin America results in many being unable to pay their debts, which leads to the adoption of structural adjustment policies.
1997		An Asian financial crisis begins when a Thai firm with billions of dollars of debt is unable to make payment on its loan, causing a domino effect in the region.
2006		The U.S. housing market peaks and home values begin to fall.
2008		The U.S. housing crisis impacts mortgage lenders and investment companies, leading the U.S. government to pump money into comp anies deemed "too big to fail" to avoid greater economic collapse.
		The G20 meets in Washington to discuss measures to steer reform of international monetary policy and manage the financial crisis.
2009	April	The G20 meets in London and pledges billions to the IMF for countries in need of assistance.
	October	In Pittsburgh the G20 agrees to the Mutual Assessment Process to monitor how domestic actions impact other countries and to minimize any negative results.
2010	June	At the G20 summit in Toronto, attention is diverted to the growing crisis of Greece's indebtedness and the potential impact on its EU member states.
	November	At the G20 conference in Seoul, unilateral, nationalist interests begin to dominate the agenda
2011		In Cannes the G20 finds it increasingly difficult to move forward with international monetary policy reform.
2012		The Mexico G20 summit fails to move reform forward.

to center on a series of crisis-managing efforts.[7] The first came in December 1971 with a meeting of industrialized countries at the Smithsonian in Washington, D.C., that brought about an agreement to realign currency values against the dollar. The net effect was to devalue the dollar. Less than two years later, in March 1973, this agreement was replaced by one that allowed the value of the dollar to "float" and be determined by market forces. The value of the dollar declined further.

Oil-exporting countries were particularly hard hit by the devaluation of the dollar. The price of oil was calculated in dollars, and thus profits now declined. The October 1973 Arab-Israeli War provided the members of the Organization of Petroleum Exporting Countries (OPEC) an opportunity to drastically increase their profits and use oil as a political weapon against Israel's allies. On October 16 OPEC announced a 70 percent increase in the price of oil; the next day it announced production cutbacks. By 1974 the price of oil had quadrupled. Along with great profits for OPEC members, this also created a global financial crisis as advanced economies shrunk under the weight of high oil prices. The response of Western bankers to the sudden increase in oil prices was to cut interest rates, a move that had the unexpected effect of producing a global stagflation—high inflation (the rapidly rising price of goods and services) and high economic stagnation (low economic growth rates).

The oil crisis brought an end to the era of cheap gasoline. It also served as a model for other developing states whose primary source of wealth was the sale of natural resources. The large profits made by OPEC provided the banks it invested those profits in with large amounts of money to lend. With advanced economies slow to recover from the oil crisis, banks began to look at developing countries, especially those with exportable natural resources, as investment targets. This set the stage for the next global financial crisis that erupted in developing economies in 1982.[8] By the end of the 1970s, the debt level of developing countries had increased significantly. At the beginning of the decade, Latin American states owed $29 billion; this figure had grown to $159 billion by 1979 and reached $327 billion in 1982. Typically these loans were adjustable interest rate loans that were reset every six months, making developing states vulnerable to changes in the international financial system. By 1982 interest rates were rising significantly and these countries found it harder to attract investors. This pattern repeated itself in the 2008 financial crisis when investment funds shrunk dramatically due to bad investments and slowed economic growth.

U.S. banks had been at the forefront of this lending spree, and they now found themselves holding dangerously large amounts of Latin American debt, with the result that their corporate bond ratings began to decline. Among those whose ratings were lowered were Chemical New York, First Chicago Trust, Bankers Trust, and Manufacturers Hanover.

The crisis broke into the open in August 1982 when Mexico announced that it could not make its next interest payment. By the end of 1982, a total of forty countries had made similar announcements. Several countries, led by Mexico, Venezuela, Argentina, and Brazil, renegotiated their debts with foreign banks. In return for having their debts renegotiated, developing economies were forced to adopt a series of structural adjustment policies. These policies included privatization, liberalization, and tax reform, and countries had to undertake them in order to get funding to reduce their debt. A reduction in government spending on domestic welfare programs was also typically required. Working with the IMF, the United States put forward two recovery plans, both of which required structural changes on the part of debtor countries. The 1985 Baker Plan coupled structural adjustments with postponing some debt payments. When this failed, the 1989 Brady Plan called for coupling structural adjustments with debt relief and debt reduction. It took more than a decade for both developing countries and banks to fully recover.[9]

At first glance it would appear that states and international organizations had been able to come together in an effective fashion to meet this monetary crisis. Closer inspection, however, reveals that this was not the case. When the next financial crisis erupted in Asia, the IMF tried to apply the same solution used here. The problem was that the root cause of the Asian financial crisis was different and thus it demanded a different solution. This tendency not to be able to learn from the past or look for signs of an impending monetary crisis has been commonplace on the pathway of conflict and cooperation in international monetary reform.

The Asian financial crisis was led by the Four Tigers (Hong Kong, South Korea, Taiwan, and Singapore). The early 1990s saw Asia become a major force in international trade through the adoption of export-led growth strategies.[10] This growth triggered an investment boom in commercial and residential property, as well as in large government-supported infrastructure projects that were financed by foreign borrowing. This wave of building resulted in a significant amount of excess capacity in the real estate market and in ill-considered infrastructure ventures brought on by the overly close relations between the government, bankers, and industrialists.

In February 1997 a major Thai property development firm announced that it could not make its next scheduled $3.1 million interest payment on an $80 billion loan. As the scope of the problem became clear, currency speculators began selling off the Thai bhat at its current dollar value in anticipation of its eventual devaluation, at which point they could repurchase bhats at a lower dollar cost. The Thai government began using its foreign reserves to buy bhats in the international market to protect the currency's value. This rescue effort failed, and on July 2 Thailand announced that the bhat would float against the dollar. Its value quickly declined by 18 percent, which deepened the Thai financial crisis because repayment had to be in dollars.

With its foreign exchange reserves now all but exhausted, Thailand called upon the IMF for help. The IMF provided assistance but insisted upon Thailand's adoption of the standard set of structural adjustment policies that it had applied to Latin America in the 1980s. Before it had run its course, the financial crisis that began in Thailand spilled over to Malaysia, Singapore, Indonesia, South Korea, and Japan. The political and economic fallout from the crisis was widespread. The value of Asian currencies fell dramatically. Millions of Asians fell below the poverty line as a result of businesses failing and reduced profits. Rulers in Indonesia and Thailand were forced to resign. Globally, the reduced economic growth in Asia led to a drop in world oil prices. Reduced oil revenues, in turn, were held responsible for a financial crisis that gripped Russia in 1998.

Box 10.2

Concept Focus

Globalization

Globalization has become the favored shorthand expression for conveying the underlying dynamics and structure of the international system today. Best defined in the abstract, globalization is the process by which economies develop and become integrated with others in the world. Common elements of globalization include a fast-paced and deeply penetrating process of interaction among states, societies, and individuals and the loss of control over that process and its consequences for all concerned. In addition, there are three typical ways in which globalization is used to help us make sense of the international system.

The first way the term *globalization* has been employed is as an ideology. Ideologies are comprehensive sets of beliefs that allow one to make sense of the world. Several different categories of globalization ideologies exist today, the most prominent of which are pro-globalization ideologies that see globalization as a positive force. Adherents of this perspective tend to see globalization as an irresistible force that promotes democracy, peace, and prosperity for all, and they define it largely in economic terms in which underlying market forces beyond the control of governments are the driving force. Standing in opposition to this perspective are two anti-globalization ideologies. On the political right is a populist-nationalist, anti-globalization ideology that sees globalization as a dangerous force that can and must be countered by national action. Proponents of this position see globalization as threatening the independence and self-sufficiency of the average citizen through the exporting of jobs, which leads to increased unemployment and the lowering of wages. On the political left, anti-globalization ideologies also stress the theme of exploitation and call for counteraction. A common theme of these anti-globalization ideologies is the demand to replace globalization from above with globalization from below, meaning that the economic and political benefits of globalization identified by pro-globalization ideologies can only be realized if the

(Continued)

(Continued)

poor citizens of developing countries are their driving force rather than multinational corporations and banks.

A second way in which globalization is used is as a vehicle for understanding how the international system came into being. Here, globalization is considered as a process. We can think of how this process operates in two different ways. One method is to differentiate between structural forces that have led to globalization and agency attributes that have moved it forward. Structural forces include capitalism and a rationalist-scientific mode of inquiry that seeks to understand and control the world rather than attribute events to forces beyond human control. Agency attributes include the ability to develop new technologies and to engage in cooperative and regulatory undertakings.

A second method by which globalization as a process can be understood is to divide it into stages. Economist Thomas Friedman, who holds a pro-globalization ideological perspective, divides the process of globalization into three stages: Globalization 1 was spread by armies and navies that colonized the world; Globalization 2 was spread by multinational corporations; and Globalization 3 is being spread by individual entrepreneurs. Some would argue we have entered Globalization 4, in which the dominant force is state capitalism in the form of sovereign wealth funds, state-owned natural resource corporations, and national champions, which are privately owned or privately controlled firms that receive special backing from governments.

The third frequent way in which globalization is used is as a way of characterizing the global condition today. Defining globalization in this manner directs our attention to two important theoretical issues. One issue is, should globalization be thought about strictly in economic terms, or is it multidimensional? And, if multidimensional, how do those dimensions interact? If we look at the responses of anti-globalists to globalization, it is clear that they see globalization in political, cultural, and societal terms, as well as in economic ones. A second issue is how do we measure globalization? How do we compare the level of globalization today with that from a decade ago or measure the degree to which a country is involved in globalization? This challenge is no different from that facing those who see the world as becoming more peaceful or democratic or for those who argue human rights abuses are on the rise. Because globalization is a concept that is subject to so many different meanings and interpretations, it presents an especially difficult global setting within which to manage conflict and cooperate for a mutually beneficial solution.

Problem Setting and Origins:
A U.S. Crisis Goes Global

In the early 2000s, the epicenter of the financial crisis moved again.[11] The chief operating office of Credit Suisse, one of the world's leading financial services company, with headquarters in Switzerland, described the 2008 financial crisis as "probably the longest anticipated crisis we have ever seen."[12] This time the crisis began in the United States, where a strong housing market had resulted in a large influx of foreign money into the country. The net result was that interest rates on home mortgages remained low while home prices rose due to high demand.[13] Historically, U.S. banks lent money to homeowners and then held on to that mortgage until it was paid off. The money they lent came from the funds people and firms deposited into savings accounts. Moreover, after the Great Depression of the 1930s, banks were required to have sufficient funds on hands to cover the deposits they held. Beginning in the late 1970s, changes were made to the way mortgages were financed. Holders of mortgages such as banks and investment houses began to bundle them together into investment pools, which were then sold and resold to investors on the stock market. These sales provided lenders with additional funds that could be used to make more mortgages, provided investors with profits from the sale and resale of these bundled loans, and lowered the risk of investment failures due to bankruptcy since each bundle contained many different mortgages. Two of the largest companies involved in creating these bundles were Fannie Mae and Freddie Mac, both congressionally created, stockholder-owned corporations.

To protect themselves against mortgage failures, investors purchased insurance contracts on their investments known as credit default swaps. As with any insurance policy, the issuer of the policy earns money so long as the event being insured against does not occur. One of the problems with this insurance program was uncertainty over the real value of the properties being insured. They were bundled together in so many ways and rebundled so often that determining the actual value of properties became almost impossible. In 2007 the face value of these credit default swaps was $62 trillion. One of the largest credit default swap providers was American International Group (AIG).

With mortgages now bundled, the credit worthiness of the individual borrower became less of an issue because so many loans were being put together in a single package that the risks of one loan going bad were dramatically reduced. Moreover, so long as the values of homes kept going up, the danger of a loan being defaulted on by a borrower who could not make payments or sell his or her house seemed very small. One result of this was that many loans were now being given to individuals who would not have otherwise been seen as being credit worthy. All of this changed in 2006 when the price of homes peaked and began to fall. Bankruptcies began to rise rapidly as borrowers who had used adjustable rate loans to buy their homes (loans whose value was not fixed but could rise periodically) found their monthly payments skyrocketing. As the rates to these loans increased, borrowers could neither obtain affordable refinancing nor sell their homes to pay off their mortgage because the prices of their homes were falling rather than going up.

The implications of this change in the housing market quickly rippled through the banking and investment industries that had been buying and selling bundles of mortgages. In September 2008 alone, Lehman Brothers investment firm, one of the largest investment companies in the United States, went bankrupt. In an effort to save it from the same fate as Lehman Brothers, the U.S. Treasury Department deemed AIG "too big to fail" and extended to it an $85 billion line of credit. Lending institutions faced a straightforward problem: having borrowed money to purchase these bundles of mortgages, they had to pay off their debts, but the mortgages were rapidly losing their value due to declining real estate prices. Even worse, paying off debts meant that there was less money available for making new investments. This set off a downward spiral. As losses mounted, wary customers pulled funds out of mortgage-backed investments, reducing the amount of money available to lending institutions to invest or pay off debts. Selling off assets—mortgages—to acquire money to pay off debts would only drive down the price of homes even more. U.S. firms now began to reduce inventories and lay off workers. This then led to reduced consumer spending because of the growing numbers of jobless workers

The crisis soon became global as panicky investors began to pull out of other investment markets for fear that U.S. economic troubles would soon spill over and impact their economies.[14] The result was a worldwide shortage of investment funds. Economies that had begun to grow rapidly were hit particularly hard because many had borrowed heavily in order to export goods to the U.S. market, where consumer demand had been strong but was now rapidly shrinking. Faced with a shortage of money, these nations now had to turn to the IMF for help in paying off their debts. In 2008 the IMF loaned Ukraine $16.5 billion and Hungary $15.7 billion. It also approved standby funding of $7.6 billion for Pakistan. Even the poorest countries could not escape the effects of U.S. economic troubles. Economic growth in Africa, for example, began to decrease in the second half of 2008. Nigeria and Angola, which depended heavily on oil exports, and Botswana, which depended on diamond sales, were among the hardest hit. Poverty reduction efforts in Africa were also negatively affected, with the IMF calculating in 2009 that the crisis would result in an additional 7 million people living below the poverty line of $1.25 per day that year and another 3 million by 2010. Globalization had allowed what began as a problem rooted in the operation of the U.S. housing market to quickly become a monetary crisis that now demanded a global response.

Problem Definition and Response: Looking Inside and Outside the State

As the full scope of the financial crisis was revealed, countries adopted a twofold response strategy that unrolled in five phases. Domestically, countries sought to contain the scope of the financial crisis by implementing a series of corrective measures. On the international scene, they sought to find a way to put the global monetary system back together.

The domestic reform efforts to deal with the growing monetary crisis followed a similar pattern in most countries.[15] A first phase sought to contain the spread of the financial crisis. Governments lowered interest rates, increased the money supply, and put together financial rescue plans for failing firms. In the second phase, they focused on taking steps to minimize societal losses due to the economic slowdown and the recession that soon followed. Stimulus packages served as the primary policy tool in this phase. Among the larger programs put together were those by China ($586 billion), the EU ($256 billion), Japan ($396 million), and Mexico ($54 billion). The global scope of the crisis created significant problems for this strategy because it greatly reduced the possibility that countries could export their way out of the recession by increasing production (and thereby employment) and selling goods abroad since consumers everywhere were hard hit by the financial crisis.

The third response phase focused on fixing the financial system and restoring confidence in financial institutions. The fourth and final domestic-centered phases, which as of 2013 remained ongoing, involved steps to move domestic economies back to their pre-crisis states. The economic challenge here is significant. Estimates produced in early 2009 calculated that as much as 40 percent of the world's wealth was lost in the 2008 crisis.

On the international front, the Group of 20 (G20) was the instrument of choice for constructing a strategic global response to the 2008 crisis.[16] Established in 1999 after the Asian financial crisis, the G20 is a forum for cooperation and consultation on international financial matters among the finance ministers and central bank governors from twenty major economies. The heads of government of the G20 countries met for the first time to address the global financial crisis in Washington, D.C., in November 2008, at the urging of European leaders. This summit came to be popularly referred to as "Bretton Woods II," a reference to the location of the founding meeting where the IMF and World Bank were created.[17] This meeting was the first in a series of G20 summit conferences dedicated to restoring the international monetary system to health.

While the G20 Washington summit conference in November 2008 was not free from conflict and controversy, it did not produce serious disagreements. The sense of crisis was now firmly established, as was the need to show unity. Chinese president Hu Jintao observed that "to effectively cope with the financial crisis, countries in the world should enhance confidence, increase coordination and intensify cooperation . . . .The reform should be conducted in a comprehensive, balanced, incremental and pragmatic manner."[18]

The major point of division among those present was the desire of European leaders to take dramatic action to build a new international financial architecture (although they disagreed on how to do this and who was

---
| **Box 10.3** |

Spotlight

Selecting a Setting for International Monetary Negotiations

One of the most difficult issues facing countries seeking to cooperate on solving a problem of mutual concern is identifying a setting. The selection of a location sends a signal as to the intent and outlook of those coming together. Three possible settings presented themselves as venues for international negotiations after the 2008 financial crisis. The first was the International Monetary Fund (IMF). After U.S. president Richard Nixon's 1971 decision to take the dollar off of the gold standard in 1971, instead allowing its value to "float" and be determined by market conditions, the IMF shifted its attention from managing international financial transactions to providing financial assistance to countries under severe economic distress.

The IMF's past experience in dealing with financial crises and its large bureaucratic base were strong reasons to rely on it during the 2008 crisis. Offsetting these advantages, however, were significant political liabilities. The IMF operated on a weighted voting system, with those countries that loaned the most money receiving the most votes. For many, this effectively made it an instrument of the most powerful countries. Reinforcing this perception was that IMF loans came with "strings attached"—the recipient was required to undertake a series of pro-market and budget-cutting reforms as a condition for receiving the loan. Finally, the IMF was perceived as having a "one-size-fits-all" mindset on how to deal with economic crises. Rather than take national conditions into account, the same rescue formula was applied everywhere. In the most recent Asian financial crisis, this strategy made the problem worse. In sum, if the IMF were selected as the site for global monetary negotiations, it would have signaled a desire by the rich to impose their will on the poor.

The second option from which to design a global strategy was the Group of 8 (G8). Originally made up of five economically developed democracies (the G5: the United States, Great Britain, France, Japan, and West Germany) it was convened in 1974 by President Gerald Ford and met informally following the 1973 oil crisis to discuss how to respond to rising oil prices and their impact on developed economies. Canada, Italy, and Russia later joined, making it the G8. (The EU also participates in G8 meetings, making its actual membership nine). The G8 has no permanent bureaucratic foundation or offices. Its presidency rotates among the members, and the country holding the presidency is responsible for planning and organizing the annual summit conferences. Over time, the agenda of these meetings has expanded beyond narrow economic issues to include such global topics as combating terrorism, providing health care, protecting the environment, and energy efficiency.

As it lacks an infrastructure to implement and oversee decisions, G8 meetings tend to focus on the setting of agendas and the proclamation of aspirational targets rather than the creation of concrete action plans. A major limitation on the G8's effectiveness as an instrument for the solving of global problems was its limited membership. In an attempt to address this problem, in 2003 Brazil, South Africa, Mexico, India, and China began participating in its meetings, creating what some refer to as the G8+5. Periodically, other countries have been extended invitations to participate as well. This increase in informal membership did little to blunt criticisms of the G8 as too small and privileged an organization to serve as a forum for addressing global problems. From the perspective of rich countries, using the G8 as a location for addressing the global monetary crisis had the advantage of involving fewer countries and allowing members to operate in a more informal and less bureaucratic fashion. As with the IMF, however, selecting the G8 would have been perceived by developing countries as a slight since their only representation there was through BRICS (Brazil, Russia, India, China, and South Africa), countries whose economic standings were far different from many of those in the G8.

The third option to oversee the global approach to handling the 2008 financial crisis—and the one selected—was the G20. Its membership consists of the finance ministers and central bank governors of nineteen countries, plus a delegate from the EU. Typically, these officials meet once a year. As with the G8, the G20 is designed to be a forum to promote cooperation on international economic matters. As a group, these economies represent some 85 percent of the world's gross national product, although they are not, strictly speaking, the largest nineteen national economies in the world. Their combined gross national product and larger number, however, does help to ensure that any decision arrived at would have the support of the world's major economies. Like the G8, the G20 lacks a permanent bureaucratic infrastructure or staff. The chair rotates among members and is responsible for establishing a temporary administrative structure and organizing summit meetings.

For developing countries, the G20 was the least objectionable of the three available alternatives, even though they continued to lack significant representation. Unlike the IMF, which uses a weighted voting system and whose meetings produce binding agreements, the G20 works by consensus and produces less restrictive statements of intent. The G20 has also taken steps to increase the representation of developing countries. After the November 2010 Seoul summit, it was agreed that up to five nonmember countries, including two African countries, would be invited to attend. Earlier, after the June 2010 Toronto summit, the G20 had decided to engage in a policy of outreach to nongovernmental organizations.

responsible for the crisis) and the desire of U.S. president George W. Bush to pursue a moderate, reformist agenda in which the G20 restricted itself to

1. developing a common understanding of the root causes of the crisis,

2. reviewing actions already taken and that would be taken to address the crisis,

3. formulating common principles for reforming financial markets,

4. identifying an action plan to implement those principles, and

5. reaffirming a commitment to free-market principles.

The reformist agenda won out, and a broad laundry list of statements emerged from the meeting that provided symbolic evidence of action but did little to address the underlying issues.

The leaders of the G20 met again in London in April 2009, and there was a greater sense of expectation that this summit would need to go beyond making broad statements of cooperation and concern. Working against this outcome was the emergence of a clear division in thinking among G20 members over how to proceed. The United States and United Kingdom favored creating a new set of stimulus plans, while France and Germany opposed such a move for fear of creating an even larger debt crisis. The depth of this disagreement was clear for all to see when Bush's successor, Barack Obama, and British prime minister Gordon Brown appeared together at one press conference and French president Nicolas Sarkozy and German chancellor Angela Merkel attended another.

In the end the London summit papered over these differences with yet another broad agreement. A declaration pledged $1.1 trillion to deal with the global financial crisis, to help countries in need of assistance, to give to multilateral development banks to help especially poor countries, and to promote world trade. It was also agreed that greater regulations and oversight in such areas as transparency and accountability would be adopted with respect to the actions of financial institutions. Finally, the new Financial Stability Board was established to promote cross-national cooperation and to serve as a financial crisis early warning system.

Six months later the G20 met in Pittsburgh to review the progress made since London and to chart the next steps forward. The key agreement here was establishing a mutual assessment process through which countries would become more aware of the international spillover effects of steps they took to help their own economies recover. This awareness, in turn, was expected to create pressure to change policies that threatened the economic health of others. The Pittsburgh summit also called for making the G20 the primary forum for international cooperation on monetary matters and for increasing the voice of emerging markets and developing countries in IMF decision making. On the development front, it called for increased IMF funding for development projects and greater access to food, fuel, and finance for the world's poorest countries.

When the G20 heads of state met for their fourth summit in Toronto in June 2010, a new division arose. Some countries, such as the United States, China, and India, wanted to bring an end to the global financial crisis's worldwide slowdown in economic activity by spending on business investment stimulus packages. Others, led by France, Germany, and the EU, favored reducing spending and balancing budgets to avoid mounting debt problems and thereby encourage economic investment and growth.

The Toronto meeting took place against the backdrop of yet another unsettling development in the international financial crisis. In May the value of the euro hit a four-year low, and stock prices in Asia tumbled. The spark was the virtual collapse of the Greek economy. For decades Greece had run large budget deficits as a means of financing government social programs. A large amount of this debt, as much as 80 percent, was held by foreign investment firms and banks. The global economic recession sparked by the U.S. financial crisis aggravated this problem by reducing government income from tourism and shipping and causing lenders to become wary of taking on new debt. In early 2010 evidence also surfaced that the Greek government had deliberately lied about the level of its indebtedness in order to maintain a favorable debt rating.

Investors now faced the prospect of losing 30 to 50 percent of their money invested in Greek securities. Greece, in turn, faced the prospect of being unable to finance some $11.3 billion of debt. The IMF and EU provided Greece with immediate loans amounting to $142 billion in an effort to deal with the situation. The EU also announced a massive rescue package for other EU states to draw upon to prevent a reccurrence of the Greek crisis. Leading candidates to default next on their national debts were Italy, Spain, Portugal, and Ireland. An even greater fear was that the European monetary union would collapse. How to respond to this crisis divided EU members, and the solutions adopted led to social unrest in the affected countries.

Once again the G20 meeting ended with a declaration that gave both sides the ability to declare victory. The United States had to accept more specific set of targets and deadlines for deficit reduction measures than it would have preferred. The members agreed to deficit cuts by 2013 and to stabilize their overall debt load by 2016. But the final report also directed veiled criticism at Germany and China. Germany, which had a large trade surplus, was urged to encourage the purchase of imports to help global economic recovery. China, which also ran a large trade surplus, was called upon to change its monetary policies so that its currency exchange rate would more accurately reflect its true value compared to other currencies. Even before the financial crisis hit, the United States had argued that China was deliberately undervaluing its currency, the yuan, relative to the U.S. dollar as a way of encouraging Chinese exports and creating balance of trade problems for the United States.

The final planned installment of G20 meetings scheduled to address the global monetary crisis was held in Seoul, South Korea, in November 2010. By the time leaders arrived in Seoul, much of the enthusiasm and commitment to global monetary reform that had spurred early discussions had vanished. IMF and World Bank officials now openly expressed fears that proposals for global cooperation would lose out to unilateral initiatives designed to further national interests. The end result, they argued, would be to allow money to flow freely to those countries with the least stringent regulatory policies, a move that potentially would set the stage for another global financial crisis.

The United States and China remained in the eye of the storm. In the case of China, the issue continued to be its growing trade surplus. That China was running a huge trade surplus was not debated. What was at issue was the extent of the danger this posed. Germany was also running a large trade surplus and was reluctant to criticize China, as were countries such as Australia, Saudi Arabia, and South Korea that benefited greatly from trade with China. The primary irritant in the case of the United States was a decision by the Federal Reserve Board to print an additional $600 billion to inject into the U.S. economy through Treasury bond purchases. The move produced criticism from Germany, Brazil, and others, who argued this was currency manipulation because it would potentially have the effect of keeping U.S. interest rates low, which would help stimulate U.S. economic recovery but also raise the value of other currencies, thereby hurting the recovery efforts of other countries.

The final outcome of the G20 meeting at Seoul was a call for further action that was short on specific details and continued to rely on peer pressure rather than new rules to bring a new financial order into existence. The core initiatives put forward by the Obama administration sought to have G20 countries adopt a formula for measuring the progress that each made in reducing its budget deficits or trade surpluses, as well as rules for determining how large such imbalances might be. The IMF would also be empowered to evaluate to what extent G20 member countries impacted others in either a positive or negative way. Opposition to setting specific targets in these areas was led by Germany and China, with the result instead being indicative guidelines and an agreement not to engage in competitive currency devaluation policies and to keep trade imbalances at a sustainable level.

Problem Evolution and Development: Fading from View

After the Seoul summit, G20 heads of government began meeting on a yearly basis. As with those earlier summits, the decisions arrived at in these summits consisted largely of a laundry list of points of agreement and action with little follow-through, an unsurprising outcome since the G20 lacked a permanent bureaucracy and its decisions take the form of policy statements rather than binding agreements. Only one of thirteen commitments made at Seoul (fiscal consolidation) received a perfect compliance score of the G20 countries.

The closing Cannes summit communiqué was characterized as inclusive, vague, and modest in its scope, a situation born of continuing disagreements among member countries on two different levels. First, the United States continued to take positions that were inconsistent with those of many of its European allies. Second, a behind-the-scenes tug-of-war continued as the core G8 countries within the G20 and the broader set of developing economies in the G20 maneuvered for influence in these deliberations.

In another point of similarity with earlier G20 summits, instead of focusing on the continuing underlying problems of reforming the global monetary system, these more recent summits came to fixate more on the problem of the moment. The crisis of the moment at Seoul was the fear of currency wars, in which countries engage in a competitive race to weaken the value of their currencies in order to stimulate their own economic growth by keeping interest rates low, thereby encouraging consumers to spend more and businesses to borrow more. A weakened currency also makes that country's exports cheaper and imports from other countries more expensive. At the Cannes summit in 2011, the euro crisis and the political, social, and economic situations in Italy and Greece had replaced the global economic slowdown brought on by the 2008 financial crisis as the major point of concern. At Los Cabos, Mexico, in 2012, side meetings between the United States and Russia on the situation in Syria garnered as much media attention as did economic issues.

By the time the Seoul summit ended in 2010, the worst of the 2008 financial crisis appeared to be over. Yet problems of slow and sluggish growth continued in the United States and other advanced economies as investors remained unsure whether the actions taken by the G20 would be sufficient to produce sustained global economic growth. Recall that the pathway travelled to the creation of the G20 summits encountered a series of earlier monetary crises, each of which took place under a different set of constraints. In 2008 globalization was the new and dominant feature of the pathway. The implications it held in terms of the speed with which the crisis spread caught policymakers unaware. Globalization's political and economic leveling effects would also require states to find a new way of responding to the problem. Earlier solutions such as the United States taking the lead in the debt crisis and the IMF taking the lead in the Asian crisis could not be repeated. The danger this holds for international monetary policy is that the further 2008 fades from view, the greater will be the tendency to assume that the problem has been solved. An appreciation for the depth of the challenges faced and the challenges of finding an agreed-upon course of action will be lost.

Conclusion: Challenges to the G20

Evaluations of the G20's efforts to construct an effective global response to the 2008 financial crisis are mixed. Generally, high marks are given to the early conferences.[19] In particular, the involvement of the emerging economies that existed beyond the boundaries of the G7 is seen as a significant achievement given the limited role they have traditionally played in international negotiations. The G20 summits are also credited with taking a pragmatic and adaptive approach to problem solving, which created a setting that encouraged countries to treat the 2008 financial crisis as an international problem requiring global cooperation rather than one that was purely domestic in nature and could be solved unilaterally.

The G20 benefitted from its early successes. As one observer noted after the Cannes summit, the G20 has gone "from being almost out of work to having its financial resources hugely increased."[20] Later conferences are seen as having produced diminishing returns as the political commitment of G20 countries to coordinated action and the effectiveness of economic coordination plans declined with the passage of time. Instead of operating in a crisis atmosphere, the G20 must now produce consensus in a time of perceived calm and normalcy. While international monetary problems continue to exist, they are no longer seen as threatening the survival of the global monetary system.

This new condition presents the G20 with a great challenge to its legitimacy as the primary source of global monetary governance. Three dimensions to this challenge stand out. The first is membership. Is the G20 too small, or is it too large? Is it still an instrument of domination by those whose currencies dominate the international monetary system? If so, can it incorporate the voice of those countries that possess the quasi currencies or pseudocurrencies found at the bottom of the international currency pyramid, such as Panama, Cambodia, Laos, Bolivia, and many of the poorer African countries?[21]

A second challenge is to gain the allegiance of rising economic powers.[22] China stands out as a country whose currency is taking on an important international dimension, yet it remains cautious if not reluctant to take on major leadership responsibilities, recognizing that in doing so it may forfeit some of its freedom to ignore G20 decisions when they might harm China's national interest. The remaining BRICS (Brazil, Russia, India, and South Africa) present another challenge to the G20's continued legitimacy as a source of international monetary governance. While all are rising economic powers, there is little else that unites them. The sources of their respective economic strengths and political orientations provide only a fragile foundation on which to base a united front, especially when the issue is making rules as opposed to dissenting from decisions made by others.

Finally, there is the problem of institutional design, or how you build global organizations to solve problems.[23] The G20's success came from its ability to serve as a type of global steering committee and not as an institution that involved itself in ground-level operations where the details of its decisions were implemented. These actions were left to national authorities. Holding on to and building upon its legitimacy would require the G20 to establish itself in the role of a global steering committee while at the same time avoiding becoming too deeply involved in dictating policy, as the IMF did in the debt and Asian crises. Two decision-making risks face the G20 here. The first is the danger of making overly lofty commitments that member countries lack the interest or capability of meeting. The second is perpetual inaction. The costs of each are high. Taken together, these dangers will likely downgrade the status of the G20 from a valuable steering committee to that of just another international organization created to solve a problem that became largely irrelevant with the passage of time. They may also increase the likelihood of another global monetary crisis catching world leaders by surprise.[24] Should that be the case, the pathway to conflict and cooperation that global monetary reform has travelled down will take yet another sharp turn as policymakers seek to formulate a global response. The constraints they find imposed by globalization will be even more pronounced on that path, as may be the need to bring in additional countries and nongovernmental organizations to solve the problem.

Case Analysis

1. Describe to what extent governments are hostage to the operation of unpredictable markets in financial matters.

2. In the Concept Focus box we noted that globalization can be seen as an ideology, a process, and a condition. In what order of importance would you put these three views of globalization in looking at the pathway of international monetary policy? Explain your reasoning. Pick another policy area and construct a similar ranking. Are they the same or different? Why?

3. To what extent are the causes of the global debt crisis, the Asian financial crisis, and the 2008 global financial crises similar in their underlying economic and political conditions?

4. How might the situation look today if, instead of using the G20 as the basis for international coordination, one of the other two options (IMF or G8) had been selected?

5. To what extent were less developed countries listened to in addressing the 2008 crisis? Should they have been listened to more?

6. Has the G20 outlived its usefulness? In looking to the pathway of cooperation and conflict that international monetary policy will travel down in the future, what type of steering committee system should be created in its place?

7. Could the United States have exerted a stronger leadership role in the G20 deliberations? If so, should it have?

8. If you were to construct a Bretton Woods II international economic management system to prevent the next global economic crisis from happening, what institutions would you create and what power would you give them?

Suggested Readings

Cohen, Benjamin. *Global Monetary Governance*. New York: Rutledge, 2008. Cohen presents a solid overview of the issues and challenges of establishing global rules for the international monetary system.

Eichengreen, Barry. "Fortifying the Financial Architecture." *Current History* 109 (January 2010): 17–23. This article presents an economist's evaluation of what has been accomplished and what issues remain. It also discusses what options are open to governments.

Helleiner, Eric. "A Bretton Woods Moment: The 2007–2008 Crisis and the Future of Global Finance." *International Affairs* 86, no. 3 (2010): 619–636. Helleiner discusses the uniqueness of the Bretton Woods meeting and proposes a four-step path forward for international financial reform.

Jickling, Mark. *Averting Financial Crisis* (Washington, DC: Congressional Research Service, 2008). This is an early account of the financial crisis that explores the question of what makes a financial crisis and identifies government options.

Kindleberger, Charles. *Power and Money.* New York: Basic Books, 1970. Kindleberger presents a classic account of the role that money plays in international politics.

Nanto, Dick. *The Global Financial Crisis: Analysis and Policy Implications* (Washington, D.C.: Congressional Research Service, 2009). This report provides an excellent discussion of the origins of the financial crisis, the issues involved, and the impact of the crisis on different regions of the world.

Web Resources

Brookings Institution, www.brookings.edu. This Washington, D.C.-based, nonprofit public policy organization offers research and commentary on issues and events such as economics and fiscal policy.

CATO Institute, www.cato.org. Find research and news from this public policy research institute on issues ranging from monetary policy and housing markets to international economics and development.

International Monetary Fund, www.imf.org/external/index.htm. The official IMF site includes research and news on individual countries, as well as a statistics database that can be explored by country or topic.

G20, www.g20.org. This site is a go-to resource for current G20 coverage in the news and information on the most recent summits.

Peterson Institute for International Economics, www.iie.com. This site for this private, nonpartisan, and nonprofit public research institution contains news and research on issues of international economic policy by country, region, and topic.

11 Uniting Europe through a Common Currency

This chapter examines efforts by European leaders to bring about a further unification of Europe through the creation of the euro. The pathway of conflict and cooperation these leaders have travelled to reach this point dates back to the end of World War II when Winston Churchill called for creating a United States of Europe. The path has been marked by a series of great successes, but more recently this success has begun to look somewhat hollow. When financial crisis struck some of the newest members of the European Union (EU) in the early twenty-first century, it threatened both further progress toward establishing a United States of Europe and even the existence of the EU itself.

A look back at international politics shows that Europe and European powers (Great Britain, France, Germany, Russia, and Austria-Hungary) were at the center of most major political, economic, and military events prior to the twentieth century. European powers fought and cooperated with each other through a series of alliances and coalitions. The central principle underlying their political and military interactions was sovereignty. The principle of sovereignty placed very real limitations on the types of cooperation that occurred between states and how that cooperation was achieved. According to it, each government was recognized as having full control over its territory and had the right to enter into, withdraw from, or reject any international agreement presented to it. Cooperation thus could not be imposed or forced upon states.

The principle of sovereignty remains a cornerstone of international politics, but where once it was highly valued and seen as protecting the rights of states, it is now increasingly seen as an outmoded idea that stands in the way of providing economic and military security. European states were among the first to confront this changing reality. They did not do so voluntarily but because of changes taking place in the structure of the international system. World War II had left them politically, militarily, and economically weakened. They were no longer at the center of world politics. Instead the United States and Soviet Union were the dominant powers, and Europe was reduced to being a potential battlefield as these two superpowers fought for global supremacy. In its now-weakened position, the need for cooperation took on a new urgency and led many to propose pathways that would strip European states of their sovereignty.

Our Concept Focus in this chapter is on integration theory, the set of ideas that provides the foundation for thinking about how to unify independent countries into a larger political unit. Our Spotlight section will examine in more detail the positions taken by Germany, France, and Great Britain in negotiations over the adoption of the euro.

| Box 11.1 |

Case Summary

The creation of the euro has unified the European political and economic landscape, though inconsistencies in policies have led to disagreements; Britain refuses to adopt the euro, preferring to keep the pound as its currency.

Global Context

At the end of the Cold War, concerns that West Germany would dominate European monetary policy and adopt a more independent stance led to efforts by its neighbors to encourage greater European cohesion through the adoption of a single currency. In the twenty-first century, a common currency has encouraged economic growth and worker mobility, but it has also linked the vulnerabilities of one euro country to all.

Key Actors

- France
- Germany
- Great Britain

Motives

- France wished to control German economic power as part of its broader goal of using European economic power as a pillar of French foreign and domestic policy initiatives.
- West German leaders wanted to secure West Germany's place in Europe and maximize the prospects for European economic stability by separating financial decisions from political influences as much as possible.
- Never fully committed to the idea of membership in the European Union, Great Britain looked with suspicion at the creation of the euro, concerned that it would result in a loss of sovereignty.

Concepts

- International political economy
- Integration theory
- Sovereignty

Creating the Euro

What began in 1950 with a French proposal to create what would be the six-country European Coal and Steel Community grew over time into what is today the twenty-seven-member European Union. The EU stands today as a symbol of prosperity, social justice, and democracy. It also serves as proof that countries with a history of repeated wars can transform their relations and create a region of peace and cooperation. The crowning achievement in this transformation came on January 1, 1999, when the euro became the official currency of eleven members of the EU.

This positive imagery has been called into question by the depth of the Greek financial crisis of 2009, the subsequent problems encountered by other EU members, and the EU's struggles to respond in a politically and economically effective fashion. It was believed by many that European unification would not and should not stop with the creation of the euro. A common metaphor used to capture the dynamics of European unification was that of riding a bicycle. No matter how slowly, the rider must constantly peddle and keep going forward. Stopping is not an option. If the rider stops peddling, the bicycle will become unbalanced and the rider will fall. The euro crisis and the EU's struggle to respond to it in a coherent fashion suggested the bicycle was in danger of falling. Now the fear is that European integration will falter and slide back, in the process creating doubts elsewhere in the world about the value of attempting to replicate the European experience. The establishment of a truly European foreign defense policy seemed likely to be the next area for greater cooperation and one that now appears in doubt.

Three different storylines compete for prominence today in the politics of the EU. The first is that "the worst is over." While the financial crisis that erupted in Greece in 2009 has not been fully resolved, the very existence of the euro and the EU itself are no longer threatened. Financial problems will continue, but they are aberrations—exceptions to the rule. Each problem is the result of country-specific issues and not an indicator of fundamental difficulties that cannot be solved through a new fiscal compact among member countries. The second storyline is that Europe stands on the cusp of the long-discussed dream of a United States of Europe. In September 2012 Jose Manuel Barroso, president of the European Commission, called for a "federation of nation states . . . that can tackle common problems," and the following week the Future of Europe Group proposed a series of reforms among which was increased "binding cooperation."[1] The third storyline is that the EU is struggling with a crisis it cannot control, in part because its existence was rushed through too quickly as European leaders sought to cope with German reunification after the end of the Cold War. Not only does the EU lack the economic tools to address its ongoing financial problems but still unresolved is the fundamental question of who pays—taxpayers in economically healthy countries or the private sector whose investments are at risk?

Timeline

European Monetary Integration

1952		The European Coal and Steel Community is established, with France, Germany, Italy, Belgium, Luxembourg, and the Netherlands as members.
1958		The European Economic Community (EEC), often referred to as the Common Market, is founded by the same six countries.
1969	December	EEC heads of state and government meet in The Hague and agree to form the Werner Committee on economic and monetary union.
1970		The Werner Report is presented.
1972		The "snake" is established.
1973		Great Britain, Denmark, and Ireland join the EEC.
1979		The European Monetary System is established. It includes the exchange rate mechanism (ERM).
1981		Greece joins the EEC.
1986		Spain and Portugal join the EEC.
1986	February	The Single European Act is signed. The act promotes the idea of a true common market and a single currency.
1989	April	The Delors Report outlines three stages to monetary union.
1989	June	The European Council adopts the Delors Report.
1990	July	Stage one of monetary union begins.
1990	December	Intergovernmental conferences (IGCs) are launched on political and economic union.
1992	February	The Treaty on European Union (Maastricht Treaty) is signed.
1992	September	The first ERM crisis hits the European Union (EU).
1994	January	Stage two of monetary union begins.
1995	January	Austria, Finland, and Sweden join the EU.
1995	December	The term *euro* is officially adopted for the common currency.

1997		The Stability and Growth Pact is agreed upon.
1998		The European Central Bank is established.
1999		Stage three of monetary union begins, with eleven countries satisfying the Maastricht criteria; the euro becomes the official currency of the EU.
2001		Greece joins the euro area.
2002	January	Euro coins and banknotes are introduced.
2002	February	All national currencies in the EU are no longer recognized as legal tender in the euro zone.
2008		The EU agrees to a stimulus package to boost its economies following a global financial crisis.
2009		Greek debt reaches its highest point in modern history.
2010		The EU and International Monetary Fund agree on a bailout package for Greece; the austerity measures called for in Greece lead to rioting in the streets.

Problem Setting and Origins: Europe's Postwar Rebalancing

Monetary union has been a recurring theme throughout European history.[2] In the mid-1800s, France led Belgium, Switzerland, and Italy in the creation of the Latin Monetary Union. Shortly thereafter, Sweden, Denmark, and Norway formed the Scandinavian Monetary Union. Most significantly, a single currency came into existence as part of German unification. Movement toward German unification began in 1818 with the establishment of the Zollverein (German Customs Union). The benefits of this trade zone were severely undermined by the maze of tolls, inspection stations, and competing currencies found within it. As late as 1871 one could find seven currency areas; 119 forms of gold, silver, and token coins; and 117 types of bank notes. This situation came to an end in 1876 when Prussia, the leading state in the German Empire that had grown around the Zollverein, forced all members to accept the mark as the only currency. Currency problems again figured prominently in German history after World War I when runaway inflation (at one point in October 1923 reaching 32,000 percent) destroyed the value of the German mark and plunged the country's economy into chaos. The social and political climate this created contributed greatly to the rise to power of Adolf Hitler.

The images of economic desperation in the 1920s and 1930s spurred a number of post–World War II policy initiatives in Europe. So too did early postwar fears that Western Europe would fall under Soviet domination. Two of the earliest steps toward European integration were the Treaty of Paris (1951), which created the European Coal and Steel Community in 1952, and the Treaty of Rome (1957), which created the European Economic Community, also referred to as the Common Market, whose members were France, Italy, West Germany, the Netherlands, Belgium, and Luxembourg.[3]

Initially, far less attention was given to questions about money than about trade, although there was some discussion between France, Belgium, Luxembourg, the Netherlands, and Great Britain about establishing a single currency. By the late 1960s, this had changed, and in 1969 the linkage between trade and finances received considerable attention from European leaders. The Barre Memorandum of October 1969 asserted that continued economic growth and raising living standards of the members of the European Common Market required the "fuller alignment of economic policies in the Community . . . [and] intensifying monetary cooperation."[4] Inflationary pressures on the U.S. dollar had grown significantly as American defense spending and the commitment to the Vietnam War increased. Investors began to switch from using dollars to the more stable German mark. As a result, the mark's value went up while those of other countries, such as France, went down, creating an imbalance in European trade relations.

Two months later, in December 1969, a European Economic Community (EEC) summit conference at The Hague, Netherlands, established the Werner Committee to develop a plan for economic and monetary union.[5] The core of the debate before the committee was which of two different German approaches to adopt in plotting out a future for Europe. In the first view, the coronation perspective, monetary union would be the final step in an integration process that had become firmly grounded in free-market principles and a commitment to budgetary-solid economic principles. The second, minimalist perspective saw parallel movement of political and economic union occurring, with both reaching their end points simultaneously. The Werner Report came down solidly on the side of the minimalist perspective. It advanced a gradual strategy for achieving European monetary union through a series of stages that would take a decade to complete. Parallel to monetary union, it envisioned movement toward European political union. There was, however, nothing automatic in this movement. Germany insisted that such movement would depend on members coordinating and harmonizing their economic policies.

In concrete terms, the major result of the Werner Report was the "snake," a system that linked European currencies to one another and, more loosely, to the U.S. dollar using a formula that permitted limited currency changes. Problems soon arose. Cooperation between EEC members on coordinating economic and fiscal policy was not forthcoming. France, in particular, was unwilling to make such a commitment. To no one's real surprise, the snake created in March 1972 failed to survive the wave of financial problems that confronted the international economy in the early 1970s, most notably the collapse of the Bretton Woods system, the inflationary impact that the 1973 oil crisis had on the global economy, and the devaluation of the U.S. dollar. Great Britain left the snake in June 1972, Italy followed in February 1973, Denmark left in June 1973, and France left twice, in 1974 and 1976, because these countries found it impossible to keep the value of their currencies within the snake's boundaries.

It would be the late 1970s before movement toward European currency unification gathered momentum again. As earlier, concerns over the stability of the U.S. dollar, along with new inflationary pressures unleashed by another round of oil price hikes, were the prime motivating factors. With hopes of creating a zone of monetary stability in Europe, the European Monetary System (EMS) was established in March 1979. It put into place a European exchange rate mechanism (ERM) and a European currency unit (ECU). The ERM effectively linked EEC currencies to one another within a narrow band of fluctuation. National banks were expected to intervene when the outer limits of this band were broken. Given the strength of the German mark compared to the currencies of other countries, this effectively made it the primary reference point. The ECU did not replace national currencies, as the euro would later do. Rather, it was an artificial accounting tool used to help fix national currencies against one another. Its value was based on a weighted basket of national EEC currencies, most notably the German mark, French franc, Dutch guilder, and British pound sterling. Membership was voluntary, and Great Britain opted not to join the ERM until 1990.

Problem Definition and Response: German Financial Dominance

The European Monetary System operated with considerable success into the late 1980s, but it also highlighted the reality of continuing German financial domination over European currency values, which gave rise in France to concern over its ability to balance German influence in Europe. Added to these fears were concerns that new Soviet leader Mikhail Gorbachev's economic and political reform agenda might tempt Germany to weaken its ties with Western Europe and strike out with a more independent political and defense foreign policy. Led by President François Mitterrand, French officials were determined to link Germany more fully into Europe and to hold its influence in check. The result was informal talks between Mitterrand, German chancellor Helmut Kohl, and EEC president Jacques Delors in 1988 to investigate how European monetary union might be achieved. The result of this initiative was the Delors Report, which was issued in 1989 and identified three stages that would lead to European monetary union.[6]

The first stage involved completion of the internal EEC market and removal of all restrictions on further financial integration, along with closer coordination of economic and monetary policies. Work on this stage began on July 1, 1990. The second stage called for establishing the European

---| **Box 11.2** |---

Concept Focus

Integration Theory

The European Union (EU) now holds a central place in European political, economic, and social policymaking. So too does the belief that conflicts among European states will be settled by negotiation and international law rather than through war. The EU's existence and expectations of the peaceful settlement of disputes are largely taken for granted by many, but not so by those who lived through WWII or came of age in the two decades that followed. Little was certain then about the political or economic future of Europe. All that was certain was the belief that war should not break out again in Europe. The troubling thing about this belief was that it was also present after WWI, and those hopes were short-lived. Peace, as well as political stability and economic growth, were shattered as the economic depression of the 1930s grew in severity and extremist parties came to power in Germany and Italy. Accordingly, scholars and policymakers began to look in earnest at strategies for avoiding a repetition of Europe's post-WWI experience.

Three different strategies were put forward to guide efforts at creating a prosperous and politically stable Europe. Collectively they were identified as integration theories because their goal was to bring together the separate states of Europe under a common authority, often characterized as a United States of Europe. One approach put forward was **federalism**. Federalism represents a frontal attack on the notion of sovereignty. The principle of sovereignty must be attacked first because it is grounded in the idea of a conflict-prone, self-help, international system in which states are not obliged to abide by international rules or agreements. In this view, the only way to create a larger political unit is to create new institutions (courts, legislatures, bureaucracies, executives) that centralize political power above states and thus make sovereignty irrelevant. Federalism holds that once these new institutions are in place, a new shared sense of common identity will develop among people who once thought of themselves as belonging to separate and competing political systems. Piecemeal approaches in which sovereign power is slowly whittled away are seen as bound to fail because they cannot generate sufficient momentum and political will to overcome the inevitable resistance of national-level policymakers to strip them of power.

A second possible path to integration considered was **functionalism**. Advocates of this strategic line of action argued that the pathway to political integration lay in first achieving economic integration. National patterns of trade, investment, and planning had to be supplanted by cross-border trade, investment, and planning, thus requiring states to coordinate policies if common problems were to be solved. Functionalists were confident that this strategy would succeed for two reasons. First, economic problems tended not to be viewed the same way as political problems. Whereas political problems were solved via bargaining, economic problems were addressed on the basis of technical and objective criteria. Second, increasingly, economic problems could not be solved by national authorities. This combination of characteristics led functionalists to argue that although policymakers could be expected to resist direct attacks on sovereignty, they would react more positively to calls for integrative steps to solve economic problems. Functionalists disagreed with federalists on another important topic: they were less interested in creating a bigger, supranational state and more open to a wide variety of institutional arrangements that would make sovereignty irrelevant.

The third approach to integration put forth was **neofunctionalism**, which has been described as federalism in functionalist clothing. Neofunctionalism shares with federalism the desire to see a larger political unit created. It shares with functionalism an "economics first" strategy of integration. Where neofunctionalism differs from functionalism is in its assertion that the areas for economic integration must be carefully selected and not left to the natural workings of the market place. Neofunctionalists optimistically argued that if approached this way, success in one area of economic integration would naturally spill over into other areas, with the cumulative effect being that sovereignty would erode. Less optimistically, however, neofunctionalists cautioned that spillover was only one possible outcome of efforts to integrate national economies. Muddling through, spill back, and spill around were other possible outcomes. Should any of these occur, national sovereignty would remain strong, if not actually be strengthened. Of the original three approaches to integration, it was neofunctionalism that provided the foundation for European integration.

A more recent addition to the strategies for pursuing integration is **constructivism**. From the constructivist perspective, what matters most is not the nature of the institutions created or the economic benefits provided by cross-national economic activity or international regulations, but the manner in which institutions and practices serve as instruments of communication and persuasion among people, altering their sense of collective identity. In the case of European integration, the key test involves the construction of a shared sense of European citizenship. The constructivist perspective on integration highlights a problem that the three original approaches tended to discount: the possibility of unequal political commitment to the new and larger unit being created. Two possible fault lines include differing levels of commitment by elites and the public at large and differing levels of commitment by citizens due to the perceived value of participating in the integration process.

Over time the successes of European integration became the standard against which other integration efforts were measured. The euro crisis brought forward renewed attention to these drivers of integration and the degree to which European integration was a success. Additionally, it called into question the value and feasibility of creating a United Europe by using any of these methods and highlighted the dangers of the gap between elite and public commitment to European unity.

Monetary Institute to strengthen central bank cooperation and plan the transition to a single currency. It was expected that, in the second stage, movement would take place away from coordinating monetary policies and towards the formation of a common monetary policy. The third and final stage involved fixing exchange rates between national currencies and replacing them with a single currency. With the acceptance of the Delors Report by the European Council in Madrid in June 1989, the question of monetary union was transformed from one of "if" to "when."

The general expectation coming out of the Madrid meeting was that movement through stages two and three would be a long, drawn-out affair that would take most of the 1990s. This timetable was scrapped with the fall of the Berlin Wall in November 1989 and the perceived need on the part of the French and others to link a new, united Germany firmly to a European union more quickly. One stumbling block to moving more rapidly to stages two and three was that, at Germany's insistence, it had been agreed that moving to these stages would require amending the 1957 Rome Treaty. An intergovernmental conference (IGC) was set up for this purpose, but no date was set for it to begin is deliberations. At the December 1989 Strasburg meeting of the European Council, it was agreed that the IGC, along with a parallel intergovernmental conference on political union, would soon convene.

A variety of settings were used in these negotiations once they began in 1991. The monetary union ICG met eleven times at the ministerial level and twice at the permanent representative level, and three informal meetings of finance ministers were held. Additionally, a series of at least eight bilateral meetings were held between German and French officials. These bodies considered, to varying degrees, plans put forward by the EEC commission as well as by Germany, France, Great Britain, Spain, Luxembourg, and the Netherlands.

The intergovernmental commissions issued their reports to the European Council at its December 9–10, 1991, meeting in the Dutch city of Maastricht. That meeting then approved the Treaty on European Union, better known as the Maastricht Treaty, which defined the European monetary union under a single currency as the official goal of the EU and established a timetable for this to happen, along with criteria for participating. It was decided that stage two was to begin on January 1, 1994, with stage three beginning no later than January 1, 1999. The agreement was signed in February 1992 and came into effect on November 1, 1993.

One of the key points determined in these negotiations was the convergence criteria that a country would have to meet to enter into stage three. In general terms, these were the economic conditions a country had to meet to be able to adopt the new single European currency. Five main requirements were established, all of which had to be met:

- A country's inflation rate could be no more than 1.5 percent, about the average inflation rate of the three lowest inflation rate countries of the EU.

- The government's debt level could not be more that 60 percent of its gross domestic product.

- The government's deficit could not exceed 3 percent of its gross domestic product.

- The country must have belonged to the ERM (exchange rate mechanism) for two years and maintained a normal exchange rate fluctuation.

- The country's long-term interest rate could not be more than 2 percent above the average of the three lowest inflation countries of the EU.

With these conditions in place, negotiations now moved to the timing of stage three. France and Italy sought a clear and firm deadline. Germany and the Netherlands called for monetary union only after economic stability had been achieved. The Maastricht Treaty tried to appease both sides by identifying two different timetables for moving to stage three. If economic stability was achieved before the end of 1996, a date could then be set for moving to stage three. If not, then stage three would begin automatically on January 1, 1999. All that would be decided in this case was which members would be eligible to enter stage three.[7]

| **Box 11.3** |

Spotlight

French, German, and British National Bargaining Priorities

On the surface, the negotiations to create a single currency in Europe proceeded in a relatively straightforward fashion. Yet the political reality was quite different. Leaders in every country had to contend with domestic political opposition, competing foreign policy goals, and the legacy of past policies. Here we look at the bargaining strategies and priorities of France, Germany, and Great Britain.

For French president François Mitterrand, monetary union was about French power and standing in international and European politics. The chief antagonists here were the United States and Germany. European monetary union was crucial to controlling the financial power of the United States as well as the political influence that flowed from it. Alone, France was not able to challenge U.S. financial dominance of the international financial system, but it could credibly hope to do so if it were sitting at the head of a European monetary union. A prerequisite for the success of this strategy was controlling Germany by bringing it into a monetary union in which its economic power could be made to serve French purposes. In pursuing these goals, Mitterrand adopted a bargaining style that centered on deepening and making irreversible Germany's commitment to monetary union and a single currency. To this end, he sought to position Germany as the country placing key EMU proposals on the negotiating table. At the same time, Mitterrand was not above selectively defining controversial issues coming before negotiators as Germany's fault in an effort to force Germany forward.

For German chancellor Helmut Kohl, monetary union was, at its base, about linking Germany to Europe in such a way as to prevent any recurrence of the balance-of-power politics that had pitted France against Germany. His goal was to do this without it appearing to Europeans that Germany was dominating the process or making it appear to Germans that monetary union would threaten German economic stability and bring back memories of inflationary pressures that arose in the 1920s and 1930s. Preventing this from happening required a preexisting commitment to economic stability on the part of all European governments and insulating banks from pressures to adjust monetary policy for political purposes.

(Continued)

(Continued)

Under Kohl's leadership German negotiators followed a rule-based negotiating style that often put them at procedural odds with their French counterparts. Whereas French negotiators were often content to leave room for discretion in the language of the agreements being negotiated, German negotiators sought to inject a maximum amount of precision and clarity into treaty language so as to increase the predictability that the final outcome would be achieved. Germany's goal was to reduce the influence of political considerations over economic ones in setting convergence and exchange rate policies. Germany also made negotiators focus on the end stage of the negotiations: stage three. From the German negotiating perspective, the central question was what stage three would look like and how to construct stage two to get to it. This approach clashed with that of those who sought a more open-ended transition process and were willing to accept a range of possible outcomes.

The Delors Report and its call for a single currency placed Great Britain on the defensive and in a minority position. The British pound lacked the strength of the German mark, making Great Britain less influential in discussions about the future of Europe's monetary system. Complicating matters further was that the British had underestimated the importance of such key steps leading to the Maastricht Treaty as the Delors Report and establishing the ERM. Not seeing themselves as Europeans or "of Europe," they failed to fully appreciate the emotional pull that led the continental states to support a single currency.

Domestic politics also created problems for the British government. Whereas Margaret Thatcher had been a supporter of British engagement with Europe earlier in her political career, by the end of her tenure she was an ardent and vocal opponent, declaring at one point in the negotiations that currency unification was premature and asserting that it would not happen within her lifetime. At another time she stated that she would "never give up the pound."[8] Her fundamental opposition to economic union was reinforced by her fears over German unification. For Thatcher, Germany was "by its very nature a destabilizing rather than stabilizing force in Europe,"[9] and she advocated a series of reunification conditions that angered Kohl. Thus, in Rome in 1990, when the other eleven members of the EEC voted to set terms for political union, Thatcher voted against it. Hers was also the only dissenting vote on setting a date for the start of stage two of economic union.

The core of the British negotiating problem was that although Great Britain opposed the decision to create a single European currency, for the longest time it lacked an alternative proposal. In the end, Great Britain presented two alternatives to a single European currency, but neither gained much support. It became clear that some means would have to be found to exempt the British from participating in the euro. One possibility was a general opt-in clause in the Maastricht Treaty, by which members would vote themselves in; another was an opt-out clause by which members could vote themselves out. Both were unacceptable to those states seeking to make currency unification automatic. The second-best solution agreed upon was to give Great Britain a specific exception with a deadline of the end of 1997 to exercise its opt-out option.

Problem Evolution and Development: The Maastricht Treaty

With the Maastricht Treaty adopted in February 1992, the next step was the ratification of the treaty by members according to their respective constitutional provisions.[10] The ratification process was anything but smooth. Voters in Denmark rejected the treaty in a referendum held on June 2, 1992, with 50.75 percent voting against it. Danish leaders subsequently negotiated four opt-out provisions in the treaty, including one for economic and monetary union. A second referendum was held on May 18, 1993, in which the treaty was approved by 56.7 percent of the voters. French voters approved the Maastricht Treaty by an even thinner margin. In a September 20, 1992, referendum, 51.05 percent voted yes. The British Parliament gave its approval in July 1993, but only after stormy deliberations in which a slim conservative majority backed by the support of Liberal Democrats overcame opposition from rebellious conservative party members reportedly supported by Margret Thatcher. Germany was the final member to give its approval to Maastricht. Both houses of the German Parliament had given their overwhelming support to the treaty, but final approval rested on the German Federal Constitutional Court's verdict on the constitutionality of the treaty. This occurred in November 1993.

Accompanying and reinforcing these political difficulties in moving forward to a single European currency were economic difficulties.[11] These problems had their roots in the ongoing process of German reunification. To counter the inflationary problems caused by the government's monetary policies, the Bundesbank raised interest rates, setting set in motion a Europe-wide recession. In September 1992 the British pound and the Italian lira were forced out of the ERM, and the French franc barely stayed in, partly due to German support. The following year, another round of economic shocks almost caused the ERM to fall apart, as Germany and France were unable to coordinate their financial positions. In a desperate act to hold the ERM together, the permissible currency fluctuation band was increased.

These economic difficulties were particularly damaging to the cause of currency union because they called into question the ability of all but a handful of countries to be ready for stage three. The possibility that only a few might join was not anticipated at Maastricht. Several problems stood out: Italy and Belgium had governmental debts far in excess of the stated permissible limits. Controversial reforms were introduced in these countries, reducing pensions and raising income taxes in order to improve their eligibility status. Germany and France ran greater government deficits than permitted in the membership criteria. Whereas Germany was intent on reaching the 3 percent limit, French leaders waffled before ultimately committing themselves to it.

Not surprisingly given the history of single-currency negotiations, political pressures emerged that pushed leaders in opposite directions. France made it clear that, in spite of these economic difficulties, Italian and Spanish participation in stage three was essential in order to lessen continuing French fears that Germany would dominate the new financial system. German leaders felt it necessary to reassure the German public that moving to the euro would not undermine the economic stability associated with the German mark. Complicating matters still further was the British position. The conservative government of John Major had given every indication that it would give the required opt-out notification by the end of 1997 and not participate in stage three. Hope that this might not be the case surfaced briefly when Tony Blair and the Labor Party came into office following the May 1997 election. These hopes were dashed when, in October of that year, Blair's government announced that Great Britain would opt out.

In the end, efforts to lessen both sets of pressures were taken. In 1997 the Stability and Growth Pact was signed that carried over the Maastricht membership or convergence criteria after countries were admitted to stage three. The pact set up a monitoring system to ensure compliance and put into place sanctions against countries that violated its terms. It was also agreed that when the European Council judged the fitness of countries for membership, an expansive or lenient interpretation of the Maastricht criteria would be used. In May 1998 it was announced that eleven of the fifteen EU members had met the standards. Only Great Britain, Denmark, Greece, and Sweden were left outside. Of these, only Greece wished to enter stage three but was judged not to have met the criteria.

The euro came into existence on January 1, 1999, as a virtual currency. It did not exist in physical form. National currencies continued to circulate, but they were now subunits of the euro, with their values fixed against one another. All debts and bonds were denominated in euros. This situation continued until January 1, 2002, when euro coins and paper notes began to circulate and national currencies began being retired from circulation. February 28, 2002, was set as the last day national currencies could be used.

It would not take a decade for the euro to face what became in the eyes of some both inside and outside the EU a life-threatening crisis.[12] The epicenter of the crisis was Greece, which was a member of the EU when the euro came into existence in 1999 but did not meet the convergence criteria and only adopted the euro as its national currency on January 1, 2002.

The global debt crisis of 2008 led to a situation in which it appeared likely that the governments of several EU countries would not be able to meet their debt obligations. Greece was at the forefront of these concerns, but Ireland, Spain, Italy, and Portugal all appeared to be in need of rescue packages as well. The causes of these sovereign-debt crises varied—in Greece and Portugal troubled government finances were the main problem, while in Ireland and Spain banking problems were paramount—but many also held the EU responsible for moving too quickly to introduce the euro without having taken the additional step of unifying banking and taxation policy within the European monetary union.

In 2010 Standard & Poor's downgraded Greek government debt to junk bond status, forcing the EU and International Monetary Fund (IMF) to provide a €110 billion bailout package for Greece that imposed stringent austerity measures and wide-ranging financial reforms as a condition for its issuance. The rescue package proved inadequate and another bailout, this time by the EU, IMF, and European Central Bank, totaling €130 billion was needed in 2011. Domestic political problems in Greece that centered on public resistance to the terms of the bailouts, the inability to form a new government, and continued economic problems led to widespread discussion of the possibility of a "Grexit": Greece leaving the euro system.

Germany played a central and complex role in constructing these rescue packages. Many held it partly responsible for the crises due to its trade surplus and strict monetary policies. For their part, Germans expressed anger at having to be a primary source of funds for bailing out EU members whose debt they saw as the result of overspending, poor banking practices, under taxing, and corruption.

In the course of negotiating the EU rescue packages, Germany advanced two highly controversial proposals. One called for amending EU treaties to permit the permanent operation of the European Financial Stability Facility, which had been created as an emergency fund in response to the Greek debt crisis. The great difficulty that many EU members encountered in passing and amending previous treaties suggested that this was a strategy fraught with danger and for which the necessary political will might be lacking. Germany's second proposal was for imposing financial losses on investors in future bailouts. German leaders argued that without the fear of financial losses, investors would continue to be attracted to the potential payoffs of high-risk bond purchases and investments in troubled EU members rather than investing in more financially secure EU countries.

Although Greece still struggles to restructure and revitalize its economy, fears of a Grexit have lessened. Problems for the euro and EU, however, remain. As many commentators have noted, there does not exist a truly European demos: "While most Europeans have an attachment to their 'European identity,' the vast majority of the people . . . use different cultural lenses when they try to understand and appreciate the European integration project. . . . They learn about it from their own politicians, and they evaluate its performance relative to their own goals."[13]

Conclusion: Political and Economic Considerations

Intuitively, we think of monetary policy as being economic policy and divorced from politics, but as the creation of the euro and subsequent developments have shown, creating monetary policy can be extremely political. Political considerations led to the euro's creation, framed discussions of how the euro would come into existence, and have been at least equal in importance to economic considerations in determining how to cope with the financial crisis that struck Europe after its creation.

Viewed in a global context, the euro marked a potentially important event in the evolving structure of global politics. For several decades after World War II, the United States and Soviet Union were the two dominant powers in world politics. After the fall of communism, the United States was left as the sole remaining superpower. Today we are in a period of global transition. American power has declined, but the United States remains the leading global power. China's power is rising, and it is a potential challenger to the United States. Should the creation of the euro lead to greater cooperation and unity among France, Germany, and Great Britain in economic policy and eventually in foreign policy, it holds the potential for elevating Europe to the status of a third major power. This would change even more the future shape of the international system and the constraints it places on conflict and cooperation among states.

In this chapter we have reviewed the history and major issues in the pathway to creating the euro as the common currency of the EU. The Case Summary box highlights the key features of our discussion so that they may be compared with the accounts of conflict and cooperation presented in other chapters. It is perhaps only right to close by noting that while we have focused on a major problem currently faced by the EU, European integration has produced a significant number of successes. Most notably, integration created a single market across Europe by eliminating tariffs, quotas, and customs duties in the trade of most goods and products among member states. It has also brought about the free movement of people across borders and established a charter of political, economic, and social rights for EU citizens and residents.

Case Analysis

1. Based on the challenges that European Union member states faced in meeting and maintaining the monetary union standards, what challenges might they face if the EU agreed to more integration with a stage four political union?

2. What does the term *United Europe* suggest to you? Does it exist today?

3. Can a European common currency exist without a strong European government? Why or why not? What does the United States' experience suggest?

4. Would any of the integration models not followed in European integration have made monetary union easier to achieve and prevented the euro crisis?

5. What were the major points of conflict on the pathway to creating the euro? Did they change over time or remain the same?

6. To what extent did policymakers listen to their publics in moving toward monetary union? How much should they have listened?

7. Was there a point of no return on the pathway of conflict and cooperation that led to the creation of the euro?

8. Do you think German, French, or British interests have been best served by the creation of the euro? Was this also true at earlier points along the pathway of conflict and cooperation that led to the euro's creation?

Suggested Readings

Brown, Bernard. "Ordeal of the European Union." *American Foreign Policy Interests* 35, no. 1 (2013): 21–30. Brown examines the political objectives of European unification and current controversies.

Issing, Otmar. *The Birth of the Euro*. Cambridge, UK: Cambridge University Press, 2008. The author, a key figure in the creation of the euro and in the early years of the European Central Bank, reviews the debates and struggles surrounding their establishment.

La Malfa, Giorgio. "The Limping Euro." *Survival* 55, no. 1 (2013): 135–144. The author, a member of the Italian Parliament, argues that because it is a political and economic orphan, the euro cannot be very strong and will continue to generate hostility to the idea of a unified Europe.

Marsh, David. *The Euro: The Battle for the New Global Currency*. New Haven: Yale University Press, 2011. This is an updated volume on the history of the euro that includes commentary on the financial crises of Greece, Ireland, and Portugal.

Mourlon-Druol, Emmanuel. *A Europe Made of Money*. Ithaca, NY: Cornell University Press, 2012. Building on integration theory, this volume examines the emergence of the European Monetary System from 1974 to 1979.

Mulhearn, Chris, and Howard Vane. *The Euro: Its Origins, Development, and Prospects*. Cheltenham, UK: Edward Elgar, 2008. This work presents a concise history of the origins of the euro, the institutions of the EU, the EU's expansion, and the beginnings of the euro crisis.

Web Resources

Bruegel, www.bruegel.org/blog/eurocrisistimeline. This European economics think tank provides a timeline on the euro crisis.

European Central Bank, www.ecb.int/home/html/index.en.html. Access statistics and information on the euro, the EU's monetary policy, and Europe's financial condition.

European Union, http://europa.eu/index_en.htm. Learn more about how the EU works, its laws and policies, and life in the union at its official Web site.

Economic and Financial Affairs, European Union, http://ec.europa.eu/ economy_finance/euro/emu. The EU describes its economic and monetary integration, why it chose the euro, how it provides financial assistance, and the financial instruments that support EU policies.

Institute for New Economic Thinking, http://ineteconomics.org/euroc risis. Get the latest news, opinions, and research on Europe from leading economists.

International Monetary Fund, www.imf.org/external/index.htm. Access statistics, IMF reports on individual countries, videos, and other publications.

PART III
Human Security

12 Humanitarian Relief after Haiti's Earthquake

International humanitarian relief efforts do not travel down a single pathway. They take place under many different circumstances. Two of the most prominent are postconflict situations, when a country is struggling to cope with the carnage and destruction left by war, and disaster relief efforts, when the challenge facing a society is how to rebuild in the aftermath of a natural or man-made disaster. Our focus here is on this second pathway—international humanitarian relief efforts in response to disasters.

On one level the humanitarian relief efforts taking place on this pathway are fundamentally nonpolitical. Rooted in practical field experience, these efforts are often referred to as the "rules of three." Two different sets of these rules exist. The first rule of three involves the fate of the people who need help and details what conditions they can be expected to withstand: three minutes without air; three days without water; three weeks without food; three months without hope.[1] Failing to provide the necessary relief for these needs within these timeframes is seen by experts as leading to failure of the humanitarian effort. The second rule of three details the three structural stages of the broader humanitarian effort: response, relief, and recovery. In the response phase, the focus is on conducting search and rescue missions to save lives. In the relief phase, attention shifts to providing life-sustaining provisions such as food, ice, clothing, and temporary shelter. The emphasis in the recovery phase is on community rebuilding and infrastructure development.

A closer look at these relief efforts points to a different reality. We find a pathway that, though marked by public statements of cooperation and expressions of great concern for the well-being of people in distress, also contains elements of conflict. Moreover, in some circumstances conflict may dominate cooperation on these pathways. Relief efforts may be geared primarily to improving a country's image. Under these circumstances the real goal is to advance a country's foreign policy objectives within a region rather than to help people.[2] The conflictual dimension to relief efforts also reveals itself in the fact that countries sometimes reject humanitarian aid even though a clear case for its need exists.[3]

The ever-present tension between conflict and cooperation not only surfaces in relations between those travelling the humanitarian relief pathway but also in the objectives being pursued. The major point of tension exists between providing security for the state (bringing an end to violence and looting, making streets safe, protecting government buildings, etc.) and providing security to those affected by the disaster. This second form of security is often referred to as human security.

In this chapter we will examine the pathway of international humanitarian relief as it worked its way through Haiti following the January 2010 earthquake. Our Concept Focus will be on human security. Our Spotlight section is on the protection cluster established by the United Nations (UN) as a central part of its emergency response to the crisis caused by the earthquake.[4] In particular we are concerned with the attention (or lack thereof) given to human rights for women and children.

Haiti as a Humanitarian Symbol

Haiti has become a symbol of both the international community's compassion in responding to a natural disaster and of the dilemmas and magnitude of the challenges that face responders. The international community, states, international organizations, and nongovernmental organizations responded with an outpouring of billions of dollars in financial and material humanitarian aid for the victims of the January 2010 Haitian earthquake. Yet, three years later, a former Haitian government official asked, "Where is the reconstruction?" and observed, "If you ask what went right and what went wrong, the answer is, almost everything went wrong."[5] Estimates are that over 357,000 Haitians still live in 496 tent camps. The symbolism of Haitian humanitarian relief continues, however. In November 2012 former president and first lady Jimmy and Roslyn Carter participated in a Habitat for Humanity mission to Haiti to build 100 one-room houses. Then eighty-eight years old, it was Jimmy Carter's second trip to post-earthquake Haiti.

Before the 7.0 magnitude earthquake occurred, Haiti was widely recognized to be the poorest country in the Western Hemisphere. Its economic and political situations were among the most troubled in the hemisphere, if not the world.[6] In 2009 the United Nations Human Development Index ranked Haiti 149 out of 171 countries. This index, which includes statistics on life expectancy, literacy, education, and other measures of the standard of living, is used to compare countries in terms of their quality of life. That same year Haiti ranked 175 out of 182 countries in the Corruptions Perception Index, a quantitative measure of how corrupt a government is seen by experts and in public opinion polls. In the immediate years leading up to the earthquake, 78 percent of Haitians were living on less than $2 per day. More than one child in five was chronically malnourished. An estimated 80 percent of the population was unemployed or working in the informal sector, which is defined as being outside of government control and

---

Box 12.1

Case Summary

After a 7.0 magnitude earthquake rocked Haiti, one of the poorest nations in the Western Hemisphere, in 2010, Haiti's government was unable to muster the resources needed to respond to the devastation. The international community scrambled to supply humanitarian relief, but, years later, Haiti is no better off than it was before the quake.

Global Context

Disaster relief efforts such as those in Haiti take place in a global context that relies heavily on voluntary contributions from states and nongovernmental organizations to provide short-term assistance. Outside of United Nations specialized agencies, no formal response mechanism exists to coordinate these efforts.

Key Actors

- Haiti
- United States, including the U.S. military and the U.S. Agency for International Development

- United Nations
- Various nongovernmental relief organizations

Motives

- Haiti needed outside assistance to provide for the health and welfare of its citizens and to help its economy and infrastructure recover.
- The United States sought to provide aid for a people and country in need, and it was also conscious of how past refugee flows created a mass exodus from Haiti to the United States.
- International organizations also sought to provide assistance for the humanitarian need in the wake of the crisis.

Concepts

- Foreign aid
- Humanitarianism
- Human security

- International organizations
- Intervention

---

consisting of black market and underground economic activity. Fifty-two percent of the country's population lived in overcrowded cities, the largest of which is Port-au-Prince. Cité Soleil, a slum district located within the city, has been described by the United Nations as the most dangerous place on earth. Those who live in the countryside were (and still are) engaged in subsistence farming. An importance source of income, amounting to 20 percent of Haiti's gross domestic product, came from remittances sent home by Haitians living and working abroad.

Two years after the earthquake and the massive outpouring of global aid, Haiti is hardly better off. In 2012 it was ranked 7 out of 177 countries on the Failed State Index, a quantitative measure of the ability of governments to exercise effective control over their territory. This ranking, although two spots better than in 2011, still earned it the designation of being in critical condition. Columbia was the nearest-ranking Latin American state, coming in at 44. In 2011 the Human Development Index placed Haiti in the low development category, ranking it 158 out of 187 countries. Nicaragua was its nearest-ranking Latin American state at 129. An estimated 72 percent of Haitians were living in poverty (on less than $2 per day) in 2011, and 80 percent were below the poverty line as established by the Haitian government.

Similarly, the human rights situation in Haiti continues to mirror its pre-earthquake profile. High levels of violent crime existed prior to the earthquake, and the UN found an increase in murders, rapes, and kidnappings after the earthquake. Violent protests and civil unrest had also increased as the political and legal systems struggled to reestablish their legitimacy and

---

| **Box 12.2**

Concept Focus

Human Security

Security is one of the most dominant themes in the study and practice of international politics. Traditionally, the focus has been on state security, but this is no longer the case. An increasingly large number of voices are calling for placing people and not states at the center of international politics. Human security is a relatively recent concept in the study of international politics, rising in visibility when the Cold War ended and the security threats facing states took on a less threatening character. As former U.S. director of central intelligence James Woolsey noted, at the time we were no longer threatened by a menacing dragon but by less dangerous poisonous snakes. The death of the dragon provided an opportunity to pursue a very different foreign policy agenda.[7]

The 1994 United Nations Human Development Report (UNHDR) put forward human security as the centerpiece of such an alternative strategy, one that centered on "the legitimate concerns of ordinary people who sought security in their daily lives."[8] The report went on to identify two broad dimensions of human security. The first centered on safety from such chronic threats as hunger, disease, and repression. The second set grew out of "sudden and hurtful disruptions in patterns of daily life."[9] The first set of threats is ongoing and requires the long-term attention of states, nongovernmental organizations, and international organizations.

(Continued)

(Continued)

The second set of threats is short-term and episodic. Responding to these threats requires immediate action.

Within these two broad categories, the 1994 UNHDR highlighted seven "vital core" dimensions to human security: (1) economic security (assured basic income); (2) food security (physical and economic access to food); (3) health security (protection form infectious and parasitic diseases): (4) environmental security (protection from pollution, environmental degradation, and the depletion of natural resources); (5) personal security (protection from war, torture, criminal acts, state violence): (6) community security (the survival of cultures and traditions): and (7) political security (respect for basic civil and political rights).

While the 1994 UNHDR is the foundation on which most government and scholarly reports on human security are based, it is not the only definition of human security. A far more restrictive definition from the Human Security Project focuses exclusively on freedom from fear, arguing that human security should be conceptualized as freedom from violence and the fear of violence. Still another element has been put forward by Kofi Annan. Speaking as UN secretary-general, Annan identified three human security pillars: freedom from want, freedom from fear, and the freedom to live in dignity.

These differing definitions are reflected in disagreement over the appropriate focus of human security efforts, creating a continuing dilemma for policymakers that is not easily resolved. For instance, should equal attention be given to freedom from fear and freedom from want, or should one be prioritized over the other? Does protection from large-scale violations of human rights guarantee that threats from poverty, disease, and malnutrition will be addressed? When does a fear or want cross the threshold to become a human security problem? Simply put, how much poverty or state violence must there be?

Among the most challenging contexts within which human security strategies have to be constructed are those involving internally displaced persons (IDP). These are people who "have been forced or obliged to flee or to leave their homes or places of habitual residence, in particular as a result of or in order to avoid the effects of armed conflict, situations of generalized violence, violations of human rights or natural or human-made disasters, and who have not crossed an internationally recognized State border."[10] According to the Internal Displacement Monitoring Center, 26.4 million people fell into this category in 2011. Of them, 14.9 million were internally displaced due to natural disasters, most often because of floods and storms.

Because they do not cross borders, IDPs often remain invisible. The effects of IDPs on a country also differ from those of refugees. Refugees threaten to bring a conflict with them when they flee if they use their new homeland as a point for staging or supporting violent action in their origin country. They may also place heavy financial burdens on their new homeland regarding the provision of basic necessities, or they may disrupt the ethnic, religious, or political balance of power in a country through their arrival. The international consequences of IDPs, however, often are minimal. This does not mean, however, that their impact on their own country is insignificant. Their movement may destroy the environment, overcrowd urban areas, spawn criminal activity, and become a recruiting source for terrorist and antigovernment military groups.

authority. Michael Joseph Martelly was elected president in March 2011 in a contested election, and it was not until October 2011 that Parliament approved a prime minister. Conflict between Martelly and Parliament then led to several seats on the Haitian Supreme Court remaining vacant as the two could not agree on whom should sit on the court.

Problem Setting and Origins: A Shaky Political-Economic Foundation

Haiti's troubled economic conditions have deep historical roots. Sharing the Caribbean island of Hispaniola with the Dominican Republic, Haiti was originally used as a base by pirates to attack French and British merchant ships. After French rule was officially established in 1697, an economy based on coffee and sugar plantations that relied on African slave labor gradually took root. A successful slave revolt broke out in 1791 and is cited by many historians as a key factor in Napoleon's decision to sell the Louisiana Territory to the United States in 1803, since without Haiti Louisiana's economic value to France was sharply reduced. In 1804 Haiti became an independent state after forces sent by Napoleon to put down the rebellion were defeated. The United States did not recognize Haitian independence until 1862, in large part due to issues of race and color. A 1826 congressional debate over establishing formal diplomatic relations with Haiti saw concerns voiced about "moral contagion" and the danger posed to the South by rewarding "the fruits of a successful Negro insurrection."[11]

Haiti's economic development suffered greatly in its early period of independence. The failure of the United States and others to recognize Haiti's sovereignty led to a period of isolation that worked against foreign investment and trade. Compounding this situation was the breakup of its large plantations into smaller subsistence farming units and the need to pay France "compensation" for the loss of Haiti as a colony.

Political instability in Haiti went hand in hand with its economic troubles. From 1853 to 1915, Haiti experienced twenty-two changes in government. Since independence it has had fifty-six presidents, of which only ten completed a full term in office. Stability of a sort arrived in the early Cold War era with the arrival of the Duvalier dynasty. Tolerated and often actively supported by the United States for their anticommunist orientation, François "Papa Doc" Duvalier and his son Jean-Claude "Baby Doc" Duvalier together ruled Haiti from 1957 to 1986. Only briefly during the John F. Kennedy administration did the widespread corruption, extreme poverty, and violent nature of Duvalier rule lead to counteraction as Haiti saw its foreign aid terminated and it was excluded from the U.S. Alliance for Progress, a foreign aid program established by President Kennedy that focused on improving economic relations with Latin America.

One significant by-product of the political-economic situation in Haiti was a steady stream of Haitians fleeing to the United States. At first

Timeline
Haiti's Humanitarian Emergency

1957–1986		Haiti, ruled by the Duvalier dynasty, comes to be known for its widespread corruption, poverty, and violence.
1991		A coup ousting Jean-Bertrand Aristide from the presidency sends thousands fleeing to the United States; most are caught by the U.S. Coast Guard and returned.
1994		The United States assists Aristide in returning to power.
2000		Aristide is reelected to the presidency.
2004		Aristide is overthrown once again; Haiti's new president requests a UN peacekeeping force, MINUSTAH.
2009		Haiti ranks as one of the world's least developed and most corrupt nations.
2010	January 12	A 7.0 magnitude earthquake rocks Haiti, damaging over 200,000 buildings, killing tens of thousands of people, and leaving 1 million people homeless.
	January 13	The United States deploys search and rescue teams to Haiti and the USAID Disaster Response team arrives.
	January 15	United Nations appeals for emergency financial assistance
	January 18	The UN and U.S. forces agree to give humanitarian concerns priority over security.
	January 23	The UN announces that emergency relief is at an end.
2011		Only 5 percent of rubble has been removed from Haiti, and only 15 percent of the required housing has been built.
2012		Only 43 percent of pledged money has been received by Haiti, most of which has not gone through the Haitian government but through non-governmental organizations.

this exodus was led by members of the upper class. Members of the urban middle class and semi-skilled workers soon followed. By the 1970s many poor and uneducated Haitians also sought refuge in the United States. In

November 1980 alone, some 1,000 Haitian "boat people" sought to enter the United States. Arriving in such large numbers on small, unsafe boats, the Haitian refugees soon overwhelmed the ability of local authorities to provide for their food, housing, and medical care, prompting calls that the U.S. Navy take action to stop their arrival in the United States. This refugee flow was temporarily ended by the Ronald Reagan administration, which threatened to cut off foreign aid to Haiti and ordered the U.S. Coast Guard to intercept the boats and return the passengers to Haiti. As a result, in November 1981 only forty-seven Haitians reached U.S. soil.

The refugee flow resumed stronger than ever a decade later in September 1991. In December 1990 Jean Bertrand Aristide, an ardent advocate of the poor and long-time opponent of the Duvalier regime, was elected president.[12] Even before his inauguration Aristide was the target of a failed coup by pro-Duvalier supporters. His presidency ended less than a year later, in September 1991, when the army led a second, successful coup against him. In the coup's aftermath, many Haitians again took to the sea. Fearing that once more the influx of Haitian refugees would far exceed the capacity of local and state governments to deal with their arrival, the U.S. Coast Guard intercepted 40,000 refugees and returned them to Haiti.

Returning Aristide to power became a priority of the Bill Clinton administration, but one that encountered many frustrations. International economic sanctions were placed on Haiti, but with little impact due to their lax enforcement. A global conference held on Governors Island in New York set a timetable for Aristide's return, but it produced little in the way of follow through. Clinton sent U.S. naval vessels and troops to Haiti, only to have them leave quickly after encountering an unruly crowd. Finally, in September 1994, supported by a United Nations Security Council resolution and with an invasion force in the air, a delegation led by former U.S. president Jimmy Carter convinced Haitian general Raoul Cédras to resign. Aristide returned from exile on October 15 to complete his presidential term, which ended in 1996.

The Haitian constitution does not permit presidents to serve consecutive terms, so Aristide did not run for the presidency in 1996, but he was again elected president in 2000 before being overthrown by another coup in 2004. Following Aristide's removal in February, Haiti's new president, Boniface Alexandre, requested that the UN send in a peacekeeping force to help restore order in Haiti and bring an end to weeks of political and economic unrest. The UN quickly agreed, citing the situation in Haiti as a "threat to international peace and security in the region."[13] A force of 1,000 U.S. Marines arrived the next day. On April 30 the UN took the added step of creating the United Nations Stabilization Mission in Haiti (MINUSTAH) force with a military capacity of up to 6,700 troops. MINUSTAH was composed almost entirely of Latin American forces and replaced the U.S.-led UN peacekeeping force on the ground in Haiti.

An immediate focal point of MINUSTAH activity was Cité Soleil, the gang-filled slum area within Port-au-Prince that was an Aristide political stronghold. Numerous skirmishes with armed gangs, some of which resulted in civilian casualties, accompanied MINUSTAH's efforts to take control of this area. One such incident in June 2005 resulted in as many as eighty deaths. Success proved to be an elusive goal, with critics arguing that, more often than not, MINUSTAH forces merely stood on the sidelines, permitting the police to commit atrocities against pro-Aristide forces. In October 2006, for the first time in three years, Haitian police, supported by MINUSTAH soldiers, were able to enter Cité Soleil for one hour. Not surprisingly, while some in Haiti came to see MINUSTAH as a force for law and order, others viewed it as an occupying army.

MINUSTAH continued to operate in Haiti in the years prior to the earthquake, providing security against gangs and helping to put down riots such as those caused by a food crisis in 2008. More generally, it was charged with promoting reconciliation and a political dialogue among Haiti's warring pro- and anti-Aristide political factions.

Problem Definition and Response: Earthquake Devastation and Relief

On Tuesday, January 12, 2010, at 4:53 p.m., a magnitude 7.0 earthquake struck Haiti, and global perceptions of the country changed dramatically. Earthquakes measuring less than 3.0 are considered so small as to be imperceptible. Those with a 7.0 or greater magnitude are held to be capable of producing severe damage over large areas. Thirty-two aftershocks, ranging in magnitude from 4.3 to 5.9, were recorded in the first two hours after the earthquake hit.[14] Over the next two weeks, more than fifty-two aftershocks were recorded. The 2010 earthquake was not unanticipated, nor was it the first to hit Haiti due to its location near the edge of the Caribbean tectonic plate. That plate had been stuck in place since 1770 when a major earthquake razed large sections of Port-au-Prince. The city had been virtually destroyed two decades earlier, when in 1751 another large earthquake occurred. The last major earthquake to strike Haiti occurred in 1860.

Seismologists judged the destruction caused by the 2010 Haitian earthquake to be more than twice as lethal as that of any previous magnitude 7.0 earthquake. This was due to decades of unsupervised building and housing construction that left structures particularly vulnerable to the seismic shocks emanating from the sudden release of massive amounts of energy from the earth's crust. Some of the buildings or structures that suffered major damage or total destruction were the Presidential Palace, the National Assembly, the Port-au-Prince Cathedral, the headquarters of MINUSTAH, the offices of the World Bank, the control tower at Haiti's international airport, the Port-au-Prince harbor, and the main jail (allowing 4,000 inmates to escape). Half of Haiti's schools and three of its universities suffered significant damage, as did several major hospitals, including ones operated by the humanitarian relief group Doctors without Borders. Haiti's communication system also suffered major damage. Its public telephone system ceased operating, fiber optic connectivity was disrupted, and many roads became blocked with debris.

Specific damage estimates vary considerably.[15] The Haitian government reported that 250,000 residences and 30,000 commercial buildings were destroyed or severely damaged. It also stated that 1 million people had been made homeless and 300,000 were injured. Most controversial are the death estimates. The Haitian government initially estimated that 230,000 Haitians died as a result of the earthquake. On the first anniversary of the quake, it raised this number to 316,000. Far different numbers of dead were put forward in February 2010 by a Radio Netherlands investigative report and in an unpublished May 2011 report by the United States Agency for International Development (USAID). Radio Netherlands placed the death toll at closer to 92,000, and USAID concluded the death toll was between 45,000 and 85,000. This discrepancy is not surprising due to both the understandable difficulty of making definitive calculations under crisis circumstances and the politics of international crisis relief efforts. It is through stressing the unprecedented and catastrophic nature of a humanitarian tragedy that countries, relief agencies, and international organizations seek to maximize the public's monetary response.[16] Whatever the true number on the loss of life in Haiti, it was catastrophic. A spokesperson for the UN Office for the Coordination of Humanitarian Affairs described the Haitian disaster as "historic" and stated that "we have never been confronted with such a disaster in the U.N. memory."[17]

Crisis relief efforts can be characterized in many different ways. For the purposes of this case study, we first break these efforts down by identifying the major responders. Next we identify the major problems the responders encountered. Then later we turn our spotlight on the global push to place human rights at the center of the relief and recovery effort. Three first responders played particularly important roles in responding to the Haitian earthquake: the UN, the United States, and nongovernmental organizations.

The UN has a long history of coming to the aid of countries struck by a natural disaster, so it was no surprise that it quickly established a Disaster Assessment and Coordination (UNDAC) team, a unit that gives the UN the capacity to respond quickly at the onset of an emergency. By the end of 2010, UNDAC teams had conducted 207 emergency operations in over ninety countries. UNDAC teams operate out of the United Nations Office for the Coordination of Humanitarian Affairs (OCHA), which was the lead agency working with the Haitian government, established donors, the military, and those on the ground in Haiti. OCHA worked to coordinate the efforts of search and rescue teams and coordinate assistance efforts. In order to coordinate and prioritize humanitarian emergency response activities, the UN sets up "clusters" and assigns lead responsibility to specific UN agencies. In Haiti, twelve clusters were established (see Table 12.1).

Table 12.1 United Nations Clusters in Haiti	
CLUSTER	**LEAD UN AGENCY**
Agriculture	Food and Agriculture Organization
Camp coordination and camp management	International Organization for Migration
Early recovery	UN Development Programme
Education	UN Children's Fund
Emergency shelter and nonfood items	International Federation of the Red Cross and Red Cross Crescent Societies
Emergency telecommunications	World Food Programme
Food	World Food Programme
Health	World Health Organization and Pan American Health Organization
Logistics	World Food Programme
Nutrition	UN Children's Fund
Protection	Office of High Commissioner of Human Rights, UN Children's Fund, UN Population Fund, MINUSTAH
Water, sanitation, and hygiene	UN Children's Fund

Each of these clusters faced serious challenges. For instance, the emergency shelter cluster faced major problems centered on the displacement of people from their homes. An estimated 500 makeshift camps housing more than 700,000 people were spontaneously created in the aftermath of the earthquake. The World Food Programme, the lead agency in the food cluster, established sixteen food distribution points in the hopes of getting two weeks' worth of rations to 2 million people in Port-au-Prince. Drinking water was being provided for more than 900,000 people each day, and more than 66,000 people were employed in a "cash-for-work" program intended to spur early recovery by removing rubble and clearing drainage canals.

MINUSTAH's presence also grew. Its mandate had been extended for one year in October 2009, and the earthquake led to a further mandate extension and an increase in its authorized force size from 2,211 police officers and 6,940 military troops to 3,711 officers and 8,940 soldiers. Evidence of its growing rule could be seen in its involvement in human rights issues. Along with the Office of the UN High Commissioner on Refugees, MINUSTAH was charged with monitoring human rights violations and assisting the Haitian police and judiciary in preventing and responding to human rights violations.

In addition to organizing activity on the ground, the UN also set out to raise funds for Haitian earthquake relief and reconstruction efforts. On January 15 the UN Humanitarian Country Team in Haiti issued a flash appeal for $575 million in emergency financial assistance. By early February $619 million (107 percent of the goal) had been committed. In mid-February, the UN raised its appeal figure to a record high of $1.44 billion.

The United States also had a two-pronged approach to the onset of the Haitian crisis.[18] Within twenty-four hours the United States had deployed search and rescue teams and a USAID Disaster Assistance Response Team had arrived in Haiti. Operational efforts to provide assistance to those on the ground were placed under the coordinating authority of USAID, which was particularly active in the water, sanitation, and hygiene; food; logistics; health; and protection clusters. The U.S. military supplied additional operational resources. The scale of the effort was staggering. By March some 40,000 U.S. military personnel were stationed in Haiti or on surrounding waters. Fifteen U.S. vessels and forty aircraft were involved in transporting relief and rescue personnel, victims of the earthquake, and supplies. A little more than one month after the earthquake, 2.6 million bottles of water, 2.3 million food rations, 15 million pounds of bulk food, 844,000 pounds of bulk fuel, and more than 125,000 pounds of medical supplies had been delivered. The United States also worked with the government of Haiti to reopen Haiti's harbors and reestablish airport service to allow relief supplies to arrive. By early March an average of seventy-five relief flights were landing per day at the Port-au-Prince airport, down from a high of 160. Commercial flights resumed on February 18.

The United States also provided financial resources to the Haitian emergency response and reconstruction effort. On January 13 the U.S. ambassador to Haiti issued a disaster declaration, making an initial $50,000 in immediate funds available for disaster relief. The following day President Barack Obama announced that the United States was making $100 million available for humanitarian assistance. By early March a total of $712.9 million had been provided to Haiti for earthquake relief efforts. In addition, the overall regular foreign aid assistance package for Haiti in fiscal year 2010 was $363 million, with specific funding set aside for global health and child survival programs, food aid, narcotics control, and law enforcement and military training and education programs.

President Obama also sought to mobilize private funds for Haiti. He reached out to former presidents Bill Clinton and George W. Bush to spearhead a fund-raising effort. In doing so he replicated a format employed by George W. Bush in 2004 when he asked Clinton and George H. W. Bush to lead fund-raising efforts for victims of the Indian Ocean tsunami that struck Indonesia, Sri Lanka, India, and Thailand particularly hard.

Estimates of how many nongovernmental organizations (NGOs) descended on Haiti are hard to come by. Newspaper accounts refer to "hundreds, maybe thousands,"[19] ranging from well-established NGOs such as Save the Children, the International Red Cross, and Doctors without Borders to virtually anonymous and nameless Baptist missionaries from Idaho (who proceeded to try to illegally smuggle out some thirty Haitian "orphans" for adoption in the United States). Many came flush with money. The American Red Cross, for one, raised $7 million in one day from pledges made via text messages alone. All total, Americans donated more than $1.4 billion. Most donors in a crisis prefer to give to NGOs rather than to the government of the country needing assistance out of concerns about how their money will be spent. So massive was the presence of NGOs in Haiti that many Haitians referred to their country as "the Republic of NGOs."

NGOs performed a wide variety of services. Doctors without Borders reported treating over 3,000 people in the first week after the earthquake. By late January it was treating fewer patients with injuries directly related to the earthquake and more with indirectly related physical problems such as diarrhea and mental trauma. In the first days following the earthquake, Catholic Relief Services announced a $200 million, five-year relief and reconstruction program for Haiti. One of its immediate projects in the wake of the earthquake was delivering shelter kits and critical shelter materials to some 6,500 families staying in makeshift camps. Two of the activities undertaken by the International Red Cross were the establishment of a physical rehabilitation center in Port-au-Prince that was capable of treating 1,000 patients per year and inspection visits to prisons and police stations to ensure the humane treatment of those in custody.

| **Box 12.3** |

Spotlight

Human Rights and the UN Protection Cluster in Haiti

A 1991 UN resolution tentatively redefined the problem of helping internally displaced people (IDPs) from a humanitarian issue of providing food, shelter, and medical aid into a human rights issue. This recognition helped quickly mobilize international action in response to Haiti's 2010 earthquake, which devastated the already poor and struggling nation. The Thirteenth Special Session of the Human Rights Council on January 27–28, 2010, passed a resolution expressing concern that "the effects of the earthquake have further exacerbated existing challenges to the full enjoyment of all human rights in Haiti." The resolution also expressed concern over the

> medium- and long-term consequences of the disaster, including its social, economic and development aspects . . . [and] call[ed] upon the international community to continue to ensure adequate and coordinated support for

the Government and the people of Haiti in their efforts to overcome the challenges arising from the earthquake, keeping in mind the importance of integrating a human rights approach.[20]

The UN's protection cluster served as the primary means through which to address Haiti's human rights situation in the aftermath of the earthquake, which was particularly challenging due to the urban setting of the relief efforts. Urban camps are not easily separated from the larger population in a way that controls population flow, the distribution of aid, or the provision of security. They are often spontaneous in their development and blend in with the existing population structure, making the cleanup of debris and reconstruction more difficult. Many who come to the camps are not necessarily displaced in the sense of having lost housing but are urban dwellers seeking access to aid and support that they feel will otherwise not be available to them. Resettlement to existing housing sites in Haiti (urban or rural) was further complicated by the challenge of establishing land ownership rights in a country where informal agreements rather than formal legal titles are common and multiple ownership claims are frequent.

Within this context of makeshift housing, lost infrastructure, scarce resources, and competing claims, human rights violations against women and children in Haiti were of particular concern.[21] Women and children are routinely the most vulnerable persons in the wake of a disaster or crisis. Human Rights Watch estimated that more than 300,000 Haitian women and children were living in camps for displaced persons after the earthquake. The Haitian government estimated that more than 100,000 children were without family protection, and UNICEF reported a rise in child trafficking and illegal adoptions. USAID reported assisting 596 women and 513 child victims of violence in Haiti in 2010.

Living conditions and the absence of medical care were major issues, particularly with regard to childbirth. The absence of security and lack of privacy in the camps were repeatedly cited as contributing factors in direct violence against women and children. So too was the behavior of police and MINUSTAH forces that were assigned to protect the camps but either failed to stop individual and gang violence against women and children or engaged in it themselves. The number of women engaging in prostitution to earn money or gain access to food and shelter also rose after the earthquake. Lack of money for transportation and health services not provided for free (such as sonograms) led to a rise in infant mortality rates.

Complicating the human rights challenge faced by relief workers even more was the traditional Haitian practice of *restavek*, in which impoverished families drop off children at the homes of better-off Haitians. These children—some 300,000, according to estimates—receive little or no education and often become servants. They also often are targets of abduction or sexual abuse and thus become infected with the HIV-AIDS virus. It was not uncommon for such children to be dropped off in the resettlement camps.

Despite these accomplishments, Haitian humanitarian relief also encountered a series of problems that led to recriminations and accusations among those involved in the mission as to who was responsible for inefficiencies in the delivery of aid and relief. Coordination of effort in a crisis situation is an inherently difficult task. As we noted at the outset of our case study, time is of the essence. Emotions of both those giving and receiving aid are on edge. Accurate information is scarce and rumors are abundant. Added to this is the ever-present potential for misperceiving motives and holding conflicting agendas. Here we highlight three common problems that arose in Haiti.

First, the UN cluster approach, which was intended to serve as a coordinating mechanism for relief efforts in various areas, soon became overwhelmed by the arrival and participation of scores of NGOs.[22] One study after the crisis concluded "the coordination system began to go round in circles."[23] Not only were there too many NGOs desiring to participate in cluster coordinating meetings, but many of them did not know Haiti well and were led by non-French speakers. This resulted in the meetings being held in English, which virtually guaranteed the exclusion of the majority of Haitians from discussions about the relief and recovery operations in their own country. Many Haitians, therefore, came to feel that Haiti had become an occupied country ruled by outsiders. Additionally, the clusters encountered great difficulty in collecting data that would allow resources to shift from problem to problem and area to area as the rescue and recovery effort progressed. Rather than adopting a common methodology to measure progress or the lack thereof, many NGOs developed their own and/or failed to coordinate their efforts with other NGOs. The result was that while a large amount of time and effort was spent in trying to assess the situation, not enough usable data was collected.

A second problem involved the establishment of priorities, especially in the early stages of the international response. The initial priority was to establish security on the ground. Without it, humanitarian relief and rescue efforts were unlikely to succeed. Security was not an abstract problem, as looting, rioting, and other forms of violence quickly surfaced. In the first week of the crisis, the UN Security Council voted to send an additional 3,500 soldiers and police officers to Haiti. But rather than being held in check by the emphasis on security, the violence grew as Haitians came to feel that the relief effort was not making enough progress. Relief agencies also complained about the priority being given to security concerns over relief efforts. Doctors without Borders, for example, complained that an aircraft carrying a field hospital was repeatedly denied permission to land. Other NGOs noted that relief trucks were left unused at the airport for lack of supplies to deliver. In each case the problem identified was the priority being given by U.S. military officials to transporting troops and security supplies. The UN and U.S. forces agreed on January 18 to give priority to humanitarian flights over security flights. Embedded in this problem was another concern, however: the large and central role of the U.S. military in the humanitarian effort. While the logic of using U.S. military capabilities for the relief effort was recognized, past U.S. military actions in Haiti left many there suspicious of U.S. motives.

A third problem with the humanitarian mission centered on the goals and capabilities of the NGOs that descended upon Haiti.[24] A study done by the nonprofit Disaster Accountability Project collected information from 196 NGOs. They found that of $1.4 billion raised through donations, only $730 million was spent on the ground in Haiti. A survey of these 196 NGOs' Web sites found that only eight provided solid information on their activities. Most relied on anecdotes and appeals to emotion. The Disaster Accountability Project report singled out for criticism what some describe as medical tourism. Too often medical volunteers arrived in Haiti with minimal equipment, no pharmaceutical supplies, and no means of verifying their clinical capabilities or those of their organizations. Rather than serving as an added source of strength in the relief efforts, they became liabilities, interfering with the effective delivery of medical care by established emergency response teams that arrived with self-contained infrastructures. Additionally, local Haitians with medical experience and skills were routinely pushed aside and ignored by these newly arrived volunteers. Critics charged that photo opportunities all too often replaced the efficient treatment of patients. Random and uncoordinated donations of medication further complicated the rescue mission by overwhelming emergency supply and distribution systems with medicines that were not always appropriate to the situations faced on the ground.

Problem Evolution and Development: Transitioning out of Crisis

No definitive point exists at which the international Haitian humanitarian relief effort passed from the crisis stage into the post-crisis stage.[25] A transition point of sorts came very early, on January 23, when, after the UN stated that the emergency phase of the relief effort was nearing an end, the Haitian government formally ended its search for survivors. By the first anniversary of the earthquake, numerous "lessons learned" studies had been carried out about the crisis response, suggesting that for international organizations and relief agencies, Haiti had entered a post-crisis stage.

The picture that emerged from Haiti at this one-year anniversary point revealed much work that remained to be accomplished. Oxfam, an international alliance of organizations that works to eliminate poverty and injustice around the world, concluded that in many respects the relief effort had reached a standstill. Only 5 percent of the rubble had been cleared, and because of this only 15 percent of the required basic and temporary housing had been built. UNICEF concluded that more than 1 million people remained displaced. Two years after the earthquake, a UN study found that of the approximately $44.5 billion pledged by UN members for reconstruction projects, only 43 percent had been delivered, which explained in part the slow pace of progress. Moreover, this money favored some projects and recipients over others. Less than half of the money allocated for agricultural projects and for health projects had been disbursed. Only 6 percent of the money had been channeled through Haitian institutions and less than 1 percent through the Haitian government, meaning that most was held and distributed by NGOs. This created a situation in which some argued that the relief effort was now de-legitimizing the Haitian government in the eyes of its own people. U.S. aid also came in for criticism. Less than 1 percent of USAID funds went directly to Haitian organizations. The largest recipient of USAID funds to be used in Haiti was a for-profit firm, Chemonics.[26]

The situation after the earthquake also recalled episodes from Haiti's economic and political past.[27] On the economic front, the showcase for Haiti's "build back better" strategy, a slogan former President Bill Clinton first penned for Haiti's recovery after a series of deadly hurricanes in 2009, was the Caracol industrial park, which went forward with little planning and was built largely with U.S. earthquake relief funds. Intended to employ 20,000 people, the park's main industrial anchor was a factory owned by a South Korean garment manufacturer who had earned a reputation in Guatemala for unfair and hostile labor practices. An earlier generation of export-oriented clothing factories in the Duvalier era resulted in a massive influx of workers who came to populate Cité Soleil, helping to transform it into the gang-filled slum it became. The land along Caracol Bay for the industrial park was obtained by the Haitian government by evicting 366 farmers. Before the earthquake, plans had designated this land to be part of Haiti's first protected maritime area.

On the political front, a sense of déjà vu came with the return of two exiled leaders on the eve of the 2011 presidential election in March. First, on January 16, 2011, after twenty-five years away, Jean-Claude "Baby Doc" Duvalier returned from exile in France, asserting he was returning to help in Haiti's reconstruction. Many suspected Baby Doc's true motive was to gain access to funds he had accumulated as president. Then, on March 18, 2011, Jean-Bertrand Aristide returned from exile in South Africa. Aristide had announced his wish to return to Haiti hours after the 2010 earthquake, but the United States asked South Africa to delay his return until after the presidential election. Aristide had declared the 2010 presidential election was not free and fair since his party had been barred from participating, and the United States feared his presence might destabilize the situation in Haiti and disrupt the election.

Added to this political and economic mix in the midst of Haiti's reconstruction efforts was an outbreak of cholera.[28] Cholera, a severe intestinal infection that if untreated is fatal in 25 percent of cases, is transmitted by water or food that has been contaminated by feces. If treated aggressively, the death rate drops to about 1 percent. Prior to October 2010 when the first cholera outbreak in Haiti was announced, there had not been a major incidence of the sickness in the country for fifty years. The outbreak was linked to river water contaminated by a sewage spill at a Nepali peace-keeping camp. In December 2011 the Pan American Health Organization placed the number of dead from cholera at almost 7,000, with over 250,000 cases being reported. This represented a serious health crisis for a country and people already vulnerable to the violence that had sprung up after the earthquake and left without homes or access to public services such as running water and reliable access to food. The passage of two additional years did nothing to improve the situation.[29] In late 2013, unable to get the UN to admit responsibility for the cholera outbreak, advocates for the Haitian victims of the epidemic announced they would bring legal action against the UN, although it was unclear at the time whether U.S. courts would accept the law suit.

The International Monetary Fund had projected 8 percent growth rates for Haiti in 2011 and 2012. The actual rates were far less—only about 2.5 percent in 2012. Homelessness remained an acute problem due in some measure to the type of housing being built. Rather than reconstruct damaged but usable slum housing or build simple homes (at the cost of $6,000 per house), donor organizations such as the Inter-American Development Bank funded the construction of new homes near major economic development projects such as Caracol at a much higher cost (in some cases over $30,000 per house). Many of the houses built remained empty due to problems ranging from an absence of doors and windows to an inability to hook them up to water supplies. Human safety remained under siege. Fourteen percent of refugee camp households reported that one or more family members had been molested. Nine percent reported that a family member had been raped. Much aid money has gone unspent for a variety of reasons, such as contracts falling through and projects being cancelled. For example, Spain provided $100 million to Haiti's water authority for infrastructure development, but only $15 million of it was spent by the end of 2012. The United States has over $1 billion money in unspent Haitian relief money. The Red Cross is holding another $500 million.

Unspent aid money is not unique to the Haiti earthquake relief efforts. Bureaucratic delays and changing government priorities are a political reality for national governments and international organizations. Relief organizations also face these problems. Additionally, they are often unwilling to admit they might have more money than they need. Turning away donations is simply not done.

Conclusion: Lessons of Haitian Relief

According to one relief official, "Haiti is the humanitarian disaster of the future . . . and we're not ready for it."[30] If this assessment is correct, Haiti offers many lessons for those engaged in humanitarian relief efforts. One set of cautionary lessons relates directly to efforts to provide human security to IDPs who are victims of natural disasters. Three such lessons stand out. First, while the great outpouring of funds for the Haitian relief effort was somewhat of an anomaly, as historically many donors have seen helping IDPs fleeing war and civil unrest as more central to their mission than helping those caught in the throes of an earthquake or tsunami, money alone does not matter. In December 2012 there were still 357,000 IDPs remaining in Haitian camps. Those who leave are often enticed into doing so by a payment of cash (in some cases $400 per family) to return home.

The second cautionary lesson is a lack of clarity on what protection means. Relief experts Elizabeth Ferris and Sara Ferro-Ribeiro assert that this was the case in Haiti.[31] They state that international actors spent too much time trying to define what protection meant and came up with a definition that was not helpful in setting human rights priorities. The end result was that those working on protection issues for women, children, prisoners, orphans, and so forth came up with different definitions that denied effective protection to the majority of Haitians. Third, for all that Haiti initially represented a symbol of the world's compassion, symbols have their limits as tools of humanitarian intervention. They cannot overcome donor fatigue, nor can they make organizations spend money or spend it effectively. Moreover, they may be overtaken by new symbols. In November 2012 Hurricane Sandy struck the northeast coast of the United States, inflicting major damage on the metropolitan New York area and bringing forward a wave of aid from concerned citizens and organizations across the United States. Earlier in its journey up the Atlantic Ocean, Hurricane Sandy struck Haiti. Along with a series of earlier fall storms, it created an additional 58,000 IDPs there. When combined with a drought in 2012, 20 percent of Haiti's population now suffered from severe food insecurity. Little was heard of this plight in the United States.

Haiti also offers lessons for the study of conflict and cooperation in world politics. When faced with a humanitarian crisis of the magnitude of the Haitian earthquake, the assumption is that the pathway being travelled by states, international organizations, and nongovernmental organizations will be one characterized by widespread cooperation and that conflict will be minimal if not totally absent. As we have seen, this is not the case. Conflict was present, although not in the form of hostile military action or deliberately aggressive policies. Instead it took the forms of conflicting priorities, a desire to control the situation or act unilaterally, and a tendency to treat Haitians as passive receivers of help rather than as partners in rebuilding their country.

Case Analysis

1. Under what conditions or for what reasons, if any, should a country reject international humanitarian disaster relief aid?

2. To what extent is the pathway of cooperation and conflict on international humanitarian disaster relief aid nonpolitical? If it is not, should it be nonpolitical? How might this be done?

3. Select another recent case of international humanitarian disaster relief and compare it to Haiti. What similarities exist? What differences do you see?

4. How much responsibility do nonprofit organizations bear for the problems that arose in Haiti?

5. What are the responsibilities and obligations of the host government when an international disaster relief humanitarian aid effort is being undertaken within a country?

6. Who should be in charge of international disaster relief humanitarian aid efforts on the ground?

7. Who should determine when the pathway being travelled by those providing international disaster relief humanitarian aid to a country should come to an end—the host government or those donating aid?

8. How would you measure the amount of human security existing in a country?

Suggested Readings

Haiti: One Year Follow Up Report on the Transparency of Relief Organizations Responding to the 2010 Haiti Earthquake (Washington, DC: Disaster Accountability Project, December 2010–January 2011). Using information from surveys sent out to nongovernmental organizations involved in Haitian relief efforts, this report presents an accounting of how numerous nongovernmental organizations performed.

Jobe, Kathleen. "Disaster Relief in Post-Earthquake Haiti: Unintended Consequences of Humanitarian Volunteerism." *Travel, Medicine and Infectious Disease* 9, no. 1 (2011): 1–5. This article summarizes U.S. humanitarian relief efforts in Haiti, giving special attention to the pharmaceutical and medical supply chain and the impact of volunteers on the health care system.

Margesson, Rhoda, and Maureen Taft-Morales. *Haiti Earthquake: Crisis and Response*. Washington, DC: Congressional Research Service, 2010. This work presents early analysis of MINUSTAH after the quake, Haiti relief operations, international relief funding, and congressional concerns.

Rencoret, Nicole, Abby Stoddard, Katherine Haver, Glyn Taylor, and Paul Harvey. *Haiti Earthquake Response: Contextual Analysis*. New York: United Nations Evaluation Group, July 2010. This work presents an overview of the political, social, and economic context within which the Haitian earthquake occurred and discusses the lessons learned from Haiti for disaster relief.

Vohr, James. "Haiti Disaster Relief: Logistics Is the Operation." *Military Review* 91 (July–August 2011): 76–82. Vohr provides an overview of lessons learned from the logistical challenges faced by the military in providing aid to Haiti.

Weisenfeld, Paul. "Successes and Challenges of the Haiti Earthquake Response: The Experience of USAID." *Emory International Law Review* 25, no. 3 (2011) 1,097–1,120. The author, who served as a

USAID administrator and was coordinator of the USAID Haiti Task Force team in Washington, discusses the need for greater efficiencies in disaster relief efforts.

Weiss, Thomas, and David Korn. *Internal Displacement: Conceptualization and Its Consequences*. Oxford, UK: Routledge, 2006. Weiss and Korn offer an analytic and conceptual discussion of the problems associated with internal displacement.

Web Resources

American Red Cross, www.redcross.org. This U.S.-based humanitarian agency provides assistance in disaster relief efforts both in the United States and abroad.

Center for Economic and Policy Research, www.cepr.net. Explore debates and reports on economic and social issues such as economic growth, inequality, and poverty, and review issues particularly concerning Latin America and the Caribbean.

UN Office for the Coordination of Humanitarian Affairs, www.unocha .org. Learn more about the UN agency responsible for bringing together humanitarian actors for a cohesive relief response.

UN Stabilization Mission in Haiti, www.un.org/en/peacekeeping/missions/ minustah. Facts, figures, and more information on MINUSTAH in Haiti are available from their official site.

World Vision, www.worldvision.org. Explore the activities of a Christian humanitarian organization engaged in disaster relief and other efforts worldwide.

13 Libya's Uprising and the Responsibility to Protect

Humanitarian intervention has become a particularly salient feature of international politics since the end of the Cold War. From Somalia to Bosnia to Kosovo, multilateral forces entering conflict zones in the name of saving lives have raised hard questions about the nature of state sovereignty versus an increasingly strong case for the world's "responsibility to protect" civilians from harm when governments are unwilling or unable to do so. In this chapter, we explore both humanitarian intervention and the narrower, newer idea of "responsibility to protect" through a case study of the 2011 intervention in Libya while that country underwent a violent uprising as part of the broader Arab Spring.

The pathway of conflict and cooperation concerning international intervention in Libya included domestic conflict between Libyan leader Muammar Gaddafi and Libyan rebels, as well as conflict from international forces bombarding the country in March 2011. Yet as we see from the cases throughout this book, conflict and cooperation cannot be separated. The international bombardment of Libya is a notable instance of cooperation among North Atlantic Treaty Organization (NATO) countries and between Western countries and members of the Arab League and United Nations (UN) Security Council to protect Libya's residents. This case is significant for many reasons. It speaks to the continued role of outside power in the region of the Middle East and North Africa (MENA), as well as to the multilateral nature of efforts to confront situations in which a government and its people are at odds within a sovereign country. What is the proper role of the outside world? Who makes decisions about what to do, when, and why?

When the conflict includes a dimension of humanitarian crisis—and deliberate, large-scale violence against the civilian population, as it did in Libya—these questions become direr. Norms of human rights coexist with norms of sovereignty and nonintervention. Sovereignty is the long-standing notion that countries are free to conduct themselves domestically without foreign interference. Nonintervention, enshrined in the Charter of the UN Article 2(4), is the idea that countries shall refrain from the threat or use of force against the territorial integrity or political independence of any state.[1] These ideas contrast with the evolving notion of universal human rights, seen broadly as freedoms guaranteed to all people by virtue of being human. Just what counts as a "right" is debated and debatable, but two that are generally agreed upon are the right to life and the protection of noncombatants from government violence.

How the world responds to these competing normative expectations leads us to this case study's Concept Focus on the related concepts of humanitarian intervention and the responsibility to protect (or R2P). We look at the differing views of this debate as applied to Libya across the West, the Arab League, the African Union, and the UN Security Council.

The case of Libya is also important as an example of how Middle East regimes and outside governments are responding to the so-called Arab Spring. Our Spotlight section considers the role of the Arab League in Libya's uprising, as well as in the broader Arab Spring, in order to help understand how the violence arose, why governments responded the way they did, and the prospects for intervention in other regions, such as Syria.

International Intervention in Libya

In December 2010 a movement that came to be called the Arab Spring burst forth in Tunisia after a fruit vendor set himself on fire in protest of that country's oppressive regime. The vendor's desperate act prompted widespread antigovernment protests that led, one month later, to President Ben Ali fleeing the country. Tunisia's success sparked a similar movement in Egypt, which led to the ousting of long-time president Hosni Mubarak. While Tunisia and Egypt saw regime change with little to no violence, when protests arose in Libya, dictator Muammar Gaddafi responded with force.

Unlike his peers in Tunisia and Egypt, who succumbed to the mass movements after brief attempts to repress them or reform their way out of trouble, Gaddafi was intent to stay. Comparing the protestors to "gangs" that were "like rats" and vowing to use force to maintain order,[2] Gaddafi put Libyans and the world on notice that he would not go quietly and would use all means of violent repression to put down the uprising. It was because of Gaddafi's crackdown that the international community grappled with the issue of whether to intervene for humanitarian reasons and protect Libya's woefully vulnerable civilians or to respect Gaddafi's sovereign right to rule and let the matter be resolved internally.

Problem Setting and Origins: The Gaddafi Regime

Like many states in the MENA region, Libya was a construct of European colonialism. In 1911 Italy succeeded the Ottoman Empire as the colonial power in control of what is today the nation of Libya. After Italy's defeat in

---

Box 13.1

Case Summary

When Libyan civilians demonstrated for greater freedoms in early 2011 as part of the larger Arab Spring and were met with a violent crackdown by leader Muammar Gaddafi, the international community determined it had a responsibility to protect the civilians in what Gaddafi said was a domestic concern.

Global Context

When civilians demonstrate for greater freedoms in a country, the international community has historically offered verbal support but considered the matter a domestic concern. In a post–Cold War world that has seen tragedies such as the Rwandan and Serbian genocides receive too little attention too late, failure to act when a regime or faction takes violent action has become a growing issue for the international community.

Key Actors

- Arab League
- Libya

- North Atlantic Treaty Organization (NATO)
- United States

Motives

- Libya's Muammar Gaddafi was determined to remain in power and described the uprising as a domestic issue of terrorism.
- France and the United Kingdom were strong advocates for forceful intervention to protect Libyan civilians.
- The United States didn't want to be seen as tolerating repression, but it also did not want to be perceived as promoting another war in the Middle East. Thus, it let its NATO allies take the lead.
- The Arab League, a bloc of twenty-two Arab countries, advocated intervention in the name of protecting Libyans from their own government.
- Other countries and outside major powers, including Russia and China, struggled to balance their resistance to setting a precedent of humanitarian intervention with their desire to side with the Libyan people.

Concepts

- Humanitarianism
- Human rights

- Right to protect
- Sovereignty

World War II, the UN administered Libya until its independence in 1951. The independent Libya's first leader, King Idris I, was well received by his people from Benghazi in the country's east, but he was reviled by others as a pawn of Western powers in what was the heyday of Arab nationalism in the 1950s and 1960s. In 1952 Egypt's Gamal Abdul Nasser stoked independent Arab nationalist sentiments in the region with the Free Officers coup that ousted the previous British-installed monarch. In September 1969 the Idris regime ended with a military coup led by General Muammar Gaddafi. Like his compatriots in Egypt (Hosni Mubarak), Syria (Hafez al-Assad), and Iraq (Saddam Hussein), Gaddafi became the self-declared ruler of Libya and advocated pan-Arab unity, anti-Westernism, and a unique populist brand of Arab socialism bent on redistributing wealth from elites and Western companies to state-run industries.

Gaddafi put his stamp on Libyan politics through the Green Book, a political treatise that served somewhat as a constitution; by calling people's congresses at the local level of government; and through the nationalization of the oil sector and much of the economy.[3] Tripoli became the new capital, and Libya's power base moved to the northwest where the Gaddafi clan was based. Despite the people's congresses, it was Gaddafi, his clan, and supporters who ruled Libya for the next several decades.

The losers in this revolution and move, then, were kinship networks from the previous regime that were separated by vast distances by desert and the Gulf of Sidra. Gaddafi faced sporadic opposition from these areas, and, like other Arab nationalists who were secular in nature, from Islamists. In the 1980s the National Front for the Liberation of Libya combined Islamists and the secular, prodemocracy Movement for Change and Reform. These early advocates for democratic reforms were unsuccessful and many ended up in prison or forced underground. In the 1990s the Libyan Islamic Fighting Group mounted a more violent campaign, including attempts on Gaddafi's life, on an Islamist agenda before mass repression and imprisonment drove the organization underground and into disarray.

Such repression did not completely eradicate protest in the country. As recently as 2006, protests originally aimed at controversial T-shirts related to cartoons of the Prophet Muhammad turned into demonstrations against the regime. The resultant deaths at the hands of Libyan police became a rallying cry for protesters, who picked the anniversary of February 17 to rally again in 2011.[4] Gaddafi's founding principles of anti-Westernism, Arab socialism, and pan-Arab policies had become dated, worn, and unproductive by the twenty-first century. Libyan youth instead pressed for political liberalization and economic hope for the future in a country where they had only known decades of curtailed civil liberties, state-controlled media, and no true elections for positions of real power. When the economic engine of Gaddafi suffered during downturns in the oil markets or due to sanctions on the country related to Gaddafi's ties to terrorism, Libya's population was left more hopeless still.

International opinion of Gaddafi's regime also worked against him. Although not beloved at home or abroad, over his more than forty years in power, Gaddafi proved himself to be a survivor. Every time protests to his regime arose, he handily put them down with an exercise in repressive violence that, while noted by the international community, was considered a sovereign prerogative. When protests arose in 2011 as part of the wider Arab Spring uprising, Gaddafi was no doubt aware of the global attention directed his way, but past experience showed he could expect no interference when he cracked down on the internal dissent.

| **Box 13.2** |

Concept Focus

Humanitarian Intervention and the Responsibility to Protect

Though they sound similar, humanitarian intervention is distinct from the responsibility to protect (R2P). **Humanitarian intervention** is the introduction of foreign forces into a sovereign country in the name of protecting or saving the lives of the country's civilian population. Such interventions have deep historical roots and have been both unilateral and multilateral. The rights that European philosophers and statesmen advocated originally applied in practice only to European peoples, then later all of humanity.[5] Political scientist Michael Barnett places the "big bang" for legitimate humanitarian intervention with eighteenth-century Enlightenment thinkers and religious movements that helped "translate sympathy into collective action."[6] However, if employed erratically and unilaterally by states, the practice runs the risk of abuse either from (1) moral justifications masking self-interested power grabs by one country against another or (2) humanitarianism given to some but not to all.

The legal status of humanitarian intervention, then, has been hotly contested, particularly in the context of the Charter of the UN paradigm and its emphasis on sovereignty and nonintervention. Given the tide of ethnic cleansing and genocide in the wake of the Cold War, the pressures to intervene despite sovereignty forced the debate to the foreground. The inaction in the Rwanda genocide in 1994, during which an estimated 800,000 were killed in three months, raised issues of moral culpability, and the 1999 NATO intervention in Kosovo in the face of ethnic cleansing created controversy over the use of force within a sovereign state (Serbia) without UN Security Council authorization. This issue came up again in late summer 2013 in the case of Syria after chemical weapons prompted U.S. and British calls for action without Security Council approval.

It is in this context that the **responsibility to protect** phenomenon emerged. Related, but distinct from humanitarian intervention, the R2P is a specific mandate enshrined in the 2005 UN World Summit Outcome Document. Building off a Canadian proposal of the International Commission on Intervention and State Sovereignty (ICISS), the UN World Summit concluded with states agreeing to three principles: (1) the responsibility of the state to protect its own people from harm, (2) the commitment of the international community to assist states in providing this protection, and (3) the responsibility of member states of the UN to respond to a crisis when a state is unable or unwilling to provide that protection.[7] The sorts of actions that are supposed to trigger R2P are war crimes, genocide, ethnic cleansing, and crimes against humanity. These principles were formally accepted in UN Security Council Resolution 1674 with an understanding that R2P is not an automatic invitation for outside interference but only a last resort and only to be undertaken with UN Security Council authorization.[8]

Problem Definition and Response:
A Violent Crackdown on Libya's Uprising

Bolstered by the success of protestors in Tunisia and Egypt, those in Libya opposed to Gaddafi's reign took to the streets, particularly in the country's eastern province, which was far from Gaddafi, Gaddafi's tribal base, and Tripoli. On February 17, 2011, five years after a protest in which police killed ten or more Libyans, people in Benghazi and other northeastern towns rallied in support of the anniversary, as well as in protest of the various problems facing Libyans, which ranged from housing to the regime itself. They faced little resistance from authorities and, emboldened by the Arab Spring, the protests widened and were broadcast from a TV station set up by activists in Benghazi. As defections from the regime became known and Gaddafi's forces engaged in the first crackdown, the initially peaceful protests transitioned to an armed insurrection.[9]

The Gaddafi regime responded with outrage. The rhetoric and actions of the Libyan regime, which vowed that "everything will burn,"[10] unsettled international observers who were anticipating further events. Defecting Libyan pilots added details about the regime's plans on February 21, 2011, saying they had been ordered to bomb the protesting throngs in Benghazi, which suggested that a massacre had been ordered.[11] International pressure to act mounted quickly, but how to do so was not clear cut.

Different countries viewed the events in Libya in different ways. France and the United Kingdom led the pro-intervention voices, with the United States a tepid partner. Others in Europe, such as Italy, were caught between the influx of refugees and the history of colonialism in Libya. Other major powers, such as Russia and China, approached the events with a skeptical eye toward Western humanitarian intervention claims while still wanting to support the will of the Arab people. To them, humanitarian intervention was perceived as an excuse through which Western powers could intervene in domestic affairs of friends and weaker states and, by extension, threaten their own states' sovereignty and domestic policies.

National policy is often presented as a unified idea shared by a country's elite, but many decisions, particularly ones involving the use of force in other countries, are highly controversial. This case study explores the U.S. decision-making process regarding Libya and explains why the United States chose to act and also why it chose to "lead from behind."[12] The Barack Obama administration was divided over what to do about Libya. Defense Secretary Robert Gates was hesitant to intervene and was skeptical about a proposed no-fly zone to combat Gaddafi's advances to recapture ground gained by rebels in the east.[13] Leading the pro-intervention case was UN ambassador Susan Rice and National Security Council member Samantha Power. Rice advocated that the United States go beyond establishing a no-fly zone and push for a broader mandate for intervention, while Power swore to "come down on the side of dramatic action."[14] The United States was the first country to cut Gaddafi's funding, freezing $32 billion in Libyan assets held by U.S. banks, and it supported the effort for a UN resolution over the situation in Libya.[15]

But how exactly to intervene, and the U.S. role in that intervention, raised issues for the Obama administration. The normative pull to "do something" within the global framework of humanitarianism competed with Middle East and world leeriness about Western militarism. Also of concern was U.S. public opposition to another American war in the region, due in part to the United States having a reputation for cultivating authoritarianism in the region despite the rhetoric of democracy from the West. For U.S. diplomats and politicians, navigating U.S. strategy during the Arab Spring, then, was a dance between images of Western imperialism and images of Western hypocrisy. Western intervention might unleash old feelings of anti-imperialism from those in the Middle East, but lack of Western intervention could yield charges of hypocrisy and propping up dictators and cronies. Add to this mix the U.S. public's opposition to intervention in the Middle East after the wars in Iraq and Afghanistan, and it was unsurprising that President Obama took a cautious and multilateral approach to Libya.

In contrast, the British and French took the lead in defining the problem as a humanitarian crisis—one with related economic and social implications for Europe. British prime minister David Cameron warned that "if Gaddafi's attacks on his own people succeed, Libya will once again become a pariah state, festering on Europe's border" and "hundreds of thousands of [Libyan] citizens could seek escape, putting huge pressure on us in Europe."[16] Britain had lately fostered economic ties with Libya through oil contracts between Libya and BP, but it also harbored a lingering resentment that was tied to Libya's complicity in the bombing of Pan Am Flight 103 over Lockerbie, Scotland, in 1988. The French were first to recognize the Libyan rebels' National Transitional Council as the country's legitimate government on March 10, 2011. Authors Lin Noueihed and Alex Warren suggest French president Nicholas Sarkozy's assertiveness was partly related to pending elections and criticisms against him for being too tepid in response to the uprisings in Tunisia at the start of the Arab Spring.[17]

Other NATO countries followed suit, although two in particular were less enthusiastic. Italy's colonialism over Libyan territory from 1911 to 1942 influenced its approach to the crisis. In the 1990s Italy and Libya forged agreements for a new relationship in which Italy acknowledged "the consequences of thirty years of occupation," which included "racist ideologies, mass punishments (deportations, hangings, forced labor)" and policies that resulted in "between 40,000 and 70,000 deaths due to forced deportations, starvation, and disease inside the concentration camps, and hangings and executions."[18]

Italy also was driven by real concerns about the influx of refugees. On February 23, 2011, Italy banded together with five other European Union (EU) Mediterranean states to demand greater European solidarity, partly in terms of money but, more importantly, in terms of parceling Libyan refugees across Europe and disrupting human trafficking syndicates. By early March more than 6,000 migrants had arrived on the Italian island of Lampedusa, which reportedly raised fears over a large influx of people fleeing North Africa's violence.[19] Gaddafi sought to stoke European, and particularly Italian, fears when he told reporters on March 7, 2011, that if he fell from power, "You will have immigration, thousands of people from Libya will invade Europe. There will be no-one to stop them anymore."[20] On March 15, 2011, a ship carrying almost 2,000 migrants from northern Africa who were working in Libya at the time of the uprising was blocked from sailing into Italian waters on the order of Interior Minister Roberto Maroni.[21]

Unlike other EU or NATO members, Italy was also highly integrated with the Libyan economy: nearly a quarter of its crude oil, 10 percent of its natural gas, and billions in Libyan investments flowed into Italy's economy. Italian companies in the manufacturing and petroleum sectors had billions invested in Libyan oil production and infrastructure development. Because of this economic entanglement, although the United States and EU froze Libyan assets abroad and prohibited foreign direct investment, Italy showed reluctance to freeze Libyan sovereign funds until a coordinated response from NATO members was forged.

As the uprising began to gain momentum in February, such economic ties might explain why Italian prime minister Silvio Berlusconi said that he did not want to "bother" Gaddafi by condemning violent crackdowns against Libyans. By the end of that month, however, Berlusconi began condemning the violence once it appeared Gaddafi's hold on power was slipping. Italy's most significant move involved the suspension of the 2008 Italian-Libyan "friendship" treaty—a major foreign policy achievement of the Italian prime minister—which contained a nonaggression clause between the two countries.[22]

Turkey, another NATO ally, is a Muslim country run by an Islamist party, the Justice and Development Party. Turkish prime minister Recep Tayyip Erdoğan opposed NATO involvement in Libya, arguing that NATO's "only task is to protect member states."[23] While Erdoğan warned Libya against taking cruel steps in crushing the uprising, he also expressed opposition to imposing sanctions on Libya, as well as to the establishment of a no-fly zone or military intervention against Gaddafi forces.[24] Representatives of the Turkish foreign ministry met with their European and Middle Eastern counterparts throughout February and cautioned that intervention in Libya could have adverse effects.

While the West decided whether it should intervene in Libya and exactly how much intervention might be needed, another debate arose much closer to home amidst the uprisings within the League of Arab States, also known as the Arab League. Created in 1945, the Arab League consists of governments of twenty-two Arab-majority countries found across Africa and Southwest Asia.

The Arab Spring represented a puzzle to the existing Arab governments, most of which were authoritarian regimes with their own share of oppressive tactics, corruption, and economic woes. If the "Arab street" was demanding change nonviolently and gaining the sympathies of the broader international community, it placed their governments in the difficult situation of needing to balance their grip on power with the potential demands of the public—without inviting international condemnation. The Gulf monarchs—Saudi Arabia, Kuwait, Bahrain, Qatar, United Arab Emirates, and Oman—were threatened by the notion of democratic uprisings, just as they had been threatened before by Arab nationalist and Islamist challenges to their dynastic rule over the past decades. Collectively, these monarchies acted under the auspices of the Gulf Cooperation Council (GCC) to help quell Arab Spring–related unrest brewing in Bahrain. But when it came to Libya, the GCC states sang a different tune. They were eager to show the West and their own citizens that they cared about the plight of Arabs, but they were worried about their own legitimacy and survival. Libya gave many regional states the chance to demonstrate their concern far from their own borders. Gaddafi had garnered little goodwill in the region over the decades and had outright threatened and insulted the traditional monarchies during his earlier years of strident Arab nationalism. These facts made it relatively easy for the Arab League to side with the rest of the international community against Gaddafi.

The Arab League as a regional organization, then, pitted GCC governments against others more suspicious of Western meddling in the region (see Box 13.3). The organization voted to suspend Gaddafi's representatives from GCC meetings, condemning what GCC secretary general Amr Moussa called "crimes against the current peaceful popular protests and demonstrations in several Libyan cities."[25] At that point, Libya's representative to the Arab League, Major Abdel-Moneim al-Huni, resigned his post and left the Gaddafi government due to the dishonor he claimed the regime had created.[26] Ahead of the UN vote, the Arab League also voted for a no-fly zone to be established, with dissenting votes only from Algeria and Syria. Such actions served as public relations fodder and contributed to the growing international consensus for intervention in Libya. In the end, the Arab League worked with the UN to authorize a restrained use of force in Libya.

Beyond NATO and the Arab League, reactions were mixed and hesitant. The African Union, of which Libya was a member, was divided over the prospect of foreign intervention into a fellow African country. Uganda's foreign minister Sam Kutesa reflected the awkward position many of these states were in when he demanded that Gaddafi reform and respond to the will of the Libyan people but also claimed he would "not accept foreign interference" and encouraged what should be "an African solution" to the problem.[27]

Problem Evolution and Development: UN Resolutions for International Action

The resulting effort of the various voices and perspectives on the Libyan uprising was a series of UN resolutions that called for international action within prescribed limits. On March 17, 2011, the UN Security Council

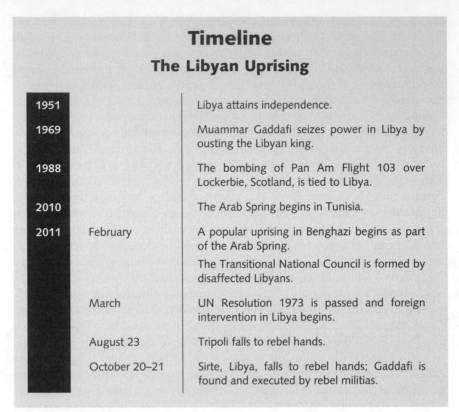

Timeline
The Libyan Uprising

1951		Libya attains independence.
1969		Muammar Gaddafi seizes power in Libya by ousting the Libyan king.
1988		The bombing of Pan Am Flight 103 over Lockerbie, Scotland, is tied to Libya.
2010		The Arab Spring begins in Tunisia.
2011	February	A popular uprising in Benghazi begins as part of the Arab Spring. The Transitional National Council is formed by disaffected Libyans.
	March	UN Resolution 1973 is passed and foreign intervention in Libya begins.
	August 23	Tripoli falls to rebel hands.
	October 20–21	Sirte, Libya, falls to rebel hands; Gaddafi is found and executed by rebel militias.

passed UN Resolution 1973 by a vote of 10–0, with five abstentions: Brazil, China, Germany, India, and Russia. The resolution began with a demand for a "complete end to violence and all attacks against, and abuses of, civilians." It placed special onus on Libyan authorities to "comply with their obligations" under "international humanitarian law" and to "take all measures to protect civilians and meet their basic needs, and to ensure the rapid and unimpeded passage of humanitarian assistance."[28] The resolution also called for a freeze of regime assets and an arms embargo.

The real punch in Resolution 1973, though, was in authorizing UN member states to take "all necessary measures . . . to protect civilians and civilian populated areas under threat of attack" in Libya. The resolution, toward that end, established a no-fly zone that empowered foreign forces to enforce "a ban on all flights in the airspace of the Libyan Arab Jamahiriya in order to help protect civilians."[29] This was intended to prevent further aerial assaults by the Gaddafi regime. Humanitarian and NATO flights continued in Libyan airspace.

Importantly, and reflective of Arab and Turkish hesitancy toward Western intervention after especially the Iraq War of 2003, Resolution 1973 prohibited a foreign occupation force within Libyan territory.[30] As UN members were eager to build consensus and legitimacy for intervention, the final resolution tried to be sensitive to regional politics and reiterated the need for participating countries to keep the UN and Arab League secretaries general informed of any measures taken in the implementation of the resolution.[31]

Implementing Resolution 1973 was a curious affair given its constraints and the different motives of the involved parties. British foreign secretary William Hague hailed the resolution as a necessary measure "to avoid greater bloodshed, to try to stop what is happening in terms of the attack on civilians."[32] Hinting that the operation might be about more than just protecting civilians, Hague also asserted that "the Libyan people must be able to have a more representative government and determine their own future."[33] Italy remained opposed to unilateral military action against Libya but did support a Libyan no-fly zone if the UN Security Council approved it within a framework acceptable to the Arab nations in the region. Yet the pressures on Italy resulting from the influx of Libyan refugees became a focal point of the domestic debate within the Italian cabinet and legislature. Succumbing to these pressures and reversing its earlier reluctance to get too involved, on March 20, 2011, Italy opened its military bases to NATO members led by Britain, France, and the United States after the UN Security Council resolution passed.[34]

The MENA regional position, including that of Turkey, also came around in favor of humanitarian intervention. In March 2011 Turkey made a priority of providing Libya with humanitarian assistance in recognition of the two countries' shared historical and cultural ties. Turkey's careful and neutrally worded statement about the assistance avoided taking sides and claimed that its only aim was to help the Libyan people.

Although Turkey had sided in favor of NATO humanitarian intervention, its representatives attempted a careful balancing act, maintaining contact with both Libyan rebels and government officials. Turkish foreign minister Ahmet Davutoğlu met with Libyan opposition member Mahmoud Jibril, who handled foreign affairs for the Transitional National Council, in the opposition stronghold of Benghazi. That same week, Davutoğlu also met with Gaddafi 's envoy, Libyan deputy foreign minister Abdelati Obeidi. This approach had consequences in Libya, where protesters attacked the Turkish consulate and demanded that the Turkish flag be lowered.[35] By July Turkey had moved solidly into a position of ousting Gaddafi and recognized the rebel government as the country's legitimate representative, promising $200 million in aid.[36]

If Resolution 1973 was meant to affect Libya's behavior, it did not work. Gaddafi scoffed at the UN's actions. U.S. secretary of state Hillary Clinton responded that coalition military action in Libya would continue until Gaddafi complied with the resolution, saying that Gaddafi was in "flagrant breach" of the resolution's terms.[37] Gaddafi's forces continued to wage war while trying to persuade the world that the rebellion was the product of foreign terrorism and meddling. Al-Qaeda, for its part, had issued a call for support for the rebellion, and at least some factions of Libyan rebels recruited fighters with ties to groups in a "cooperative relationship" with al-Qaeda.[38] This aspect of the Arab Spring uprisings, in Libya as well as Syria and elsewhere, complicated support for rebellion by both Western powers and regional regimes wary of radical Islamist attempts at revolution. Still, in Libya the main thrust of the opposition seemed to be Libyan nationalists and local Gaddafi opposition eager for change after decades of abuse.

In April 2011 Gaddafi called for a cease-fire and negotiations, which could have been an opportunity for cooperation to resolve the problem. But the condition for talks was a cessation of air strikes. The United States, United Kingdom, and France refused to accept this condition, pointing out that "the regime has announced ceasefires several times before and continued attacking cities and civilians."[39]

An April 30 air strike by NATO struck Gaddafi's Tripoli home, killing members of his family, including children. This became a point of controversy not just because of the killing of civilians and children by the intervening powers but also for the targeting of government leadership, which seemed to go beyond the mandate of "protecting civilians." Had the UN mission become—or was it always meant to be—one of regime change? This perception frayed the prospects for cooperation from the international community and confirmed the suspicions of those who had been hesitant to permit the authorization of force.

Pressing the case against Gaddafi in the international arena, in June the International Criminal Court issued a warrant for the arrest of Gaddafi, his son Saif al-Islam, and his intelligence chief Abdullah al-Senussi, charging them with crimes against humanity and opening the legal avenue to capture the Libyan leaders to bring them to justice. At this point, cooperation or resolution seemed to be out of reach, and the battle for the future of Libya was in the hands of the UN-supported rebels who fought against the increasingly marginalized Gaddafi regime.

The fighting continued throughout the summer, with the rebels making gains and pushing west towards the capital, Tripoli. On August 21, 2011, the rebel forces entered Tripoli as Gaddafi made radio appeals to rise against the rebel "rats." By August 23, 2011, the rebels had taken Tripoli, sending Gaddafi and his allies fleeing to his hometown of Sirte.

The interim government gained international recognition as the legitimate voice of the Libyan people at a Paris conference on September 1 and moved into Tripoli under interim prime minister Mahmoud Jibril. Once established, the interim government began pumping Libya's oil on behalf of the new regime, and the UN Security Council removed sanctions on the country. The UN General Assembly granted recognition to the National Transitional Council, capping the rise to power of the rebel factions as Gaddafi and his dwindling loyalist forces fought for their lives in a few remaining towns, including Sirte. In October 2011 Sirte fell and Gaddafi went into hiding. He was found and handled severely by his captors. He died from his injuries, bringing an inauspicious end to a forty-year reign.

| **Box 13.3** |

Spotlight

The Arab League's Approach to the Arab Spring

The Arab League cast its support with the NATO-led intervention in Libya. Gaddafi lacked friends in the league and the broader Middle East, and, as such, he was an easy target to turn against, allowing Arab nations to support Libyan citizens' quest for reform and greater freedoms without committing to anything at home. But the case of Libya cannot be understood outside the context of the so-called Arab Spring. With the relatively nonviolent falls of the regimes in Tunisia and Egypt providing inspiration to the citizens of other authoritarian regimes, similar protests arose in Libya, as well as Yemen, Bahrain, and Syria. To date, only Libya has been the recipient of international humanitarian intervention, in part because not all countries faced widespread threats to their regimes.

Many countries saw Arab Spring protests of different degrees, and their governments responded with different degrees of reform and repression. The Arab League, of which most of these countries were members, also responded in different ways. Yemeni president Ali Abdullah Saleh stepped down after escalating violence occurred in his country, but only after quiet prodding from the Saudis, who were initially reluctant to see him go. Bahrain's monarchy also fended off popular challenge with the help of Saudi Arabia's military intervention under the Gulf Cooperation Council. In both of these cases, the Arab League did not promote intervention and, in fact, major players reiterated the sovereign right of countries to handle internal affairs.

Syria's Arab Spring uprising has been the most deadly in the region, with an estimated 100,000 killed as of the summer of 2013. Like Libya, Syria spiraled into a bloody, militarized civil war, with armed factions and defections combining with international sanctions from the United States and European Union. Unlike with Libya, however, the United Nations could not agree on intervention, with Russia threatening to veto calls for the use of force. The Arab League voted to suspend the regime of President Bashar al-Assad from the league's proceedings. In subsequent meetings the Arab League also approved sanctions on Syria and support for arming the opposition groups. In spring 2013 the Syrian opposition group, the so-called National Coalition, assumed the Syrian seat in the Arab League, even as the civil war languished on.

While the Arab Spring speaks to a set of common conditions—economic deprivation, corruption, authoritarianism, and bulging unemployed youth populations increasingly plugged into social media—each country's story has had a different outcome. These outcomes have relied decisively on the role of the regime's military and whether outside powers went in or stayed out. The Arab League's role, while not integral to the fate of regimes under attack, is important since the league can legitimize governments or their opposition and legitimize or undermine international action.

Conclusion: Causes and Consequences of Intervention

By the end of 2011, Libya had undergone historic transformation. As of August 2013 it had become a fledgling democracy, though many questions of security and liberty were still unanswered. An attack on the U.S. consulate on September 11, 2012, killed the U.S. ambassador, and the perpetrators are still unaccounted for. Weapons from Libya have spread to conflict areas in Algeria and Mali, fueling regional instability in North Africa and adding complexity to the debate about the virtues and consequences of foreign intervention. Ending an old problem—tyranny—may beget new problems of chaos if not handled carefully. Could Libya have come to such a fate without international intervention? Could intervention have been avoided if Gaddafi had been willing to cooperate in the first place? As we see again, lack of cooperation is one side of a coin and conflict the other. The NATO-led military operation was originally a humanitarian mission, yet the implementation of UN Resolution 1973 facilitated the success of the rebellion and the ouster of the Gaddafi regime. Whether regime change was originally the ultimate purpose or just the consequence of a humanitarian intervention is hotly debated. Some fear that humanitarianism is a cloak for more instrumental or imperial agendas. Whether or not the UN and Arab League endorsements legitimized the actions in Libya, the question of how to protect civilians from their own governments within the context of sovereignty remains a daunting puzzle for the future to solve.

The lessons of Libya—the causes and consequences of foreign intervention there—will echo throughout the region in other hot spots, especially Syria. After the August 2013 allegations of chemical weapons use in Syria, debate ramped up in the UN about whether to intervene, how to intervene, and what resolution would be sought. The Arab League representative to the UN walked a line, claiming to be horrified over the deaths of hundreds of innocent civilians but noting "international law says that military action must be taken after a decision by the [Security] Council"—a caution against possible Western attacks without UN approval.[40] Whether conflict in Syria goes the way of that in Libya will have a lot to do with whether there is cooperation in the UN and Arab League in support or opposition to intervention.

Case Analysis

1. How did different governments view the crisis in Libya? Consider the elements that influence decision making in foreign policy. Explain what motivations you attribute to the different views.

2. How does humanitarian intervention get shaped through multilateralism— when many governments participate in the debate about policy and how to

implement it? What are the trade-offs of intervening alone (unilaterally) as opposed to with others?

3. How did the multilateral pathway to intervention in Libya affect how the NATO operation was conducted? How did acting in an alliance and under UN resolution guidelines shape the course of intervention?

4. Describe how the Arab League's position toward Libya differed from its approach to other uprisings in the Arab Spring. What do you think was behind its shift in position?

5. The United States is described as taking the position of "leading from behind" in Libya. How did it do so? What domestic politics may have led President Obama to want to avoid looking like he was taking the United States to war in the Middle East?

6. Why was it important for Resolution 1973 to ban foreign troops in Libya? How may have this also helped the Obama administration with its domestic politics?

7. Consider Libya's pathway of conflict and cooperation that led to its Arab Spring uprising. Were there missed opportunities for cooperation? Explain your response.

8. Given the events in Rwanda, Kosovo, and Libya that gave increasing attention to the international community's sense of a responsibility to protect, identify a similar current crisis and make an argument for R2P.

Suggested Readings

Barnett, Michael. *Empire of Humanity: A History of Humanitarianism*. Ithaca, NY: Cornell University Press, 2011. This book is an in-depth look at the politics of promoting and enforcing humanitarianism.

Bellamy, Alex. *Global Politics and the Responsibility to Protect: From Words to Deeds*. New York: Routledge, 2011. This book surveys the origins of R2P and the shortcomings of the international community to implement it consistently.

Daalder, Ivo, and James Stavridis, "NATO's Victory in Libya: The Right Way to Run an Intervention." *Foreign Affairs* 91, no. 2 (2012). Available online at www.foreignaffairs.com/articles/137073/ivo-h-daalder-and-james-g-stavridis/natos-victory-in-libya. This article presents a favorable analysis of the NATO intervention in Libya.

Dawisha, Adeed. *The Second Arab Awakening: Revolution, Democracy and the Islamist Challenge from Tunis to Damascus*. New York: W. W. Norton, 2013. This book situates the "Arab Spring" in the historical context of the region that has known previous periods of social upheaval.

Noueihed, Lin, and Alex Warren. *The Battle for the Arab Spring: Revolution, Counter-Revolution and the Making of a New Era.* Cambridge: Yale University Press, 2012. An excellent survey of the early cases of the "Arab Spring," including other governments' responses in the region.

Pape, Robert. "When Duty Calls: A Pragmatic Standard of Humanitarian Intervention." *International Security* 37, no. 1 (2012): 41–80. This article attempts to situate military intervention between interests and moral obligation.

Web Resources

Arab Spring Timeline, *The Guardian,* www.theguardian.com/world/interactive/2011/mar/22/middle-east-protest-interactive-timeline. The British newspaper *The Guardian* presents an interactive guide to the events of the Arab Spring in Libya and the rest of the Middle East.

League of Arab States, www.lasportal.org. The official site for the League of Arab States (in Arabic and English) gives an overview of the Arab League and its members. It also includes statements of the organization's position on issues, including Libya and Syria.

NATO, Operation Unified Protector, www.nato.int/cps/en/natolive/71679.htm. This resource provides official statements and documents related to the NATO operation in Libya.

UN Resolution 1973, www.un.org/News/Press/docs/2011/sc10200.doc.htm. Access the complete text of the UN resolution passed on March 17, 2011.

14 Governing the Global Commons of the Arctic

In this chapter we examine the challenges of cooperating on a pathway that is still very much under construction. Our concern is with the Arctic, a region that for two very different reasons has long lacked any clear set of international rules promoting cooperation among states or limiting conflict between countries operating within its boundaries. First, in the past the Arctic was considered a remote geographic area of little economic value, so countries had little reason to be interested in it. Second, flying over the Arctic or going underneath its waters constituted the shortest route for Russian and American missiles and submarines to reach each other's territory.

These reasons are no longer valid. The Arctic is now viewed as a potentially valuable economic resource because of the oil that lies beneath its waters and because the shrinking polar ice cap has opened up shipping waterways that bring Europe and Asia much closer together. And, while the end of the Cold War did not transform the United States and Russia into allies, it opened up space for cooperation that once did not exist. The increased value of the Arctic is not without its costs, including the potential for threatening a fragile environment and disrupting the lifestyles of traditional inhabitants of the region.

As a result of these unique features, the Arctic pathway of conflict and cooperation that countries currently are travelling is one marked more by a record of neglect rather than conflict. The challenge countries face is not one of overcoming past distrust of an adversary but of finding common ground for the future among neighbors long preoccupied with other interests. Our Concept Focus in this chapter is concerned with international regimes. Our Spotlight section highlights the regional and global challenges that have emerged to face the Arctic Council, which is the intergovernmental forum that promotes cooperation and coordination among the Arctic states.

The Arctic Rediscovered and Redefined

Whereas the world's average temperature in 2012 was almost 0.5 degrees centigrade above the average seen from 1951 to 1980, in the Arctic it was almost two degrees centigrade higher. The results of this rising

---

Box 14.1

Case Summary

Environmental and economic changes, as well as increasing globalization, have resulted in contention between nations seeking to manage the Arctic and its resources—a global commons—for their benefit. These factors have also raised the possibility of future military competition in the region.

Global Context

The ending of the Cold War and the increased significance of globalization, as well as environmental changes (the melting of the polar ice pack) and economic changes (the increased importance of oil and year-round waterways connecting Europe and Asia), have served to catapult the Arctic onto the global agenda.

Key Actors

- United States
- Russia
- Canada
- China and Japan
- The Inuit, represented through organizations

Motives

- The United States and Russia are most concerned with protecting national access to key Arctic resources, particularly in relation to military and economic security issues.
- Canada wishes to maintain its sovereignty over key aspects of the Arctic.
- Although China and Japan have no territory in the Arctic, they seek to have a voice in Arctic decision making to represent their own national interests.
- The Inuit are concerned about representing their lifestyle, culture, and native environment.

Concepts:

- Global commons
- Human rights
- International regimes
- National security
- Sustainable development

---

temperature were evident for all to see. By September 2012 the Arctic Ocean's ice sheet had shrunk to half of what it was in 1979. Two of the most common images of the Arctic today are that it is a cold, distant region and one threatened by environmental degradation and threats to native

species. In a sense, both views are correct. Traditional geographic definitions stress its northern location either by virtue of its (1) lying north of
the Arctic Circle (66° 33'N), (2) existing above the northernmost tree line,
or (3) having an average temperature that is below 50°F in the warmest
month. It is also a region that quite literally is vanishing. Arctic glaciers
are thawing at an astonishing rate. The area covered by snow in June is
about one-fifth less than it was in the 1960s, and parts of Alaska are losing
territory at the rate of 454 feet per year. If the melting trend continues, the
sea level may rise to the point where many of the world's largest cities may
become imperiled by rising waters. From 20,000 to 25,000 polar bears live
in the wild in Canada, the United States, Russia, Denmark, and Norway.
Rising demand for polar bears in China and Russia, along with increased
hunting quotas for indigenous populations in Canada, has created alarm
among advocates of endangered species who seek a global ban on trade in
polar bears.

These truths also mask a changing political reality: the Arctic has been
rediscovered and redefined. Once a peripheral region whose fate could be
safely left in the hands of second- and third-ranking diplomats and bureaucrats, now its environmental and endangered species concerns monopolize
headlines. The Arctic today is a region that commands the attention of presidents and secretaries of state. Its oil reserves and navigational waterways
could be useful in constructing thriving economies in an era of globalization
and rising energy prices, but at the same time, they suggest points of lever-
age that could be used against a country's national interests. The Arctic is
now less of a self-contained region whose problems are defined in terms of
its particular history, culture, and norms than it is a region in which global
geopolitical concerns define an agenda for action.[1]

Left unanswered in its rise to prominence is the question of how should
the Arctic, with its vast swaths of land and ice and no developed infrastructure or administration, be governed? Should countries be allowed to claim
portions of it as their own territory, thus carving it up into pieces, or should
the Arctic be treated as a global commons that belongs to no country or set
of countries? If the first option were to come to fruition, the rules set up
for governing the Arctic ought to advance a country's national interest. Of
course, issues of which states could claim it as property and on what basis
sovereignty could be claimed would need to be addressed. If the global commons option took prominence, the rules should be formulated with an eye
to preserving the Arctic as a global inheritance for all people and for future
generations.

International regimes are one way of establishing rules for governing
the use of a global commons territory.[2] What makes the case of the Arctic
regime different from other contemporary efforts of regime-building is that
here we are concerned with a regime for a specific geographic area, where
in most cases regimes are being constructed or debated for functional areas
such as the environment, natural resources, or cyberspace.

| **Box 14.2** |

Concept Focus

International Regimes

We tend to speak of foreign policy as if it is a singular course of action, as in U.S. foreign policy or Chinese foreign policy. In reality, at any one point in time a country's foreign policy reaches out in multiple ways and in multiple directions. Among the types of foreign policy problems that confront policymakers with the greatest challenges are those whose solution or effective management lies beyond their unilateral control. Foremost among these types of problems are those involving a global commons. The concept of a global commons dates back to old English law and refers to land that is owned by the village as a whole and not by any one individual. Accordingly, it was land that was to be used for the common good and could be used by all villagers. The concept of a commons was originally applied to the international politics of natural resources, oceans, climate, pollution, and outer space. More recently, it also has been applied to such human creations as the Internet and open source software.

To treat a problem or region as a commons does not mean conflict among states does not exist. States may hold potentially contradictory policy goals in using the commons. They may seek to use the commons for their own benefit and gain and in the process deny or reduce access to the commons to competitors, or they may seek to preserve the commons so that it may be used by all members of the community and by future generations. The cumulative end result of giving priority to narrowly defined state interests over the global interest is the destruction of the commons, which is typically referred to as the "tragedy of the commons" because the long-term destruction was not intended, nor were the goals of advancing short-term state interests necessarily irrational.

One strategy available to countries trying to respond to the challenges of using and preserving a commons is to create regimes. A regime is a set of norms, rules, and decision-making procedures that allow participating members to coordinate their actions and jointly achieve their foreign policy goals.

Regimes are not synonymous with international organizations. Regimes may be built *around* international organizations, but this is not necessary. What is essential to the successful operation of a regime so that it increases the ability of countries to cooperate are that it carries out three functions: (1) it provides information about the actions of members, thus reducing the number of misunderstandings among members and fears of being exploited by others who are breaking or manipulating the rules; (2) it reduces transaction costs, or the time and effort of reaching future agreements; and (3) it creates an overall expectation of cooperation among members.

Although regimes share these common functions, they can also be differentiated in a number of ways. Two of these ways are particularly important in understanding the ability of a regime to foster cooperation and the types of policy goals it is trying to advance. First, we can distinguish between strong and weak regimes depending on whether or not consensus exists among members over the nature of the problem and the correct course of action to take, whether clearly stated standards of behavior exist, whether a well-developed monitoring system of member behavior exists, and whether there is an ability to punish or sanction members that violate regime norms. The more of these conditions present, the stronger the regime.

Second, regimes can be differentiated in terms of the dynamics that led to their creation. On the one hand, they may be created out of a shared sense of purpose rooted in the conviction that cooperative action is necessary to address a problem. Under these circumstances regimes are negotiated into existence. The other option is for a powerful country to create a regime largely to legitimize its dominance and facilitate the pursuit of its own exclusive foreign policy interests.

Regimes are not without their critics. One commonly cited problem is the democratic deficit. In this situation, as key decisions are made in accordance with regime rules and norms or through international organizations, citizens have less and less control over those decisions. A second argument against regimes is that they on occasion make problems worse rather than better. This can occur because they prevent governments and local political authorities from responding in accordance with solutions geared to a particular context and replace them with generic global solutions.

Problem Setting and Origins:
Internationally Claimed and Resource Rich

The uniquely defining political characteristics of the Arctic as a region in world politics today emerge from the intersection of its three essential features. Where much of Antarctica in the south is a single continent surrounded by oceans, the northern region of the Arctic is largely an ice-covered ocean surrounded by several continents. It includes a large portion of Greenland, which is a not an independent country but a self-governing part of Denmark; the Spitsbergen Peninsula belonging to Norway; and parts of Finland, Sweden, Iceland, Russia, Canada, and the United States. Thus, the Arctic lacks a political center.

The world is concerned with the Arctic as a political region because it contains passageways connecting more important areas and because it is the source of economically valuable natural resources. One of the more famous passageways in the Arctic is the Northwest Passage, which Canada holds to be part of its inland waterway and which the United States considers to be an international strait. Another long-standing dispute involving the United States and Canada is over the Beaufort Sea, which lies between the Yukon Territory and Alaska. The Beaufort Sea holds valuable fish stocks and potentially significant oil reserves.

A second defining feature of the Arctic is the role it played in the Cold War. Not unlike Antarctica, the Arctic long existed on the fringes of world politics. The countries along its perimeter reached out to it only tentatively and for varied purposes. Russians entered Siberia in the sixteenth century in pursuit of fur trade. The British, through their possession of Canada, turned to the Arctic in hopes of finding a route to China (the Northwest Passage) that would not only reduce travel time but allow them to avoid the powerful Portuguese and Spanish navies patrolling the warm water oceans.

The United States became an Arctic power with the purchase of Alaska from Russia in 1867. While the primary interests they had in the Arctic varied for each of these major powers, perhaps the primary benefit the Arctic provided them all with was a wall of security that sealed them off from a northern attack on their core territories.

The Arctic's isolation from the broader pattern of world politics lessened considerably with the onset of the Cold War after World War II. Rather than serve as a protective barrier from attack, the Arctic now became a primary route through which both the Soviet Union and the United States feared such attacks might occur. Most significantly, the so-called great circle route across the North Pole provides the shortest direct line for aircraft to follow when travelling between the two countries. Elaborate early warning systems were set up to provide protection from long-range bomber and missile attacks that might travel this route. The distant early warning (DEW) line was the most notable early warning system, consisting of a series of sixty-three radar stations located above the Arctic Circle running from Greenland and Iceland through Canada and into the United States. The stations were authorized in 1954 and became operational in 1957. Submarines also benefitted from using the Arctic waters. Some 5,000 miles were saved by sending submarines covertly to the Pacific by Arctic waters rather than passing them publicly through the Panama Canal.

The third defining characteristic of the Arctic is its indigenous population.[3] Unlike Antarctica, which has no permanent residents, the Arctic was home to approximately 4 million people in 2013. This figure combined the indigenous population, whose roots go back thousands of years, and the nonindigenous population. Estimates from 1910 placed the total Arctic population at less than 300,000 residents. The most politically significant indigenous population in the Arctic then and now is the Inuit, who live in Canada, Russia, Greenland (Denmark), and the United States. Inuit leaders placed their number at approximately 100,000 in the late 1970s. Current estimates place the number at 160,000.

A core issue for the Inuit has long been control over natural resources and land rights, which lie at the heart of an even larger issue—that of self-determination. These concerns have shaped pan-Inuit cooperation across national boundaries and were, in turn, shaped by the discovery of oil in the Arctic. Oil was discovered in Arctic Alaska in 1957, and by 1963, 1,000 indigenous people from twenty-four Alaskan villages had petitioned for a land freeze in the state until issues of native rights were resolved. The Inuit of the North Slope of Prudhoe Bay, where oil was discovered, soon organized the Arctic Slope Native Association and laid claim to over 88,000 square miles of traditional Inuit hunting land. Resource exploration led indigenous peoples to also organize in Canada. The announcement of the intent to construct a hydroelectric power dam at James Bay led Inuit and Cree leaders to join together in opposition by forming the Indians of Quebec Association.

The political organization of indigenous people took on an international dimension in 1973 when the first Arctic Peoples Conference was held in

Copenhagen, Denmark. Inuit from Canada were represented, but absent were representatives from Alaska and the Soviet Union. Four years later, in 1977, the first Inuit Circumpolar Conference (ICC) was held.[4] In attendance were representatives from Greenland, Canada, and the United States. Inuit from the Soviet Union did not participate until a later ICC meeting.

While formal transnational cooperation among the Inuit gave the international politics of the Arctic a dimension not found in other regions, other, more traditional, forms of state-to-state cooperation were also present. As early as 1911, the United States, Russia, Japan, and Great Britain (for Canada) signed the North Pacific Sealing Convention, which was designed in part to help restore the stock of seals in the Bearing Sea. More than half a century later, in 1973, five Arctic states, including the United States and Soviet Union, signed the Agreement on the Conservation of Polar Bears. The 1920 Svalbard Treaty broke new ground by demilitarizing the Svalbard archipelago. Originally signed by fourteen states, the treaty awarded this contested piece of Arctic territory to Norway but at the same time prohibited Norway from building naval and military fortifications there. Norway was also required to respect the environment and the rights of other states to engage in such varied forms of economic activity as fishing, hunting, mining, and trade.

This treaty is seen by many as the model on which the 1959 Antarctic Treaty was based. The Antarctic Treaty was the first Cold War arms control agreement. It established the region as a scientific preserve and one only to be used for peaceful purposes. All forms of military activity are prohibited. Quite explicitly, the treaty does not recognize or establish any claims of territorial sovereignty to the Antarctic. Additionally, it states that "no new claims shall be asserted while the treaty is in force."[5]

Problem Definition and Response: The Battle for Arctic Governance

The tendency to see the Antarctic and the Arctic as similar rather than quite distinct international regions led to the widespread belief that a treaty similar to the Antarctic Treaty would soon be negotiated for the Arctic. This did not happen. The combination of the absence of a single large landmass, geographic proximity to the two superpowers, the presence of natural resources, and a permanent population made the Arctic a far more politically sensitive region during the Cold War than was Antarctica. Calls for the creation of nuclear-free zones did appear periodically in the 1960s, but even they tended to focus on regions adjacent to the Arctic rather than in the Arctic itself.

It was not until the late 1980s that the impetus for creating an international governing structure for the Arctic appeared on the international political agenda in the form of an October 1987 speech given by Soviet premier Mikhail Gorbachev in Murmansk. Gorbachev had assumed the leadership of the Soviet Union's Communist Party in 1985 following a series of

Timeline
Global Interest in the Arctic

1903–1906	The Northwest Passage is first navigated.
1911	The North Pacific Sealing Convention is signed.
1957	The distant early warning line becomes operational. Oil is discovered in Alaska.
1959	The Antarctic Treaty is signed.
1973	The First Arctic Peoples Conference is held. The Agreement on the Conservation of Polar Bears is signed
1977	The First Inuit Circumpolar Conference is held.
1987	Gorbachev gives a speech calling for denuclearization of the Arctic.
1991	The Arctic Environmental Protection Strategy is signed. The Northern Forum is established.
1996	The Arctic Council is founded.
2007	A Russian explorer plants the Russian flag on the Arctic Ocean floor.
2009	President George W. Bush's National Security Document identifies the United States as having fundamental security interests in the Arctic.
2012	Russian president Vladimir Putin calls for stronger Russian naval presence in the Arctic. A treaty on search and rescue protocols in the Arctic is signed.

predecessors who ruled only for a year or two, and he faced the challenge of addressing massive economic difficulties at home. To this end, he instituted the twin policies of *glasnost* (restructuring) and *perestroika* (openness). Recognizing the need for trade and the inability to sustain the high level of military spending that had characterized Soviet foreign policy, Gorbachev also put forward a "new thinking" policy that emphasized toning down Cold War hostilities with the United States. One element of this new thinking was to embrace the language of arms control and disarmament.

One of the first signs of the extent to which Gorbachev's ascendance to power had changed Soviet foreign policy was his speech in Murmansk on October 1, 1987. In this speech Gorbachev outlined both military security and nonmilitary cooperation agendas for the Arctic. In the area of military security, he called for denuclearization of the Arctic, naval arms control, and the development of confidence-building measures. As for the non-military agendas, Gorbachev proposed cooperation in developing natural resources/energy, the coordination of scientific research, and coordination on protecting the environment. He also called for a change in Soviet policy that would allow indigenous people within the Soviet Union to attend international meetings of Arctic peoples.

The impact of Gorbachev's speech on Arctic governance varied by major topic area. Those in the military security area received it with skepticism and produced little by way of meaningful diplomatic activity. The superpower public relations battle over arms control in Europe was very much alive, and the Intermediate Nuclear Forces Treaty limiting the size of nuclear deployments in Europe would not be signed by Gorbachev and Reagan for two more months. In contrast, calls for cooperation in the areas of environment, science, and natural resources set in motion a diplomatic process that began in 1989 at the initiative of Finland and led to the creation of the Arctic Environmental Protection Strategy (AEPS) in June 1991. This nonbinding agreement was signed by Canada, the United States, Denmark, Finland, Iceland, Norway, Sweden, and the Soviet Union. It pledged signatories to preserve the environmental quality and natural resources of the Arctic environment and to meet the needs and traditions of the Arctic Native peoples. This meeting is considered historic because three indigenous peoples groups attended as observers and were designated as permanent participants.

It was not long before proposals for a more formal vehicle for Arctic cooperation emerged, crystallizing in the creation of the Arctic Council in 1996.[6] A number of contentious issues divided the founding members of the Arctic Council. The council membership was the same as that of the AEPS, which was absorbed into this new body. One issue was the scope of the council's concern. The United States was adamant that the council's focus should be narrowly restricted to environmental issues and rejected proposals to extend its jurisdiction to include military security issues or development issues, especially in cases where natural resources were to be defined as belonging to a common or shared region. Russia (the Soviet Union had formally ended on December 25, 1991) shared the U.S. objection to any discussions on a common security approach or to looking at nuclear contamination in the Arctic. Canada, on the other hand, favored a more expansive definition of the Arctic Council's jurisdiction, one that included developing a common maritime policy.

A second issue dividing the Arctic Council was the role of indigenous groups. The AEPS had established the principle of formally certifying indigenous groups as permanent participants. The question now became whether this status should be extended to others. Fears existed in some quarters that so many indigenous groups would seek to become permanent participants that it would dilute the voice of indigenous peoples. Others called for having indigenous groups participate as part of national delegations. This issue had been left purposely vague at the founding of the AEPS, with it being noted that "different situations in the arctic countries may call for different ways of achieving" representation.[7]

The third issue dividing the founding members was the official status of the Arctic Council. The United States insisted that the council was not to be seen as a body that could make decisions or take action that was legally binding on its members. It was not to have any formal role in coordinating Arctic policies other than those agreed to by its members. The Arctic Council was to be an arena for political discussion—a forum for exchanging views. Accordingly, it would not be established by a treaty but through a declaration. To drive home the point that the Arctic Council was not a formal international institution with a headquarters and secretariat, U.S. secretary of state Warren Christopher indicated that he would not attend the signing ceremony creating the council. Russia then followed suit by not sending its minister of foreign affairs.

Movement toward the transitional organization of regional and local governments followed soon after that to organize indigenous peoples. The foundation was laid in 1974 at the First International Conference on Human Environment in the Northern Region that was held in Japan. It was attended by officials from Canadian provincial governments; U.S. states such as North Dakota, Washington, Alaska, Idaho, and Minnesota; and cities in Finland, Sweden, and Norway. Little movement toward action occurred until after the Soviet Union fell, at which point representatives from Russian *oblasts* (administrative regions) became active members. At this time, discussions among northern regional and local governments took on a more formal shape with the founding of the Northern Forum. Like the Inuit Circumpolar Council, the forum also has observer status in the Arctic Council.

Established in 1991, the same year the AEPS was formulated, the Northern Forum has a more diverse membership than the Arctic Council. Founding members included representatives from China, Japan, and the Republic of Korea. Greenland, on the other hand, has no members on the Arctic Forum. The forum's central focus is on sustainable development, which is an economic development strategy that emphasizes conserving natural resources for use by future generations as opposed to a "growth now" strategy that sees natural resources as tools to be used to the maximum extent possible in the present. This stands in sharp contrast to the AEPS and the Arctic Council, where pressure from the United States marginalized discussions of sustainable development. The roots of this difference in focus provided one of the primary forces that led to the establishment of the National Forum. In a very real sense, a political fault line divides local leaders and national leaders in how they view the Arctic region. For national leaders, the Arctic is viewed through a lens that emphasizes resource extraction and national security. From their national vantage point, the local population benefits greatly by virtue of the monies directed to the Arctic in support of these priorities. From the local perspective, however, in the rush to provide military security and exploit natural resources, too little attention is given to providing for the social welfare of the northern inhabitants, and, as they have little voting strength, their concerns are easily ignored in national capitals.

The result of these differences in perspective is that, according to one observer, the Arctic Council and Northern Forum are like ships passing in the night. Little collaboration has taken place between them, and only a few joint projects have occurred.[8] It is as if the countries involved in seeking to establish rules governing behavior in the Arctic are travelling down two separate pathways with different sets of priorities and views that occasionally come together but then go their own ways again. Not unexpectedly under these circumstances, cooperative efforts have been slow to develop.

Problem Evolution and Development: Globalization and Competition

The ability of the Arctic Council to serve as the basis for a regime governing the Arctic has faced serious challenges from two different sources. One is the rapid increase in the pace of globalization and its consequences for the Arctic. The second is the emergence of competing arenas of regional cooperation.

In the late 1980s, the existing barriers to cooperation in the Arctic were ideological and strategic. The end of the Cold War reduced the security dimension in superpower relations and, in the eyes of some, left just one superpower standing. It created space for a greater degree of cooperation between states and reduced fears of cheating and exploitation in these new arrangements, although, as we have seen, parties still entered into these agreements with a great deal of caution and did not invest significant powers in the transnational bodies created.[9]

The impact of globalization on the pattern of cooperation was somewhat different. The basic structures within which cooperation could occur were already in place. What globalization did was change the negotiating agenda. Cooperation on military security issues remained stalled and, to some extent, military competition actually intensified. U.S. president George W. Bush's 2009 National Security Document, for example, asserted that the "United States has broad and fundamental security interests in the Arctic region and is prepared to operate either independently or in conjunction with other states to safeguard these interests."[10] Specifically mentioned were missile defense, maritime security operations, and the deployment of sea and air systems for strategic airlift. In 2012 Russian president Vladimir Putin called for building a stronger Russian naval presence in the Arctic in response to the military actions of other states and to better protect Russian strategic and economic interests.[11] The smaller Arctic states have also taken symbolic steps to make their military presences in the region more visible. In 2006 Canada strengthened its Canadian Rangers, a volunteer and largely native force that operates in the north, and in 2009 Norway became the first Arctic state to position its military command leadership in the Arctic.[12]

Changes in technology and the increasing demand for energy associated with globalization have transformed the long-standing interest in Arctic natural resources and waterways from a scientific concern to an issue high on the economic agenda of states. Globalization has not been the only factor contributing to this surge of interest in the Arctic's economic resources; climate change has also played a major role. Since 1951 the Arctic has been warming at about two times the global average. The Arctic sea ice has shrunk in size some 12 percent each decade since the 1970s. In 2011 the summer average ice coverage was nearly half the average of the 1960s, and Inuit hunters now often find the sea ice too thin to support their sleds. Greenland's ice shed is losing 200 gigatons of ice per year, four times the amount from a decade ago. Estimates now variously predict that the Arctic oceans will be ice free by 2037, or at least by the end of this century. These climatic changes will also result in a 25 percent increase in plant growth as the frozen tundra shrinks.

A Danish study concluded that 97 percent of the Arctic's mineral resources are located in clearly defined territorial borders; these include those beneath the ocean's surface on the continental shelf. BP estimates that hydrocarbon reserves in the Arctic constitute 25 to 50 percent of the untapped total available in the world. Hydrocarbons are found in crude oil and are a major source of the world's electric energy. The U.S. Geological Survey estimates that 30 percent of the world's undiscovered natural gas (1,669 trillion cubic feet) lies in the Arctic and that 13 percent of the world's undiscovered oil reserves (90 billion barrels) will be found there. Eighty-four percent of these oil reserves are believed to be offshore. This does not necessarily place them in international waters, however. The Arctic lands of the United Sates, Greenland, and Canada are believed to hold the most oil, while U.S., Russian, and Norwegian Arctic territories are seen as having the most natural gas resources. By 2012 Shell Oil had spent over $4 billion on Arctic oil exploration without yet having drilled one oil well. That same year, ExxonMobil agreed to invest $500 billion in a joint project with Russia's Rosneft oil company to develop offshore oil reserves. In sharp contrast to this current interest in Arctic oil exploration, consider that in 2004 Greenland held an auction for offshore oil drilling rights and received one bid.

A similar situation exists with regard to exploration for key metals. Greenland has issued over 100 exploration permits, and recently a consortium paid $590 million for a large iron ore deposit in the Arctic. Taken as a whole, these figures highlight the extent to which the environmental changes taking place in the Arctic have moved economic considerations ahead of military ones in the pattern of conflict and cooperation taking place today on the Arctic pathway. Melting Arctic sea ice has also raised the specter of increased shipping. The most favorable route is the Northern Sea Route, which winds along the Siberian coast. Currently this route is open for only four to five months each year due to sea ice. In 2010 only four ships made the voyage; in 2011, thirty-four did. Why the increased traffic? The Northern Sea Route holds the potential for reducing the shipping time between Europe and East Asia by one-third. The principal alternative shipping route from East Asia to Europe now goes through the Suez Canal and is 40 percent longer in distance. Shipping through the Northern Sea Route would reduce the distance between Shanghai and Rotterdam by 22 percent. Using the Northwest Passage, which passes through waters claimed by Canada but defined by the United States as an international waterway, would reduce the travel distance by 15 percent. China, Japan, and South Korea have already begun to invest in new ice-capable vessels. The increased expense of building these vessels is offset by the reduced premiums that would be offered by insurance companies compared to what they now charge ships for passing through pirate-infested waters such as those off the coast of Africa. These insurance premiums, along with ransoms and disruptions to shipping, are estimated to cost shipping companies $7-12 billion per year.

Nothing has better symbolized the growing importance of the Arctic and its resources to economies in a globalized world than two recent incidents involving Russian claims. The first happened on August 2, 2007, when a mini-submarine expedition led by Russian explorer Artur Chilingarov reached the ocean floor beneath the North Pole. Chilingarov planted a Russian flag, declaring that "the Arctic is Russian." This prompted a Canadian official to respond, "You can't go around the world these days dropping a flag somewhere. . . . This isn't the 14th or 15th century."[13] Still, the media was quick to pick up on this act and christen it as the beginning of a new gold rush into the northland. The second incident occurred in September 2013 when a Greenpeace International ship with thirty crew members from eighteen different countries sailed into Russian territorial waters in the Arctic to protest its oil exploration efforts. Russian border guards descended from helicopters onto the ship and arrested the crew, charging them with piracy.

Three distinct issues surround the question of how to move forward in creating an international regime to govern the Arctic. The first issue is the type of law that must be followed. International law is commonly divided into two types: soft and hard. Soft international law generally establishes principles to be followed and guidelines for action. It is found in United Nations international resolutions and declarations and the action plans that emerge from international gatherings. Most importantly, there exists no enforcement mechanism, and soft law is not binding on those who agree to it. In contrast, hard laws establish strict obligations on signatories. They are legally enforceable commitments and as such are considered binding. Hard laws are generally found in international treaties and in customary principles of international law, such as respect for diplomatic immunity.

From its inception, the Arctic Council was to operate and exert its influence through soft law. No permanent secretariat or bureaucracy was established. The council was established by declaration and not by a treaty. As we saw, the United States intentionally downplayed the council's powers by not having Secretary of State Christopher attend the Ottawa meeting at which the council was founded. It was not until the council's 2012 meeting, its seventh since its founding, that the first tentative steps to hard law were taken. In what Secretary of State Hillary Clinton characterized as a "historic meeting," the Arctic Council's eight members signed a legally binding treaty

---

| Box 14.3 |

Spotlight

Conflicting Interests with the Arctic Five

Spurred on by the Russian flag-planting and news stories heralding "a battle for resources" and "a scramble for territory," five members of the Arctic Council—those that have territory that extends into the Arctic Ocean—met in Ilulissat, Greenland, in 2008 to discuss the future of Arctic governance. The Arctic Five, as they became known, were the United States, Russia, Denmark, Norway, and Canada.[14] At the meeting sharply differing views were expressed concerning how Arctic governance should proceed. Canada expressed a desire to involve the remaining three members of the Arctic Council (Finland, Iceland, and Sweden) in the discussions of governance. It also wanted to keep the indigenous groups involved. The United States asserted that while the Arctic Council had a role in the future of Arctic governance, the Arctic Five was a preferable venue for "political discussions" because the Arctic Council was too "unwieldy." General agreement among the Arctic Five did exist on not enlarging the Arctic Council by extending permanent observer status to other states, such as the European Union (EU). Canada was particularly concerned with the EU interest in banning seal hunting. Russia was also opposed to extending observer status to the EU, as well as China, for fear this would dilute its own power within the Arctic region.

In May 2008 the Arctic Five concluded their meeting by issuing the Ilulissat Declaration. It began by asserting that "by virtue of their sovereignty, sovereign rights and jurisdiction of the Arctic Ocean the five coast states are in a unique position" to address the possibilities and challenges facing the region. It went on to note that the law of the sea framework "provides for important rights and obligations . . . .We remain committed to this legal framework and to the orderly settlement of any possible overlapping claims." Finally, it observed that "this framework provides a solid foundation for responsible management by the five coastal States and other users of this Ocean through national implementation and application of relevant provisions. We therefore see no need to develop a new comprehensive international legal regime to govern the Arctic Ocean."

The Ilulissat Declaration did not put an end to the question of how to best organize the Arctic regime. In October the European Parliament called for an international treaty for protecting the Arctic, citing the Antarctica Treaty as a model. The feasibility and benefits of a similar treaty for the Arctic are not uniformly accepted by experts because of fundamental differences between the two regions.[15] Whereas Antarctica is characterized as a landmass surrounded by water, the Arctic is frozen water surrounded by pieces of land. Additionally, whereas Antarctica has no permanent population, this is not true of the Arctic. Finally, when the Antarctica Treaty was signed, the region was of little political, economic, or strategic interests to countries. This is not the case today for the Arctic. These differences lead many to conclude that the effort needed to negotiate and ratify a treaty would not be worth it.[16]

The Inuit also reacted negatively to the Ilulissat Declaration, seeing it as inconsistent with their efforts to be included as full partners in Arctic decision making. The April 2009 meeting of the Inuit Circumpolar Council passed a declaration stating that "from time immemorial the Inuit have been living in the Arctic" and that while the Inuit live throughout the Arctic region and are found within the boundaries of several states, they are "united as a single people."[17]

Even the members of the Arctic Five changed their minds about the proper way to govern the Arctic. In 2010 the United States and Canada reversed their positions. Canada became the leading advocate of the Arctic Five, and the United States sought to reestablish the Arctic Council as the key political decision-making unit. The Arctic Council was still not ready to expand its number of states and denied all requests for permanent observer status, including those from the EU and China.

covering Arctic search and rescue missions. Clinton became the first secretary of state to attend an Arctic Council meeting.

The second issue concerns which countries should be members of the Arctic Council. This question is of central importance to countries that are not Arctic by standard geographic definition but that have maritime and shipping interests in the region (especially as shipping lanes become open for longer periods of time). As we noted above, China, Japan, and South Korea have already begun to make major investments in creating an Arctic shipping capability. In 2009 China, South Korea, the European Union (EU), and Italy sought permanent observer status in the Arctic Council. Japan has now also requested this status. These requests have been denied as the Arctic Council states struggle with the question of what rights go along with this status.

The third point of controversy is closely related to the second. Should the regime created to govern the Arctic be separate and distinct from the operation of larger agreements on governing the global commons, or should it be subsumed under them? This raises the questions of who decides what those rules are (the question we just noted above) and what interests and values will guide the establishment of those rules. The principal alternative to a regime based on the preferences of Arctic states is one organized around the 1982 Law of the Sea (LOS) Convention.

The LOS Convention, which required almost a decade to be negotiated, has been ratified by 162 countries and the EU. According to its provisions, all coastal states are entitled to national jurisdiction over a continental shelf of a minimum of 200 nautical miles. This distance coincides with an exclusive economic zone in which each country has special rights to the use of marine resources, including energy production. Mineral resources on the ocean floor beyond national jurisdictions are judged to a common heritage of all peoples and are placed under the jurisdiction of the International Seabed Authority. The key operative phrase is "a minimum of 200 nautical miles." Under the LOS Convention, coastal states are allowed to extend their area of national control by presenting evidence to the Commission on the Limits of the Continental Shelf that proves the contiguous seafloor is a natural extension of their continental shelf. Signatories to the LOS Convention have ten years from the time they sign the treaty to provide this evidence.[18]

Russia was the first Arctic state to file a petition. It claimed 1.2 million kilometers, a territory known as the Lomonosov Ridge that runs from Siberia to Greenland and includes the North Pole. Denmark, Canada, and the United States challenged that claim, with the United States arguing that the ridge was traditionally part of the Arctic Ocean basin. Russia's claim was denied for lack of sufficient scientific evidence. Norway and Denmark (for Greenland) also have made submissions, and Canada is expected to do likewise before the window to act closes. The United States is in an unusual position that complicates its role in these proceedings and threatens to undermine the legitimacy of the LOS process. It has not signed the LOS Convention and thus is not bound by its procedures regarding how to establish a claim, nor is it in a position to submit a claim.

The commission's powers in dealing with land claims are quite limited, putting its agreements firmly in the category of soft law. It may not impose its own judgment on the case. Coastal states determine their boundaries through the submission of evidence. The commission is also not authorized to rule on competing or overlapping claims to a particular territory. It is not a court. According to the LOS Convention, it is up to states to work out disputes between themselves. The commission is limited in its authority to making recommendations, but those recommendations are important to the Arctic coastal states since they hold the potential to form the basis for hard law if they are adopted by the International Seabed Authority.

Conclusion: Who Should Rule?

The specter of soon-to-be-unleashed cutthroat competition for Arctic resources generated by the planting of the Russian flag on the Arctic floor was overstated in at least two regards. First, the prospects for outright military confrontation are slim. For all states concerned, the benefits of cooperation vastly outweigh the costs of calculated sustained confrontation or heightened international tensions.[19] Second, as enticing as the economic potential of the region is, there are real technological challenges to realizing this wealth.[20] The Exxon-Rosneft partnership will not make a final investment decision until almost 2020 and does not expect to drill for oil for another ten to fifteen years. Likewise, Greenland's oil production is at least two decades in the future. Still, the fundamental dilemma remains: What type of governing system should be put into place in the Arctic? Should it be one that is organized by the states that surround the Arctic, should it be a set of rules constructed by all of those with economic interests in the Arctic regardless of their location, or should it be a global treaty?

Answering this question would go a long way to determining what countries should join together in travelling the Arctic pathway of conflict and cooperation. Historically, it has been a lightly travelled pathway and one that has not received consistently high priority even by those most affected by the situation. Changing environmental conditions have helped generate renewed interest and emphasis on the region, and economic considerations have become of paramount importance. Oil, natural resources, and transportation waterways all offer the possibility of large profits but also have the potential for destroying the Arctic for its traditional inhabitants. Those who wish to see the Arctic preserved as a global commons join the mix as a new round of military competition and conflict sets in and countries with economic stakes in the Arctic seek to protect their investments.

Case Analysis

1. Rank in order of most important to least important the major issues being dealt with on the Arctic pathway of conflict and cooperation: protecting the environment, economic gain, and military security. Why did you rank them this way? What trade-offs are involved among them?

2. Should the Arctic be considered a global commons?

3. What is the best governing system for the Arctic: a regional agreement, an international treaty signed by all states, or extending national jurisdictions into the region?

4. Should the Inuit and other indigenous peoples have a voice in governing the commons? What is the best way of accomplishing this?

5. Which is better suited for governing the Arctic, a hard international regime or a soft one?

6. As the world's dominant economic and military power, does the United States have a special responsibility for leading the global effort to set up rules for governing the Arctic?

7. Given the importance of economic issues in the future of the Arctic, should multinational corporations be given a voice in deciding the rules of an international regime for the Arctic?

8. States were relatively indifferent about the Arctic for a long period of time. Did this create any special problems in moving down the pathway of conflict and cooperation? Identify a strategy that might be used by states in building cooperation on a foundation of indifference.

Suggested Readings

Antrim, Caitlyn. "The Next Geographic Pivot: The Russian Arctic in the Twenty-First Century." *Naval War College Review* 63, no. 3 (2010): 15–37. Antrim provides an overview of Russian military and economic interests in the Arctic region, along with a discussion of implications for the future.

Arctic Council. *Arctic Climate Impact Assessment*. Cambridge: Cambridge University Press, 2005. The council provides a thorough discussion of the nature of climate change in the Arctic and its implications for the future.

Bloomfield, Lincoln. "The Arctic: Last Unmanaged Frontier." *Foreign Affairs* 60 (Fall 1981): 87–105. Written during the Cold War, this account provides an overview of Russian, American, and Canadian thinking on key Arctic issues during that time period.

Blunden, Margaret. "The New Problem of Arctic Stability." *Survival* 51, no. 5 (2009), 121–142. Blunden notes that the sense of common space that once defined the Arctic is under pressure as states jockey for a competitive economic advantage in the region.

Howard, Roger. *The Arctic Gold Rush: The Race for Tomorrow's Natural Resources.* London: Continuum, 2009. Howard presents a solid overview of the states competing for economic gain in the Arctic and the natural resources they seek to control.

Murray, Robert. "Arctic Politics in the Emerging Multipolar System: Challenges and Consequences." *The Polar Journal* 2, no. 1 (2012): 7–20. Murray views the international politics of the Arctic from the vantage point of a multipolar system, giving special attention to the possibility of military competition there.

Young, Oran. "Governing the Arctic: From Cold War Theater to Mosaic of Cooperation." *Global Governance* 11, no. 1 (2005): 9–15. This is a solid overview piece on the problem of Arctic governance written by one of the leading specialists on the subject of international regimes.

Zellen, Barry. *On Thin Ice: The Inuit, the State and the Challenge of Arctic Sovereignty.* Lanham, MD: Lexington, 2009. Zellen's work looks at the place of the Inuit in the evolving debate over how to treat the role of indigenous peoples in constructing an international regime for the Arctic.

Web Resources

Arctic Council, www.arctic-council.org/index.php/en. Explore the official site of the Arctic Council.

Atlantic Council of the United States, www.acus.org. Access publications and press accounts from this nonpartisan institution promoting transatlantic cooperation and international security.

Barents Euro-Arctic Council, www.beac.st/in_English/Barents_Euro-Arctic_Council.iw3. Explore documents and reports from this intergovernmental and interregional organization aimed at sustainable development of the Euro-Arctic region.

Center for Strategic and International Studies, http://csis.org. This U.S.-based bipartisan nonprofit contains research and analysis, including audio and video, on numerous issues concerning international security, governance, and the environment, among other topics.

Inuit Circumpolar Council, www.inuitcircumpolar.com. Learn more about this major international nongovernmental organization that represents the interests of Inuit in the Arctic region.

15 Immigration Tensions over the U.S.- Mexico Border

T he U.S.-Mexico border is the most frequently crossed international border in the world, with approximately 350 million people crossing legally each year.[1] Running 1,969 miles, or 3,369 kilometers, in length, the border extends from Imperial Beach, California/Tijuana, Baja California, to Brownsville, Texas/Matamoros, Tamaulipas. It traverses four U.S. states, six Mexican states, and diverse terrains that range from urban areas such as El Paso, Texas/Ciudad Juarez, Chihuahua, to vast deserts such as the Sonoran.

The southwestern United States was once formally a part of Mexico, and thus the two share cultural and family ties and, in many regions, a common language. Moreover, the Mexican-born U.S. immigrant population is one of the largest, topping out at 30 percent in 2000, though that number has dropped since the onset of the economic recession in 2008. Economically, the United States is Mexico's largest trading partner, and Mexico is the third-largest U.S. trading partner.[2] Furthermore, the two countries are connected, along with Canada, via the North American Free Trade Agreement (NAFTA). Politically, they are neighbors and allies, with governments that see the benefits of unity, as represented though the peace parks and friendship parks along the border. As this information reflects, the United States and Mexico are indelibly interconnected, and migration over the U.S.-Mexico border has always existed—at times the exchange of people has been fluid; at other times it has been difficult and controversial.

In this chapter we examine the long history of conflict and cooperation concerning immigration between the United States and Mexico. At the center of this sometimes contentious relationship is an issue that is both domestic and international: the illegal influx of Mexican workers who cross the border to work in the United States. We begin with a review of the history of immigration across the U.S.-Mexico border, then address Mexico's role in the U.S. immigration system, and finally examine the importance of the bilateral relationship that creates opportunities and challenges for the two countries. We will also focus on the inevitable conditions that globalization creates, such as the search for lower labor costs and "free trade," the issue of transnational threats, and the undeniable linkages of the U.S.-Mexico border region—including cultural and familial ties—that can be stronger than government regulations.

Two questions with regard to Mexican-U.S. relations are particularly controversial. First, given the historic and current political, social, and economic interconnectedness of neighboring countries—in this case the United States and Mexico—how is it possible to manage immigration along borders? History reveals both a need and a desire for interchange in order to build and maintain an economically and politically strong nation-state. Yet there are also times of isolation as countries sometimes want to minimize costs and influences associated with cross-border interactions. Second, with increasing globalization, what is the purpose of borders? Today, the boundaries of most nation-states do not represent firm shells that divide one country from another; instead they often represent filters, with governments seeking the benefits gained from a fluid border and attempting to hold back the disadvantages, such as the high costs of maintaining security and the loss of jobs to immigrants.

In this chapter our approach to the problem definition and response phase will vary somewhat from other case studies. Rather than simply focusing on the problem definition and response at one point along the pathway, we will show how it has evolved over time from early attempts to control the border through current policy efforts. Our Concept Focus in this chapter is on transregional immigration and globalization. It explores immigrant networks and the economic and social forces that draw immigrants to the United States. Our Spotlight section will take a closer look at border control, paying special attention to the work of Border Patrol agents and to the fencing that creates a physical divide along the U.S.-Mexico border.

Immigration and the U.S.-Mexico Border Today

On September 4, 2001, Mexican president Vicente Fox arrived in Washington, D.C., to meet with President George W. Bush. At the top of Fox's agenda was the status of the more than 3 million Mexicans living illegally in the United States. Fox supported a blanket amnesty for these immigrants who had entered the United States illegally. Bush agreed that the issue was vital to their bilateral relationship but repeatedly noted that immigration was a complex issue that could not be dealt with quickly. Bush opposed the amnesty proposal, but he supported the idea of expanding a temporary worker program that would permit Mexicans living illegally in the United States to gain permanent legal residency. Although full agreement on immigration was not expected, the two leaders issued a set of principles and a framework that would guide the development of proposals to

---

| **Box 15.1** |

Case Summary

Illegal immigration has been a recurring problem along the U.S.-Mexico border. Securing the border presents many challenges, not the least of which is the determination of Mexican workers to obtain jobs in the north and of U.S. employers to hire them.

Global Context

The September 11, 2001 (or 9/11), terrorist attacks shifted U.S. attention more strongly toward national security concerns, and particularly to the porous border with Mexico, which is seen as a vulnerability.

Key Actors

- Mexico
- United States

Motives

- Mexican workers are motivated to cross the U.S.-Mexico border for jobs that pay substantially more than what they could get at home.
- Some U.S. employers seek to maximize profits, and the hiring of illegal workers allows them to pay low wages and provide substandard conditions toward this end.
- Mexico benefits economically from the remittances sent back from its laborers in the United States. The work of these laborers in the north also decreases unemployment burdens on the Mexican government.
- The United States wants to maintain secure borders for its national security. It also must balance domestic concerns about "U.S. jobs for U.S. citizens" with the reality that there are jobs that U.S. citizens are not willing to take and an economy that needs them to be filled.

Concepts

- Globalization
- Migration
- National security
- Supply and demand

---

regulate the flow of Mexican immigrants into the United States and set the stage for further talks.

Reactions to the principles and framework were, not surprisingly, mixed. What *was* unexpected was the presidents' approach. As noted by one U.S. expert, "In the past it has been the United States that made all the specific proposals, and the Mexicans who said 'yes,' but never said when. This time, President Fox made all the proposals, and it was his good friend President

Bush who had to say 'yes,' but couldn't say when."³ The meeting was viewed as having built new trust within the bilateral relationship and as a promise for greater cooperation, particularly on issues concerning the U.S.-Mexico border. Unfortunately, the September 11, 2001, terrorist attacks pushed U.S.-Mexico issues into the background, decimating what looked like a new focus on problems that had existed for years.

History and geography give Mexicans unique status in the U.S. immigration system. Not only do Mexicans represent the largest migration flow in the world, they are also the largest group of migrants to the United States—and their numbers have doubled during each decade since 1970, mainly due to unauthorized migrants.⁴ By 2013 the Mexican-born population in the United States numbered around 11.7 million.⁵ Compared to other migrants, Mexicans tend to be younger, less educated, work in lower-skilled occupations, and live at lower socioeconomic levels. Furthermore, today's Mexican migrants are the product of previous immigration policy decisions as well as the complex, interlinked history of the U.S. and Mexican economies, labor markets, and societies. For Mexico, the loss of these immigrants to the United States is two-sided. The Mexican government recognizes that it loses a portion of its labor force— predominately a young and healthy albeit generally less educated portion—but it gains economically through remittances, an economic boost that totals $22 billion (about 2.5 percent of Mexico's GDP in 2010).⁶ Most Mexican immigrants arrive in the United States by crossing the U.S.-Mexico border.

The truth about immigration along the U.S.-Mexico border is that there are not only a large number of legal crossings each year but a vast number of illegal crossings as well. Although impossible to document the precise number of these illegal crossings, estimates range from 400,000 to 500,000 per year.⁷ Those who cross represent linkages between the two countries—the majority of them are seeking work and a better life for their families; however, there are also those who come for more nefarious reasons such as running drugs and weapons or human trafficking. There is thus a darker side of the political reality of the border. As such, current border policies have led to the U.S.-Mexico border becoming a more militarized, walled divide. This is seen by some as a means to control the interaction and exchange between the United States and Mexico and by others as an affront to the interconnectedness of the two countries. This shifting reality is based on the region's history and national interpretations of current trends.

Problem Setting and Origins: Labor Demands and the Bracero Program

The United States is considered a country of immigrants due to the fact that nearly every U.S. citizen, aside from Native Americans, is descended from someone who emigrated from another country. Until the 1840s immigration to the United States remained relatively small and was minimally regulated. Beginning in the mid-1840s, however, an upsurge in immigration due to events such as Ireland's potato famine led to the highest influx of newcomers seen up to that time. Between 1845 and 1850, a reported 1,397,286 immigrants, mainly from northern Europe, came to the United States, and another 2,598,214 arrived between 1851 and 1860.[8] After a period of slight decline, immigration once again peaked from 1900 to 1914, with nearly 900,000 immigrants entering the United States each year. [9] This increase set the stage for Congress to address immigration issues, beginning with a 1917 act implementing a literacy test for immigrants over the age of sixteen. Congress also raised the tax paid by new immigrants upon arrival.[10]

As World War I began in 1914, immigration to the United States changed from being historically more European-based to include people from the larger Western Hemisphere. Mexicans immigrants were exempted from certain restrictions that others faced during wartime; although Asian and European immigration numbers were curtailed, U.S. agricultural, transportation, and mining industries successfully lobbied Congress to not restrict Mexican immigration. Mexicans were admitted into the country as guest workers, and their influx for jobs set a trend that continues to this day. Then, as now, Mexicans saw their wealthy neighbor to the north as a place where they could find work and earn money to support and improve the lives of their family members. Unlike today, the Mexican laborers of the early twentieth century—most of whom worked in the agricultural sector—tended to be both migratory and seasonal, and many returned to Mexico in the winter rather than live in the United States for extended periods of time.

Following the end of World War I and with the onset of the Great Depression, more than 500,000 Mexican Americans were "repatriated"—that is, deported or pressured to leave the United States. As the nation turned more insular, it was believed that U.S. jobs should be held by U.S. citizens and that deporting Mexicans would open more employment possibilities for U.S. citizens. This way of thinking was accepted for a time, but by the start of World War II, the United States once again faced a labor shortage as many men of working age were sent off to war. It was again necessary to draw labor from other groups, and, in keeping with the goal of maintaining U.S. jobs for U.S. citizens, women became one of the first groups called upon to address the labor shortages. This did not fully alleviate the dearth of laborers needed in U.S. industry, however, and to address the continuing demand, the United States once again looked to Mexico. This situation led to the creation of the Mexican Farm Labor Program, commonly referred to as the Bracero Program. The Bracero Program legally allowed Mexicans passage into the United States specifically to fill needs within the labor market. Both the U.S. government and the Mexican government championed the start of the program, which began a new phase of cooperation in Mexican immigration to the United States and increased the number of Mexicans crossing the border.

The Bracero Program was created in 1942 and consisted of a series of laws and bilateral diplomatic agreements to allow for the importation of temporary contract laborers from Mexico to the United States. It was originally intended to focus on a need for manual labor—specifically agricultural laborers experienced in harvesting sugar beets in California. Noting the improved production in Californian agriculture, other states became interested in the program, and, within a couple of years, the Bracero Program expanded to cover most of the United States. By 1944 it provided agricultural labor to vast areas of the United States, with the notable exception of Texas. (At this point, Texas still maintained an open border policy with Mexico and thus attracted laborers in that manner. Additionally, Texas was perceived by the Mexican government as mistreating Mexican laborers so the Mexican government refused to allow Texas access to the policies of the Bracero Program.) Like the agriculture industry, U.S. railroads were also experiencing a lack of employees for manual labor, and a corollary program was created to allow Mexican workers to fill jobs such as track maintenance.

Labor from the program provided the needed services for U.S. agriculture and railroads throughout World War II as Mexico nationals desperate for work willingly took on these arduous jobs at wages scorned by most U.S. citizens. Yet in 1945, with the end of the war and the return of U.S. servicemen, the influx in U.S. citizens able to fill positions brought an end to the railroad Bracero Program. The agricultural industry did not experience the same increase in U.S. labor, and Mexican employment endured by means of a variety of acts of Congress and governmental agreements. U.S. legislators argued that continuing the agricultural portion of the Bracero Program through 1947 would serve as an alternative to illegal immigration along the U.S.-Mexico border. Congress agreed, with many legislators noting that regulating the crossings over the border via guest worker permits was preferential to unregulated passage.

In 1951 U.S. president Harry S. Truman signed Public Law 78, creating a renewable two-year program formalizing protections for Mexican laborers. This program was renewed every two years until 1963 when criticisms concerning abuses to the program and to the Mexican laborers brought about only a one-year renewal and a formal end to the program. Although a small number of agricultural bracero contracts were renewed until 1967, the majority ended in 1964, again shifting the type of immigration over the U.S.-Mexico border from legal agricultural workers to growing numbers of illegal Mexicans.

During the time of the Bracero Program, 4.6 million crossings of temporary guest Mexican workers occurred, creating a situation in which legal immigration was possible and, thus, the numbers of those attempting to cross the border illegally were minimal.[11] Of the Mexicans who received these guest worker visas, many secured green cards and ultimately legal U.S. residency; others simply left the agricultural areas and illegally found work in the cities. Although bracero workers reported what appear to be many cases of abuse, it is also worth mentioning that the program proved popular among migrants because it offered work and more money than they could make in Mexico. As a result of this, in some cases it also offered a renewed sense of dignity. All of these latter elements, in addition to demographic, economic, and social conditions in Mexico, led to an increasing desire of Mexican workers to cross the border and find jobs—legally or illegally. Additionally, the remittances the laborers sent back to Mexico helped to strengthen the Mexican economy, and U.S. employment opportunities lessened pressure on the Mexican government to deal with its own unemployment. Therefore, the program was generally supported by the Mexican government and people.

After the Bracero Program ended, there was a lack of political will to address U.S.-Mexico border immigration issues despite a desire for low-skilled, cheap labor in the United States and a desire by Mexicans to work what they perceived as decent-paying jobs. The supervision and standards in place under the program ended with it, beginning a new phase of Mexican migration to the United States that included the creation of a well-developed underground system to illegally cross the border for jobs. Workers were no longer able to acquire Bracero Program work visas, yet many who arrived in the United States illegally found the employment they sought. Due to the "under-the-table" nature of the employment, however, it often involved lower wages and substandard conditions for workers, which allowed companies to hire illegal immigrants for less than legal ones. This reality led to eroding support, particularly within the U.S. agricultural sector, for the legal importation of workers from Mexico. By the late 1960s and early 1970s, the number of legal immigrants from Mexico to the United States was down, while the numbers of illegal immigrants had risen. Simply put, the possibility of a job in the United States led Mexicans to cross the U.S.-Mexico border any way they could, despite the fact they would have to toil for low wages and often face substandard living conditions and environmental risks in those jobs. Those who crossed the border illegally did not report workplace violations for fear of not getting paid and being deported.

Despite these less than advantageous conditions, by the 1980s the United States saw another rise in legal and illegal immigration from Mexico. In fact, legal emigration from Mexico roughly doubled over the decade of the 1980s, encouraged to some degree by the Mexican government, which was dealing with economic uncertainty associated with the oil shocks of the 1970s.[12] Mexicans arrived in the United States in increasing numbers, particularly in 1982 when the Mexican economy suffered a severe breakdown. Within the United States, some employers willingly hired illegal immigrants for what was less than minimum wage but higher pay than Mexicans would receive in their home country; Mexican workers could earn in the United States up to six times what they would earn in Mexico, which was a powerful incentive.[13] In addition, the U.S. market received needed, low-skilled, and cheap labor that helped improve profit margins. (The United States produces very few people who are willing to work seasonal, low-skilled jobs). Despite certain benefits to both sides of the border, the issue of illegal immigration ultimately needed to be addressed, and in 1986 Congress passed the Immigration Reform and Control Act, which reformed immigration law by requiring employers to attest to their employees' immigration status and making it illegal to knowingly hire unauthorized immigrants. It also legalized certain seasonal agricultural immigrants and immigrants who had entered the U.S. before 1982.

Despite this reform and subsequent physical boundaries being erected within urban centers along the border, the vast network of people working to sustain the illegal crossing of immigrants from Mexico into the United States persevered until 2001. Presidents Bush and Fox, who met September 4–5, 2001, had hoped the year would see a change in the illegal immigration situation, perhaps in the form of greater cooperation between the two countries. What neither expected, however, was that the change would be a tightening of the borders and a lack of focus on immigration issues due to the terrorist attacks of September 11, 2001.

Since the 9/11 attacks, increased technology, infrastructure, and enforcement has made passage across the U.S.-Mexico border complicated. Among other factors, the number of checkpoints within the United States has increased, forcing illegal Mexican immigrants to utilize the services of coyotes, smugglers paid to help immigrants cross the border under the government's radar. The fees charged by coyotes easily run into the thousands of U.S. dollars per individual; it is a significant expense for the immigrant and not something he or she can afford to repeat. Consequently, once in the United States, many immigrants choose to stay for extended periods of time rather than following the historic method of working seasonally and then returning to Mexico.

Over time Mexico again voiced criticism against the U.S. stance to stop immigrants from illegally entering the United States to work. After the 2001 meeting between Bush and Fox, Mexico believed there would be a more equal standing for the two countries and that the United States would recognize the benefits it received from both legal and illegal Mexican immigrants. When this did not happen, Mexico protested the U.S. government's unilateral measures to secure its borders, claiming they only led to greater discrimination and exacerbated the mistreatment of the Mexican immigrants.

Evidence currently shows that the number of illegal immigrants crossing the U.S.-Mexico border is diminishing. This is due in part to increased border security and tougher immigration laws, although it is also associated with the economic downturn, which has resulted in a loss of jobs within the U.S. economy and led to more people competing for fewer jobs.[14]

Problem Definition and Response: Border Control Policies

Throughout the years, U.S. immigration policy has created a platform for debate. Policymakers must weigh the desire to maintain global economic competitiveness against the need to curb illegal immigration and secure U.S. borders. On the one hand, economic sectors suggest there is a need to both lower the costs of labor—i.e., find inexpensive labor either within the United States or export manufacturing and production outside the country—and to

---

| Box 15.2 |

Concept Focus

Transregional Migration and Globalization

Long-standing concepts of the immigrant experience prove inadequate at capturing the new realities of immigrant populations and movement. **Transregional migration**—the movement of people from one country or region to another, often for work—occurs around the world and is not a one-way street, with immigrants simply adapting to their new country and new way of life. Immigrants are both affected by and affect what transpires in their new communities and in their country of origin.

Economic liberalization, which contributes to globalization, is a broad term that refers to the minimizing of government regulations and restrictions in the economy in exchange for greater participation from private entities. The benefits of economic liberalization include greater efficiency and effectiveness of the economy and the ability to attain better skills and technology. The drawbacks include loss of domestic industry, risk of brain drain, and environmental degradation. In today's globalized world, most economically developed countries have liberalized in order to remain globally competitive. This is reflected in changes such as partial or full privatization of government institutions and assets, fewer restrictions on domestic and foreign capital, open markets, lower tax rates for businesses, and greater labor-market flexibility. In the less economically developed countries, economic liberalization refers more to increasing the possibilities for foreign capital and investments into their economies. For many countries, economic liberalization is seen as a necessity in order to remain or become competitive in our globalized economy.

In the United States, the **North American Free Trade Agreement (NAFTA)** seeks to create a continent-wide free trade zone (economic liberalization and increased globalization) within which goods, capital, and information circulate freely. However, the participating governments (the United States, Canada, and Mexico) have chosen not to address the issue of the movement of labor, leaving unauthorized labor migration to be suppressed by police actions at the border and via coercive internal sanctions. In the context of free trade, however, the free circulation of goods, capital, and information promotes rather than excludes emigration from labor-rich countries, as is the case with Mexican immigration to the United States.

As trade relations expand among the North American countries, a continent-wide infrastructure of transportation and communication is also arising to facilitate circulation of labor. This can lead to an expanding network of interpersonal ties, creating a means for immigrants to achieve their goals of participating in an economy as workers, producers, and consumers. First, by sending a family member abroad to work, households diversify their labor portfolios, reducing risks to income for the family. This alters the consumption pattern within the country of origin, allowing people to purchase more goods due to remittances received from the immigrant family member. Second, the existence of these immigrants creates target communities for future immigrants—making additional immigration more likely. Aspiring immigrants turn to friends and relatives with migratory experience to help them get into another country and to find a job. This creates a network for

(Continued)

(Continued)

immigration, further expanding the pool of people with social connections and immigration experiences and drawing more immigrants. Additionally, within the United States it has also led to the development of Mexican communities that maintain elements of their home culture and traditions, thus creating both economic and social forces that reinforce immigration.

Efforts within the United States to increase the cost of international movement of labor (and discourage illegal immigration) have the unintended consequence of lowering the odds of immigrants returning to their home countries. This increases the stock of "permanent" immigrants within the United States, which increases the immigrant network, and leads to more immigration. Similar situations and efforts are found throughout the developed world. European governments are attempting to stop illegal emigration from their former colonies and from northern Africa in order to absorb citizens from less prosperous European Union countries. All of these immigrants are looking for a better life and higher standard of living. The citizens in these countries are also reacting to the societal, economic, and environmental impacts of a large influx of people over a short period of time. Just as in the United States, rather than addressing the changes brought on by a mobilized labor force within a globalized world, European countries are looking at the possibility of becoming more isolationist in order to protect their own. Alternatively, rather than suppressing immigration, if these countries embraced labor as a natural outgrowth of market forces and social processes associated with free trade, NAFTA countries and the European Union could work to increase the economic strength of families, communities, and, ultimately, countries of origin. This could create a situation in which immigrants would then choose to return home rather than stay permanently in the more developed countries such as the United States.

attract top foreign talent. On the other hand, there is a necessity to maintain security for the country, which is often achieved by limiting immigration in order to secure more jobs for U.S. citizens and to keep harmful outside forces from entering the country. As a part of the sometimes competing interests of these economic and security aims, the U.S. immigration debate often focuses on how to streamline a heavy bureaucratic visa application process and address millions of current, undocumented immigrants already living in the country—all without alienating existing ethnic communities within the United States. The methods to achieve these goals have taken a variety of forms over the years, some of which have had the support and cooperation of the Mexican government and people. Often, however, they have created greater conflict between the two neighbors.

In 1924 the U.S. government created the U.S. Border Patrol, a quasi-military presence that mans the U.S.-Mexico border, with the passage of the Labor Appropriation Act. Although the impacts were not immediately clear, over time this act and the Border Patrol provided impetus for great change. Among other consequences, the advent of the Border Patrol created the idea of the "illegal alien." The Labor Appropriation Act also stated that undocumented workers were fugitives, leaving many Mexicans north of the border subject to suspicion and resulting in an increased targeting of immigrants by law enforcement. This in turn perpetuated increased regulations for the hiring of labor within the United States, as well as for those wanting to cross the U.S.-Mexico border, particularly during times of economic downturn.

In 1953, after World War II yet during the time of the Bracero Program, the U.S. government felt pressured to respond to the rising number of immigrants and launched Operation Wetback. Though ostensibly targeted at all "illegal aliens," the operation tended to focus specifically on Mexicans, and they made up a large number of the 3.8 million immigrants deported under the program's auspices. By 1965 U.S. policy took another form with the Immigration and Naturalization Act, which eliminated previously set "country of origin" quotas for immigrants coming to the United States. This ultimately resulted in doors opening for more legal immigrants from Mexico, as well as from other non-Western European locations, based on skills and family relationships. Yet even with the increased slots for legal entry, many Mexicans seeking labor did not meet the requirements and thus illegal immigration continued over the border.

In September 1993 the U.S. Border Patrol initiated a program called Operation Blockade that was designed to form a human and vehicle blockade along the border across the length of El Paso, Texas. The operation, consisting of 400 agents and vehicles spaced every 100 yards, successfully prevented illegal immigration while it was in force.[15] The U.S. Immigration and Naturalization Services (INS) saw the success of the program and permanently funded it, renaming it Operation Hold the Line. This nationally funded program represented a shift in the ideology of policing illegal immigration. Rather than finding and deporting illegal immigrants within the United States, Operation Hold the Line focused on intercepting and preventing illegal entries at the U.S.-Mexico border, specifically near El Paso, Texas. The operation was credited with a 72 percent drop in apprehensions in the region surrounding El Paso between 1993 and 1994.[16] The sharp reduction in the El Paso region's illegal immigration—146,000 apprehended in 1996 compared to 286,000 in 1994—was also attributed to Operation Hold the Line.[17] This success led to Congress passing legislation focusing on border security, strengthening border control, and allocating resources to busy border crossings—in other words, policies which directly targeted the U.S.-Mexico border.

In light of the success of Operation Hold the Line, in 1994 the INS launched Operation Gatekeeper, which was designed to crack down on illegal immigrants entering the United States through San Diego, California. The operation militarized the border, increasing the number of U.S. Border Patrol agents and resources. Just as Operation Hold the Line was successful in slowing illegal crossing in the El Paso region, Operation Gatekeeper was successful in deterring immigrants from crossing the border into San Diego. The United States was focusing policies on strategic regions—in the early

1990s, the El Paso and San Diego regions accounted for two out of every three apprehensions along the southwest border.[18]

The sustained effect of these policies, however, was not the desired deterrence from crossing, but rather a pushing of immigrants to other regions along the border. In Texas, McAllen surpassed El Paso as the region with the most apprehensions, increasing from 124,251 in 1994 to 243,793 in 1997.[19] And with San Diego under scrutiny, immigrants chose to cross further east, often via the Imperial Desert and over the mountains north of Tecate, Mexico, which caused El Centro, California, to see an increase in apprehensions from 27,654 in 1994 to 616,346 in 2000.[20] This created a deadly situation. Since 1994 several thousand immigrants have died trying to cross the U.S.-Mexico border, mainly from exposure, hypothermia, dehydration, or heat stress. The increased effort at deterrence has also led to a situation in which migrants who successfully cross the border stay in the United States longer than before rather than risk the harsh conditions or arrest traveling back and forth across the border. Additionally, because of the increasing difficulty of crossing the border, illegal immigrants from Mexico are more likely to settle in the United States with spouses and children. This change has increased the pressure on local schools, hospitals, and other social services where these people settle, particularly along the U.S.-Mexico border.

Another shift in policy occurred in 1996. Again the U.S. Border Patrol was bolstered, and this time fencing was added along the border in California and Texas. This emphasis on a physical wall dividing the two countries was strengthened after 9/11 when calls for increased closure were renewed. The construction of border fencing and walls is an ongoing process; by 2013 the border fencing covered 651 miles.[21] While most U.S. citizens are in favor of increasing border security and maintaining U.S. jobs for U.S. citizens, some aspects of the fencing give many people pause. The suggested benefits of the wall include enforcement of laws, discouraging illegal immigration, containment of the illegal drug trade, and protection from terrorists. These benefits seem to outweigh the drawbacks of the expense to build the wall, environmental degradation, damage to the United States' international reputation, and a straining of relations with Mexico. The increased risks of crossing the border have resulted in a decrease in the undocumented labor force, a group which Texas governor Rick Perry states is important to "continue to grow the [U.S.] economy."[22] Actions taken to expand the wall and increase security along the border have intensified the trends that were already apparent with the 1994 policies.

Prior to July 2001 when President Fox and President Bush began discussing how to cooperatively address the issue of illegal crossings and the status of the 3 million undocumented Mexicans in the United States, many U.S. and Mexican economic and immigration policies counteracted each other, and the issue largely lacked emphasis. In 1986 U.S. president Ronald Reagan signed an immigration bill designed to curtail the increasing flow of Mexicans to the United States, but since Mexico had been benefitting from the remittances sent from Mexican workers back to their home communities, it was not in a hurry to minimize the immigration or its resultant monetary gains. By 2001, however, Mexico's economy was improving, and both presidents recognized the supply and demand issue for laborers. They also acknowledged the connections between the two countries and expressed a desire to work together to minimize or eliminate deaths along their shared border. Additionally, U.S. congressman Luis Gutierrez (D-Ill.) backed a bill to legalize immigrants who could prove U.S. residence since 1996, and business and labor interests pushed for a guest worker program to allow Mexican workers to freely come and go across the border but not permanently stay in the country.

These potential shifts in policy were derailed that fall after the 9/11 attacks. U.S. officials told the Mexican government that immigration reform was unlikely due to increased terrorism fears. In addition, the 9/11 attacks led to the creation of the U.S. Department of Homeland Security (DHS), which was designed to institutionalize the link between border security and terrorism. The DHS merged three border control agencies: the Customs Service, the INS, and the Coast Guard. The idea behind the DHS was to formulate a sustained campaign to gain control over the U.S. borders, create a system in which the U.S. government would decide exactly who was allowed to enter the country, and provide the government with the capacity to enforce its decisions. Again, this was a policy targeting immigration, both legal and illegal, including that along the U.S.-Mexico border.

Two legislative acts in the mid-2000s were designed to both increase security and make it more difficult for undocumented workers to enter and stay in the United States. In 2005 the Real ID Act was put into place, and in 2006 the Secure Fence Act was enacted. The Real ID Act established federal standards for state-issued driver's licenses and identification cards, changed visa limits for temporary workers, updated and tightened laws on applications for asylum and the deportation of aliens for terrorist activity, and waived laws that interfered with the construction of physical barriers at the borders. The Secure Fence Act was designed to make the border more secure by decreasing illegal entry through the construction of 700 miles of physical barriers along the border. In addition, the law authorized more vehicle barriers, more expansive lighting, additional checkpoints, and the use of technology such as cameras, satellites, and unmanned aerial vehicles to reinforce infrastructure at the border.

Again, as with most U.S. legislation that impacts immigration policies, the Mexican government was not supportive of the changes. In 2007 Mexican president Felipe Calderón blasted U.S. immigration policies and promised to protect the rights of Mexicans in the United States. Calderón stated that "Mexico does not end at its borders" and "where there is a Mexican there is Mexico."[23] The Mexican government, although likely in part responding to the repercussions from receiving fewer remittances, based its criticisms on U.S. insensitivity toward those who supported the U.S. economy and the harm the new policies were having by dividing Mexican families.

Amid stalled federal comprehensive legislation and complaints that the federal government has not satisfactorily stemmed the tide of illegal immigrants crossing the U.S.-Mexico border, several states have passed their own measures to handle immigration matters. Of the states that have passed restrictive laws focused on curbing illegal immigration along the border, the most notorious is Arizona. In April 2010 Arizona passed SB 1070 (amended by HB 2162), a controversial law that requires state and local law enforcement agencies to determine the immigration status of anyone they stop or arrest if they have reason to suspect illegal status. The bill also imposes criminal punishments on illegal immigrants and those who harbor, employ, or transport them. Proponents advocate the bill will protect jobs for U.S. citizens and help maintain security. Critics suggest this piece of legislation targets mainly people of Mexican descent, legal or illegal, and amounts to racial profiling. Shortly after Arizona governor Jan Brewer signed the bill, legal challenges were filed. The complaints included alleged violations against federal immigration laws, the supremacy clause, the First Amendment, the Fourth Amendment, the due process clause, the privileges and immunities clause, the equal protection clause, and the commerce clause. The legal arguments were brought to the U.S. Supreme Court, and in June 2012 a split decision was delivered. The Court upheld the provision requiring state law enforcement officials to check the immigration status of individuals they encounter but blocked other provisions on the ground that they interfered with the federal government's role in setting immigration policy.

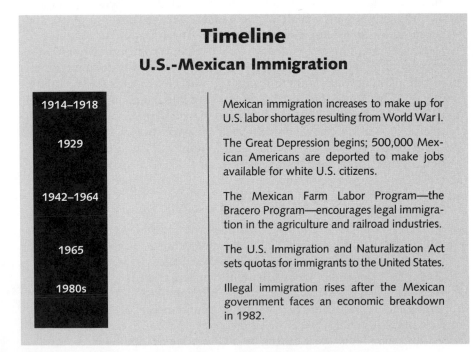

Timeline
U.S.-Mexican Immigration

1914–1918	Mexican immigration increases to make up for U.S. labor shortages resulting from World War I.
1929	The Great Depression begins; 500,000 Mexican Americans are deported to make jobs available for white U.S. citizens.
1942–1964	The Mexican Farm Labor Program—the Bracero Program—encourages legal immigration in the agriculture and railroad industries.
1965	The U.S. Immigration and Naturalization Act sets quotas for immigrants to the United States.
1980s	Illegal immigration rises after the Mexican government faces an economic breakdown in 1982.

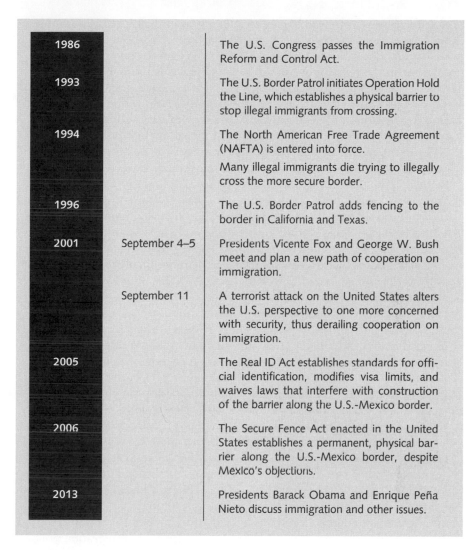

1986		The U.S. Congress passes the Immigration Reform and Control Act.
1993		The U.S. Border Patrol initiates Operation Hold the Line, which establishes a physical barrier to stop illegal immigrants from crossing.
1994		The North American Free Trade Agreement (NAFTA) is entered into force.
		Many illegal immigrants die trying to illegally cross the more secure border.
1996		The U.S. Border Patrol adds fencing to the border in California and Texas.
2001	September 4–5	Presidents Vicente Fox and George W. Bush meet and plan a new path of cooperation on immigration.
	September 11	A terrorist attack on the United States alters the U.S. perspective to one more concerned with security, thus derailing cooperation on immigration.
2005		The Real ID Act establishes standards for official identification, modifies visa limits, and waives laws that interfere with construction of the barrier along the U.S.-Mexico border.
2006		The Secure Fence Act enacted in the United States establishes a permanent, physical barrier along the U.S.-Mexico border, despite Mexico's objections.
2013		Presidents Barack Obama and Enrique Peña Nieto discuss immigration and other issues.

Problem Evolution and Development: Globalization's Discontent

The U.S.-Mexico border region is the most demographically dynamic region in the United States.[24] By 2010 the population on the border was 14.4 million; by 2020 it is expected to be 19.5 million.[25] This growth is outpacing the two governments' abilities to provide adequate infrastructure for basic necessities or border control. Added to that, the much-anticipated economic development and well-paying jobs from NAFTA have not been realized on either side of the border. Thus, although NAFTA has produced a large increase in trade and investment across the U.S.-Mexico border, it has not created prosperity in U.S. border communities. Furthermore, many higher-paying assembly and manufacturing jobs in the United States moved to Mexico and elsewhere offshore and were replaced with low-skilled, low-paying jobs, causing increasing levels of unemployment and underemployment in the U.S. border states. This, coupled with increased vehicular border crossings due to increased trade, set the stage for renewed conflict. U.S. citizens did not want to see jobs lost to Mexico, and the increased vehicular crossings provided greater access to Mexicans wishing to cross the border, making it easier for both legal and illegal immigrants.

The development of this situation stems from the fact that immigration is the forgotten stepchild of the current movement toward globalization. Over the past half century, the United States consciously and deliberately freed up trade in goods and lifted controls on capital and investment; it also urged and pressured other nations to do the same. Immigration policy or the movement of people—the third leg of freer economic movement—was not addressed; rather, it was developed largely by accident. Thus, while there was discontent surrounding the problem of unauthorized immigration into the United States, especially on the border region, the pressure to do something was overridden by economic interests that opposed the sort of heavy-handed government intervention required to gain greater control. Additionally, the Mexican government was benefitting from the economic linkages created with immigration and thus often did not discourage its citizens from seeking work in the United States. Add to this the increased focus on security issues and securing U.S. borders after 9/11 and it becomes clear that diverse interests have created a difficult situation for the U.S. government with regard to immigration on the U.S.-Mexico border.

One of the main problems is that U.S. federal legislation on comprehensive immigration reform is stalled. The diverse interests within the United States, in addition to concerns surrounding the bilateral relationship with Mexico, including the Mexican government's desire to see greater freedom in movement of labor across the U.S.-Mexico border, have led to a complex situation. In addition, many of the programs put forward within the U.S. federal government contradict restrictive state-level immigration laws, creating a blurry divide between state and federal authority over immigration policy. The current Barack Obama administration leans toward enforcement-based policies for curbing illegal immigration. These policies include increasing nationwide immigration sweeps to arrest illegal immigrants that are criminal offenders and increasing audits of companies that hire undocumented laborers. As a part of this, in an attempt to directly target the border, the administration expanded border security measures utilizing the U.S. Border Patrol.

Mexico, on the other hand, would like to see movement toward greater acceptance of the immigrants that it believes are helping grow the U.S. economy. It is estimated that about 12 million Mexicans, 15 percent of Mexico's labor force, live in the United States.[26] Reversing some of the strict U.S. immigration policies and instead looking at a guest worker policy could benefit Mexico through increased remittances, fewer illegal crossing attempts, and greater interaction with family members still in Mexico.

Box 15.3

Spotlight

Patrolling the U.S.-Mexico Border

Many of the most contentious issues of the U.S.-Mexico bilateral relationship—from illegal immigration to contraband trafficking—play out along the U.S.-Mexico border. Many people are unaware of the vast challenges of managing a border between a technologically advanced, capital-rich country and a modernizing, labor-exporting one, as well as the ways in which the United States and Mexico are attempting to mitigate the conflicts and meet these challenges. The governments and citizens of both countries desire a border that facilitates trade by moving people and goods quickly and efficiently. They also, however, want the border to enhance the security of both nations.

The main U.S. entity that addresses these goals is the U.S. Border Patrol, which was established in 1924. For most of its existence, the Border Patrol was little more than a token presence between the land border points of entry into the United States. Now, however, it is the single largest law enforcement agency in the country. Since the mid-1990s, it has worked alongside vehicle and pedestrian fencing on the U.S.-Mexico border. In addition, the border is also monitored by electronic sensing devices and aerial drones with cameras transmitting data, allowing Border Patrol agents to respond quickly to breaches. Mexico does not have a specific border enforcement agency. Its Customs authorities and Federal Police address the border issues. The last two presidents of Mexico sought to engineer a more secure, yet more prosperous, border with the United States.

Determining the effectiveness of border enforcement is difficult and imprecise. As it is driven mainly by economic conditions and opportunities, emigration from Mexico will continue into the United States as long as there are U.S. jobs offering wages that are higher than those in Mexico. Since the economic downturn in the United States in 2008 minimized job possibilities, the number of illegal immigrants coming from Mexico appears to have dropped. Data from recent years, however, suggest that the increased enforcement and fencing have also played a substantial role in discouraging illegal entry across the border. Within the United States, the number of apprehensions has fallen by more than 50 percent since 2006, a decline that has coincided with the border fence development and increased Border Patrol efforts began under the George W. Bush and Felipe Calderón administrations and that predates the onset of the recession in 2008. (Although it is important to note that the construction market, which is a magnet for illegal labor, had begun to weaken prior to 2008.)

In the mid-1990s, prior to the development of the border fence, the Border Patrol reported approximately 600,000 annual arrests in both California and Texas and about 300,000 in Arizona.[27] As this was before Operation Gatekeeper, crossing was much easier in the urban regions of California and Texas than in the harsh desert region of Arizona. This pattern changed following development of the fence in urban areas during the mid-1990s. Apprehensions rose substantially in Arizona and fell sharply in California and Texas, suggesting that illegal immigrants were

(Continued)

(Continued)

responding to the tougher enforcement by choosing the less delineated, although harsher, routes through the desert. Similarly, with the expansion of fencing and an increase in Border Patrol agents in Arizona since 2005, apprehension numbers have fallen there as well.

Under U.S. presidents George W. Bush and Barack Obama and Mexican presidents Felipe Calderón and Enrique Peña Nieto, the two countries have developed a considerable range of policy tools for border issues. These have ranged from the Merida Initiative and a twenty-first-century border management plan to the establishment of Border Enforcement Security Task Force teams for both countries. The two countries' law enforcement authorities also share sensitive intelligence and work together to address terrorism and transnational criminal organizations. Military-to-military cooperation, addressing but not militarizing the fight against transnational crime, has also improved. In general, both the United States and Mexico want to eliminate the criminal elements along the border and enhance trade, and the cooperation between the two countries will likely continue to grow.

In addition to the expanded Border Patrol and fencing, current U.S. border enforcement also increasingly includes technology. Cameras along the border, infrared glasses, and drones transmitting images of the border region increase the "eyes" of enforcement agents and thus the level of enforcement on the border. These increased enforcement techniques have helped bring the estimated apprehension rate of illegal immigrants along the border up to around 80 percent.[28] Realistically, it is impossible for a large, open, economically capitalist and democratic country like the United States to construct and maintain perfect border defenses. Thus, the possibility of what the government can realistically achieve is at odds with what many in the U.S. public desire.

Public opinion on illegal immigration from Mexico is divided. Opponents to immigration claim that immigrants are a drain on the U.S. economy, taking jobs that would otherwise go to U.S. workers. They also suggest that many illegal immigrants do not pay taxes yet use the U.S. health care and educational systems. Proponents believe immigrants are an economic boon because they do work that U.S. workers are unwilling to undertake. Furthermore, proponents note that even illegal immigrants pay sales tax, some pay income tax, and they do not frequently use the health care system due to fear of being caught and deported.

Entering the United States legally is a huge undertaking, and millions of people try to work through the system every year. This is one of the reasons the issue with illegal immigration has intensified: policymakers have not sufficiently addressed the hurdles to legal immigration. Consequently, many experts believe that legal immigration must be addressed and made more efficient in order to deter illegal immigration and attract needed skilled foreign workers. The current U.S. administration is looking at reforming the cumbersome visa and citizenship process for immigrants, particularly in the high-demand science, technology, engineering, and math (STEM) fields. It is also considering the implementation of guest worker programs for unskilled workers, particularly those in the agricultural sectors. Movement on these issues is slow, however. Even though these changes would focus only on specific labor sectors, suggestions for easing the immigration process continue to be the subject of heated debates.

One thing is clear; many U.S. citizens believe the U.S. immigration system is urgently in need of reform. According to a January 2012 Gallup poll, nearly two-thirds of U.S. citizens are dissatisfied with the current level of immigration into the United States, with 42 percent of the respondents saying U.S. immigration levels should be decreased.[29] Debates among U.S. citizens center primarily on immigrants entering from Mexico, despite the fact that the Pew Hispanic Center shows that migration flows between Mexico and the United States have been at net zero since 2007, mainly due to declining U.S. economic opportunities.[30] Another troubling issue is that the U.S. Latino population, which now comprises the largest and fastest-growing minority group within the country, is experiencing an ongoing deterioration of trust in law enforcement.

Currently, U.S. federal government policies dealing with illegal immigration along the U.S.-Mexico border are being criticized by immigration advocates and hard-liners alike. Hard-liners argue that the administration is not doing enough to curb the illegal immigration and often support the idea of even more fencing along the U.S.-Mexico border. Advocates argue that an enforcement-heavy approach instills a culture of fear in immigrant communities, which creates difficulties in truly understanding the problem, and also limits needed low-skill labor, which ultimately hurts the economy. Overall, legal immigration levels and border security are intimately linked and thus must be addressed simultaneously—many of the existing immigration problems may be due to a failure to integrate these two issues rather than a failure of border control.

Meetings between Obama and Peña Nieto in May 2013 came at a time when the two countries were attempting to address the border problems and work to forge closer economic ties. Also at this time, citizens of both countries were focused on immigration reform proposals in the U.S. Congress. Both countries recognize the need for change, but since the 9/11 terrorist attacks, they also recognize the complications. In his meetings with Obama, Peña Nieto appeared to want to replicate the power balance of the Bush-Fox meetings by shifting the public conversation away from the security and border issues that have traditionally dominated such visits. Peña Nieto has suggested scaling back the U.S. role in confronting transnational crime, particularly drug trafficking and organized crime based in Mexico. Peña Nieto's actions have not had the same effect as did those of Fox, although Peña Nieto, like Fox, has found it necessary to dismiss reports of unraveling of cross-border ties between security agencies. Clearly, immigration concerns regarding the U.S.-Mexico border are again shifting, but only time will tell if this round will bring real change.

Conclusion: Reconciling Security and Immigration

The United States is unlikely to ever have an open border with Mexico that allows for the free crossing of immigrants. U.S. political coalitions that favor tough border control are strong and likely durable, and they cite threats of terrorism and transnational crime as reasons to necessitate effective border measures. At the same time, the desire of Mexicans to migrate to the United States however they can is unlikely to change as Mexico attempts to rebuild its economy, and it will likely always be possible to find employers in the United States willing to hire illegal workers in order to lower overhead costs. This leaves the U.S.-Mexico border as a location of continuing cooperation and conflict.

Revisiting the questions addressed at the beginning of this chapter, how is it possible to manage immigration along borders? And, with increasing globalization, what is the purpose of borders? First, ultimately the challenge becomes how to allow cooperation and avoid conflict on issues concerning the crossing of the U.S.-Mexico border. Is it possible to make border security compatible with a sensible immigration system that strengthens the U.S. economy and social and political connections to Mexico? And is a more flexible legal immigration system that would allow greater access into the United States for needed Mexican labor the answer? Much of the United States' global advantage comes from its wealth and superior technology, along with a labor force willing to produce goods. Retaining this advantage depends on the ability of the United States to attract and keep people who can help it maintain these standards—people who have historically included those who crossed the U.S.-Mexico border both legally and illegally. This brings us to the second question, the purpose of borders. With increasing globalization and the need for efficient economic interchange in order to maintain the strength of a nation-state, the role of a border can no longer be that of a shell—isolating a country from others. On the other hand, countries' needs for increased security measures to deal with new threats demand some type of contiguous perimeter. These two necessities often challenge, if not contradict, one another. Thus, the answer to this question is complex and will likely continue the historic trend of shifting as national and global conditions change. Over time the United States and Mexico will redefine both the issues of immigration between them and the role of the border that divides their lands. The responses to these issues will play a large role in influencing the cooperation and conflict between the two countries.

Case Analysis

1. Given that a more open border in the past encouraged migrant workers to return home for a time, should the United States ease its efforts to tighten the border? Why or why not?

2. Describe the relationship between illegal immigration and globalization. Explain how conflicts on immigration arise from labor needs and social change.

3. Consider the fence the United States established on the U.S.-Mexico border. Describe what efforts you suggest to control illegal immigration.

4. Given that Mexico benefits economically from remittances sent home from workers in the United States, what motivates Mexico to help the United States deal with the illegal immigration situation?

5. Describe the dynamics you see as the main contributors to conflict on the pathway traveled by Mexico and the United States when it comes to illegal immigration. Consider both the structure of world politics and the elements that influence foreign policy decision-making.

6. What recommendations would you make to change U.S. policies in order to address the issue of illegal immigration on the U.S.-Mexico border?

7. Why have U.S. immigration reform efforts failed to stop illegal immigration?

Suggested Readings

Andreas, Peter. *Border Games: Policing the U.S.-Mexico Divide*. 2nd ed. Cornell, NY: Cornell University Press, 2012. This book focuses on border policing in our post-September 11 world of economic interconnectedness with increased security, increased numbers of players, and higher stakes.

Cornelius, Wayne, and Jessa M. Lewis, eds. *Impacts of Border Enforcement on Mexican Migration: The View from Sending Communities*. Boulder, CO: Lynne Rienner Publisher, 2007. This anthology of essays addresses illegal immigration and the effects efforts to control migrant passage have on the behavior of migrants.

Danelo, David. *The Border: Exploring the U.S.-Mexican Divide*. Mechanicsburg, PA: Stackpole Books, 2008. This investigative report examines immigration and border security by exposing the complexities of geography, economic and emotional ties and histories through the stories of people on the border.

Johnson, Kevin, and Bernard Trujillo. *Immigration Law and the U.S.-Mexican Border: Si se puede?* (The Mexican American Experience). Tucson: University of Arizona Press, 2011. This book explores the long history of Mexican immigration to the US by explaining US immigration law and policy and its impacts.

Maril, Robert Lee. *The Fence: National Security, Public Safety and Illegal Immigration along the U.S.-Mexico Border.* Lubbock: Texas Tech University Press, 2012. Maril presents the U.S. border fence project through human and financial costs as told by those who live and work on the border.

Massey, Douglas. *Five Myths about Immigration: Common Misconceptions Underlying U.S. Border-Enforcement Policy.* Washington, DC: Immigration Policy Center, 2005. This work looks at the fundamental misunderstandings about the motivation behind immigration to the U.S., and suggests effective immigration policies require overcoming five basic myths.

Nevins, Joseph. *Operation Gatekeeper and Beyond: The War on "Illegals" and the Remaking of the U.S.-Mexico Boundary.* New York, NY: Routledge, 2010. This study examines the complex social, political and economic forces that gave rise to the criminalization of undocumented immigrants.

Web Resources

Center for Immigration Studies, www.cis.org. Explore information about the social, economic, environmental, security, and fiscal consequences of legal and illegal immigration into the United States at the site of this independent, nonprofit research organization.

Mexican Migration Project, http://mmp.opr.princeton.edu/home-en.aspx. Data and assessments are provided by this multidisciplinary research effort between the United States and Mexico.

Migration Policy Institute, www.migrationpolicy.org. Issues of migration worldwide are addressed by this independent nonprofit think tank.

Pew Hispanic Research Center, www.pewhispanic.org. This U.S.-based nonprofit research organization publishes surveys and research that seek to improve the understanding of the U.S. Hispanic population.

U.S. Border Patrol, www.cbp.gov/xp/cgov/enforcement/border_patrol. Access information and data about legal and illegal crossings into the United States from the official site of the U.S. Border Patrol.

16 Social Responsibility and the BP Oil Spill

In this chapter we will review the events that led up to the 2010 Deepwater Horizon oil spill, in which millions of barrels of oil, or petroleum, seeped into the Gulf of Mexico, and the actions taken by the United States and international entities involved in the event. The Deepwater Horizon spill brought to the forefront the difficult balance that exists between today's modern world—generally a petroleum-dependent society—and the need to protect the environment. It also made the world's interconnectedness apparent. Many countries and people are interested in the existing global reserve of petroleum and are willing to pay good money for access to it. Additionally, the world now functions under an economic system filled with multinational corporations (MNCs) that work together to provide goods—in this case petroleum products—for governments and individuals while drawing a profit. This integration leads to interwoven roles and actions, which results in increasing difficulty to assign responsibility or demand accountability when something goes wrong. The Deepwater Horizon oil spill and the focus it brought on the MNC BP, formerly known as British Petroleum, highlight many of these issues.

The big question that remains unanswered in the wake of the Deepwater Horizon spill is, how can we protect the environment in a setting where so many diverse entities function, where not only governments but also MNCs have political and economic power, and where no one is solely responsible for mistakes? No longer is one country's government responsible for maintaining the environment. Rather, in situations such as the Deepwater Horizon spill, which involved a variety of countries, a government, and MNCs, and which impacted the Gulf of Mexico—a global commons—we must address multifaceted responsibility. This case study will examine two particularly controversial aspects of this debate. First, what can be done to deal with massive environmental degradation from such crises when no one wants to take responsibility? Second, how do we assign responsibility for events that involve many entities? One argument suggests that responsibility lies with the overarching entity that both manages the situation and benefits most from it; in this case, BP. BP was the overarching manager of the Deepwater Horizon rig in the Gulf of Mexico and should have been on top of all aspects of the drilling, of the oil rig, and of the rig's maintenance. The other side of the argument suggests blame should be equally distributed to all involved, from the rig's main supervisor to the companies that made each part, to the government regulatory bodies that failed at oversight. We will review the pathway of conflict and cooperation that led to the Deepwater Horizon spill and its aftermath, examining the events that led up to the spill and how the various entities involved chose to handle it.

The Concept Focus in this chapter looks at multinational corporations in the globalized world and the issue of social responsibility. The Spotlight

---

Box 16.1

Case Summary

On April 20, 2010, an explosion occurred on the Deepwater Horizon, a drilling rig located in the Gulf of Mexico, killing eleven workers, sinking the rig, and prompting one of the largest oil spills—and environmental crises—in U.S. history.

Global Context

Multinational corporations have developed extensive reach and influence in an increasingly globalized economy and have become vital parts of advanced and developing economies. They often work together on joint ventures, with national governments responsible for oversight. Due to this intertwining of relationships, determining responsibility and meting out accountability after an economic and environmental disaster is difficult and complex.

Key Actors

- BP
- United States

Motives

- The United States sought to hold the responsible parties legally and financially accountable for the disaster and its economic impacts; it also recognized the failings of its own regulatory agencies.
- MNCs such as BP are money-making businesses, and those involved in this event were seeking to profit from deepwater offshore drilling in the Gulf of Mexico; all of the MNCs involved wanted to avoid taking full responsibility for the spill—including financial responsibility.

Concepts:

- Corporate social responsibility
- Globalization
- Environmentalism

section examines how federal regulatory agencies can find themselves captured by those they are supposed to be regulating and looks at the case of the U.S. Minerals Management Service (MMS).

The Deepwater Horizon Oil Spill

On April 20, 2010, an explosion occurred on the Deepwater Horizon, a drilling rig licensed to BP and located in the Gulf of Mexico, forty-two miles southeast of Venice, Louisiana. The explosion killed eleven workers, injured seventeen others, and led to the sinking of the $560 million rig. Part of BP's Macondo prospect, a petroleum exploration area in the Gulf of Mexico, the rig drilled a reported 13,000 feet below the seabed before something went wrong and the explosion occurred. The rig sank two days after the explosion, and the resulting oil slick ultimately covered some 28,958 square miles of the Gulf.[1] Dubbed the "BP oil spill," it is the largest offshore oil spill in U.S. history; an estimated 4.9 million barrels of oil seeped into Gulf waters over a three-month period. The spill caused extensive damage to marine and wildlife habitat, public and private lands, and ultimately fishing and tourism economies from Louisiana to Florida. Although the U.S. government placed blame on multiple entities, including its own regulatory agency, the Minerals Management Service, it ultimately named BP the responsible party. After an internal investigation, BP admitted to mistakes that led to the oil spill, although the multinational company claims its partners in the joint venture also hold responsibility.

At the time of the explosion, there were 126 people on the rig; of these, 115 were evacuated. The U.S. Coast Guard launched a rescue operation for the remaining eleven people, but after a three-day search, the operation was called off because reasonable expectations for survival had passed. Cleanup of the spill began after the rescue efforts concluded, with BP assuming responsibility for the initial cleanup and mitigation efforts. BP performed controlled burns to remove oil from open water, spread chemical dispersants to accelerate the process of natural dispersion of the oil, agreed to pay for the state of Louisiana to construct sand berms to capture oil before it entered bays and wetlands, and hired thousands of workers to clean oil off the Gulf Coast beaches. The U.S. government also participated in the cleanup, contributing military staff and governmental personnel from agencies such as the National Oceanic and Atmospheric Administration, the Environmental Protection Agency, and the U.S. Geological Survey to the operation, and setting up a command structure to coordinate cleanup activities.

The costs of the spill continue to mount. As of June 2013, the spill has cost BP an estimated $32 billion, including $14 billion in cleanup costs and $8 billion in compensation to Gulf Coast residents.[2] Furthermore, there is no cap for the settlements to Gulf Coast residents and businesses, and new claims can be submitted until April 2014, thus the total of claims will continue to rise. And finally, BP faces potentially billions of dollars in fines under the Clean Water Act, the outcome of which will likely be determined in 2014. Estimated costs to the U.S. government vary widely depending on what is included in the assessment. Calculating economic and environmental damage from any spill, particularly one of the magnitude of the Deepwater Horizon spill, is difficult: Should unemployment be included? Future health costs? And how does one assess the cost of the loss of coral reefs and other wildlife? It is hard to calculate the tangible ecosystem services that are lost or impaired when parts of the environment such as marshes or bays are damaged, let alone the subtle impacts that are identified after the initial impact of the oil spill. Similarly, the states impacted have a hard time assigning a cost to the damage given the domino effect to local businesses—the loss of a part of the fisheries industry impacts grocery stores, restaurants, and all others whose livelihoods are closely tied to the waters of the Gulf Coast.

| Box 16.2 |

Concept Focus

Multinational Corporations and Social Responsibility

Three movements are increasingly prevalent in today's globalized economic setting: privatization (shifting a resource or business from state to private ownership), deregulation (the reduction or elimination of government control from an industry or commodity), and liberalization (the removal or reduction of government restrictions in social and economic policy). The changes in the market brought on by these three movements have created more space for companies and corporations to pursue their own objectives. They are able to set their own agendas and follow what they see as the necessary regulations rather than those imposed upon them by a government, and they do so in increasingly vast regions of the world. Multinational corporations (MNCs), companies that operate across multiple countries and regions, are large beneficiaries of greater privatization, deregulation, and liberalization. Their expansion as powerful economic entities gives them increasing influence on the development of many economies.

The sheer size of major MNCs—the largest have budgets that exceed those of many small countries—means that their influence and impact on individuals, governments, and even the global economy is substantial. The economic and employment contributions of MNCs can sustain nations, regions, and communities, in many cases exceeding the influence of the host nation's economy. MNCs such as Coca-Cola, Toshiba, ExxonMobil, Walmart, and BP improve technology and create jobs, and thus wealth, for host countries. Because they are a major force in the globalization of business practices, knowledge, and technology, they often influence countries' policies and actions economically, socially, and politically—to some degree even eroding state sovereignty in key areas of decision making and occasionally finding themselves entangled in conflicts and even wars among developing nations.[3] In an increasingly global economy, it has become necessary to recognize the growing influence of MNCs and to examine the social responsibility that comes with this influence.

In the course of their operations, most MNCs create externalities, such as pollution, that impact the livelihoods, lifestyles, and health of those around them. To maintain a positive image amongst the public, MNCs may try to substantially impact communities in a positive way, such as by using responsible and sustainable means to utilize the environment to extract natural resources. Many MNCs understand that they are reaping profits from extracting a community's resources and are conscious that their business can be seen as either a lucrative benefit or an undesired stain on the community. This mutual interdependence between communities and corporations leads to discussions of corporate social responsibility and how it can be addressed.

When talk of corporate social responsibility first began in the late 1960s, MNCs considered it to be a passing fad. However, as customers, employees, and, in many cases, entire communities have placed increasing importance on it, MNCs have found it difficult to ignore. As such, corporate social responsibility tends to peak in times when corporations need "good press," but many companies now view it as a good practice both for their bottom line (happier employees, support from local communities) and for the communities in which they work.[4] This buy-in from many MNCs muddies the water for corporations that have not practiced corporate social responsibility and puts those corporations in a position of needing good press.

BP's response to the Deepwater Horizon oil spill included a strong corporate responsibility program. As U.S. citizens and consumer watchdog groups set up boycotts and anti-BP campaigns that resulted in lost revenue and a worsening reputation for the company, BP responded with an increased commitment to social responsibility. The company had engaged in corporate responsibility initiatives before the spill, but increased its commitment afterwards, sending money to environmental groups and tourism boards, sending its employees to the Gulf region to engage in physical labor and help with the cleanup, and televising its efforts to the nation through commercials that continued to run into 2013.

Critics suggest this situation highlighted how MNCs such as BP choose to act in ways that raise their profit margin, thus MNCs utilize corporate social responsibility when it is helpful to them and ignore it when it is not. Proponents, however, suggest that corporate social responsibility is a movement that is becoming institutionalized in MNCs. What is certain is that this responsibility provides a means by which communities can benefit from MNCs within their region.

Problem Setting and Origins:
Growing Demand for Oil

Countries around the globe started using petroleum products as a major energy source in the 1950s. Prior to that time, timber, whale blubber, and coal were used as the major sources of energy. Within Europe and the United States, coal and natural gas were used for transportation, heating, and industry starting in the nineteenth century, with coal supplying the bulk of energy needs well into the twentieth century. Over time, with the expansion of petroleum-dependent industries, the demand for petroleum increased, stimulating the development of an industry to supply the resource. The petroleum companies that were established are both state-owned, such as Saudi Aramco, Gazprom (Russia), and Petróleos de Venezuela, and MNC-owned, such as BP, ExxonMobil, and ConocoPhillips,[5] and the resulting industry has come to impact global technology, development, economics, and politics.

The first commercial oil wells began appearing in the mid-1800s, and by the 1890s, with mass production of automobiles, the demand for gasoline and oil began its steep incline. During the world wars, petroleum facilities became major strategic assets for militaries, therefore increasing the political importance of the resource and creating an expansion in petroleum exploration. By the 1950s, post–World War II, due to the growing use of automobiles and increasing numbers of oil-fired electricity plants, oil become the most-used energy source in many countries, including the United States.[6] The availability of petroleum from sources such as California, Texas, Oklahoma, Canada, and Mexico, together with the ease of transportation, high-energy density, and relatively low costs, led to a sustained increasing use of the resource.

By 1960 the importance of petroleum was clear to domestic and international interests alike. As the industry was largely dominated by MNCs, a number of governments took note and joined together in order to strengthen their state-owned petroleum production companies. Iran, Iraq, Kuwait, Saudi Arabia, and Venezuela formed the Organization of Petroleum Exporting Countries (OPEC), an organization that today includes eleven member countries. By the 1970s the OPEC countries produced close to 50 percent of the world's oil.[7] The growing market for petroleum products, along with the creation of OPEC, drew the United States and many other countries into Middle Eastern politics. They supported oil-producing countries such as Saudi Arabia and participated in protecting the transportation of petroleum via sea lanes in the Persian Gulf and through the Suez Canal.[8]

Within the United States, the production of petroleum increased until 1970, topping out at 9.637 million barrels per day.[9] Since 1970 U.S. production has declined due to the geologic reality that oil is a nonrenewable, limited resource. Such was the demand for oil in the United States that the country could not develop a domestic supply to meet that demand; furthermore, demand was increasing around the world as well, creating a tighter world market. These facts, coupled with the military and economic needs for petroleum, led to the U.S. government's acknowledgement of the importance of the resource, which resulted in increased political emphasis on petroleum both domestically and internationally. Domestically, President Richard Nixon set price controls starting in 1971 in order to address the rapid rise of petroleum prices; internationally, the power to control petroleum production levels, which was held by the major OPEC countries, was recognized.

In 1973 several Arab OPEC countries stopped selling oil to the United States and the Netherlands as a protest to these countries' support of Israel in the Arab-Israeli "Yom Kippur" War. The embargo ultimately was extended to South Africa, Rhodesia, and Portugal and led to OPEC dropping production by 25 percent, which caused temporary shortages of petroleum products such as automobile oil and gasoline in many areas around the globe. Within the United States, the embargo caused a shortage of gas, triggering long lines at gas stations, rationing, and a tripling of prices. The embargo itself revealed the increasing interdependence of the global economy—OPEC was able to impact many countries' economies and many citizens' daily lives, particularly in the United States.

In reaction to the embargo, the U.S. Congress passed the Emergency Petroleum Allocation Act of 1973 (EPAA) to protect consumers from gasoline shortages and high prices. Ultimately the EPAA was deemed a failure because its complex regulations exacerbated the shortages it was supposed to ameliorate. In effect, by attempting to insulate the United States market from world oil prices, the EPAA created incentives to hoard oil at times when it should have been released to the market. In 1975, when the EPAA regulations were scheduled to expire, Congress replaced many of them with new rules under the Energy Policy and Conservation Act (EPCA). The last vestiges of the EPAA were repealed in 1981.

The EPCA reflected a change in approach. Whereas in 1973 Congress sought economic protections, through the EPCA in 1975 it focused on energy reliability and prices within the United States, as well as on international concerns about economic and national security. This shift increased the petroleum industry's status globally, giving the industry the idea that it was helping to protect a country's national security as well as its economic security. In addition, the act established the Strategic Petroleum Reserve, an emergency fuel supply of up to 1 billion barrels of petroleum designed to mitigate future temporary supply disruptions. The act also encouraged energy conservation and aimed to increase oil production by giving price incentives for the development of domestic crude oil. Behind it all was an overarching goal of U.S. energy independence.

Energy independence for the United States was again reemphasized in 1978 with the Iranian Revolution, which overthrew Iran's leader and U.S. ally and brought to power a fundamentalist Islamic regime less interested in maintaining good relations with the West. The revolution resulted in a drop of 3.9 million barrels per day of Iran's crude oil for three years, from 1978 to 1981.[10] Although initially other OPEC countries filled the gap in production, by 1980, with the start of the Iran-Iraq War, many Persian Gulf nations reduced output. By 1981 oil production from OPEC countries was about one-quarter lower than 1978 levels, and prices had doubled. In response, the U.S. government removed price and allocation controls on the petroleum industry, allowing market forces to set domestic crude oil prices for the first time since the early 1970s. This provided petroleum companies with an incentive to move forward with oil exploration activities, including increased offshore drilling, which was gaining support due to fears of becoming dependent on foreign oil. Despite these incentives for drilling, in

1981 Congress placed a moratorium on the leasing of increasingly large areas of the U.S. Outer Continental Shelf for oil and gas drilling. The moratorium, viewed as a delayed congressional action to address California's concerns stemming from the 1969 Santa Barbara Channel oil spill, originally focused on the waters off central and northern California.[11] As the economic importance of tourism grew for coastal communities around the United States, however, the ban was extended to most of the United States' coastal waters except the Gulf of Mexico and areas around Alaska. This moratorium was extended again in 1990 when President George H. W. Bush put into place an executive ban on offshore drilling, restricting federal offshore leasing to Texas, Louisiana, Mississippi, Alabama, and parts of Alaska. Bush's successor, Bill Clinton, also extended the ban.

Although the executive order banned drilling in parts of the United States, petroleum energy consumption in the country increased dramatically in the late 1980s as a result of low oil prices brought on by a surplus of oil. But in August 1990 Iraq invaded Kuwait, causing petroleum prices to rise sharply. The price increase was further accentuated when the United Nations limited the amount of oil that could be purchased from Iraqi controlled reserves in order to, first, attempt to convince Iraq to restore the authority of the legitimate government of Kuwait, and, later, to end the Iraqi government's repression of all Iraqi citizens.[12] Over the next two decades, petroleum prices rose and fell due to a variety of world events, including a lowering of U.S. oil production, the Asian financial crisis, and increased production from countries in Latin America.

For many countries, including the United States, the most evident impact from increasing petroleum use was not the environmental effects, but rather an emphasis on the need for greater energy independence. Within the United States, this emphasis came from a desire to counteract international control of the markets and the desire for greater security, most notably following the al-Qaeda attacks on the United States on September 11, 2001. Among the nation's many responses to the 9/11 attacks was a subsequent desire for fewer ties to Middle Eastern, oil-producing countries. This resulted in increased pressure from within the United States for additional drilling in U.S. territory.

In 2008 President George W. Bush lifted the 1990 executive order banning offshore drilling.[13] Although the executive order was mainly symbolic due to federal law banning offshore drilling, the move signaled a growing push for greater U.S. domestic oil production. Response to these efforts was mixed. Environmentalists expressed concern for marine habitat, while others suggested offshore drilling would help the United States become less dependent on imported oil and could lower gasoline prices. A number of states and communities responded by passing their own bans on offshore drilling while others, namely Texas and Louisiana, expanded (and have continued to periodically expand) production. The 2006 opening of the Gulf of Mexico's Lease 181 of the Macondo prospect—the location of the Deepwater Horizon—for exploration was one of these expansions.[14]

On March 31, 2010, President Barack Obama proposed to expand offshore oil and gas drilling, potentially opening large areas of the Atlantic Coast from Delaware to central Florida, the eastern Gulf of Mexico, and the northern coast of Alaska. The proposal was intended to reduce dependence on foreign oil supplies and generate revenue at a time when the country and many parts of the world were struggling under the impact of the 2008 financial crisis. The move pleased petroleum companies and domestic drilling advocates, but it angered environmental organizations and some residents of the affected states who feared damage to coastlines, fisheries, popular beaches, and wildlife. The proposal would have meant a substantial change for the petroleum industry, allowing them access and furthering their "done for national security" prestige. The proposal, however, did not move forward due to the complications of an existing offshore rig, the Deepwater Horizon.

Timeline
The Deepwater Horizon Spill

2010		
	April 20	The Deepwater Horizon Rig explodes, and eleven workers are unaccounted for after the explosion.
	April 22	The Deepwater Horizon rig sinks after burning for thirty-six hours.
	April 24	The Coast Guard reports an oil leak from the well.
	April 27	Homeland Security and the Department of the Interior launch a joint federal investigation into the explosion; the Coast Guard and Minerals Management Service share jurisdiction for the investigation.
	April 29	Louisiana governor Bobby Jindal declares a state of emergency; President Obama commits resources to the disaster.
	April 30	The Obama administration stops permits for new offshore drilling until the cause of the explosion is found.
	May 2	BP begins work on relief wells to stop oil from escaping.
	May 3	High numbers of wildlife mortality are reported.
	May 11	BP, Transocean, and Halliburton executives appear before a Senate committee; each blames the others.

(Continued)

(Continued)

	May 16	BP successfully attaches a pipe to the well allowing capture of some of the oil, but the well continues to leak.
	May 19	Oil begins to wash ashore in Louisiana.
	May 22	Obama announces a bipartisan commission to investigate the cause of the BP spill.
	May 27	Scientists announce the BP spill is the worst in U.S. history; President Obama halts all deepwater drilling in the Gulf of Mexico and announces a six-month moratorium on new deepwater drilling in the Gulf and Pacific.
	June 16	With oil still leaking from the well, BP agrees to set up a $20 billion fund for damages and claims.
	July 7	Tarballs wash up on the Texas coast, meaning all the U.S. states along the Gulf are impacted.
	July 12–15	BP successfully installs a containment cap to stop the flow of oil but notes it is not a permanent fix.
	August	The U.S. government reports that 4.9 million barrels of oil leaked into the Gulf from the spill.
	September 8	BP releases an internal report on the oil spill, accepting some responsibility but claiming other companies must bear some of the blame.
	September 19	BP officially declares the oil well completely and permanently sealed.
	December	The U.S. government files suit against BP and its partners over the accident.
2011	January	The White House National Oil Spill Commission concludes the BP spill was the result of systematic management failure at BP, Transocean, and Halliburton.
2012	November	BP agrees to pay $4.5 billion in a settlement with the U.S. government and to plead guilty to felony counts related to the deaths of the eleven workers.
2013	January	Transocean agrees to pay more than $1.4 billion to settle the Justice Department's criminal and civil allegations.
2013	February	The civil trial begins to determine BP's liability for violations of environmental protection laws.
	July	Halliburton agrees to plead guilty to destruction of critical evidence after the explosion and oil spill in 2010.

Problem Definition and
Response: Economic and Safety Interests

Problems with the Deepwater Horizon rig can be traced back to its beginnings. In March 2008 the U.S. Minerals Management Service (MMS) leased
the mineral rights to drill for oil at the Macondo prospect. This well is
located in Mississippi Canyon Block 252 in the U.S. sector of the Gulf of
Mexico, approximately forty miles off of the Louisiana coast. BP purchased
the rights at Lease Sale #206 in New Orleans, Louisiana. Although it was
under the supervision of the MMS, it would later become clear that the
development of the Macondo prospect was not regulated in an effective and
efficient manner.

Nearly one year after the leasing of the mineral rights to drill for oil at
the Macondo prospect, the MMS received BP's exploration and environmental impact plan. The plan stated that an accidental surface or subsurface
spill would be unlikely, but that if a spill did occur, no significant adverse
impacts would be expected due to the distance from shore and the response
capabilities that would be implemented.[15] Shortly thereafter, the U.S.
Department of the Interior concluded that a massive oil spill was unlikely
and thus exempted BP's Gulf of Mexico drilling operation from a detailed
environmental impact study.[16] Although some suggest this shows that neither the federal regulators nor the company could envision an accident on
the scale of the BP spill,[17] others say the exclusions exempting proposed
activity from environmental impact studies, given because such studies cost
the MNCs time and money, reveal another manner in which the MNCs
were influencing the regulatory bodies.[18]

With the needed go-ahead from U.S. government agencies, BP commenced with its plan of developing the Macondo prospect. Although a
senior drilling engineer at BP warned that the metal casing for the blowout
preventer, a valve used to seal, control, and monitor gas and oil wells, might
collapse under high pressure, by October 2009 drilling began. The following February the Deepwater Horizon rig began drilling on the Macondo
prospect. The Deepwater Horizon was built by the South Korean company Hyundai Heavy Industries, owned by Swiss-based Transocean Ltd.
and leased to BP, which contracted construction work to the U.S. MNC
Halliburton. The deepwater drilling (drilling at depths over 1,000 feet) took
place at a water depth of approximate 5,000 feet.

Over the next two months, a variety of events suggested possible problems with the development of the offshore well. In March 2010 an accident
damaged a gasket on the blowout preventer on the rig, and in early April
a Halliburton employee warned those in charge that BP's use of cement
did not follow best practices. Furthermore, despite Halliburton recommendations for greater barriers to ensure the petroleum would not leak into
the surrounding ocean, the MMS approved BP's amended permit to use a
single liner, or steel pipe that encases the petroleum as it is pumped, with
fewer barriers. In addition, BP circulated only a fraction of the mud in the
well, minimizing a technique designed to remove air pockets and debris

that can contaminate cement used in the well. By mid-April drilling was completed by the Deepwater Horizon rig and the well was prepared for cementing so that another rig for oil retrieval could be put in place. The blowout preventer was tested and determined to be functioning. By late April the cementing of the final production casing string, the steel pipe set in the well to prevent petroleum leaking, was completed by Halliburton, and a recommended cement bond log test, which would have taken from nine to twelve hours at a cost of $128,000 and would have evaluated the integrity of the cement work, was canceled.

Box 16.3

Spotlight

The Capture of the Minerals Management Service

Established within the U.S Department of the Interior (DOI) in 1982, the Minerals Management Service (MMS) was designed to address problems with federal minerals management programs. Specifically, it managed the natural gas, oil, and other mineral resources on the outer continental shelf of the United States in order to insure adequate collection of royalties owed to the United States from leaseholders. It was also intended to provide adequate protection against physical theft of resources in the field.

Prior to the Deepwater Horizon spill in 2010, the DOI and congressional investigators had identified a number of management shortcomings and conflicts of interest within the MMS. The MMS was in charge of three possibly conflicting areas: energy development, safety and environmental regulation enforcement, and royalty collection and disbursement. Concerns surrounding management failings and conflicts of interest were being addressed by Congress and the Obama administration prior to the spill. In the aftermath these concerns became even more urgent, and the issue of conflicts of interest and the MMS's competing missions came under intense review.

The heart of the issue was the fact that the MMS issued energy leases and collected royalties from oil and gas produced on federal lands while at the same time policing offshore drilling to protect against theft and environmental damage. In other words, the MMS was responsible for policing those who put the money into its revenue stream, a situation many viewed as a conflict of interest and one that often resulted in negative consequences for the environment. Critics of the MMS claimed this was a case of regulatory capture.[19] An investigation revealed MMS employees had accepted generous gifts from petroleum companies, allowed company employees to fill out the inspection reports, and ignored repeated warnings from government scientists about safety and environmental risks in order to more quickly process energy exploration plans. Additionally, investigations after the spill found a severe shortage of inspectors, a dearth of regulations, and a "completely backward" approach to investigating spills and accidents.[20]

Overall, investigations suggested that the MMS was, at minimum, perceived to be under undue influence by the petroleum industry due to the agency's heavy reliance on the revenue from the industry. Over its twenty-eight year history, the

MMS was one of the government's largest revenue collectors thanks to the influx of money from the petroleum industry.[21] In addition, the MMS received assistance from the industry, such as its expertise in drilling within risky waters, allowing the industry that the MMS regulated to determine if its own practices were safe.[22] Overall, the relationship between the MMS and the petroleum industry illustrated the economic and political power and influence the petroleum industry can perpetuate within a government agency.

In response to the investigation, Interior Secretary Ken Salazar announced a plan to divide the MMS into three divisions to separate its energy development functions and the management of leasing and permitting for energy development; its safety and environmental enforcement functions, including inspections; and its revenue collection and disbursement functions. Additionally, the MMS was renamed the Bureau of Ocean Energy Management, Regulation, and Enforcement. The director of the MMS, Elizabeth Birnbaum, resigned after what many believe was pressure from the government.

Effective in October 2011, the MMS was reorganized, splitting the duties among the Bureau of Ocean Energy Management, the Bureau of Safety and Environmental Enforcement, and the Office of Natural Resources Revenue. Proponents suggest problems have been addressed, but critics note that even though the agency names have changed, many of the people remain the same. Only time will tell if the agencies created from the former MMS are truly independent from the MNCs that are economically vital to their existence. For now it appears that the new government agencies have clear mandates on issues of responsibility and accountability in place to avoid future conflicts of interest.

At 9:45 p.m. CST on April 20, 2010, oil, gas, and concrete from the Deepwater Horizon rig exploded. Interviews with rig workers suggest that a bubble of methane gas moved up the drill column before exploding and catching the rig on fire, killing eleven platform workers and injuring seventeen others. According to Transocean, work prior to the explosion had been routine and there were no indications of problems. Furthermore, although the Deepwater Horizon rig was drilling the well hole, it was not yet bringing up the petroleum—there were plans to replace the rig with another before commencing with the oil retrieval. Transocean suggested the event was caused by a sudden catastrophic failure of the cement, the casting, or both.

In addition to the loss of life on the rig, there was extensive environmental damage to the region. The fire that followed the explosion engulfed the rig platform and burned for more than a day before the Deepwater Horizon sank on April 22. That same day, a U.S. Coast Guard officer was quoted saying that oil was leaking from the rig at a rate of approximately 8,000 barrels of crude per day.[23] Over the next four months, estimates of the amount of oil spilled varied, with the final consensus reporting that roughly 5 million barrels of oil were released from the Macondo prospect into the Gulf of Mexico. The determination of the extent of the spill and the damage produced by it was, and to some degree remains, controversial. To some, particularly those personally impacted by the spill, the variation in the estimates of the amount of oil that flowed into the Gulf of Mexico undermined confidence in the petroleum industry and the federal government's response to the spill. Initial estimates from the federal government for the amount of oil were, as we now know, low and inaccurate. The government used data supplied by BP— data based on the belief that there was no oil emanating from the wellhead at the ocean floor. At the same time, nongovernmental scientists suggested much higher, and ultimately much more accurate, estimates based on the small amount of flow data publically available. The disparity between the two sets of initial estimates, and the fact the U.S. federal government was using data supplied by BP, created the impression that the government was either not capable of handling the spill or not being candid about the size and scope of it. Management of the issue needed to be addressed independent of influence from BP and the other MNCs involved in order to eliminate the appearance of cooperating with BP to hide the extent of the disaster.

By the second week of the spill, the U.S. government increased the official estimate from 1,000 barrels per day to 5,000 barrels per day based on input from the National Oceanic and Atmospheric Administration (NOAA). Even the NOAA data, however, did not take into account leakage from a kink in a riser, a 5,000-foot pipe connecting the well at the ocean floor to the drilling platform on the surface, producing another imprecise estimate. Despite acknowledged deficiency in the data that caused inaccuracies, NOAA's estimate of 5,000 barrels per day was held up as the government's official flow-rate estimate for nearly a month.

In mid-May BP released a video showing oil flowing from the end of a broken riser. Within hours of the video release, scientists began producing estimates of 50,000 to 100,000 barrels per day from the riser. The video allowed greater insight into the problem to those not directly connected to the companies associated with the spill. This led to intense pressure and criticism directed toward BP for not being more forthcoming about the size of the leak and consequently the spill and damage done. It was suggested the company was impeding independent scientific inquiry, compelling Rep. Edward J. Markey of Massachusetts to request that BP release more video footage. Bowing to the pressure and the congressman's request, on May 20, 2010, BP made public a live feed of the oil spill.

In order to gain control of the constantly changing information and publicity, including public perceptions of the government that ranged from "lackluster performance" to "inept bureaucrats," on May 19, 2010, the U.S. government's National Incident Command organized the creation of the interagency Flow Rate Technical Group. This group, headed by Dr. Marcia McNutt, director of the U.S. Geological Survey and science advisor to the secretary of the interior, was charged with quickly determining a preliminary flow rate and then, over the following two months, using peer-reviewed methodologies to determine a final flow rate. Enlisting the help of nongovernmental scientists with expertise and experience, many of whom had been making estimates of the flow rate, the group got to work. On August 2, 2010, a final estimate was produced: 62,000 barrel per day for the first weeks after the explosion, declining to 53,000 barrels per day by June, when the well was capped. These figures suggest that the Deepwater Horizon incident spilled approximately 4,900,000 barrels of oil in total, making it the worst oil spill in U.S. history and the second worst globally.[24] The final estimate by independent scientists at Columbia University's Lamont-Doherty Earth Observatory and scientists at Woods Hole Oceanographic Institution suggest the total release was higher. These scientists noted that the oil pouring into the Gulf of Mexico was rising to the surface and spreading out, creating mass damage, but they also mentioned that some oil remained on the ocean floor, damaging marine environment and making estimations difficult. Discrepancies between the government and independent scientists' estimates appear to stem from the fact that nongovernmental scientists used different, more refined, methodologies, including technology such as satellite imagery.

In an attempt to gain control of the situation, BP attempted a number of techniques. However, due to the location of the well—5,000 below the surface of the Gulf of Mexico—these attempts were experiments at best. BP drilled two deepwater intercept relief wells to release the pressure and allow BP to pump in cement in order to cap the well. Another attempt sought to use remotely operated vehicles (ROVs) to activate the blowout preventer, which the company hoped would help regulate the pressure of the well and kill the well, preventing the oil flow. BP also placed a ninety-eight-ton steel containment dome over the leaks to trap the oil, which would then be piped to the surface. All of these procedures failed. It was not until May 17, 2010, when a riser insertion tube tool was inserted into Horizon's riser to suck leaking oil into a tanker that BP experienced success at reducing the amount of oil flowing into the Gulf of Mexico.

Then, on May 26, 2010, with approval from the U.S. government, BP began to proceed with a "top kill" operation—an injection of heavy drilling fluids into the well, intended to stem the flow of oil and gas. Within days, BP reported that both the top kill and a "junk shot" procedure, shooting debris such as shredded tires into the blowout preventer in an attempt to clog the well and stop the leak, had both failed. BP, after consulting with U.S. government officials, next tried placing a custom-built cap over the blowout preventer in an attempt to capture the oil flowing from the well and pipe it to the surface where oil tankers waited. Finally, on July 15, 2010, BP announced that the capping procedure had worked and oil had stopped leaking from the well. On September 19, 2010, BP declared that it had successfully intersected the well from a relief well, which allowed the pumping of cement into the Macondo prospect to stop the oil from flowing. Due to this procedure, the well was successfully sealed.

While BP was struggling to contain the spill, communities along the Gulf of Mexico were facing their own difficulties. Damage to the environment impacted not only wildlife and habitat but also the people who relied on these features for their livelihood. Marine animal deaths were extensive and included thousands of birds, hundreds of sea turtles, and hundreds of mammals, including dolphins. Damage occurred to deepwater corals and other habitats for fish, shrimp, and crabs. On shore, approximately 1,100 miles of coastal wetlands were affected by the spill, leading to the destruction of vegetation and habitat and also ultimately to sediment erosion, which destroyed boundary islands and converted marshlands to open water, thus exposing the area to greater future storm damage.[25] By May the region, which relies heavily on tourism, saw an almost complete cessation of visitors, and the once-vibrant fishing and seafood industries were shut down in anticipation of oil contamination in, particularly, fish and shrimp. By June it was confirmed that the Deepwater Horizon spill was the largest offshore oil spill in U.S. history, and President Obama declared it the worst environmental disaster ever faced by the nation. Obama articulated the need to allocate resources to not only clean up the spill but to also compensate workers and business owners whose livelihoods were harmed, and he advocated the development of a coastal restoration plan to restore wetlands and habitats and to address both the environmental and economic conditions of the region.

From the moment the spill began, elements within the U.S. government wanted to help manage the issue. Two days after the explosion, a National Response Team comprised of sixteen federal departments and agencies, including the White House; U.S. Coast Guard; Departments of Commerce, Homeland Security, Interior, and Defense; and the Environmental Protection Agency, held its first meeting. This group was charged with coordinating emergency preparedness and response to oil and hazardous substance pollution events. Additionally, Congress held nine hearings and three briefings within the first few weeks after the oil spill. Within a month, ten House and Senate committees were investigating the circumstances surrounding the spill. Results from the hearings included convincing BP and Transocean to reveal their timelines and hand over test dates from the damaged well, pressuring BP to release live video of the well, and pressuring the companies to take a broader look at options of dispersants to break up the oil. The U.S. government, influenced by President Obama's comments and the congressional response to public distress, particularly the distress of the public directly impacted by the spill, pushed to not only address the issues stemming from the spill but also to examine whose and which actions were responsible for the spill and how it was possible to minimize the possibility of another spill of this magnitude.

Finally, in mid-May 2010, President Obama issued an executive order creating the National Commission on the BP Deepwater Horizon Oil Spill and Offshore Drilling. The commission, headed by former administrator of the Environmental Protection Agency William K. Reilly and former Florida senator Bob Graham, was a bipartisan entity with a diverse representation of experts with relevant expertise.

At about this same time, NOAA reported that oil from the BP spill had reached the Loop Current. The Loop Current is a warm ocean current in the Gulf of Mexico that flows northward between Cuba and the Yucatan Peninsula, looping through the Gulf of Mexico before exiting through the Florida Straits into the Atlantic Ocean. Thus, although not immediately impacted, other counties do eventually feel the effects of environmental disasters of the magnitude of the BP spill through not only actual petroleum in their water but also the reduction of resources such as fish and seafood. By the first of June, scientists on the coasts of Alabama and Mississippi recorded the arrival of oil, and by the fourth of June, the first substantial amount of oil arrived on the Florida coast. In addition, large plumes of oil in the deep water of the Gulf of Mexico were reported on May 12, 2010. These plumes, said to be depleting the oxygen dissolved in the water, posed a threat to marine life forms such as fish, mammals, and deepwater coral reefs.

The extent of the oil spill is of vital concern because the Gulf of Mexico and its coastal areas are some of the world's most productive marine and coastal ecosystems. The waters contain large numbers of fish and shellfish that are important to U.S. and international fishermen and seafood industries. In addition, the coastal wetlands provide recreation, water purification, storm buffers, wildlife habitats, shorebird rookeries, and nursery grounds for aquatic life.

Overall, the damage was extensive. The impact created when organisms and ecosystems encounter large amounts of oil is well documented. For wildlife, physically contacting, ingesting, inhaling, or absorbing oil causes harm. Birds and mammals are exposed to oil as they float on, dive into, or surface in oil-slicked water. Even land-based animals such as raccoons are exposed by feeding on carcasses of contaminated fish and wildlife.

The economic impacts are just as broad, and those from the BP oil spill touched not only the communities along the Gulf of Mexico but ultimately much of the nation. Commercial fishing in the Gulf of Mexico region was closed or limited in many areas. The reduction in fish, along with lower harvests of oysters and shrimp, caused seafood prices to rise sharply. The tourism industry, hotels, restaurants, tour boats, and related businesses on the Gulf Coast were severely impacted as people chose to go elsewhere—to locations where there was no oil washing ashore. These effects resulted not only in short-term drops in revenue but also a long-term decline in property tax values, a reduction in services, and, due to the loss or lessening of the fishing industry, a loss of community. The impact to communities outside of the United States has not been as well documented and, although an issue in some diplomatic discussions, for many countries the issues surrounding the spill were simply not addressed.

Finally, on the broader scale, in early June 2010, the Dow Jones Industrial Average fell 120 points after the Obama administration announced a criminal investigation into the BP oil spill. On that same day, BP stock lost

15 percent of its market value, the beginning of a trend that drove down the market valuation of the company.

The petroleum industry, and most specifically BP, was concerned with loss of profit. In addition to the loss in market value, BP was also facing expensive mitigation of the spill to lessen the long-term impacts to the environment and economy of the Gulf region. And the U.S. government placed a moratorium on offshore drilling, which impacted the entire petroleum industry. The petroleum industry suggested this moratorium would hurt economic growth and job creation in the Gulf states most impacted by the spill. To the relief of the industry, the moratorium was lifted on October 12, 2010. The reason for the lifting, which occurred early as it was scheduled for November 30, 2010, was twofold: Interior Secretary Ken Salazar noted new rules were imposed and in place that strengthened safely measures for offshore operations, and the Obama administration was under intense pressure to lift the moratorium, as economists and the petroleum industry suggested it would result in billions of dollars in lost income and forced layoffs.[26]

Problem Evolution and Development: Restitution and Future Safeguards

In an attempt to mitigate the damage done (to the environment, to people, and, ultimately, to the company), BP assumed responsibility for the initial cleanup and mitigation efforts. These efforts included physically cleaning the oil from the water and shores and also managing situations where people could show legitimate claims for personal damages. The first part of this proved to be easier than the second part.

The "on the ground" cleanup was begun by a number of entities, including private companies and local fishermen hired by BP to capture oil floating in the Gulf. In addition, the U.S. government contributed military staff to the cleanup efforts, established a command structure to monitor the response to the spill, coordinated decision making on how best to address situations, and created communication networks among organizations responding to the incident. The command structure, which coordinated efforts to clean up the spill, included individuals from BP and Transocean, along with experts from a dozen federal agencies, including the MMS; the NOAA; the Environmental Protection Agency; the Departments of the Interior, Defense, and Homeland Security; the Fish and Wildlife Service; the Coast Guard; the Centers for Disease Control; and others. The idea behind this command structure was to take advantage of the strengths and expertise a variety of entities had to offer. The MNCs had knowledge of the process behind deepwater drilling and thus could work on the process of stopping the leak, while the government agencies were able to address economic, security, and environmental concerns.

The cleanup actions included the recovery of oily water, controlled burns to remove small oil patches, the application of chemicals to accelerate natural dispersion, and the construction of berms along barrier islands and wetlands to capture oil. These coordinated efforts, along with the natural evaporation and dissolution processes and the direct recovery of oil from the wellhead, removed nearly three-quarters of the oil from the spill. The remaining oil left in the Gulf is reported to be below the surface of the water, has washed ashore as tarballs, or is buried in the sand and sediments.

Economic concerns were also addressed. U.S. commerce secretary Gary Locke declared a "fishery disaster" for commercial and recreational fisheries in Louisiana, Mississippi, and Alabama. This declaration allowed for greater mobilization of federal relief efforts. President Obama rescinded a proposal for expanded offshore drilling, announced a six-month moratorium on new deepwater oil drilling permits in 500 feet of water or more, and instituted new safety requirements for drilling, including new standards for equipment and procedures with a focus on casing and cementing, blowout preventers, and well control systems. In addition, the Department of the Interior and the Council of Environmental Quality announced a review of the National Environmental Policy Act procedures as followed by the MMS—in particular an examination of the procedures for outer continental shelf oil and gas exploration and development. Finally, the Justice Department began reviewing violations of the Clean Water Act, the Endangered Species Act, the Migratory Bird Treaty Act, and the Oil Pollution Act of 1990, and the Department of the Interior issued a directive implementing stronger safety requirements for offshore drilling on the outer continental shelf.

While the U.S. government identified issues within the MMS and took measures to correct them, it did not go so far as to suggest that the conflicts of interest in the MMS were responsible for the Deepwater Horizon spill. Subsequently, BP and Transocean were named by the Justice Department to be the responsible parties. In order to address the economic impacts of the spill, after negotiations with the government and a meeting with President Obama, BP agreed to create an independent $20 billion fund to pay claims arising from the oil spill. This action allowed the Obama administration to boast of creating a large pot of money to help the affected residents, while BP got a public platform to apologize, point to efforts at social responsibility, and note that BP was still a strong and viable MNC. In addition to the $20 billion fund, BP also agreed to suspend paying dividends to shareholders for the rest of 2010 in order to help compensate oil field workers for lost wages. Over time, BP paid out $25 million to the state of Florida to finance tourism advertising. And on November 15, 2012, thirty-one months after the spill, BP pleaded guilty to criminal changes and reached a $4.5 billion settlement with the U.S. government.

Two other MNCs were involved in the joint venture: Anadarko Petroleum Corporation owned 25 percent of the Gulf drilling operation, and Moex Offshore, a subsidiary of Mitsui, owned 10 percent. Anadarko and Moex agreed to pay BP, the joint-venture operator of the exploratory well, $4 billion and $1.1 billion, respectively, after U.S. government investigators spread blame for the spill across a number of companies involved rather than singling out BP.[27] In January 2013 Transocean agreed to settle civil and criminal claims with the U.S. federal government for $1.4 billion.[28] Both BP and Transocean still face a multistate civil case, scheduled to begin in February 2014 in New Orleans. This civil suit will be divided into three phases to determine liability, the amount of oil leaked, and financial penalties. It is not expected to conclude before 2014 ends.

Clearly, conflict over responsibility and accountability in the Deepwater Horizon oil spill still exists. One arena in which there does appear to be some reconciliation, however, involves the new rules issued by the Department of the Interior. The new rules heighten standards for barriers at underwater well and blowout preventers and transfer the cost and accountability of verification, certification, and inspection for safety from the government directly to the leaseholder. More specifically, CEOs are required to certify that their operations comply with all government regulations, that their equipment has been tested, and that personnel have been appropriately trained.

The Oil Pollution Act of 1990 mandates that responsible parties pay for the entire cost of cleanup after spills from offshore drilling. This includes payments for lost profits, destroyed property, and lost tax revenue. The act caps liability at $75 million for economic damages, although BP noted that this was largely irrelevant since BP would honor and pay all legitimate claims. BP's CEO at the time, Tony Hayward, noted that BP was prepared to pay out more than $75 million without seeking reimbursement from the U.S. government or the Oil Spill Liability Trust Fund, which is money set aside to cover oil spill costs over the $75 million limit or when the responsible party is unknown or refuses to pay. As of February 2011, BP reported more than 490,000 individuals had submitted claims, nearly half of which had been turned down. The company, however, has handed out $3.4 billion to 169,000 claimants and estimates the costs will ultimately total nearly $40 billion.

Conclusion: Responsibility and Accountability in Disaster

With the Deepwater Horizon oil spill, millions of gallons of oil poured into the Gulf of Mexico, creating an economic and environmental disaster the repercussions of which continue to be felt in the region today. Although the spill originated from a well 5,000 feet below an open sea and approximately forty miles from the nearest land, within weeks the oil flowed in thin lines into broken marshes, river deltas, and open bays, and onto barrier islands and coasts. Scientists predicted that the oil would continue to show up in these areas for months, if not years, after the capping of the well. Many people, livelihoods, and environments were impacted. Although government investigations and lawsuits have resulted in policy changes and payments for some damages from the spill, the issues of ultimate responsibility and accountability for a disaster of this magnitude have not been fully resolved.

To date, all entities involved have taken some measure of responsibility, but civil suits continue. Phase one of the civil trial, which will determine the liability of BP, Transocean, Halliburton and other MNCs, concluded in mid April 2013, but the court is not expected to issue a ruling on the matter for up to a year. Phase two, which will determine the number of barrels of oil that leaked into the Gulf of Mexico, is set to begin in September 2013, and the third and final phase to determine the financial penalty for the spill will be scheduled for sometime in 2014.

The impacts of the disaster have led many of those affected to question the social responsibility of the MNCs involved. BP, Transocean, and Halliburton have all agreed to pay restitution for their deficiencies, each corporation admitting that it played a role in the disaster. But simply paying fines and settling suits does not prove social responsibility. Following the lead of the National Oil Spill Commission, which found these MNCs guilty of creating unreasonable risk due to time- and money-saving decisions, many living along the Gulf Coast do not believe the MNCs had follow-through for their stated corporate social responsibility. It is clear that these corporations are working to show their social responsibility today, if not as a means to rectify the situation, at least as a means to improve their public image. Whether they learned a lesson and will engage more fully in social responsibility in the long term remains to be seen. BP has regained most of its stock price and is considered strong financially; the same is true of Transocean and Halliburton. Thus, these MNCs have the ability to move forward, maintaining their global strength while working to remain efficient and act responsibly toward local communities and the environment. The choice to cooperate with governments, citizens, and other corporations or to attempt to use economic or political pressure to sway actions and policies to their favor is mainly up to the MNCs, although final settlement on the civil trials will affect the situation.

In today's world of increased global economic integration, in which numerous companies or organizations are involved in activities such as off-shore drilling, assigning responsibility and accountability is difficult. This is made even more complex when government regulatory agencies turn out to be captured by conflicts of interest and thus are a part of the problem. As globalization continues, this type of issue will demand greater attention, as well as a stronger delineation of roles and responsibilities.

Case Analysis

1. Have the parties involved in the BP oil spill—the MNCs and the government—taken full responsibility and accountability for the crisis? Explain your position.

2. Identify other MNCs outside of the petroleum industry that have benefitted in power and influence from globalization. Where can their influence be seen?

3. Should the activities of MNCs be regulated by a third party to keep them from exerting undue influence on governments—for example, governments of developing countries? Why or why not?

4. Think of other instances in which MNCs such as Walmart or Coca-Cola have engaged in corporate social responsibility, either nationally or within your community. What actions have they taken and what is your impression of their reputation? Why? Has their social responsibility program influenced your opinion?

5. Describe how the relationship between the petroleum industry and the Mineral Management System became compromised by the power and influence of the MNCs. How did each side benefit from the agency's capture?

6. Does the reorganization of the MMS into multiple agencies with narrower agendas make it less likely to be captured? What safeguards would you recommend be put into place to prevent future agency capture?

7. Consider the power disparity between developing countries and MNCs. Who is more powerful in today's world—a nation-state such as Nigeria or a MNC such as Shell Oil Company (also known as Royal Dutch Shell)? Explain your reasoning.

8. Describe why it is important to understand the effects of globalization and MNCs on today's world when looking at issues such as energy development.

Suggested Readings

Achenbach, Joel. *A Hole at the Bottom of the Sea: The Race to Kill the BP Oil Gusher*. New York: Simon and Shuster, 2011. This book is a retelling of the account of the Deepwater Horizon and aftermath with a focus on the technology involved in the resolution.

Bourne Jr., Joel K. 2010. "Is Another Deepwater Disaster Inevitable?" *National Geographic Magazine*. October 2010. http://ngm.national-geographic.com/2010/10/gulf-oil-spill/bourne-text. This article details the events of the spill and aftermath.

Cavnar, Bob. *Disaster on the Horizon: High Stakes, High Risks, and the Story behind the Deepwater Well Blowout*. White River Junction, VT: Chelsea Green Publishing Company, 2010. This book examines deepwater drilling, personal accounts of the Deepwater Horizon spill and aftermath, and suggest how to avoid future disasters.

Cleveland, Cutler J. "Deepwater Horizon Oil Spill." In *Encyclopedia of Earth*, updated version. February 22, 2013. www.eoearth.org/view/article/161185/. This work examines the events that led up to the Deepwater Horizon spill, the spill itself, and the actions taken as a result of the spill.

Hoffman, Andrew J., and P. Devereaux Jennings. 2011. "The BP Oil Spill as a Cultural Anomaly? Institutional Context, Conflict, and Change." *Journal of Management Inquiry* 20, no. 2 (2011): 100–112. This article examines the Deepwater Horizon spill and the institutional management related to drilling, and argues change is yet to come.

National Commission on the BP Deepwater Horizon Oil Spill and Offshore Drilling. "Deep Water: The Gulf Oil Disaster and the Future of Offshore Drilling—Report to the President." Washington, DC: Government Printing Office, 2011. A government document criticizing the government for mismanagement of its response to the Deepwater Horizon spill.

Safina, Carl. *A Sea in Flames: The Deepwater Horizon Blowout.* New York: Crown Publishers, 2011. A conservationist's view of the political and corporate causes and the environmental effects of the Deepwater Horizon spill.

Web Resources

BP Oil Disaster, BBC News, www.bbc.co.uk/news/special_reports/oil_disaster. Explore articles, maps, photos, and other information on the BP oil spill, efforts to stop it, and its environmental impact.

Deepwater Horizon Headlines, Rigzone, www.rigzone.com/news/incident.asp?inc_id=1. Access an archive of Deepwater Horizon news from this for-profit company that focuses on oil news and jobs.

Deepwater Horizon Response and Restoration, U.S. Department of the Interior, www.doi.gov/deepwaterhorizon/index.cfm. Here you can examine government documents relating to the Deepwater Horizon spill and the response to it and view additional related government links.

National Oceanic and Atmospheric Administration's Deepwater Horizon Archive, www.noaa.gov/deepwaterhorizon. Access archived data, reports, maps, articles, and more about the Deepwater Horizon spill.

Sustainability: Gulf of Mexico, BP, www.bp.com/en/global/corporate/sustainability/gulf-of-mexico.html. BP's Web page on corporate sustainability records what it has done and what it continues to do to help restore the Gulf of Mexico.

Notes

Chapter 1

1. David Dreyer, "One Issue Leads to Another: Issue Spirals and the Sino-Vietnamese War," *Foreign Policy Analysis* 6, no. 4 (2010): 297–315.
2. An early realist writer who stressed the importance of both possessive and atmospheric goals to the national interest was Arnold Wolfers, *Discord and Collaboration* (Baltimore: Johns Hopkins University Press, 1962).
3. See Barry Posen, "The Security Dilemma and Ethnic Conflict," *Survival* 35, no. 1 (1993): 27–47; and Shiping Tang, "Fear in International Politics," *International Studies Review* 10, no. 3 (2008): 451–471.
4. See Joseph Nye, *The Future of Power* (New York: Public Affairs Press, 2011).
5. Stephen John Stedman, "Spoiler Problems in Peace Processes," *International Security* 22, no. 2 (1997): 5–53.
6. Thom Brooks, "The Real Challenge of Climate Change," *PS: Political Science and Politics* 46 (January 2013): 34–36.

Chapter 2

1. Marvin Ott, "Deep Danger, Competing Claims in the South China Sea," *Current History* 110 (September 2011): 236–241.
2. Robert D. Kaplan, "The South China Sea Is the Future of Conflict," *Foreign Policy* (September–October 2011): 78–85.
3. Ibid.; and *Monsoon: The Indian Ocean and the Future of American Power* (New York: Random House, 2010).
4. "ASEAN Secretary General: South China Sea Risks Becoming 'Asia's Palestine,'" AmCham Vietnam, www.amchamvietnam.com/6096/asean-secretary-general-south-china-sea-risks-becoming-asia-s-palestine/.
5. Nguyen Hong Thao and Ramses Amer, "A New Legal Arrangement for the South China Sea?" *Ocean Development and International Law* 40, no. 4 (2009): 333–349; Dana R. Dillon, "Countering Beijing in the South China Sea," *Policy Review* 167 (June–July 2011): 51–67.

6. See Zhao Hong, "Energy, Security Concerns of China and ASEAN: Trigger for Conflict or Cooperation in the South China Sea?," *Asia Europe Journal* 8, no. 3 (2010): 413–426.; M. Taylor Fravel, "China's Strategy in the South China Sea," *Contemporary Southeast Asia* 33, no. 3 (2011): 292–319.

7. See Zhiguo Gao, "The South China Sea: From Conflict to Cooperation?," *Ocean Development and International Law* 25, no. 3 (1994): 345–359; Ralf Emmers, "The Changing Power Distribution in the South China Sea: Implications for Conflict Management and Avoidance," *Political Science* 62, no. 2 (2010): 118–131; Thao and Amer, "A New Legal Arrangement for the South China Sea?"

8. Denny Roy, *China's Foreign Policy* (Lanham, MD: Rowman and Littlefield, 1988), 74.

9. For a detailed account of the development of China's strategy, see John W. Garver, "China's Push through the South China Sea: The Interaction of Bureaucratic and National Interest," *China Quarterly* 132 (December 1992): 999–1,028. The Spotlight section that follows draws heavily on his account.

10. Chi-kin Lo, *China's Policy toward Territorial Disputes* (New York: Routledge, 1989), 93.

11. Justin Ho Cheng Lun, "Sino-Vietnamese Tensions in the South China Sea," East Asia Forum, December 15, 2012, www.eastasiaforum.org/2012/12/15/sino-vietnamese-tensions-in-the-south-china-sea/.

12. Ralf Emmers, *Cooperative Security and the Balance of Power in ASEAN and the ARF* (New York: Routledge, 2003), 151

13. See U.S. State Department, Daily Press Briefing, May 10, 1995, http://dosfan.lib.uic.edu/ERC/briefing/daily_briefings/1995/9505/950510db.html.

14. Leszek Buszynski, "ASEAN, the Declaration on Conduct and the South China Sea," *Contemporary Southeast Asia* 25, no. 3 (2003): 343–362.

15. Ian James Storey, "Creeping Assertiveness: China, the Philippines and the South China Sea Dispute," *Contemporary Southeast Asia* 21, no. 1 (1999): 95–117.

16. Leszek Buszynski, "Rising Tensions in the South China Sea: Prospects for a Resolution of the Issue," *Security Challenges* 6, no. 2 (2010): 85–104; and Fravel, "China's Strategy in the South China Sea."

17. See "Remarks at the US-ASEAN Ministerial Meeting," U.S. Department of State, July 11, 2012, www.state.gov/secretary/rm/2012/07/194843.htm.

18. The islands are known as the Senkaku Islands in Japan and as the Diaoyu Islands in China.

19. "Viewpoints: How Serious Are China-Japan Tensions?" BBC News, February 7, 2013, www.bbc.co.uk/news/world-asia-2129034.

Chapter 3

1. J. David Singer and Melvin Small, *The Wages of War, 1816–1965* (New York: John Wiley & Sons, 1972); and Meredith Reid Sarkees, "Inter-State Wars: Definitions and Variables," www.correlatesof war.org/COW2%20Data/WarData_NEW/Inter-StateWars_Code book.pdf.
2. John Mueller, "The Obsolescence of Major War," *Bulletin of Peace Proposals* 21, no. 3 (1990): 321–328; and Stephen Pinker, *The Better Angels of Our Nature* (New York: Viking, 2011).
3. Kenneth Waltz, *Theory of International Politics* (New York: McGraw-Hill, 1979); and John Mearsheimer, *The Tragedy of Great Power Politics* (New York: W. W. Norton and Company, 2001).
4. Stephen Van Evera, *Causes of War: Power and the Roots of Conflict* (Ithaca, NY: Cornell University Press, 1999), 6–11.
5. Charter of the United Nations, Chapter I: Purposes and Principals, www.un.org/en/documents/charter/chapter1.shtml.
6. Charter of the United Nations, Chapter VII: Action with Respect to Threats to the Peace, Breaches of the Peace, and Acts of Aggression, www.un.org/en/documents/charter/chapter7.shtml.
7. See, for example, James J. Wirtz and James A. Russell, "U.S. Policy on Preventive War and Preemption," *The Nonproliferation Review* 10 (Spring 2003): 113–123. Available online at http://cns.miis.edu/ npr/pdfs/101wirtz.pdf.
8. Charter of the United Nations, Chapter VII.
9. Ibid.
10. Shibley Telhami, *The Stakes: America in the Middle East* (Westview Press, 2004), 140–147.
11. Geoffrey Kemp and Robert Harkavy, *Strategic Geography and the Changing Middle East* (Washington, DC: Carnegie Endowment and Brookings, 1997), 110–114.
12. United Nations Security Council Resolution 687, 1991, www .un.org/depts/unmovic/new/documents/resolutions/s-res-687.pdf.
13. Elliott Abrams et al., Letter to President Bill Clinton, Project for the New American Century, January 26, 1998, www.newamericancen tury.org/iraqclintonletter.htm.
14. Bob Woodward, *Bush at War* (New York: Simon & Schuster, 2002).
15. PBS Frontline: The War behind Closed Doors, www.pbs.org/wgbh/ pages/frontline/shows/iraq/.
16. Mark Thompson, "Was There an Anthrax Push into War with Iraq?," *Time,* June 27, 2011, http://nation.time.com/2011/06/27/ was-there-an-anthrax-push-into-war-with-iraq/.

17. Quoted in Peter Hahn, *Crisis and Crossfire: The United States and the Middle East since 1945* (Washington, DC: Potomac Books), 123.
18. "Saudis Warn US over Iraq War," BBC News, February 17, 2003, http://news.bbc.co.uk/2/hi/middle_east/2773759.stm.
19. Turkey Rejects U.S. Troop Proposal," CNN.com, March 1, 2003, www.cnn.com/2003/WORLD/meast/03/01/sprj.irq.main/.
20. Ibid.
21. "EU Allies Unite against Iraq War," BBC News, January 22, 2003, http://news.bbc.co.uk/2/hi/europe/2683409.stm.
22. David Kinsella, *Regime Change: Origins, Executions, and Aftermath of the Iraq War,* 2nd ed. (Belmont, CA: Thompson/Wadsworth, 2007).
23. Walter Pincus, "WMD Commission Releases Scathing Report," *The Washington Post,* March 31, 2005.
24. Barton Gellman, "Iraq's Arsenal of Ambitions," *The Washington Post,* January 7, 2004, 22.
25. JoAnne Allen. "FBI Says Saddam's Weapons Bluff Aimed at Iran." Reuters, July 2, 2009, www.reuters.com/article/2009/07/02/us-iran-saddam-idUSTRE56113020090702.
26. "Full Text: UN Security Council Resolution 1441 on Iraq," *The Guardian,* December 20, 2002, www.guardian.co.uk/world/2002/dec/20/iraq.foreignpolicy2.
27. Ibid.
28. United Nations Monitoring, Verification, and Inspections Commission: Basic Facts, www.unmovic.org/.
29. "Bush Ultimatum to Saddam: Text." BBC News, March 18, 2003, http://news.bbc.co.uk/2/hi/americas/2859269.stm.
30. H.J. Res. 114 (107th): Authorization for Use of Military Force against Iraq Resolution of 2002, www.govtrack.us/congress/bills/107/hjres114/text.
31. Ibid.
32. Ibid.
33. Jerrold Post, *The Psychological Assessment of Political Leaders* (Ann Arbor: University of Michigan Press, 2003).
34. Vaughn Shannon and Jonathan Keller, "Leadership Style and International Norm Violation: The Case of the Iraq War," *Foreign Policy Analysis* 3, no. 1 (2007): 79–104 .
35. Daniel Trotta, "Iraq War Costs U.S. More Than $2 Trillion: Study," Reuters, March 14, 2013, www.reuters.com/article/2013/03/14/us-iraq-war-anniversary-idUSBRE92D0PG20130314; and Seth Cline, "The Underestimated Costs, and Price Tag, of the Iraqi War," March 20, 2013, www.usnews.com/news/blogs/press-past/2013/03/20/the-underestimated-costs-and-price-tag-of-the-iraq-war.

36. Andrew Tilghman, "Little U.S. Military Influence Remains in Iraq," *Army Times*, March 4, 2013, 16.

Chapter 4

1. Shibley Telhami, *The Stakes: America and the Middle East* (New York: Basic Books, 2002).
2. Greg Cashman and Leonard C. Robinson, *An Introduction to the Causes of War* (Lanham, MD: Rowman and Littlefield, 2007), 157–197.
3. Avraham Sela, *The Decline of the Arab-Israeli Conflict: Middle East Politics and the Quest for Regional Order* (Albany: State University of New York Press, 1998).
4. Hemda Ben-Yehuda and Shmuel Sandler, *The Arab-Israeli Conflict Transformed: Fifty Years of Interstate and Ethnic Crises* (Albany: SUNY Press, 2002).
5. Rashid Khalidi, *The Iron Cage: The Story of the Palestinian Struggle for Statehood* (Boston: Beacon Press, 2007).
6. Marvin Gettleman and Stuart Schaar, eds, *The Middle East and Islamic World Reader* (New York: Grove Press, 2003), 170.
7. Ibid., 171–172.
8. J. A. Simpson and E. S. C. Weiner, *The Compact Oxford English Dictionary*, 2nd ed. (Oxford, UK: Clarendon Press, 1991), 231, 234.
9. Cashman and Robinson, *An Introduction to the Causes of War*, 15.
10. Chester Crocker, Fen Osler Hampson, and Pamela Aall, *Grasping the Nettle: Analyzing Cases of Intractable Conflict* (Washington, DC: USIP Press, 2005), 5.
11. William Zartman, "The Timing of Peace Initiatives: Hurting Stalemates and Ripe Moments," *The Global Review of Ethnopolitics* 1, n0.1 (2001): 8–18.
12. Naim al-Ashhab, "Lessons from the Past," Bitterlemons.org, www.bitterlemons.org/previous/b1130904ed34.html#is2.
13. Ibid.
14. Khalidi, *The Iron Cage*.
15. Benny Morris, ed. *Making Israel* (Ann Arbor: University of Michigan Press, 2007).
16. Ibid.
17. Al-Ashhab, "Lessons from the Past."
18. Morris, *Making Israel*.
19. Official Documents System of the United Nations, http://daccess-dds-ny.un.org/doc/RESOLUTION/GEN/NR0/043/65/IMG/NR004365.pdf?OpenElement.
20. Cashman and Robinson, *An Introduction to the Causes of War*, 167; and Fred Khouri, *The Arab-Israeli Dilemma*, 3rd ed. (Syracuse, NY: Syracuse University Press, 1985), 182–183.

21. Ranan Kuperman, *Cycles of Violence: The Evolution of the Israeli Decision Regime Governing the Use of Limited Military Force* (Lanham, MD: Lexington Books, 2005).

22. Michael Oren, *Six Days of War: June 1967 and the Making of the Modern Middle East* (New York: Presidio Press, 2003), 8–9.

23. Cashman and Robinson, *An Introduction to the Causes of War,* 14.

24. Some of this is adapted from Vaughn Shannon, *Balancing Act: U.S. Foreign Policy and the Arab-Israeli Conflict* (Burlington, VT: Ashgate Press, 2003).

25. Committee for Accuracy in Middle East Reporting in America, "The Six-Day War: Precursors to War: Arab Threats against Israel," www.sixdaywar.org/content/threats.asp.

26. George Lenczowski, *The Middle East in World Affairs,* 4th ed. (Ithaca, NY: Cornell University Press, 1980), 559.

27. Shannon, *Balancing Act.*

28. H. W. Brands, *Into the Labyrinth: The United States and the Middle East, 1945–1993* (New York: McGraw-Hill, 1994), 128.

29. Steven Spiegel, *The Other Arab-Israeli Conflict* (Chicago: University of Chicago Press, 1985), 186.

30. Ibid., 187–188.

31. Brands, *Into the Labyrinth,* 125.

32. Ibid., 127.

33. See Camille Mansour, *Beyond Alliance: Israel in U.S. Foreign Policy* (New York: Columbia University Press, 1994), chapter 3.

34. Richard Nixon, *The Memoirs of Richard Nixon* (New York: Grosset and Dunlap, 1978), 921; and William Quandt, *Peace Process: American Diplomacy and the Arab-Israeli Conflict since 1967* (Washington, DC: Brookings Institution Press, 1993), 157.

35. Brands, *Into the Labyrinth,* 134.

36. Ian J. Klausner and Carla L. Bickerton, *A Concise History of the Arab-Israeli Conflict* (Upper Saddle River, NJ: Prentice Hall, 1998), 183.

37. Deborah Gerner, *One Land, Two Peoples: The Conflict Over Palestine.* Boulder: Westview Press, 1991, p. 76.

38. Bernard Reich, *Quest for Peace: U.S.-Israel Relations and the Arab-Israeli Conflict* (New Brunswick, NJ: Transaction Books, 1977).

39. Quandt, *Peace Process,* 326–329.

40. Ziva Flamhaft, *Israel on the Road to Peace: Accepting the Unacceptable* (Boulder, CO: Westview Press, 1996), 119.

41. See Gerner, *One Land, Two Peoples,* 95, for a comprehensive list. These annexations were condemned by the international community and have not been recognized.

42. Wendy Pearlman, "Spoiling Inside and Out: Internal Political Contestation and the Middle East Peace Process," *International Security* 33, no. 3 (2008–2009): 79–109.

43. Spiegel, *The Other Arab-Israeli Conflict,* 419–420.
44. Flamhaft, *Israel on the Road to Peace,* 39–41. Importantly, Israel's Labor Party approved the Reagan Plan and, when in power, moved on negotiations in due course.
45. Gerner, *One Land, Two Peoples,* 94.
46. Flamhaft, *Israel on the Road to Peace,* 53–56.
47. This turned out to be the first of two uprisings that occurred by the time this book went to press; the other, the al-Aqsa *intifada,* began in September 2000.
48. Gerner, *One Land, Two Peoples,* 97–99. Many of the Palestinian casualties in the later years of the uprising were inflicted by other Palestinians; see Mitchell G. Bard and Joel Himelfarb, *Myth and Facts: A Concise Record of the Arab-Israeli Conflict* (Washington, DC: Near East Report, 1992), 170.
49. Gerner, *One Land, Two Peoples,* 126. Twenty-seven states recognized the new Palestinian state, including the Soviet Union, Egypt, and other regional powers, and by the mid-1990s more states recognized Palestine than Israel. Still, the United States refused to grant recognition, which is why Palestine is still not a sovereign state. (Klausner and Bickerton, *A Concise History of the Arab-Israeli Conflict,* 233).
50. Bickerton and Klausner, *A Concise History of the Arab-Israeli Conflict,* 235.
51. James Baker, *The Politics of Diplomacy* (New York: G. P. Putnam's Sons, 1995), 122; and Flamhaft, *Israel on the Road to Peace,* 69–71. Carter had declared the settlements illegal, and Reagan called them "an obstacle to peace."
52. Gorbachev opened up the Soviet Union to the emigration of some 650,000 Jews to Israel between 1990 and 1995. Congress voted for the loan guarantees anyway, which led the White House to hold up their disbursement (Bickerton and Klausner, *A Concise History of the Arab-Israeli Conflict,* 249).
53. Flamhaft, *Israel on the Road to Peace,* 131–132.
54. A/Res/52/250.
55. Dennis Ross, *The Missing Peace* (New York: Farrar, Straus and Giroux, 2004).
56. John J. Mearsheimer and Stephen M. Walt, *The Israel Lobby and U.S. Foreign Policy* (New York: Farrar, Straus and Giroux, 2007).
57. Andy Mosher, "Abbas Says Violence by Palestinians Should End," *The Washington Post,* December 15, 2004, www.washingtonpost.com/wp-dyn/articles/A62928–2004Dec14.html.
58. "Abbas Says Olmert Was 'Two Months' from Peace Deal," Reuters, October 14, 2012, www.reuters.com/article/2012/10/14/us-palestinians-israel-abbas-olmert-idUSBRE89D0G420121014.
59. Khaled Abu Toameh, "U.S. Softening Opposition to Fatah-Hamas Unity," *Jerusalem Post,* April 8, 2013, www.jpost.com/Diplomacy-and-Politics/PA-official-US-softening-opposition-to-Fatah-Hamas-unity-309120.

60. "Kerry to Defend Syria Policy in Mideast Visit," *Jerusalem Post,* June 21, 2013, www.jpost.com/Diplomacy-and-Politics/Kerry-to-defend-Syria-policy-in-upcoming-Mideast-visit-317318.

Chapter 5

1. William Broad, John Markoff, and David Sanger, "Israeli Test on Worm Called Crucial in Iran Nuclear Delay," *The New York Times,* January 15, 2011.
2. Malcolm Kerr, *The Arab Cold War,* 3rd ed. (London: Oxford University Press, 1971).
3. Kenneth Katzman, "Iran: U.S. Concerns and Policy Responses," CRS Report for Congress, November 1, 2006, www.fas.org/sgp/crs/mideast/RL32048.pdf.
4. Richard Clarke, *Against All Enemies* (New York: Free Press, 2004), 103–104.
5. Ibid., 112–121.
6. Mohammed Khatami, President of the Islamic Republic of Iran, "Dialogue among Civilizations," September 5, 2000, www.unesco.org/dialogue/en/khatami.htm.
7. John Limbert. "Why Can't Arabs and Iranians Just Get Along?," *Foreign Policy,* December 1, 2012, www.foreignpolicy.com/articles/2010/12/01/why_can_t_arabs_and_iranians_just_get_along.
8. Trita Parsi, *Treacherous Alliance: The Secret Dealings of Israel, Iran and the U.S.* (Cambridge: Yale University Press, 2007).
9. Peter Lavoy, "Predicting Nuclear Proliferation: A Declassified Documentary Record," *Strategic Insights* 3, no. 1 (2004). Available online at www.fas.org/man/eprint/lavoy.pdf.
10. "The Treaty on the Non-Proliferation of Nuclear Weapons," United Nations, .www.un.org/en/conf/npt/2010/npttext.shtml.
11. Some of the following is excerpted from Vaughn Shannon, "Iran and the Middle East: The Pursuit of Security and Legitimacy in the American Age," in *Strategic Interests in the Middle East,* ed. Jack Covarrubias and Tom Lansford (Aldershot, UK: Ashgate, 2007), 171–196; and Vaughn Shannon, "The U.S. Reaction to the 2009 Iranian Election: The End of 'Regime Change' Politics," *Journal of Iranian Research and Analysis* 26, no. 2 (2009): 47–63.
12. Parsi, *Treacherous Alliance.*
13. Shai Feldman, *Nuclear Weapons and Arms Control in the Middle East* (Cambridge: MIT Press, 1997), 47.
14. Graham Allison, *Nuclear Terrorism: The Ultimate Preventable Catastrophe* (New York: Times Books, 2004), 161.
15. R. Jeffrey Smith and Joby Warrick, "Pakistani Scientist Khan Describes Iranian Efforts to buy Nuclear Bombs," *The Washington Post,* March 14, 2010, www.washingtonpost.com/wp-dyn/content/article/2010/03/13/AR2010031302258.html.

16. See, for example, Patrick Clawson, Michael Eisenstadt, Eliyahu Kanovsky, and David Menashri, "Iran under Khatami: A Political, Economic, and Military Assessment," The Washington Institute, October 1998, www.washingtoninstitute.org/policy-analysis/view/iran-under-khatami-a-political-economic-and-military-assessment.

17. Feldman, *Nuclear Weapons and Arms Control in the Middle East,* 47.

18. Allison, *Nuclear Terrorism,* 161.

19. Ibid., 162.

20. Frederic Wherey, Dalia Dassa Kaye, Jessica Watkins, Jeffrey Martini, and Robert A. Guffey, *The Iraq Effect: The Middle East after the Iraq War* (Santa Monica: Rand Corporation, 2010).

21. Ibid.

22. Fouad Ajami. *The Foreigner's Gift* (New York: Simon & Schuster, 2007), 108.

23. Bernd Kaussler and Anthony Newkirk, "Diplomacy in Bad Faith: American-Iranian Relations Today," *Diplomacy and Statecraft* 23, no. 2 (2012): 347–380.

24. The poll bases its results on telephone interviews with 1,000 adults throughout Iran, which raises problems about the validity of the responses from a Western polling organization. See Mohammad Ali Shabani, "Iranians Support Nuclear Program, Blame West for Sanctions, Says Poll." Al-Monitor, February 14, 2013, www.al-monitor.com/pulse/originals/2013/02/iranian-poll-support-nuclear-program-blame-sanctions.html#ixzz2MsfxFs3X.

25. Glenn Kessler, "Did Ahmadinejad Really Say Israel Should Be 'Wiped off the Map?,'" *The Washington Post,* October 5, 2011, www.washingtonpost.com/blogs/fact-checker/post/did-ahmadinejad-really-say-israel-should-be-wiped-off-the-map/2011/10/04/gIQABJIKML_blog.html.

26. Jonathan Broder. "Israel's Nuclear Blind Spot," *The Washington Post National Weekly Edition,* March 19–15, 2001, 22.

27. Feldman, *Nuclear Weapons and Arms Control in the Middle East,* 44.

28. Broder, "Israel's Nuclear Blind Spot."

29. Dean Nelson, "A. Q. Khan Boasts of Help Iran's Nuclear Programme," *The Telegraph,* September 10, 2009, www.telegraph.co.uk/news/worldnews/asia/pakistan/6170145/A.Q.-Khan-boasts-of-helping-Irans-nuclear-programme.html.

30. Vali Nasr, *The Shia Revival* (New York: W. W. Norton & Company, 2007); and Deborah Amos, *The Eclipse of the Sunni: Power, Exile, and Upheaval in the Middle East* (New York: PublicAffairs, 2010).

31. "U.S. Embassy Cables: Saudi King Urges U.S. Strike on Iran." *The Guardian,* November 28, 2010, www.theguardian.com/world/us-embassy-cables-documents/150519.

32. Ali Gharib and Jim Lobe, "Wikileaks Reveals Treacherous Terrain for Iran Policy," Inter Press Service, November 29, 2010, http://ips news.net/news.asp?idnews=53704.

33. Barbara Slavin, "Poll: Sectarianism, Syria Drive Negative Image of Iran," Al-Monitor, March 5, 2013, www.al-monitor.com/pulse/originals/2013/03/zogby-poll-negative-arab-attitudes-iran-syria.html#ixzz2MhuBwrf1.

34. www.armscontrol.org/pdf/2003_Spring_Iran_Proposal.pdf.

35. "Europe's Iran Diplomacy," European Union Center of North Carolina, March 2008, www.unc.edu/depts/europe/business_media/mediabriefs/Brief7–0803-iran.pdf.

36. Seyed Hossein Mousavian, "Embrace the Fatwa," Foreign Policy, February 7, 2013, www.foreignpolicy.com/articles/2013/02/07/Embrace_the_Fatwa_Iran.

37. "Iran: Ayatollah Khamenei Re-Issues Fatwa against Nuclear Weapons," YouTube, June 11, 2012, www.youtube.com/watch?v=95HuFUiAEig.

38. Mousavian, "Embrace the Fatwa."

39. Michael Eisenstadt and Mehdi Khalaji, "Nuclear Fatwa: Religion and Politics in Iran's Proliferation Strategy," WINEP Policy Focus #115, September 2011, www.washingtoninstitute.org/uploads/Documents/pubs/PolicyFocus115.pdf.

40. Walter Rodgers, "Iran Breaks Seals at Nuclear Plant," CNN.com, August 10, 2005, www.cnn.com/2005/WORLD/europe/08/10/iran.iaea.1350/index.html.

41. Seymour Hersh, "Last Stand," New Yorker, July 10, 2006, www.newyorker.com/archive/2006/07/10/060710fa_fact.

42. IAEA Board of Governors, "Implementation of the NPT Safeguards Agreement in the Islamic Republic of Iran," Febuary 4, 2006, www.iaea.org/Publications/Documents/Board/2006/gov2006–14.pdf; IAEA Board of Governors, "Implementation of the NPT Safeguards Agreement in the Islamic Republic of Iran," August 31, 2006, www.iaea.org/Publications/Documents/Board/2006/gov2006–53.pdf.

43. Robert Tait and Ewen MacAskill, "Revealed: The Letter Obama Team Hope Will Heal Iran Rift," The Guardian, January 28, 2009, www.guardian.co.uk/world/2009/jan/28/barack-obama-letter to iran.

44. John Limbert, "The Obama Administration," United States Institute of Peace: The Iran Primer, http://iranprimer.usip.org/resource/obama-administration.

45. "Timeline of Nuclear Diplomacy with Iran," Arms Control Association, October 2013, www.armscontrol.org/factsheet/Timeline-of-Nuclear-Diplomacy-With-Iran#2009.

46. Robert Jervis, "Getting to Yes with Iran: The Challenges of Coercive Diplomacy," Foreign Affairs (January–February 2013): 105–115.

47. "U.S. 'Won't Stand in the Way' of Israel Attack on Iran," *New Zealand Herald,* July 6, 2009, www.nzherald.co.nz/world/news/article .cfm?c_id=2&objectid=10582822.

48. "Iran Attacks Biden's Israel Remarks," Al Jazeera, July 7, 2009, http:// english.aljazeera.net/news/middleeast/2009/07/200977602190659 .html.

49. David Sanger, "U.S. Says Iran Could Expedite Nuclear Bomb," *The New York Times,* September 9, 2009, www.nytimes.com/2009/09/10/ world/middleeast/10intel.html?_r=1&ref=world&pagewanted=all.

50. Richard Russell, "Future Gulf War: Arab and American Forces against Iranian Capabilities," *JFQ* 55, no. 4 (2009): 40.

51. Barak Ravid, "Iran's Khameini: We Will Destroy Israeli Cities if Attacked," *Haaretz,* March 21, 2013, www.haaretz.com/news/ diplomacy-defense/iran-s-khamenei-we-will-destroy-israeli-cities-if-attacked-1.511071.

52. Scott Peterson, "Iran's Rohani Vows Not to Surrender to Sanctions," *Christian Science Monitor,* August 4, 2013, www.csmonitor.com/ World/Middle-East/2013/0804/Iran-s-Rohani-vows-not-to-surren der-to-sanctions.

53. For overviews and assessments of the debate, see Colin Kahl, Melissa Dalton, and Matthew Irvine, "Atomic Kingdom: If Iran Builds the Bomb, Will Saudi Arabia Be Next?," Center for New American Security, February 19, 2013, www.cnas.org/files/docu ments/publications/CNAS_AtomicKingdom_Kahl.pdf; and Thomas W. Lippman, "Saudi Arabia's Nuclear Policy," Saudi-U.S. Relations Information Service, August 5, 2011, www.susris.com/2011/08/05/ saudi-arabia%E2%80%99s-nuclear-policy-lippman/.

54. Samer al-Atrush, "Iran Leads Nuclear Drive in the Middle East," AFP, September 18, 2010, www.google.com/hostednews/afp/article/ ALeqM5gh-97JFOTRtYHECmj8Rx4U7xvjdQ.

Chapter 6

1. Steven Metz, "Strategic Horizons: U.S. Must Prioritize among Al-Qaeda Franchise Threats," World Politics Review, July 31, 2013, www.worldpoliticsreview.com/articles/13130/strategic-horizons-u-s-must-prioritize-among-al-qaida-franchise-threats.

2. Vaughn Shannon, "Why *Who* Hates Us? Distinguishing Militants from the Merely Muslim," *Harvard International Review,* 2006, http://hir.harvard.edu/why-iwhoi-hates-us.

3. John Esposito, "It's the Policy Stupid: Political Islam and U.S. Foreign Policy," Georgetown University Research and Publications, http://acmcu.georgetown.edu/135400.html; and Shibley Telhami, *The Stakes: America and the Middle East* (New York: Basic Books, 2002).

4. Barak Mendohlson, *Combating Jihadism* (Chicago: University of Chicago Press, 2009).

5. John Esposito, *Unholy War: Terror in the Name of Islam* (Oxford, UK: Oxford University Press, 2002), 45–46.

6. Daniel Benjamin and Steven Simon, *The Age of Sacred Terror: Radical Islam's War against America* (New York: Random House, 2003), 57.

7. Greg Mortensen, *Three Cups of Tea: One Man's Mission to Promote Peace One School at a Time* (New York: Viking, 2006).

8. Jan Goodwin, *Price of Honor* (Boston: Little, Brown & Company, 1994), 82.

9. Ibid., 82–83.

10. Ahmed Rashid. *Taliban* (New Haven: Yale University Press, 2001) 129.

11. World Islamic Front, "Jihad against Jews and Crusaders," February 23, 1998, www.fas.org/irp/world/para/docs/980223-fatwa.htm.

12. Peter Bergen, *Holy War Inc: Inside the Secret World of Osama bin Laden* (London: Weidenfeld & Nicolson, 2001), 119.

13. "Wadih El Hage Resentenced to Life in Prison for His Role in the 1998 Bombings of the American Embassies in Kenya and Tanzania," United States Attorney's Office, Southern District of New York, April 23, 2013, www.justice.gov/usao/nys/pressreleases/April13/ElHagSentencingPR.php?print=1.

14. "U.S. Captures Al-Qaeda Leader Wanted over 1998 Embassy Bombings," Al Jazeera America, October 5, 2013, http://america.aljazeera.com/articles/2013/10/5/libyan-al-qaeda-leadercapturedintripoli.html.

15. Richard Clarke, *Against All Enemies: Inside America's War on Terror* (New York: Free Press, 2004).

16. U.S. Department of Defense, DOD Dictionary of Military and Associated Terms, http://www.dtic.mil/doctrine/dod_dictionary/.

17. See a typology of political violence in Ariel Merari, "Terrorism as a Strategy of Insurgency," *Terrorism and Political Violence 5*, no. 4 (1993): 213–251.

18. Daniel Byman, "U.S. Counter-Terrorism Options: A Taxonomy," *Survival 49*, no. 3 (2007): 121.

19. Paul Pillar, *Terrorism and U.S. Foreign Policy* (Washington, DC: Brookings Institute, 2001).

20. Mark Mazzetti, Charlie Savage, and Scott Shane. "How a U.S. Citizen Came to Be in America's Cross Hairs," *The New York Times*, March 9, 2013, www.nytimes.com/2013/03/10/world/middleeast/anwar-al-awlaki-a-us-citizen-in-americas-cross-hairs.html?_r=0.

21. Sabrina Siddiqui, "Obama Administration Skips Senate Drone Hearing," The Huffington Post, April 23, 2013, www.huffingtonpost.com/2013/04/23/obama-drone-hearing_n_3142144.html.

22. Richard Betts, "The Soft Underbelly of American Primacy: Tactical Advantages of Terror," *Political Science Quarterly* 117, no. 1 (2002): 19–36.

23. Mendelsohn, *Combating Jihadism.*

24. Ahmed Rashid, *Taliban: Militant Islam, Oil, and Fundamentalism in Central Asia* (New Haven: Yale University Press, 2001), 133–134.

25. "Bush Rejects Taliban Offer to Hand Bin Laden Over," *The Guardian,* October 14, 2001, www.guardian.co.uk/world/2001/oct/14/afghanistan.terrorism5.

26. Steven Saideman and David Auerswald, "Comparing Caveats: Understanding the Sources of National Restrictions upon NATO's Mission in Afghanistan," *International Studies Quarterly* 56, no. 1 (2012): 72.

27. "Al Qaeda, Taliban Have Joined Hands in Pakistan," Sify News, November 21, 2010, http://sify.com/news/al-qaeda-taliban-have-joined-hands-in-pakistan-malik-news-international-klvrkfigbha.html.

28. Aryn Baker and Loi Kolay, "The Longest War," *Time,* April 20, 2009, 27.

29. Rod Nordland, "American and Afghan Troops Begin Combat for Kandahar," *The New York Times,* September 26, 2010, www.nytimes.com/2010/09/27/world/asia/27afghan.html?_r=1.

30. "Afghan, NATO Forces Launch Anti-Taliban Air-and-Ground Push in Kandahar," Voice of America, September 27, 2010, www.voanews.com/english/news/Afghan-NATO-Forces-Launch-Anti-Taliban-Push-in-Kandahar-103854658.html.

31. Zeeshan Haider, "Pakistan Army Says in Final Phase of Swat Offensive," Reuters, June 22, 2009, www.reuters.com/article/worldNews/idUSISL49834220090622.

32. "U.S. Drone Strike Kills Four Taliban Militants in Pak," India.com, October 7, 2010, www.dnaindia.com/world/report_us-drone-strike-kills-four-taliban-militants-in-pak_1449064-all.

33. Behroz Khan and Ben Arnoldy, "Pakistan Taliban: U.S. Drone Strikes Forcing Militants Underground," Christian Science Monitor, March 15, 2010, www.csmonitor.com/World/Asia-South-Central/2010/0315/Pakistan-Taliban-US-drone-strikes-forcing-militants-underground.

34. "Pakistan Taliban Threaten Attacks in U.S., Europe," Reuters, September 3, 2010, www.rcuters.com/article/idUSTRE68230220100903.

35. Ewen MacAskill, "Osama bin Laden: It Took Years to Find Him but Just Minutes to Kill Him," *The Guardian,* May 2, 2011, www.guardian.co.uk/world/2011/may/02/how-osama-bin-laden-found.

36. Aryn Baker and Loi Kolay, The U.S. in Afghanistan: The Longest War," *Time,* April 18, 2009, http://content.time.com/time/magazine/article/0,9171,1890410,00.html.

37. Daniel Byman, Daniel, "Friends Like These: Counterinsurgency and the War on Terrorism," *International Security* 31, no. 2 (2006): 79–115.

38. Nic Robertson, "Taliban Split with Al-Qaeda, Seek Peace," CNN .com, October 6, 2008, www.cnn.com/2008/WORLD/asiapcf/10/06/afghan.saudi.talks.

39. Jason Motlagh, "Talks with the Taliban Still Face Many Hurdles," *Time*, Oct. 25, 2010, www.time.com/time/world/article/0,8599,2027300,00.html.

40. Nick Schifrin and Kirit Radia, "Afghan Impostor: U.S. Officials Confirm Talks with Phony Taliban Leader," ABC News, November 23, 2010, http://abcnews.go.com/Politics/american officials-confirm -talks-phony-taliban-impostor/story?id=12223116.

41. Paul Tait, "Afghan Taliban Reject Talks Again," Reuters, November 15, 2010, http://mobile.reuters.com/article/topNews/ idUSLDE6AD0GK20101115.

42. Katharine Houreld, "Karzai Stresses Need for Pakistani Help in Taliban Peace Process," Reuters, August 26, 2013, www.reuters .com/article/2013/08/26/us-pakistan-afghanistan-idUSBRE97P02 X20130826.

43. Eric Schmitt and Mark Mazzetti, "Secret Order Lets U.S. Raid Al Qaeda," *The New York Times,* November 9, 2008, www.nytimes .com/2008/11/10/washington/10military.html?pagewanted=all.

44. Eric Schmitt and Mark Mazzetti, "Secret Order Lets U.S. Raid Al-Qaeda in Many Countries," *New York Times,* November 10, 2008, www.nytimes.com/2008/11/10/washington/10military.html?_r= 2&hp=&oref=slogi . . . &.

45. Gregory Johnsen, "Ignoring Yemen at Our Peril," Foreign Policy, October 31, 2010, www.foreignpolicy.com/articles/2010/10/31/ ignoring_yemen_at_our_peril.

46. Paula Newton, "Purported al-Awlaki Message Calls for Jihad against U.S," CNN.com, March 17, 2010, www.cnn.com/2010/ WORLD/europe/03/17/al.awlaki.message/index.html?hpt=T2.

47. Roger Runningen, "Obama Counterterror Aide Confers with Yemen's Saleh on Fighting Al-Qaeda," Bloomberg Report, September 20, 2010, www.bloomberg.com/news/2010–09–20/obama-counter- terror-aide-confers-with-yemen-s-saleh-on-fighting-al-qaeda.html.

48. Mark Mazzetti, Eric Schmidt, and Robert Worth, "Two Year Manhunt Led to Killing of Awlaki in Yemen," *The New York Times,* September 30, 2011, www.nytimes.com/2011/10/01/world/middle east/anwar-al-awlaki-is-killed-in-yemen.html?ref=anwaralaw laki&_r=0.

49. Ellen Knickmeyer, "Yemen: Al-Qaeda 2.0," Global Post, September 27, 2010, www.globalpost.com/dispatch/middle-east/100926/yemen- al-qaeda.

50. Rob Lever, "14 Charged with Aiding Al-Qaeda-Linked Somali Group," AFP, August 5, 2010, www.google.com/hostednews/afp/article/ALeqM5h48tZOap_5pVDMUnQwJ68D2g6Wdw.
51. Ibid.
52. Andrew Hansen, "Al-Qaeda in the Islamic Maghreb," *The Washington Post,* December 11, 2007, www.washingtonpost.com/wp-dyn/content/article/2007/12/11/AR2007121101404.html.
53. Ravi Somaiya, "The Rise of Al-Qaeda in North Africa," *Newsweek,* September 16, 2010, www.newsweek.com/2010/09/16/the-rise-of-al-qaeda-in-north-africa.html.
54. Al-Qaida Ask France to Negotiate with Osama," PTI, November 19, 2010, http://timesofindia.indiatimes.com/world/europe/Al-Qaida-ask-France-to-negotiate-with-Osama/articleshow/6953787.cms.
55. Ravi Somaiya, "The Rise of Al-Qaeda in North Africa," *Newsweek,* September 16, 2010, www.newsweek.com/2010/09/16/the-rise-of-al-qaeda-in-north-africa.html.
56. Jason Lyall and Isaiah Wilson III, "Rage against the Machines: Explaining Outcomes in Counterinsurgency Wars," *International Organization* 63 (Winter 2009): 67–106.
57. Tom Finn, "Yemen: Islam's Billy Graham Takes on Al-Qaeda," Global Post, November 30, 2010, www.tucsonsentinel.com/nationworld/report/113010_yemen_alqaeda.
58. Fred Kaplan, "The End of the Age of Petraeus: The Rise and Fall of Counterinsurgency," *Foreign Affairs* (January–February 2013): 75–90.

Chapter 7

1. Michael Hayden, "The Future of Things Cyber," *Strategic Studies Quarterly* 5 (Spring 2011): 3.
2. George Friedman, *The Next 100 Years* (New York: Anchor Books, 2009), chapters 9–11.
3. Sam Byford, "Obama Warns China That Cyber Attacks Could Be 'Inhibitor' in Relations," The Verge, June 8, 2013, www.theverge.com/2013/6/8/4410372/obama-holds-summit-with-xi-jinping-on-hacking.
4. "Preventing a U.S.-China Cyberwar," *The New York Times,* May 25, 2013, www.nytimes.com/2013/05/26/opinion/sunday/preventing-a-us-china-cyberwar.html.
5. Jane Perlez, "U.S. and China Put Focus on Cybersecurity," *The New York Times,* April 24, 2013, www.nytimes.com/2013/04/23/world/asia/united-states-and-china-hold-military-talks-with-cybersecurity-a-focus.html.
6. David Sanger, "U.S. Directly Blames China's Military for Cyberattacks," *The New York Times,* May 6, 2013, www.nytimes.com/

2013/05/07/world/asia/us-accuses-chinas-military-in-cyberattacks
.html?pagewanted=all.

7. Ibid.

8. For a listing of major Chinese cyberattacks on the United States and other countries from 1999–2009, see Brian Krekel, "Capability of the People's Republic of China to Conduct Cyber Warfare and Computer Network Exploitation," prepared for The U.S.-China Economic and Security Review Committee by Northrop Grumman Corporation, October 9, 2009, www2.gwu.edu/~nsarchiv/NSAEBB/ NSAEBB424/docs/Cyber-030.pdf.

9. Michael Kelley, "Pentagon: Chinese Hackers Have Stolen Data from 'Almost Every Major U.S. Defense Contractor'," Business Insider, May 7, 2013, www.businessinsider.com/china-stole-us-military-secrets-2013–5.

10. Ellen Nakashima, "Confidential Report Lists U.S. Weapons System Designs Compromised by Chinese Cyberspies," *The Washington Post,* May 27, 2013, http://articles.washingtonpost.com/2013–05–27/world/39554997_1_u-s-missile-defenses-weapons-combat-aircraft.

11. For an expanded list see Joseph S. Nye Jr., "Nuclear Lessons for Cyber Security?," *Strategic Studies Quarterly* 5, no. 4 (2011): 18–38.

12. Barlow, John Perry, "A Declaration of Independence of Cyberspace," https://projects.eff.org/~barlow/Declaration-Final.html.

13. Martin Libicki, *Conquest in Cyberspace* (New York: Cambridge University Press, 2007), 84–85.

14. Stephen Korns, "Cyber Operations: The New Balance," *Joint Force Quarterly* 54, no. 3 (2009): 99–100.

15. Federal Bureau of Investigations, "DNS Malware: Is Your Computer Infected?," November 2011, www.fbi.gov/news/stories/2011/november/malware_110911/malware_110911.

16. Paulo Shakarian, "The 2008 Russian Cyber Campaign against Georgia," *Military Review* 91 (November–December 2011): 63–68.

17. David Sanger, *Confront and Conceal: Obama's Secret Wars and the Surprising Use of American Power* (New York: Crown, 2012).

18. Christopher Bronk and Eneken Tikk-Ringas, "The Cyber Attack on Saudi Aramco," *Survival* 55, no. 2 (2013), 81–96.

19. For an assessment of cyberterrorism, see Robert Knake, "Cyberterrorism Hype vs. Fact," February 16, 2010, www.cfr.org/terrorism-and-technology/cyberterrorism-hype-v-fact/p21434.

20. Jody Prescott, "War by Analogy," *The RUSI Journal* 156, no. 6 (2011): 35.

21. Tom Gjelten, "First Strike: U.S. Cyber Warriors Seize the Offensive, *World Affairs* 175 (January–February 2013): 33–43.

22. Prescott, "War by Analogy," 32–39.

23. Paul Meyer, "Diplomatic Alternatives to Cyber-Warfare," *The RUSI Journal* 157, no. 1 (2012): 14–19.
24. "London Hosts Cyberspace Security Conference," BBC News, November 1, 2011, www.bbc.co.uk/news/technology-15533786.
25. Meyer, "Diplomatic Alternatives to Cyber-Warfare."
26. On China, see Nigel Inkster, "Chinese Intelligence in the Cyber Age," *Survival* 55, no. 1 (2013): 45–66; Edward Wong, "Hackers Find China Is Land of Opportunity," *The New York Times*, May 23, 2013; and Alexander Klimburg, "Mobilising Cyber Power," *Survival* 53, no. 1 (2011): 41–60.
27. Klimburg, "Mobilising Cyber Power."
28. See John Arquilla and David Ronfeldt, "Cyberwar Is Coming," *Comparative Strategy* 12, no. 2 (1993): 141–165.
29. See Colin Gray, *Making Strategic Sense of Cyber Power: Why the Sky Is Not Falling* (Carlisle Barracks, PA: U.S. Army War College Press, 2013); and Strategic Studies Institute, www.StrategicStudies Institute.army.mil/.
30. Andrew Mumford, "Proxy Wars and the Future of Conflict," *The RUSI Journal* 158, no. 2 (2013): 40–46.
31. Martin Libicki, "Cyberwar as a Confidence Game," *Strategic Studies Quarterly* 5, no. 1 (2011): 132–146.

Chapter 8

1. John Barton et al., *The Evolution of the Trade Regime: Politics, Law and the Economics of GATT and the WTO* (Princeton, NJ: Princeton University Press, 2006); and C. Fred Bergsten, "Fifty Years of Trade Policy: The Policy Lessons," *The World Economy* 24 (2001): 1–13.
2. For a brief discussion of the International Trade Organization see Judith Goldstein, *Ideas, Interests, and American Trade Policy* (Ithaca, NY: Cornell University Press, 1993), 158–163.
3. Silva Nenci, "The Rise of the Southern Economies: Implications for the WTO-Multilateral Trading System," UNU-Wider Research Paper 2008/10, February 2008, www.wider.unu.edu/publica tions/working-papers/research-papers/2008/en_GB/rp2008–10/.; and A. Narlikar, "Fairness in International Trade Negotiations: Developing Countries in the GATT and WTO," *The World Economy* 29, no. 8 (2006): 1,005–1,028.
4. David Gantz, "Failed Efforts to Initiate the "Millennium Round' in Seattle: Lessons for Future Global Trade Negotiations," *Arizona Journal of International and Comparative Law* 17, no. 2 (2000): 349; Ewell Murphy Jr., "The Lessons of Seattle: Learning from the Failed Third WTO Ministerial Conference," *Transnational Law* 13 (Fall 2000): 273–287.

5. Andreas Marschner, "The New Lobbying: Interest Groups, Governments and the WTO in Seattle," *SAIS Review* 21, no. 1 (2001): 159–177.

6. "Empty Promises: What Happened to 'Development' in the WTO's Doha Round?," Oxfam Briefing Paper, July 16, 2009, www.oxfam .org/sites/www.oxfam.org/files/bp131-empty-promises.pdf.

7. United States General Accounting Office, "World Trade Organization: Cancun Ministerial Fails to Move Global Trade Negotiations Forward; Next Steps Uncertain," January 2004, www.gao.gov/ assets/250/241196.pdf.

8. Amrita Narlikar and Diane Tussie, "The G20 at the Cancun Ministerial: Developing Countries and Their Evolving Coalitions," *The World Economy* 27, no. 7 (2004): 947–966.

9. The G20 countries at the Cancun talks are not to be confused with the G20 countries at international monetary talks. The trade grouping is made up of developing economies while the monetary grouping is made up of developed and developing economies. The G20 countries referred to here are Argentina, Bolivia, Brazil, China, Cuba, Benin, Botswana, China, Congo, Cote d'Ivoire, Djibouti, Egypt, Gabon, Gambia, Ghana, Guinea, Guineas Bissau, Kenya, Lesotho, Madagascar, Malawi, Mail, Mauritania, Morocco, Namibia, Niger, Nigeria, Rwanda, Senegal, Sierra Leone, South Africa, Swaziland, Tanzania, Togo, Tunisia, Uganda, Zambia, and Zimbabwe.

10. "Empty Promises."

11. Lamy's comments can be found at www.wto.org/english/news_e/ sppl_e/sppl_e.htm.

12. Mark Thirlwell, *After Doha: 1. The Search for Plan B* (Sydney, Australia: Lowry Institute for International Policy 2006); Peter Gallagher and Andrew Stoler, "Critical Mass as an Alternative Framework for Multilateral Trade Negotiations," *Global Governance* 15, no. 3 (2009): 375–392.

13. Heribert Dieter, "The Multilateral Trading System and Preferential Trade Agreements: Can the Negative Effects Be Minimized?," *Global Governance* 15, no. 3 (2009): 393–408.

14. See Ian Bremmer, *The End of the Free Market* (New York: Penguin, 2010).

Chapter 9

1. For overviews see Lucile Newman, ed., *Hunger in History* (Cambridge: Blackwell, 1990); and Joanna MacRae and Anthony Zwi, eds., *War and Hunger: Rethinking International Responses to Complex Emergencies* (London: Zed Books, 1994).

2. Jonatan Lassa, "Famine, Drought, and Malnutrition: Defining and Fighting Hunger," *The Jakarta Post,* July 3, 2006, www.thejakar

      tapost.com/news/2006/07/03/famine-drought-malnutrition-defin
      ing-and-fighting-hunger.html.

3. Mark W. Rosegrant, Michael S. Paisner, Siet Meijer, and Julie Wit-
cover, "2020 Global Food Outlook: Trends, Analysis, and Choices,"
August 2001, www.fcrn.org.uk/sites/default/files/fpr30_0.pdf.

4. Ruth Jachertz and Alexander Nutzenadel, "Coping with Hunger?
Visions of a Global Food System, 1930–1960," *Journal of Global
History* 6, no. 1 (2011): 99–119; and Jennifer Clapp, *Hunger in the
Balance: The New Politics of International Food Aid* (Ithaca, NY:
Cornell University Press, 2012).

5. Jachertz and Nutzenadel, "Coping with Hunger," 102.

6. Simon Maxwell, "Food Security: A Post-Modern Perspective," *Food
Policy* 21, no. 2 (1996): 155–170.

7. International organizations are organizations whose members
are states. This is different from international nongovernmental
organizations, which are made up of nonstate actors such as relief
organizations, professional associations, or scientific groups.

8. Ramesh Thakur, *The United Nations, Peace and Security*
(Cambridge: Cambridge University Press, 2006).

9. See "The Vision of FAO's Founders," www.fao.org/docrep/meet
ing/010/j6285e/j6285e03.htm.

10. Jachertz and Nutzenadel, "Coping with Hunger," 111.

11. See Michael Hogan, *The Marshall Plan: America, Britain and
the Reconstruction of Western Europe, 1947–1952* (Cambridge:
Cambridge University Press, 1987).

12. "Hunger in a World of Plenty," Greenpeace, www.greenpeace.org/
usa/en/campaigns/genetic-engineering/big-challenges/hunger/.

13. Peter Toma, *The Politics of Food For Peace: Executive-Legislative
Interaction* (Tucson: University of Arizona Press, 1967).

14. See D. John Shaw, *The World Food Programme and the Development of Food Aid* (New York: Palgrave Macmillan, 2001).

15. Dale Hathaway, *The World Food Crisis: Periodic or Perpetual?*
(Washington, DC: International Food Policy Research Institute,
1975).

16. Dan Morgan, *Merchants of Grain* (New York: Penguin, 1980); and
Michael Atkin, *The International Grain Trade,* 2nd ed. (Cambridge,
UK: Woodhead Publishing, 1995).

17. Hathaway, *The World Food Crisis;* and D. John Shaw, *World Food
Security: A History since 1945* (New York: Palgrave Macmillan,
2007).

18. On the World Food Conference, see Shaw, *World Food Security;*
Thomas G. Weiss and Robert S. Jordan, "Bureaucratic Politics and
the World Food Conference: A Research Note on the International
Policy Process," *World Politics* 28, no. 3 (1976): 422–439; Thomas
G. Weiss and Robert S. Jordan, *The World Food Conference and*

Global Problem Solving (New York: Praeger, 1975); and Margaret Biswas, "The World Food Conference: A Perspective," *Agriculture and Environment* 2, no. 1 (1975): 15–37.

19. Shaw, *World Food Security,* 128.
20. Ibid., 131.
21. See Pedro Conceicao and Ronald U. Mendoza, "Anatomy of the Global Food Crisis," *Third World Quarterly* 30, no. 6 (2009): 1,159–1,182; and Thomas Molony and James Smith, "Briefing: Biofuels, Food Security, and Africa," *African Affairs* 109 (April 2010), 489–498.
22. See Maxwell, "Food Security"; and Mitchel Wallerstein and James Austin, "World Food Council at 3 Years: Global Food System Manager?," *Food Policy* 3, no. 3 (1978): 191–201.
23. Shaw, *World Food Security,* 144–148.
24. World Food Council, "The Global State of Hunger and Malnutrition: 1992 Report" (New York: United Nations, 1992).
25. On the World Food Summit, see U.S. Government Accountability Office, International Food Security, GAO Report 08–680 (Washington, DC: Government Accountability Office, 2008); and *World Food Summit on Food Security Bulletin* 150, no. 7, November 2009, www.iisd.ca/download/pdf/sd/ymbv01150num7e.pdf.
26. "Rome Declaration on World Food Security," FAO Corporate Document Repository, November 1996, www.fao.org/docrep/003/w3613e/w3613e00.HTM.
27. Shaw, *World Food Security,* 461.
28. *The Washington Post*'s Global Food Crisis Series, April 29, 2008, http://davd.i8.com/R/080429WashngtnPostGlobalFoodCrisisSeries.html.
29. Anthony Faiola, "The New Economics of Hunger," *The Washington Post,* April 27, 2008, 1.
30. Clapp, *Hunger in the Balance*, presents this argument.
31. Christopher Barrett and Daniel Maxwell, "Towards a Global Food Aid Compact," *Food Policy* 31, no. 2 (2006): 105–118.
32. Maxwell, "Food Security."

Chapter 10

1. Benjamin Cohen, *The Future of Money* (Princeton, NJ: Princeton University Press, 2004), especially chapters 1 and 8.
2. Benjamin Cohen, *Global Monetary Governance* (New York: Routledge, 2008), 11.
3. Susan Strange, *Casino Capitalism* (New York: Blackwell, 1986).
4. James Rosenau and Ernest-Otto Czempiel, eds., *Governance without Government: Order and Change in World Politics* (New York: Cambridge University Press, 1992).

5. James Boughton, *The IMF and the Force of History: Ten Events and Ten Ideas That Have Shaped the Institution* (Washington DC: International Monetary Fund, 2004).

6. Benjamin Rowland, ed. *Charles DeGaulle's Legacy of Ideas* (Lanham MD: Lexington Books, 2001), 12–15.

7. For a history of past financial crises see Luc Laeven and Fabian Valencia, "Systemic Banking Crises: A New Database," International Monetary Fund Working Paper WP/08/224, October 2008, www.imf.org/external/pubs/ft/wp/2008/wp08224.pdf.

8. Anne O. Krueger, "Origins of the Developing Countries' Debt Crisis, 1970 to 1982," *Journal of Development Economics* 27, no. 1–2 (1987): 165–187.

9. See William R. Cline, "The Baker Plan and the Brady Referendum: An Evaluation," in *Dealing with the Debt Crisis,* ed. Ishrat Husain and Ishac Diwan (Washington, DC: The World Bank, 1989); and Manuel Monteagudo, "Debt Problem: The Baker Plan and the Brady Initiative: A Latin American Perspective," *International Lawyer* 28, no. 1 (1994): 74–75, www.lexisnexis.com/hottopics/lnacademic/?verb=sr&csi=3317.

10. For discussions of the Asian crisis, see Steven Radelet and Jeffrey D. Sachs, "Onset of the Asian Financial Crisis," in *Currency Crises,* ed. Paul Kruger (Cambridge: Cambridge University Press, 2010), 105–162; and Gregory Noble and John Ravenhill, eds., *The Asian Financial Crisis and the Architecture of Global Finances* (Cambridge: Cambridge University Press, 2000).

11. See Dick Nanto, *The Global Financial Crisis: Analysis and Policy Implications* (Washington, DC: Congressional Research Service, 2009).

12. Quoted in Mark Jickling, *Containing Financial Crisis* (Washington, DC: Congressional Research Service, 2008), 1.

13. Nanto, *The Global Financial Crisis.*

14. Ibid.

15. For a discussion of the four phases of domestic responses to the global financial crisis, see Nanto, *The Global Financial Crisis,* 10–31. For lists of stimulus packages see p. 157.

16. For discussions of the G20, see Peter Hajnal *The G8 System and the G20: Evolution, Role and Documentation* (Burlington, VT: Ashgate, 2007); Judith Cherry and Hugo Dobson, "Seoul-Searching: the 201 G-20 Seoul Summit," *Global Governance* 18, no. 3 (2012): 363–381; and A. F. Cooper, "The G20 as an Improvised Crisis Committee and/ or a Contested 'Steering Committee' for the World," *International Affairs* 86, no. 3 (2010): 741–757.

17. Nanto, *The Global Financial Crisis,* 15.

18. Jinato's full statement can be found at www.chinausfocus.com/library/government-resources/chinese-resources/remarks/hu-jintao-

addresses-the-g20-summit-on-financial-markets-and-the-world-economy-in-washington-november-16–2008/.

19. See Katharina Gnath, Stormy-Annika Mildner, and Claudia Schmucker, "G20, IMF and WTO in Turbulent Times," SWP Research Paper, August 2012, www.swp-berlin.org/fileadmin/contents/products/research_papers/2012_RP10_Gnath_mdn_Schmucker.pdf.

20. Nicholas Bayne, "The G20 after the Cannes Summit Speaking Notes for the Paris Seminar," G20 Information Center, November 7, 2011, www.g20.utoronto.ca/events/111107-bayne.html.

21. Cohen, *The Future of Money*, 14–16.

22. Stewart Patrick, "Irresponsible Stakeholders," *Foreign Affairs* 89 (November–December 2010), 44–53.

23. Cooper, "The G-20 as an Improvised Crisis Committee."

24. Uri Dadush and Kari Suominen, "Is There Life for the G20 after the Global Financial Crisis?," *Journal of Globalization and Democracy* 2, no. 2 (2011), article 7.

Chapter 11

1. Quoted in Bernard E. Brown, "The Ordeal of European Union," *American Foreign Policy Interests* 35, no. 1 (2013): 24.

2. See Emmanuel Mourlon-Druol, *A Europe Made of Money: The Emergence of the European Monetary System* (Ithaca, NY: Cornell University Press, 2012), 15–30.; Luca Einaudi, "From Franc to the 'Europe': The Attempted Transformation of the Latin Monetary Union into a European Monetary Union, 1865–1873," *Economic History Review* 53, no. 2 (2000): 284–308; and Carsten Hefeker, "Interest Groups, Coalitions, and Monetary Integration in the XIXth Century," *Journal of European Economic History* 24 (Winter 1995): 489–537.

3. See John Gillingham, *European Integration, 1950–2003* (Cambridge: Cambridge University Press, 2003).

4. Quoted in Chris Mulhearn and Howard Vein, *The Euro: Its Origins, Development and Propsects* (Cheltenham, UK: Edward Elgar, 2008), 28.

5. On the Werner Committee, see Mourlon-Druol, *A Europe Made of Money*; and Mulhearn and Vane, *The Euro*.

6. See David Marsh, *The Euro: The Politics of the New Global Currency* (New Haven: Yale University Press, 2009).

7. Otmar Issing, *The Birth of the Euro* (Cambridge: Cambridge University Press, 2008); and Marsh, *The Euro*.

8. See George Jones and Rachel Sylvester, "I Would Never Give Up the Pound, Declares Thatcher," *The Telegraph,* May 23, 2001, www.telegraph.co.uk/news/uknews/1331328/I-would-never-give-up-the-pound-declares-Thatcher.html.

9. Quoted in Frederic Bozo, *Mitterrand: The End of the Cold War and German Unification* (New York: Berghahn, 2009), 196.

10. Mulhearn and Vane, *The Euro,* 120–168.

11. Ibid., 169–190.

12. Paul Mercier and Francesco Papadia, eds., *The Concrete Euro: Implementing Monetary Policy in the Euro Area* (Oxford: Oxford University Press, 2011); and Eleanor Zeff and Ellen Pirro, eds., *The European Union and The Member States* (Boulder, CO: Lynne Reinner, 2006).

13. See Erik Jones, "Europe's Threatened Solidarity," *Current History* 111 (March 2012): 88–93; Daniel Gros, "The Misdiagnosed Debt Crisis," *Current History* 111 (March 2012), 83–87; and Nicholas Crafts, "Saving the Eurozone: Is a Real Marshall Plan the Answer?," CAGE-Chatham House Series #1, June 2012, www2.warwick .ac.uk/fac/soc/economics/research/centres/cage/chh1669_eurozone_ bp_v6.pdf.

Chapter 12

1. William Lang, "Causes of Complex Emergencies," *Encyclopedia of Natural Disasters* (Los Angeles: Sage, 2011), 49–53.

2. Eugene S. Yim et al., "Disaster Diplomacy: Current Controversies and Future Prospects," *Prehospital and Disaster Medicine* 24 (July–August 2009), 291–293.

3. DeMond Miller and Derrick Miller, "Rejection of International Aid," in *Encyclopedia of Disaster Relief,* ed. K. Bradley Penuel and Matt Statler (Los Angeles: Sage, 2011), 573–575.

4. Allehone Mulugeta Abebe, "Special Report: Human Rights in the Context of Disasters: The Special Session of the UN Human Rights Council on Haiti," *Journal of Human Rights* 10, no. 1 (2011): 99–111.

5. Deborah Sontag, "Rebuilding in Haiti Lags after Billions in Post-Quake Aid," *New York Times,* December 23, 2012, 1.

6. United Nations Evaluation Group, "Haiti Earthquake Response: Contex Analysis," July 2010.

7. Douglas Jehl, "CIA Nominee Wary of Budget Cuts," *The New York Times,* February 3, 1993, www.nytimes.com/1993/02/03/us/cia-nominee-wary-of-budget-cuts.html.

8. See Chapter 2 of the 1994 United Nations Human Development Report, http://hdr.undp.org/en/media/hdr_1994_en_chap2.pdf, 22.

9. Ibid., 23.

10. The definition is that used by the Internal Displacement Monitoring Center; see "About Internal Displacement," Norwegian Refugee Council, www.nrc.no/?did=9429592.

11. Glenn Hastedt, "U.S. Foreign Policy toward Haiti," in *Encyclopedia of American Foreign Policy* (New York: Facts on File, Inc., 2004), 204.

12. Alex Dupuy, *The Prophet and Power: Jean-Bertrand Aristide, Haiti, and the International Community and Haiti* (Lanham MD, Rowman and Littlefield, 2007).

13. United Nations Security Council, Resolution 1542, April 30, 2004, www.un.org/ga/search/view_doc.asp?symbol=S/RES/1542(2004).

14. Roger Bilham, "Lessons from the Haiti Earthquake," *Nature* 463 (February 2010): 878–879.

15. Maura R. O'Connor, "Two Years Later, Haitian Earthquake Death Toll in Dispute," *Columbia Journalism Review,* January 12, 2012, www.cjr.org/behind_the_news/one_year_later_haitian_earthqu .php?page=all.

16. David Rieff, "Millions May Die . . . or Not," *Foreign Policy* 188 (September–October 2011): 22–24.

17. Philip Sherwell and Colin Freeman, "Haiti Earthquake: Police Open Fire on Looters," *The Telegraph,* January 17, 2010, www .telegraph.co.uk/news/worldnews/centralamericaandthecaribbean/ haiti/7005853/Haiti-carthquake-police-open-fire-on-looters.html.

18. Rhoda Margesson and Maureen Taft-Morales, "Haiti Earthquake: Crisis and Response," Congressional Research Service, February 2, 2010, www.fas.org/sgp/crs/row/R41023.pdf; and Paul E. Weisenfeld," Success and Challenges of the Haiti Earthquake Response: The Experience of USAID," *Emory International Law Review* 25, no. 3 (2011): 1,097–1,120.

19. William Booth, "NGOs in Haiti Face New Question about Effectiveness," *Washington Post,* February 1, 2011, www.washington post.com/wp-dyn/content/article/2011/02/01/AR2011020102030 .html.

20. Abebe, "Special Report: Human Rights in the Context of Disasters, 104.

21. United Nations Evaluation Group, "Haiti Earthquake Response: Context Analysis"; Weisenfeld, "Success and Challenges of the Haiti Earthquake Response"; United Nations General Assembly, Human Rights Council, "Report of the Independent Expert on the Situation of Human Rights in Haiti, Michael Forst," February 7, 2013, www.ohchr.org/Documents/HRBodies/HRCouncil/RegularSession/ Session22/A-HRC-22–65_EN.pdf; Patrice K. Nicholas et. al., "Orphans and At-Risk Children in Haiti," *Advances in Nursing Science* 35, no. 2 (2012): 182–189; and Human Rights Watch, *Nobody Remembers Us: Failure to Protect Women's and Girls' Right to Health and Security in Post-Earthquake Haiti,* 2011, www.hrw.org/ sites/default/files/reports/haiti0811webwcover.pdf.

22. Elizabeth Ferris and Sara Ferro-Ribeiro, "Protecting People in Cities: The Disturbing Case of Haiti," *Disasters* 36 (July 2012): 43–63.

23. Kerren Hedlund, "Strength in Numbers: A Review of NGO Coordination in the Field, Case Study: Haiti 2010," https://icvanetwork .org/system/files/versions/doc00004599.pdf.

24. William Booth, "NGOs in Haiti Face New Questions about Effectiveness," *Washington Post,* February 1, 2011; Kathleen Jobe, "Disaster Relief in Post-Earthquake Haiti: Unintended Consequences of Humanitarian Volunteerism," *Travel Medicine and Infectious Disease* 9, no. 1 (2011): 1–5; and Daniel J. Van Hoving et al., "Haiti Disaster Tourism—A Medical Shame," *Prehospital and Disaster Medicine* 25, no. 3 (2010), 201–202.

25. Human Rights Watch, "World Report 2012: Haiti," January 2012, www.hrw.org/world-report-2012/haiti.

26. Center for Economic and Policy Research, "U.S. Aid to Haiti: 'Troubling' Lack of Transparency, Effectiveness," Global Research, April 3, 2013, www.globalresearch.ca/u-s-aid-to-haiti-troubling-lack-of-transparency-effectiveness/5329600.

27. Deborah Sontag, "Earthquake Relief Where Haiti Wasn't Broken," *The New York Times,* July 5, 2012.

28. Jordan W. Tappero and Robert V. Tauxe, "Lessons Learned during Public Health Response to Cholera Epidemic in Haiti and the Dominican Republic," *Emerging Infectious Diseases* 17, no. 11 (2011): 2,087–2,093.

29. See Sontag, "Rebuilding in Haiti Lags after Billions in Post-Quake Aid"; and "Haiti: A Humanitarian Crisis in Need of a Development Solution," Internal Displacement Monitoring Centre, December 20, 2012, www.internal-displacement.org/8025708F004CE90B/(httpCountry Summaries)/0EAAA419CFB5D39DC1257ADA0037ECF6?Open Document&count=10000.

30. Quoted in Elizabeth Ferris, "Haiti and Future Humanitarian Disasters" (Washington, DC: Brookings Institution, January 12, 2011).

31. Elizabeth Ferris and Sara Ferro-Ribeiro, "Protecting People in Cities: The Disturbing Case of Haiti," *Disasters* 36 (July 2012): 43–63.

Chapter 13

1. Charter of the United Nations, www.un.org/en/documents/charter/chapter1.shtml.

2. Hebah Saleh and Andrew England, "Defiant Gaddafi Vows Fight to Death," *Financial Times,* February 23, 2011.

3. Noueihed, Lin, and Alex Warren, *The Battle for the Arab Spring: Revolution, Counter-Revolution and the Making of a New Era* (Cambridge: Yale University Press, 2012), 167.

4. Ibid., 178–179.

5. Wayne Sandholtz, *International Norms and Cycles of Change* (Oxford, UK: Oxford University Press, 2009); and Martha Finnemore, "Constructing Norms of Humanitarian Intervention," in *The Culture of National Security,* ed. Peter Katzenstein (New York: Columbia University Press, 1996), 153–185.

6. Michael Barnett, *Empire of Humanity: A History of Humanitarianism* (Ithaca, NY: Cornell University Press, 2011), 51.

7. Mark Amstutz, *International Ethics: Concepts, Theories, and Cases in Global Politics,* 4th ed. (Lanham, MD: Rowman & Littlefield, 2013), 188.

8. Ibid.

9. Noueihed and Warren, *The Battle for the Arab Spring,* 179.

10. Saleh and England, "Defiant Gaddafi Vows Fight to Death."

11. Noueihed and Warren, *The Battle for the Arab Spring,* 180.

12. Simon Chesterman, "'Leading from Behind': The Responsibility to Protect, the Obama Doctrine, and Humanitarian Intervention after Libya," New York University Public Law and Legal Theory Working Papers, Paper 282, 2011, http://lsr.nellco.org/nyu_plltwp/282.

13. Massimo Calabresi. "Susan Rice: A Voice for Intervention," *Time,* March 24, 2011, www.time.com/time/magazine/article/0,9171,2061224,00.html.

14. Ibid.

15. Ivo Daalder and James Stavridis, "NATO's Victory in Libya: The Right Way to Run an Intervention" *Foreign Affairs* 91, no. 2 (2012): 2.

16. Andrew Black, "David Cameron: Libya Action 'In National Interest,'" BBC News, March 18, 2011, www.bbc.co.uk/news/uk-scotland-12761264. Thanks to Matt Conaway for his collaboration on research into this area. See Matt Conaway and Vaughn Shannon, "The Political Psychology of R2P: Analogies and Multilateral Intervention in Libya," Paper Presented at the Annual Meeting of the ISA Northeast Regional Meeting, Baltimore, MD, November 2–4, 2012.

17. Noueihed and Warren, *The Battle for the Arab Spring,* 181.

18. Angelo Del Boca, *Mohamed Fekini and the Fight to Free Libya* (New York: Palgrave Macmillan, 2011), 3, 5.

19. "Italy Prepares for Wave of Refugees," BBC News, March 3, 2011, www.bbc.co.uk/news/world-europe-12631456.

20. "Migrants Fleeing North Africa Turmoil Land on Lampedusa," BBC News, March 7, 2011, www.bbc.co.uk/news/world-europe-12662756.

21. "Italy Blocks Ferry of Moroccans Fleeing Libya," BBC News, March 15, 2011, www.bbc.co.uk/news/world-europe-12743356.

22. Rachel Donadio, "Turmoil in Libya Poses Threat to Italian Economy," *The New York Times,* March 5, 2011, www.nytimes.com/2011/03/06/world/europe/06italy.html?pagewanted=all.

23. Şaban Kardaş. "Turkey's 'Moral Politics' in Libya: Seduction by Analogy?," Today's Zaman, March 20, 2011, www.todayszaman.com/news-238664-turkeys-moral-politics-in-libya-seduction-by-analogy-by-saban-kardas*—.html.

24. Ibid.

25. Ola Galal, "Arab League Bars Libya from Meetings, Citing Forces' Crimes," Bloomberg Report, February 22, 2011, www.bloomberg .com/news/2011–02–22/arab-league-bars-libya-from-meetings-cit ing-forces-crimes-.html.

26. Ahmed Eleiba, "Libya's representative to the Arab League resigns," Ahram Online, February 22, 2011, http://english.ahram.org.eg/ NewsContent/2/8/6188/World/Region/Libya%E2%80%99s-repre sentative-to-the-Arab-League-resigns.aspx.

27. "Gaddafi Must Stop Killings—Kutesa." *Daily Monitor,* March 18, 2011, www.monitor.co.ug/News/National/-/688334/1128316/-/c3vh lwz/-/.

28. "UN Security Council Resolution 1973 (2011) on Libya: Full Text," *The Guardian,* March 17, 2011, www.guardian.co.uk/world/2011/ mar/17/un-security-council-resolution.

29. Ibid.

30. Ibid.

31. Ibid.

32. "Libya Unrest: UK Reaction to UN Vote in Quotes." BBC News, March 18, 2011, www.bbc.co.uk/news/uk-politics-12781476.

33. Ibid.

34. Agence France Presse, "Europe Divided over Allied Campaign in Libya," New Age, March 21, 2011, http://newagebd.com/newspa per1/archive_details.php?date=2011–03–21&nid=12436.

35. "Time for Gadhafi Family Exit, Says Turkish Foreign Ministry," *Hürriyet Daily News,* April 6, 2011, www.hurriyetdailynews .com/default.aspx?pageid=438&n=meeting-libyan-rebels-turkey-supports-end-of-gadhafi-family-rule-in-libya-2011–04–06.

36. Selcan Hacaoglu, "Turkey Recognizes Libya Rebels," NBC News, July 3, 2011, www.msnbc.msn.com/id/43626058/ns/world_news-mideast_n_africa/t/turkey-recognizes-libya-rebels/; and "Turkey's Foreign Minister Meets Libyan Rebels," *The National,* July 4, 2011, www.thenational.ae/news/world/europe/turkeys-foreign-minis ter-meets-libyan-rebels.

37. Nicholas Watt, "Libya Military Action Will Continue until Gaddafi Bows to UN Demand—Clinton." *The Guardian,* March 29, 2011, www.guardian.co.uk/world/2011/mar/29/gaddafi-un-resolutions-cameron.

38. Praveen Swami, "Libyan Rebel Commander Admits His Fighters Have al-Qaeda Links," *The Telegraph,* March 25, 2011, www.tele graph.co.uk/news/worldnews/africaandindianocean/libya/8407047/ Libyan-rebel-commander-admits-his-fighters-have-al-Qaeda-links .html.

39. "Libya: Rebels and NATO Dismiss Gaddafi Ceasefire Offer," BBC News, April 30, 2011, www.bbc.co.uk/news/world-africa-132 49923.

40. "UN Showdown Set over Action against Syria," AFP, August 28, 2013, http://news.yahoo.com/obama-cameron-no-doubt-syria-regime-waged-chem-071600422.html.

Chapter 14

1. Lassi Heininen, "Circumpolar International Relations and Geopolitics," *Arctic Human Development Report*, www.svs.is/ahdr/ahdr%20chapters/english%20version/AHDR_chp%2012.pdf.

2. Oran R. Young, "Arctic Waters: The Politics of Regime Formation," *Ocean Development and International Law* 18, no. 1 (1987): 101–114; and Lincoln Bloomfield, "The Arctic: The Last Unmanaged Frontier," *Foreign Affairs* 60 (Fall 1981): 87–105.

3. Barry Zellen, "The Inuit, the State, and the Battle for the Arctic," *Georgetown Journal of International Affairs* 11 (Winter–Spring 2010): 57–64.

4. Jessica Shadin, "Remaking Arctic Governance: The Construction of an Arctic Inuit Polity," *Polar Record* 42, no. 3 (2006): 249–259.

5. For a text of the treaty, see www.antarctica.ac.uk/about_antarctica/geopolitical/treaty/update_1959.php.

6. Timo Koivurova, "Limits and Possibilities of the Arctic Council in a Rapidly Changing Scene of Arctic Governments," *Polar Record* 46 (2010): 146–156.

7. For the text of the AEPS founding document, see www.grida.no/polar/resources.aspx?id=1385.

8. Oran R. Young, "Can the Arctic Council and the Northern Forum Find Common Ground?," *Polar Record* 38 (October 2002): 289–296.

9. Oran R. Young, "Governing the Arctic: From Cold War Theater to Mosaic of Cooperation," *Global Governance* 11, no. 1 (2005): 9–15.

10. The 2009 National Security Strategy can be found at www.whitehouse.gov/sites/default/files/rss_viewer/national_security_strategy.pdf.

11. "Newly Sworn President Putin Orders Arctic Naval Boost," *Alaska Dispatch*, May 10, 2012, www.alaskadispatch.com/article/newly-sworn-president-putin-orders-arctic-naval-boost.

12. Robert W. Murray, "Arctic Politics in the Emerging Multipolar System: Challenges and Responses," *Polar Journal* 2, no. 1 (2012): 7–20.

13. Barry Zellen, Cold Front Rising as Global Warming Melts Polar Ice Pack," *Strategic Insights* 2, no. 8 (2008), http://calhoun.nps.edu/public/bitstream/handle/10945/25391/Cold_Front_Rising_As_Global_Warming_Melts_Polar_Ice_Pack%2c_a_New_Race_for_the_Arctic%27s_Resources_Begins.pdf?sequence=1.

14. Torbjorn Pederson, "Debates over the Role of the Arctic Council," *Ocean Development and International Law* 43, no. 2 (2012): 146–156.

15. Brandon Luedtke and Adrian Howkins, "Polarized Climates: The Distinctive Histories of Climate Change and Politics in the Arctic and Antarctic since the Beginnings of the Cold War," *WIREs Climate Change* 3, no. 2 (2012): 145–159.

16. Oran R. Young, "If an Arctic Ocean Treaty Is Not the Solution, What Is the Alternative?," *Polar Record* 47 (October 2011): 327–334.

17. Timo Koivurova, "The Actions of the Arctic States Respecting the Continental Shelf: A Reflective Essay," *Ocean Development and International Law* 42, no. 3 (2011): 211–226.

18. On the Law of the Sea Convention and related issues see Ted McDorman, "The Continental Shelf beyond 200 NM: Law and Politics in the Arctic Ocean," *Journal of Transnational Law & Policy* 18, no. 2 (2009): 155–187.

19. Margaret Blunden, "The New Problem of Arctic Stability," *Survival* 51, no. 5 (2009): 121–142.

20. For a discussion of the positions of the Arctic states on key issues, see Ian Brosnan, Thomas Leschine, and Edward Miles, "Cooperation or Conflict in a Changing Arctic?," *Ocean Development and International Law* 42 (January 2011): 173–210.

Chapter 15

1. Edwin Mora, "Senate Democratic Whip Compares Sealing the Mexican Border to Trying to Keep Drugs Off of I-95," Cybercast News Service, May 19, 2010, www.cnsnews.com/news/article/senate-democratic-whip-compares-sealing-mexican-border-trying-keep-drugs-i-95; and Rachel St. John, *Line in the Sand: A History of the Western U.S.-Mexico Border* (Princeton, NJ: Princeton University Press, 2012).

2. Embassy of the United States, Mexico, http://mexico.usembassy.gov/eng/eataglance_trade.html.

3. Mark Stevenson, "Fox Visits Bush," *Migration News* 8, no. 10 (2001), http://migration.ucdavis.edu/mn/more.php?id=2463_0_2_0.

4. Marc Rosenblum, William Kandel, Clare Ribando Seelke, and Ruth Ellen Wasem, "Mexican Migration to the United States: Policy and Trends," Congressional Research Service, June 7, 2012, www.fas.org/sgp/crs/row/R42560.pdf.

5. Ibid.

6. Raymundo Campos-Vazques and Horacio Sobarzo, *The Development and Fiscal Effects of Emigration on Mexico* (Washington, DC: Migration Policy Institute, 2012).

7. Ginger Thompson, "Beyond the Border," *The New York Times*, May 9, 2011, http://teacher.scholastic.com/scholasticnews/indepth/upfront/features/index.asp?article=f1128b.

8. U.S. Department of Homeland Security, *2004 Yearbook of Immigration Statistics* (Washington, DC: U.S. Department of Homeland Security, Office of Immigration Statistics, 2006).

9. U.S. Department of Commerce, *Historical Statistics of the United States* (Washington, DC: U.S. Department of Commerce, 1976).

10. U.S. Department of State, "The Immigration Act of 1924," Office of the Historian, http://history.state.gov/milestones/1921–1936/ImmigrationAct.

11. Rosenblum et al., "Mexican Migration to the United States.

12. Kate Brick, A. E. Challinor, and Marc R. Rosenblum, *Mexican and Central American Immigrants in the United States* (Washington, DC: Migration Policy Institute, 2011).

13. Barry R. Chiswick, "Illegal Immigration and Immigration Control," *The Journal of Economic Perspectives* 2, no. 3 (1988): 101–115.

14. Oliver C. Anderson, *Illegal Immigration: Causes, Methods, and Effects* (New York: Nova Science, 2010).

15. Vincent Dowd, "Operation Hold the Line," National Border, National Park: A History of Organ Pipe Cactus National Monument, http://organpipehistory.wordpress.com/orpi-a-z/operation-hold-the-line-2/.

16. Ibid.

17. Department of Agricultural Economics, University of California-Davis, "Enforcement and Databases," *Migration News* 4, no. 10 (1997), http://migration.ucdavis.edu/mn/more.php?id=1332_0_2_0.

18. U.S. Immigration and Naturalization Service, "Enforcement, Fiscal Year 2000," *Statistical Yearbook of the Immigration and Naturalization Service, 2000* (Washington, DC: U.S. Government Printing Office, 2002).

19. Ibid.

20. Ibid.

21. Elizabeth Dwoskin, "The U.S.-Mexico Border Got Secured. Problem Solved?," Bloomberg Business Week, February 21, 2013, www.businessweek.com/articles/2013–02–21/the-u-dot-s-dot-mexico-border-got-secured-dot-problem-solved.

22. "Texas Gov Says U.S. Needs Migrants, Not Border Wall," August 28, 2007, www.reuters.com/article/2007/08/28/mexico-texas-idUSN2827524820070828.

23. Traci Carl, "Mexico Blasts U.S. Immigration Policies," *The Washington Post*, September 2, 2007, www.washingtonpost.com/wp-dyn/content/article/2007/09/02/AR2007090200958.html.

24. Good Neighbor Environmental Board, "A Blueprint for Action on the U.S.-Mexico Border, https://docs.google.com/a/isu.edu/viewer?

a=v&q=cache:x5g-WvPPQ1gJ:www.epa.gov/ocem/gneb/gneb13thre
port/English-GNEB-13th-Report.pdf+&hl=en&gl=us&pid=bl&sr
cid=ADGEESgYLK5ZoksB680JL1wtM9hFWBLpZnpmfrbtT9PrH
aLNc20AWve-RyH9Y16j24WdUWI8h-ntlPkTYT10i1Tkpz
K46UeuHsh4893_030RT-38awWrsuRa11zME9j3X3M-Nx4Pk_
uz&sig=AHIEtbQ_rqY18r_5KsXZlzGHH5aDUb603g.

25. Ibid.
26. Nick Miroff, "Three Ways U.S. Immigration Reform Might Impact Mexico," *The Washington Post,* January 31, 2013, www.washing tonpost.com/blogs/worldviews/wp/2013/01/31/three-ways-u-s-im migration-reform-might-impact-mexico/.
27. Edward Alden, "Immigration and Border Control," *Cato Journal* 31 no. 1, www.cato.org/sites/cato.org/files/serials/files/cato-journal/ 2012/1/cj32n1–8.pdf.
28. Emily Badger, "Report: U.S.-Mexico Border More Secure than Ever, *Pacific Standard,* August 16, 2011, www.psmag.com/politics/ report-u-s-mexico-border-more-secure-than-ever-35079/.
29. Lymari Morales, "Americans' Immigration Concerns Linger," Gallup Politics, January 17, 2012, www.gallup.com/poll/152072/ americans-immigration-concerns-linger.aspx.
30. Jeffrey S. Passel, D'Vera Cohn, and Ana Gonzalez-Barrera, "Net Migration from Mexico Falls to Zero—and Perhaps Less," Pew Research, Hispanic Trends Project, April 23, 2012, www.pewhis panic.org/2012/04/23/net-migration-from-mexico-falls-to-zero-and- perhaps-less/.

Chapter 16

1. Cutler J. Cleveland, "Deepwater Horizon Oil Spill," in *Encyclo- pedia of Earth,* February 22, 2013, www.eoearth.org/view/arti cle/161185/.
2. Matt Smith, "Coast Guard, BP End Gulf Cleanup in 3 States," CNN .com, June 11, 2013, www.cnn.com/2013/06/10/us/gulf-oil-spill.
3. Steve Coll, *Private Empire: Exxon Mobil and American Power* (New York: Penguin Books, 2012).
4. Devin Thorpe, "Why CSR? The Benefits of Corporate Social Respon- sibility Will Move You to Act," Forbes, May 18, 2013, www.forbes .com/sites/devinthorpe/2013/05/18/why-csr-the-benefits-of-corpo rate-social-responsibility-will-move-you-to-act/.
5. Ian Bremmer, "The Long Shadow of the Visible Hand," *The Wall Street Journal,* May 22, 2012, http://online.wsj.com/article/SB1000 1424052748704852004575258541875590852.html.
6. U.S. Energy Information Administration, "Energy Timelines: Oil (Petroleum)," www.eia.gov/kids/energy.cfm?page=tl_petroleum.
7. Paul Robert, *The End of Oil: The Decline of the Petroleum Econ- omy and the Rise of a New Energy Order* (New York: Houghton Mifflin Company, 2004).

8. U.S. Energy Information Administration, 'History of Energy 1635–2000," September 27, 2012, www.eia.gov/totalenergy/data/annual/index.cfm.

9. Marc Humphries, "CRS Report for Congress: Oil Development on Federal Lands and the Outer Continental Shelf," August 6, 2008, http://fpc.state.gov/documents/organization/109517.pdf.

10. U.S. Energy Information Administration, 'History of Energy 1635–2000."

11. Margaret Haerens, *Offshore Drilling* (Detroit: Greenhaven Press, 2010).

12. United Nations Iraq-Kuwait Observation Mission, "Iraq/Kuwait-UNI KOM-Background," 2003, www.un.org/en/peacekeeping/missions/past/unikom/background.html.

13. "Bush Lifts Executive Ban on Offshore Oil Drilling," CNN.com, July 14, 2008, http://edition.cnn.com/2008/POLITICS/07/14/bush.offshore/index.html.

14. Steven Mufson, "Offshore Drilling Backed as Remedy for Oil Prices," *The Washington Post,* July 14, 2008, http://articles.washingtonpost.com/2008–07–14/business/36814397_1_oil-and-gas-outer-continental-shelf-exploration.

15. Michael Knuzelman, "Document: BP Didn't Plan for Major Oil Spill," *The Guardian,* April 30, 2010, www.guardian.co.uk/world/feedarticle/9056218/print.

16. Juliet Eilperin, "U.S. Exempted BP's Gulf of Mexico Drilling from Environmental Impact Study," *The Washington Post,* May 5, 2010, www.washingtonpost.com/wp-dyn/content/article/2010/05/04/AR2010050404118.html.

17. Ibid.

18. Ibid.

19. Thomas Frank, "The Gulf Spill and the Revolving Door," *The Wall Street Journal,* May 12, 2010, http://online.wsj.com/article/SB10001424052748704250104575238562718885050.html.

20. Mark Clayton, "BP Oil Spill: MMS Shortcomings Include 'Dearth of Regulations,'" The Christian Science Monitor, June 17, 2010, www.csmonitor.com/USA/Politics/2010/0617/BP-oil-spill-MMS-shortcomings-include-dearth-of-regulations.

21. Juliet Eilperin and Scott Higham, "How the Minerals Management Service's Partnership with Industry Led to Failure," *The Washington Post,* August 24, 2010, www.washingtonpost.com/wp-dyn/content/article/2010/08/24/AR2010082406754.html.

22. Henry Hogue, "Reorganization of the Minerals Management Service in the Aftermath of the Deepwater Horizon Oil Spill," Congressional Research Service, November 10, 2010, http://www.fas.org/sgp/crs/misc/R41485.pdf.

23. John Solomon and Aaron Mehta, "Coast Guard Logs Reveal Early Spill Estimate of 8,000 Barrels a Day," The Center for Public Integrity, June 3, 2010, www.publicintegrity.org/2010/06/03/2663/coast-guard-logs-reveal-early-spill-estimate-8000-barrels-day.

24. The Ocean Portal Team, "Gulf Oil Spill," Smithsonian National Museum of Natural History, http://ocean.si.edu/gulf-oil-spill.

25. "Assessing Impacts of the Deepwater Horizon Oil Spill in the Gulf of Mexico," Science Daily, July 10, 2013, www.sciencedaily.com/releases/2013/07/130710122004.htm.

26. Peter Baker and John M. Border, "White House Lifts Ban on Deepwater Drilling," *The New York Times,* October 12, 2010, www.nytimes.com/2010/10/13/us/13drill.html?pagewanted=all&_r=0.

27. Guy Chazan, "Anadarko to Pay BP $4 Billion," *The Wall Street Journal,* October 18, 2011, http://online.wsj.com/article/SB10001424052970204346104576636264279485124.html.

28. John Schwartz, "Rig Owner Will Settle with U.S. in Gulf Spill," *The New York Times,* January 3, 2013, www.nytimes.com/2013/01/04/business/energy-environment/transocean-settles-with-us-over-oil-spill-in-gulf-of-mexico.html?_r=0.

Index

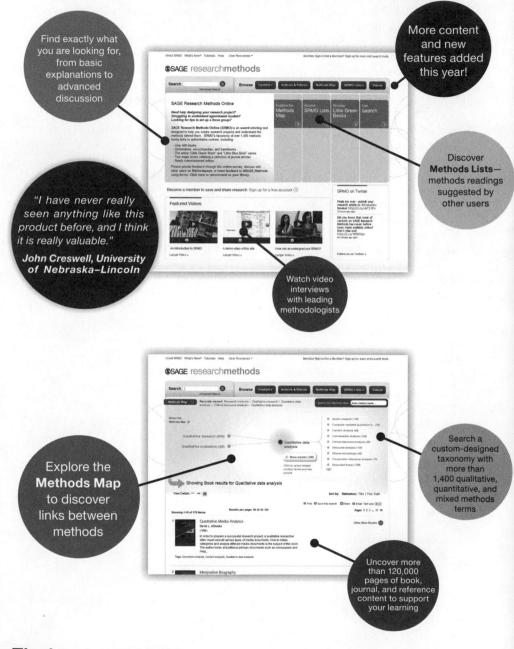